PHILOSOPHY OF RELIGION

Philosophy of
RELIGION

THE IMPACT OF MODERN KNOWLEDGE ON RELIGION

BY

FULTON J. SHEEN

Professor of Philosophy Catholic University of America
Agrégé en Philosophie à L'Université de Louvain

New York

APPLETON-CENTURY-CROFTS, INC.

COPYRIGHT, 1948, BY
FULTON J. SHEEN

Nihil obstat

Imprimatur

John M. A. Fearns, S.T.D.
Censor Librorum

✠ Francis Cardinal Spellman,
Archbishop of New York

May 7, 1948

PRINTED IN THE UNITED STATES OF AMERICA

Acknowledgments

The author and Appleton-Century-Crofts, Inc. wish to thank the many authors, agents, and publishers for their kind permission to reprint quotations from the titles listed below. All possible care has been taken to trace the ownership of every quotation included and to make full acknowledgment for its use. If any errors have accidentally occurred, they will be corrected in subsequent editions.

AGAR, HERBERT.—*A Time for Greatness.* Copyright, 1942, by Little, Brown & Company. Reprinted by permission of the publishers.

ALEXANDER, SAMUEL.—*Space, Time, and Deity.* Copyright, 1920, by The Macmillan Company. Used by permission of The Macmillan Company, publishers.

ALIOTTA, ANTONIO.—*The Idealistic Reaction Against Science.* Copyright, 1914, by The Macmillan Company. Used by permission of The Macmillan Company, publishers.

BABBITT, IRVING.—*Rousseau and Romanticism.* Copyright, 1919, by Houghton Mifflin Company. Reprinted by permission of the publishers.

BEARD, CHARLES AND MARY.—*The Rise of American Civilization.* Copyright, 1927, by The Macmillan Company. Used by permission of The Macmillan Company, publishers.

BERDYAEV, NICHOLAS.—*The Destiny of Man.* Copyright, 1937, by Charles Scribner's Sons. Reprinted by permission of the publishers.

BERDYAEV, NICHOLAS.—*The Meaning of History.* Copyright, 1936, by Geoffrey Bles, Ltd. Reprinted by permission of the publishers.

BERGSON, HENRI.—*Two Sources of Morality and Religion.* Copyright, 1935, by Henry Holt & Company. Reprinted by permission of the publishers.

BOSANQUET, BERNARD.—*The Principle of Individuality and Value.* Copyright, 1912, by The Macmillan Company. Used by permission of The Macmillan Company, publishers.

BRIGHTMAN, EDGAR S.—*The Problem of God.* Copyright, 1930, by Abingdon-Cokesbury Press. Reprinted by permission of the publishers.

BURTT, EDWIN A.—*Metaphysical Foundations of Modern Physical Science.* Copyright, 1925, by Harcourt, Brace & Company, Inc. Reprinted by permission of the publishers.

BURY, JOHN.—*The Idea of Progress.* Copyright, 1932, by The Macmillan Company. Used by permission of The Macmillan Company, publishers.

CARR, H. W.—*The General Principle of Relativity.* Copyright, 1920, by The Macmillan Company. Used by permission of The Macmillan Company, publishers.

CHANDLER, ARTHUR.—*Christian Religious Experience.* Copyright, 1929, by Longmans, Green & Company, Inc. Reprinted by permission of the publishers.

CHESTERTON, G. K.—*The Everlasting Man.* Copyright, 1925, by Dodd, Mead & Company, Inc. Reprinted by permission of the publishers.

v

COMPTON, ARTHUR H.—*The Freedom of Man*. Copyright, 1935, by Yale University Press. Reprinted by permission of the publishers.

DAMPIER-WHETHAM, WILLIAM C.—*A History of Science*. Copyright, 1936, by The Macmillan Company. Used by permission of The Macmillan Company, publishers.

DAWSON, CHRISTOPHER.—*Progress and Religion*. Copyright, 1929, by Sheed & Ward, Ltd. Reprinted by permission of the publishers.

DE BROGLIE, ALBERT.—*Religion et Critique*. Copyright, 1897, Librairie Victor Lecoffre.

DOSTOEVSKI, FYODOR.—*The Brothers Karamazov*. Copyright, 1943, by Random House, Inc. Reprinted by courtesy of the publishers.

DOSTOEVSKI, FYODOR.—*Pages from the Journal of an Author*. Copyright, 1916, Maunsel & Co., Dublin.

DUNNING, WILLIAM A.—*A History of Political Theories from Rousseau to Spencer*. Copyright, 1920, by The Macmillan Company. Used by permission of The Macmillan Company, publishers.

EDDINGTON, ARTHUR S.—*The Nature of the Physical World*. Copyright, 1937, by The Macmillan Company. Used by permission of The Macmillan Company, publishers.

EDDINGTON, ARTHUR S.—*Science and Religion*. Copyright, 1936. Reprinted by permission of John Lane, The Bodley Head, Ltd.

EDDINGTON, ARTHUR S.—*Science and the Unseen World*. Copyright, 1930, by The Macmillan Company. Used by permission of The Macmillan Company, publishers.

ENGELS, FRIEDRICH.—*Anti-Dühring*. Copyright, 1907, by Charles H. Kerr & Company. Reprinted by permission of the publishers.

ENGELS, FRIEDRICH.—*Ludwig Feuerbach*. Copyright, 1934, by M. Lawrence. Reprinted by permission of Lawrence & Wishart, Ltd.

FOSDICK, HARRY E.—*The Meaning of Faith*. Copyright, 1922, by Association Press. Reprinted by permission of the publishers.

FRANK, SEMÏON L.—*God With Us*. Copyright, 1946, by Jonathan Cape. Reprinted by permission of Yale University Press.

GILSON, ETIENNE.—*The Unity of Philosophical Experience*. Copyright, 1937, by Charles Scribner's Sons. Reprinted by permission of the publishers.

GOLDENWEISER, ALEXANDER A.—*History and Prospects of the Social Sciences*. Edited by H. E. Barnes. Copyright, 1925, by Alfred A. Knopf, Inc. Reprinted by permission of the publishers.

HALDANE, JOHN S.—*The Sciences and Philosophy*. Copyright, 1929, by Hodder & Stoughton, Ltd. Reprinted by permission of the publishers.

HOCKING, WILLIAM.—*Science and the Idea of God*. Copyright, 1944, by The University of North Carolina Press. Reprinted by permission of the publishers.

HOCKING, WILLIAM.—*What Man Can Make of Man*. Copyright, 1942, by Harper & Brothers. Reprinted by permission of the publishers.

HÖFFDING, HARALD.—*A History of Modern Philosophy*. Copyright, 1900, by The Macmillan Company. Used by permission of The Macmillan Company, publishers.

MARX, KARL.—"Theses on Ludwig Feuerbach" from *The German Ideology.* Copyright, 1938, by Lawrence & Wishart, Ltd. Reprinted by permission of the publishers.

MARX, KARL.—*On Feuerbach's Essence of Christianity.* Copyright, 1893. Reprinted by permission of Routledge & Kegan Paul, Ltd.

MARX, KARL.—*The Poverty of Philosophy.* Copyright, 1936, by M. Lawrence. Reprinted by permission of Lawrence & Wishart, Ltd.

MARX, KARL.—"A Contribution to the Critique of Political Economy" from *Selected Works,* Vol. I. Reprinted by permission of Lawrence & Wishart, Ltd.

McGIFFERT, ARTHUR C.—*The Rise of Modern Religious Ideas.* Copyright, 1915, by The Macmillan Company.

McKEON, RICHARD.—*The Basic Works of Aristotle.* Copyright, 1941. Reprinted by courtesy of Random House, Inc.

McWILLIAMS, JAMES A.—From an article which appeared in *The Modern Schoolman* (January, 1935). Reprinted by permission of *The Modern Schoolman.*

MEIKLEJOHN, ALEXANDER.—*Education Between Two Worlds.* Copyright, 1942, by Harper & Brothers. Reprinted by permission of the publishers.

MENCKEN, H. L.—*Treatise on the Gods.* Copyright, 1930, by Alfred A. Knopf, Inc. Reprinted by permission of the publishers.

MONTAGUE, WILLIAM P.—*Belief Unbound.* Copyright, 1931, by Yale University Press. Reprinted by permission of the publishers.

MOTTE, ANDREW.—*Newton's Principles of Natural Philosophy.* Revised by Cajori. Copyright, 1934, by The University of California Press. Reprinted by permission of the publishers.

MUMFORD, LEWIS.—*Faith for Living.* Copyright, 1940, by Harcourt, Brace & Company. Reprinted by permission of the publishers.

NEWMAN, CARDINAL.—*Grammar of Assent.* Copyright, 1895, by Longmans, Green & Company, Inc. Reprinted by permission of the publishers.

OVERSTREET, H. A.—*The Enduring Quest.* Copyright, 1931, by W. W. Norton & Company, Inc. Reprinted by permission of the publishers.

PARRINGTON, VERNON L.—*Romantic Revolution in America,* Vol. II of *Main Currents in American Thought.* Copyright, 1927, by Harcourt, Brace & Company. Reprinted by permission of the publishers.

PERRY, RALPH B.—*Philosophy of the Recent Past.* Copyright, 1926, by Charles Scribner's Sons. Reprinted by permission of the publishers.

PLANCK, MAX.—*Where Is Science Going?* Copyright, 1932, by W. W. Norton & Company, Inc. Reprinted by permission of the publishers.

PLEKHAVOV, GEORGE U.—*The Role of the Individual in History.* Copyright, 1940, by International Publishers.

PRATT, J. B.—*Interpretation of Psychology of Religion.* Copyright, 1928, by Charles Scribner's Sons. Reprinted by permission of the publishers.

RADIN, PAUL.—*Primitive Man as a Philosopher.* Copyright, 1927, by D. Appleton & Company. Reprinted by permission of Appleton-Century-Crofts, Inc.

RANDALL, J. H.—*The Making of the Modern Mind.* Copyright, 1940, by Houghton Mifflin Company. Reprinted by permission of the publishers.

RUSSELL, BERTRAND.—*The Scientific Outlook*. Copyright, 1931, by Bertrand Russell. Reprinted by permission of W. W. Norton & Company, Inc., publishers.

SCHMIDT, W.—*The Origin and Growth of Religion*. Copyright, 1935, by The Dial Press. Reprinted by permission of the publishers.

SERTILLANGES, A. G.—*St. Thomas*, Vol. II. Copyright, 1910, by T. Alcan.

SOROKIN, PITIRIM.—*Social and Cultural Dynamics*. Copyright, 1937, by American Book Company. Reprinted by permission of the publishers.

SPENGLER, OSWALD.—*Decline of the West*. Copyright, 1926, by Alfred A. Knopf, Inc. Reprinted by permission of the publishers.

STEIN, GERTRUDE.—*What Are Masterpieces*. Copyright, 1940, by the Conference Press.

TAYLOR, A. E.—"The Vindication of Religion" in *Essays Catholic and Critical*, edited by Selwyn. Copyright, 1930, by The Macmillan Company. Used by permission of The Macmillan Company, publishers.

THOULESS, R. H.—*Introduction to the Psychology of Religion*. Copyright, 1923, by The Macmillan Company. Used by permission of The Macmillan Company, publishers.

TOYNBEE, ARNOLD J.—*A Study of History*. Copyright, 1946, by Oxford University Press. Reprinted by permission of the publishers.

UREN, A. R.—*Recent Religious Psychology*. Copyright, 1929, by Charles Scribner's Sons. Reprinted by permission of the publishers.

WATKIN, EDWARD I.—*Theism, Agnosticism, and Atheism*. Copyright, 1936, by The Unicorn Press, Ltd. Reprinted by permission of the publishers.

WELLS, H. G.—*Fate of Homo Sapiens*. Copyright, 1939, by Martin Secker & Warburg, Ltd. Reprinted by permission of the publishers and executors.

WELLS, H. G.—*God, the Invisible King*. Copyright, 1917, by The Macmillan Company. Used by permission of The Macmillan Company, publishers.

WHITEHEAD, A. N.—*Religion in the Making*. Copyright, 1926, by The Macmillan Company. Used by permission of The Macmillan Company, publishers.

WHITEHEAD, A. N.—*Science and the Modern World*. Copyright, 1925, by The Macmillan Company. Used by permission of The Macmillan Company, publishers.

ZANGWILL, ISRAEL.—*Voice of Jerusalem*. Copyright, 1921, by The Jewish Publication Society of America. Reprinted by permission of the publisher.

REGINAE SINE LABE ORIGINALI CONCEPTAE
QUAE DUM CREATOREM TERRAE
PARIT IN TERRIS INCARNATUM
RERUM RECREANDARUM FACTA EST PRINCIPIUM
HOC QUALECUMQUE EST OPUS
IN EIUSDEM CREATORIS HONOREM EXARATUM
MILLE BENEFICIORUM MEMOR
EIUSDEM VIRGINIS PATROCINIO
DUM EXCOGITAT DUM SCRIBIT DUM RETRACTAT
IMPETRATORUM
DEDICAT AUCTOR INDIGNUS
ALTERI SI POSSIT NEMINI
LIBENTIORI ANIMO PLACITURUS

Preface

The purpose of this book is to show the relationship between human reason and religion. This involves four distinct problems: first, the history of the abandonment of reason and the final descent into irrationalism; second, a recall to the right use of reason in discovering the existence and nature of God; third, a study of the impact of the physical and historical sciences on religion; fourth, the value of the new approach to religion from man instead of nature.

In Part I it is suggested that once philosophy broke away from the great traditions which respected reason as the revealer and interpreter of purpose, it yielded to lyricism, which made philosophy dance to the tune piped for it by the spirit of an age. Actually philosophy has reached a point of irrationalism where there is an utter contempt of universals, and where, as Hermann Rauschning says: "There is nothing to protect man from feeling himself a creature of creation, *natura naturata:* he is bludgeoned into the Limbo of gloomy reality without any place to set his feet."

In order to correct this irrationalism and the reduction of philosophical principles to symbolic systems, Part II undertakes to prove the transcendence and the immanence of God by a restatement of metaphysical principles. Not to mathematics, but to what Henri Bergson was forced to admit was the "natural science of the human mind," namely, *being*, reason must turn if it is to discover the purpose of life and, therefore, the value of man. The five ways of proving the existence of God in Saint Thomas are restated in terms of modern knowledge, and shown to be independent of the cosmology either of his times, or those of Aristotle.

In Part III there is an evaluation of the impact of the empirical sciences on religion, such as an investigation of Professor Albert North Whitehead's statement that "a new cosmology suggests a new religion," and of the theory of the modern physicists that determinism in physics is a proof of the freedom of man.

From the physical sciences one passes on to a study of comparative religions and their relationship to philosophy and religion. Here, continuing the ideas suggested by De Broglie, there is a study of the problem of resemblances between religions as well as of the transcendence of Christianity.

The third branch of science to be investigated in relation to religion is the historical, for very often in time of crisis, as philosophy becomes confused, men turn to the past for a key to the solution of their problems. *Philosophy of religion* here suggests that any theory of history which denies the extratemporal, or which makes man the plaything of economic or cosmic forces, robs progress of goals and history of meaning.

Part IV takes cognizance not only of the contemporary indifference to metaphysics but also of the importance of the study of man, whose personality has been challenged by the collectivity. The Middle Ages studied the problems of man, but the modern world studies man as a problem. There is a suggestion in this part that religion can be approached from the starting point of frustrated man as well as from the point of view of nature and the cosmos. As in part II, the philosophy of Aquinas here serves as a guide to the understanding of human nature, both in itself and in relation to the cosmos.

In brief, this work attempts to recall the philosophical world to the value of reason, which, though not always under direct attack, has nevertheless been undermined from the flanks through recurrent demonstrations that humanity has been governed, from time to time, by other forces than those of reason. When Marx makes the ethical and philosophical the unstable superstructure of economic methods of production; when the Freudian tradition makes reason the marionette of the unconscious, and asserts that man's true nature is in the fulfillment of the libido; when sociologists make culture and religion the expression of an environment; when psychology becomes physiology, and physiology, chemistry, so that man is reduced to matter, and therefore a thing—then not only does reason lose its primacy, but man himself has no other value than that of being an instrument of power, political or other.

It is a curious paradox that the modern world which started out to glorify rationalism ended in irrationalism. Despite this denial of reason, its principles are still valid and have a transcendent value. It can not only prove a God Whose existence makes the universe intelligible, but also critically judge the excursions of physics, history, and comparative religion in the domain of philosophy. Finally, it can explain how man became frustrated through a loss of purpose, and by recalling this purpose can pave the way for Faith.

Contents

PART I

The Spirit of the Times and the Great Tradition

Chapter I

RATIONALISM

There is such a thing as a *Zeitgeist*, or a Spirit of the Times, varying with the times and overflowing into all the disciplines of the human mind. The spirit of one age is not clearly demarcated from another, for history is not rigid in its divisions. The fringe of one age touches that of another and sometimes is even woven through a succeeding age. A study of these various *Zeitgeists* reveals that what one generation believes to be true, the next generation believes to be false. Rationalism was true for one age, but the Romanticism of the next age believed it to be false. Scientism refused in the next age to accept Romanticism, and in our day Temporalism repudiates Scientism.

Lyricism always accompanies this Spirit of the Age. Lyricism is the interpretation of philosophy, politics, religion, literature, art and God, in terms of the particular Spirit of the Age enjoying popularity at the moment. The progress from one Spirit of the Age to another is not vital like the growth of cell from cell, but mechanical like the swing of a pendulum. The thought of the Spirit of the Age grows by contradictions, rather than by intussusception and assimilation.

A spiritual decline has been operative since the sixteenth century. One by one the spiritual realities have been rejected—the sixteenth century, for example, demanded a new Church, the eighteenth a new Christ, the nineteenth a new God, and the twentieth a new religion. There is rarely any spiritual recuperation from the loss of these great and tremendous realities, spiritual recuperation being oftentimes more difficult than physical recuperation. Instead of working towards an ideal, each Spirit of the Age changes its ideal and this changing of the ideal is frequently called Progress. Classical philosophy and traditional Christian religion, which remain outside the *Zeitgeist*, are generally regarded by the particular *Zeitgeist* as obscurantist and reactionary.

THE SPIRIT OF RATIONALISM

At the end of the eighteenth century the philosophical spirit of the times was rationalism, not the rationalism of Descartes but a poor, shabby travesty of it. Descartes believed that it was possible for the mind to deduce from a few abstract principles, in a geometrical fashion, a great *summa* of knowledge. As Christopher Dawson writes:

This is the foundation of the Cartesian method for the reform of the whole body of sciences. All the vast accumulation of knowledge and tradition which was the heritage of European culture, all the ideas and beliefs that men acquire from experience and literature and the contact with other minds were to be set aside as an impure and uncertain compound of truth and error, and to be replaced by the new knowledge of mathematical certitude which was derived from the infallible light of the pure reason.[1]

Newton gave a new form to Cartesian Rationalism by asserting that there was a rational principle valid throughout the whole universe, which principle should serve as the true foundation of thought. Fontenelle, one of the popularizers of Descartes, wrote once:

The geometric spirit is not so bound up with geometry that it cannot be disentangled and carried into other fields. A work of morals, of politics, of criticism, perhaps even of eloquence, will be the finer, other things being equal, if it is written by the hand of a geometer.[2]

Newton did this very thing; he so effectively carried over the mathematical spirit into the temper of the times that he saturated all other departments of life and thought with it, and did more than anyone else to make the natural synonymous with the rational. In 1687, Newton published his *Philosophiae Naturalis Principia Mathematica*, in which he revealed that his great ideal was to explain everything in this universe, every motion, every planet, every fall of the sparrow, by one universal law. He was, in effect, asserting that every event in the universe could be deduced mathematically from the fundamental principles of mechanical action, and more particularly from the law of gravitation, which was valid throughout the whole universe. Anything which could not be deduced from this universal law with mathematical precision was, in his opinion, unworthy of the name of science.

The ideal seemed excellent, and gained impetus when Newton, working on his universal principle of gravitation, proved mathematically that Kepler's inductive law of planetary motion must be a fact. Every day it was becoming clearer that not an appeal to sense experience, but a direct intuition of mathematical and geometrical axioms was the ideal. It was not necessary to turn the telescope on the sun; one needed merely to work out the sun's laws and movements from first principles, for the universe was regarded as a uniform mathematical universe. The physical laws which held good on the earth would be valid throughout the whole universe. Thus did Newton perfect the mechanical conception of nature inaugurated by Kepler, Descartes, and Galileo.

In laying down a universal scientific principle valid throughout the cosmos, and from which all other laws could be deduced, Newton also postulated a philosophical method that he earnestly desired should be followed. He asked that his scientific method become a philosophical method, and opened the way in his day for that same distortion of philosophy which exists in our time, namely, making religion and metaphysics conform to the rules of science. How clearly he meant to found a philosophical system based on his deductive first principle is evident from the Preface to his work:

By the proposition mathematically demonstrated in the first book, we then derive from the celestial phenomena the force of gravity with which bodies tend to the sun and the several planets. Then, from these sources, by other propositions which are also mathematical, we deduce the motions of the planets, the comets, the moon and the sea. I wish we could derive the rest of the phenomena of nature by the same kind of reasoning from mechanical principles; for I am induced by many reasons to suspect that they may all depend upon certain forces by which the particles of bodies, by some causes hitherto unknown, are either mutually impelled towards each other, and cohere in regular figures, or are repelled and recede from each other: which forces being unknown, philosophers have hitherto attempted the search in vain; but I hope the principles here laid down will afford some light either to that or some truer method of philosophy.[3]

To guide philosophers in the deductive method, Newton lays down four principles, the first three of which are rationalistic and a priori:

1. We are to admit no more causes of natural things than such as are both true and sufficient to explain their appearances.

2. To the same natural effects, we must, so far as possible, assign the same causes.

3. The qualities of bodies which admit neither intention nor remission of degrees, and which are to be found to belong to all bodies within the reach of our experiments, are to be esteemed universal qualities of all bodies whatsoever.[4]

The first philosophical principle is a solicitation to cling to natural causes, the second touches on the uniformity of nature, and the third is the typical Newtonian supposition that what is true in one part of the universe is true throughout the whole of it.[5] It was this last rule which had more to do with establishing rationalism than any other single force.

For Newton, then, science was composed of laws stating the mathematical behaviours of nature solely—laws clearly deducible from phenomena and exactly verifiable in phenomena: everything further is to be swept out of science, which thus becomes a body of absolutely certain truth about the doings of the physical world.[6]

Although Newton was by no means an atheist, he was interpreted and misunderstood by his followers to be at least deistic. His distinction between primary and secondary causes was quite justified, but his queer mingling of the two to account for irregularities in the universe left him open to censure. Partly through his own fault, therefore, and partly through the narrow mindedness of others, he caused a break with the traditional concept of God.

The influence of Newton was tremendous. In 1727 he was given a royal funeral. Voltaire popularized his ideas in the *Elements of the Newtonian Philosophy* in 1738. In 1789, forty books had been written in English about the *Principia*, seventeen in French, three in German, eleven in Latin, one in Portuguese, and one in Italian. Count Algarotti, feeling that Newton had a special appeal for the ladies, wrote *Le Newtonianisme pour les dames*, which went through many editions. And finally Pope immortalized him:

> Nature and Nature's laws lay hid in Night:
> God said, *Let* Newton *be!* And all was light.

In those days men were saying that "the backgrounds of religion and philosophy are changing." "Science has suggested a new outlook"—and so it had. Its method was: first, to find some rational principle in philosophy, as Newton found one in science; next, to apply this principle throughout the whole field of knowledge, as Newton applied his principle throughout the whole universe.

It is a fact verifiable by history that whenever there has been a great change made in scientific outlook, there arise thinkers who demand that even fundamental truths be revised to conform to the new viewpoint. There were some even in those days who claimed that "a new cosmology demands a new religion," and immediately a new religion was born. There were others who asked that ethics, literature and metaphysics change their very essence to be more in keeping with the new scientific outlook.

Lyricism of Religion

Rationalism produced a distorted kind of optimism. Beginning with the principle that God is the perfect and absolute good, and applying strictly rationalistic principles, it was concluded that God could only do what was best and perfect; hence this world must be the best possible world. Such was the thought of Leibnitz early in the eighteenth century (1710) when he published his *Theodicy*. He missed the point that this may be the best possible world for the purpose God had in mind in creating it, but not necessarily the best possible world considered in itself. His optimism was a false optimism, and from it followed a double consequence which manifested itself in England, France, and Germany: the negation of the supernatural and the denial of Providence and of God.

For if this is the best possible world, then nothing can be added to make it better. Reason alone suffices. Since faith is an addition to reason, and grace something above nature, and miracles and prophecies something above the natural scientific order, they are therefore impossible, for how can something be added to the best? The supernatural, by its very definition, was considered as outside the natural order, for it supposes something added to nature. Furthermore, since this is the best possible world, and this best possible world runs according to certain determined and mechanical laws valid throughout the whole cosmos, it was concluded that a miracle is an interference with the orderliness and the rationalistic character of the universe.

The truth of the Christian religion rests not on subjective feeling, but on objective bases for credibility, such as miracles and prophecies. On rationalistic principles, these criteria are, as indicated above, beyond the nature of the best possible world and superfluous to it. The general principles which made for the elimination of the supernatural had already been stated; they merely awaited application by two philosophers of the times who lyricized the Newtonian rationalist universe and rejected the external foundation for faith in Christ and Christianity: Anthony Collins and Thomas Woolston, who respectively denied the possibility of proof to either prophecies or miracles.[7]

Up to this point no one had attacked revelation and the Scriptures in their entirety. Locke had proclaimed the autonomy of reason; Toland had substituted pantheism, and Shaftesbury skepticism, for Christianity. It remained for Tindal to attack Christianity from all sides, for Morgan to deny the revealed character of the Old Testament, and Chubb, the revealed character of the New.[8]

France, at this time intoxicated by the power of reason, denied the supernatural. Pierre Bayle (1647-1706), one of the protagonists of the rational against the supernatural, urged contempt of everything mysterious.

Do not try to understand mysteries: if you could understand them they would be mysteries no longer. Do not even try to lessen their apparent absurdity. Your reason here is utterly powerless; and who knows but that absurdity may be an essential ingredient of mystery. Believe as Christians, but as philosophers, abstain.

Bayle believed that from the point of view of knowledge, the mysteries of religion and belief in the supernatural were offensive to reason and therefore absurd. From the point of view of morals, they did not make man any better, and hence were useless. The choice with him was imperative. Either one must be rationalist and cease to be a Christian, or be a Christian and forego reason altogether.

Voltaire (1694-1778) directed shafts of ridicule against the supernatural. "Before his journey to England, Voltaire was a dissatisfied poet; England made him a philosopher." [9] He arrived in England at a time when Collins was writing against prophecies, and Woolston against miracles. Both of these attacks inspired him, as did the sensationalism of Locke.

Voltaire did not criticize the Bible or revelation or the supernatural; he did not discuss these points; he did not reason, he only burlesqued. "I ask for only five or six good words each day [to crush that infamy]; that will suffice; it will never rise again. Laugh, Democritus; make others laugh and the sages will triumph." [10] He deliberately distorted facts in the Bible to serve his purposes as a clown. "Lie like the devil, not timidly, not merely for a time, but bravely and always.... Lie, my friends, lie." [11] In order to prove miracles impossible he gave his own definition, and then drew his conclusion. "A miracle is the violation of mathematical, divine, immutable and eternal laws. By this very statement, a miracle is a contradiction in its terms; a law cannot be at the same time immutable and violated." [12] There is nothing new in his polemics against Sacred Scripture. Much of what he says is found in Toland and Woolston and Bolingbroke. What is new is his cynicism. Truth counts for nothing with Voltaire; success is everything. He flattered himself that he had done far more to destroy Christianity than certain Reformers. *"J'ai fait plus en mon temps que Luther et Calvin."* [13]

In Germany three elements combined to produce a denial of the supernatural: English deism, French impiety, and the rationalism of Christian Wolff (1679-1754). In 1719 Wolff published his principal work, *Vernunftige Gedanken von Gott,* the purpose of which was to vulgarize the idea of Leibnitz, while modifying it considerably. The work completely eliminated the supernatural. He taught that it required a God less powerful to produce miracles than to produce natural events. God could never produce anything miraculously, for if He did He would be acting without sufficient reason and contrary to His infinite perfection. Wolff reasoned the same way concerning revelation: a revealed truth cannot be contrary to reason. Our reason has the right to judge and appreciate it. Furthermore there is no necessity for revelation since all truths can be known by the reason of man. The application of these principles destroyed Christian beliefs touching the Old and the New Testament.

As a result of his rationalistic ideas, Wolff was obliged to leave Germany within forty-eight hours. Persecution, however, made him glorious. He became celebrated in Europe: *Nova lux Germaniae, professor generis humani;* in the year 1738 there were one hundred and seven writers inspired by his principles. Under his inspiration, preachers were calling Christ a "supernatural entelechy, an adorable monad." He returned in triumph to Halle in 1740, but although he taught until his death in 1754, he had very few pupils.

Up to this point, men of limited caliber were active in theological controversy. Then came Gotthold Ephraim Lessing (1729-1781), who waged war on the supernatural with a different kind of sword, namely, incredulity and indifference, supported by his theory of unlimited progress which explained religion in a natural way, the Christian religion not excepted. In 1774-1778 he published anonymously *The Fragments of Wolfenbüttel*, a violent work against Christianity. He published it as an old manuscript presumed to have been found in the library of Wolfenbüttel, though he knew very well the name of the author, Herman Samuel Reimarus (1694-1768). Reimarus, on dying, left to his daughter Elsie a voluminous manuscript of four thousand pages, which had for its title, *Apologie oder Schutzschrift für die Vernunftigen Verehrer Gottes*. He had thought the work too bitter, so he left it to posterity to publish. Elsie was a friend of Lessing and she put it into his hands. If the work had appeared with the name of the author, it would have excited much less attention. Curiosity made its appeal more powerful. In this work the author pretends that Jesus and John the Baptist were partners in restoring the ancient Jewish regime. But the entrance into Jerusalem on Palm Sunday raised up the established authority against His plans. He was then condemned to death and died abandoned by God.[14]

The second consequence of false optimism induced by the rationalistic thinkers was the denial of Providence. How is it, if this is the best possible world, that things happen in it which are not the best? How can there be evil, pain, waste, war, and carnage? Rationalism, not being able to answer these questions, led to irrationalism. Rationalists concluded that there is no God, because the world is not perfect; if there were a God, the world would be perfect. But the irreligion which came was not at first purely atheistic. Deism paved its way, and deism owed its origin to the philosophy of Newton, who held that God is just the creator of this world machine and that He needs only to interfere with it when it requires mending. As science advanced, it became more and more clear that the laws which operated in the cosmos were universal, and there was less room for God—rationalists could not see that every increase in knowledge of the law of the universe meant an additional proof of God the Law Giver.

Newton believed that Nature proved the existence of God. In his work on Optics, he explicitly stated that every study of the universe brings us closer to the knowledge of the First Cause. As he explained: "The main business of natural philosophy is to argue from phenomena without feigning hypotheses, and to deduce causes from their effects, till we come to the very first Cause which certainly is not mechanical." [15]

Thus far Newton was in keeping with common-sense philosophy. But he went astray when he touched the point of the relation existing between God and His handiwork, for here he paved the way for deism. According to traditional thought, God not only created the world, but conserves it in being, conservation being a kind of continued creation. God is therefore Providence as well as Creator. But Newton thought of God as doing little more than creating the mass of the universe, and throwing it out into the great absolute space and absolute time which figured so prominently in his science. God made the world, it is true, but when it was finished He gave it a little flick of his thumb, or, as some have put it, "gave it a kick into space and let it go." Newton's writings in many places betray this theodicy in which God is just a little more than a Creator, who, after constructing the universe, practically let it go on independently of Him.

According to Newton, there are only two duties which God has left in this universe. First, He prevents the fixed stars from falling; and secondly, He repairs the machine of the universe whenever it needs it, lest the comets which move in eccentric orbs and the planets in concentric orbs run amuck. Dr. Edwin A. Burtt in his work entitled *Metaphysical Foundations of Modern Physical Science*, has given much attention to Newtonian theodicy and characterizes it in these words:

God, now the chief mechanic of the universe, has become the cosmic conservative. His aim is to maintain the *status quo*. The day of novelty is all in the past, there is no further advance in Time. Periodic reformations when necessary, by the addition of the indicated masses at the points of space required, but no new creative activity—to this routine of temporal housekeeping is the Deity at present confined.

Historically, the Newtonian attempt thus to keep God on duty was of the very deepest import. It proved a veritable boomerang to his cherished philosophy of religion, that as the result of all his pious ransackings, the main providential function he could attribute to Deity was this cosmic plumbing, this meticulous defence of His arbitrarily imposed laws against the threatened encroachments of irregularity. Really, the notion of the Divine eye as constantly roaming the universe, on the search for leaks to mend, or gears to replace in the mighty machinery would have been quite laughable, did not its pitifulness become earlier evident. For to stake the present existence and activity of God on imperfections in the cosmic engine was to court rapid disaster for theology.[16]

If the sole and unique function of God in the universe is to take care of the irregularities which Newton could not account for by his science, it is only natural that, as scientists find laws for such apparent irregularities, they will thereby find reasons for dispensing with God. If God's purpose in the universe is to take care of that part which science cannot yet grasp, then the advance of science will mean the retreat of God. This process of eliminating the Providential in the world order actually reached its climax in Laplace, who demonstrated the inherent stability of the universe by showing that all of its irregularities are periodical and subject to an eternal law which prevents them from exceeding certain limits. It is a queer mentality which concludes that the discovery of a scientific law dispenses with the necessity of a Scientific Lawgiver, but such was the process of thought set in motion by Newton. Having made God synonymous with the unscientific, the progress of science naturally came to mean a disbelief in God. The day that philosophy returns to the conception that the existence of God is not founded on the scientifically inexplicable, but on the rationally explicable, it will undo a false principle that has been haunting the philosophy of religion since the days of Newton.

Rationalism was not solely negative, in eliminating the supernatural and Providence; in its constructive moments it built up a religion in perfect keeping with its rationalist principles: a religion based uniquely upon reason and principles of reason—the religion of deism.

John Locke in 1695 published *The Reasonableness of Christianity*, in which he plods steadily through Scriptures accumulating proofs of his thesis, that Christ, on admitting converts to His Church, did not ask them to signify a belief in the Athanasian Creed, or the Thirty-nine Articles, but only to make acknowledgment that He was the Messias. Thus was Locke's venture into a religion, like

Newton's venture into the universe, an attempt to reduce all religion to a single formula. For Locke the transcendence of Christianity was its coincidence with the conclusions of unassisted reason. Christianity was just a great reform; it was bringing back rational sanctions which previously had been obscured. What Christ did, in the eyes of Locke, was simply to give a new weight and force to the authority of reason. There were, Locke would admit, certain great glimpses of the depths of the Life and Wisdom of God, but these were a Holy of Holies which we should not touch. We should, however, reverence them.

Locke thus did not completely eliminate the supernatural. He had too much regard and reverence for the Christian past. He rather threw it into the background by his strong emphasis on the rational character of Christianity. The formulae of the past he would keep, though they filled him with disgust. This was not so with his successors. If the formulae have no reasonable basis, if they retain their force only because of a sentimental reverence, why not purge them out of religion altogether, and reduce everything to the natural and rational? So ran their thoughts.

Samuel Clarke, author of the Boyle lectures of 1705, entitled *A Discourse concerning the Unchangeable obligations of natural religion, and the Truth and Certainty of Christian Revelation*, in keeping with the spirit of the age, believed that a new cosmology demanded a new religion, just as Professor Whitehead has taught. Clarke sought to reduce all theology to some simple principle, so that all its propositions would dovetail. His basis was intuitive truths, axioms and their corollaries. Twelve propositions which flow one from the other like the principles of Euclid are supposed to demonstrate the existence and the attributes of God. This was his foundation of Natural Religion. He proceeded to justify the supernatural on exactly the same grounds, but here the chain consists of fifteen links. The foundation is Nature (sometimes identified with God) always made up of unalterable propositions like those of mathematics. From these propositions all morality is derived. Instead of relativizing theology, as is the custom today, philosophers in those days astronomized and mathematized it. Hence we find such a statement as this: To deny that a man should love his neighbor is "as unreasonable as that he should affirm one number of quantity to be equal to another, and yet that other at the same time not equal to the first."

David Hume convinced himself and many of his contemporaries that he had found a universal principle comparable to the law of gravitation in physics, namely, the law of association of ideas. Just as the law of gravitation explained the movement of masses, so the law of association explained the groupings or the massing of mental phenomena. Attaching himself to the tradition of Newton on this point, he allied himself to the tradition of Locke by his theory concerning ideas and judgments, which arise only from "images and sometimes faint images."

Christian Wolff, who has already been quoted in reference to anti-supernaturalism, deserves mention once again for his attempt to build up a rational religion and rational ethics. He confessed that mathematicians were sure of their ground and their method, and that he hoped to give theology the same certainty. He even went so far as to believe that what could not be mathematically demonstrated could not be true. His method was Cartesian in the sense that it was mathematical. Entering the University of Jena in 1702, he studied Descartes and wrote a thesis entitled *Philosophia practica universalis mathematica methodo conscripta*. In this thesis Wolff sought to give the ontological proof of the existence of God a mathematical form, which won for him the praise of Leibnitz. What the law of gravitation was to Newton, the principle of sufficient reason was to Wolff. From it he deduces, in accordance with Newton's first three principles, the laws of inertia and continuity, the existence of God, and the necessity of revelation.[17]

On the religion of the period, Christopher Dawson writes:

Eighteenth century Deism was but the ghost or shadow of Christianity, a mental abstraction from the reality of a historical religion, which possessed no independent life of its own. It retained certain fundamental Christian conceptions—the belief in a beneficent Creator, the idea of an overruling Providence which ordered all things for the best, and the chief precepts of the Christian moral law, but all these were desupernaturalized and fitted into the utilitarian rational scheme of contemporary philosophy. Thus the moral law was divested of all ascetic and other-worldly elements and assimilated to practical philanthropy, and the order of Providence was transformed into a mechanistic natural law. Above all, this was the case with the idea of Progress, for while the new philosophy had no place for the supernaturalism of the Christian eschatology, it could not divest itself of the Christian teleological conception of life. Thus the belief in the moral perfectibility and the indefinite progress of the human race took the place of the Christian faith in the life of the world to come, as the final goal of human effort. This idea lies at the root of the whole philosophic movement, and it was fully formulated long before the days of the Encyclopaedist propaganda. And it is quite in accordance with what I have said regarding the origins of this circle of ideas, that its author should have been a priest—the first of that long line of sceptical and reforming clerics, such as Mably, Condillac, Morellet, Raynal and Sieyès, who were so characteristic of the Age of Enlightenment.[18]

LYRICISM OF THE MORAL AND POLITICAL SCIENCES

The time-spirit overflowed religion and passed into the domain of political sciences as well. It was assumed that nature contained a moral law as well as a physical law. The problem was to discover this moral law. David Hartley (1705-1757), in his work, the *Observations on Man*, writes:

The proper method of philosophizing seems to be to discover and establish the general laws of action, affecting the subject under consideration, from certain select, well-defined and well-attested phenomena, then to explain and predict the other phenomena by these laws. This is the method of analysis and synthesis resumed and followed by Isaac Newton.[19]

Just as physics was discovered to be independent of theology and governed by its own laws, so too were ethics and moral philosophy and social thought. God might have given them, it is true, as he gave the physical universe, but they could be discovered by a rational method, just as science discovered the laws of the universe. Quite naturally, social sciences of this kind would in reality be social physics. As Dr. J. H. Randall has said:

The eighteenth-century thinkers, combining at last the two strains of the humanistic emphasis upon the dignity and worth of man's life upon this earth, and of the scientific emphasis upon universal law and a harmonious causal order in every part of nature, created a science of human nature in the individual and in society. Carrying on their work as they did, profoundly influenced by the reigning Newtonian ideal of science and of scientific method, they could hardly have failed to produce a science that resembled, as closely as their new subject matter would let them—indeed, probably far too closely—the ideal and the method of mathematical physics. They went so far as to claim to have discovered a veritable mental and social physics.[20]

Inspired by the Newtonian method of analyzing a few simple cases to discover fundamental axioms, a number of social philosophies were developed. Among the more important ones was that of the already mentioned John Locke, who with other theorists of his time used the world "natural" in the sense of the rational, the identification made by Newton. From natural laws he deduced social laws. In his *Treatise on Civil Government* (1689), Locke starts his argument with a "state of nature," or a pre-political state, where there was a harmonious relation between all men:

To understand political power of right and to derive it from his original, we must consider what state all men are naturally in, and that is a state of perfect freedom to order their actions and dispose of their persons and possessions as they think fit, within the bounds of the laws of nature without depending upon the will of any other man.... The state of nature has a law of nature to govern it which obliges everyone, and reason which is that law teaches all mankind who will but consult it, that being all equal and independent no one ought to harm another in his life, health, liberty or possessions.[21]

This general statement of the end and purpose of government marks the conclusion of an attempt to base society on a religious foundation, and the beginning of the progressive secularization of the English state. The first duty of the State, according to Locke, had nothing whatever to do with safeguarding the spiritual interests of society, but was to secure the rights of private property, "for the sake of which men enter into society." Applying his rational method, Locke went further and held that under certain conditions when governments had infringed upon the rights of individuals, a revolution was naturally justified:

Whensoever therefore the legislative shall transgress this fundamental rule of society and either by ambition, fear, folly or corruption endeavor to grasp themselves or put into the hands of any other an absolute power over the lives, liberties and estates of the people; by this breach of their trust they forfeit the power the people had put in their hands for quite contrary ends, and it devolves to the people who have a right to resume their original liberty, by the establishment of a new legislation (such as they shall think fit) provide for their own safety and security which is the end for which they are in society.[22]

Thus was the Whig revolution of the middle classes against the Stuarts justified, and the same rational principle was evoked to justify the revolution of the American colonies against England.[28]

David Hartley published his *Observations on Man* in 1749. Association is for man, Hartley held, what gravitation is for the planets. Just how far the mathematical method influenced his thoughts is evident from his vest-pocket formula for social sciences: "Let W," he said, "represent the love of the world, F the fear of God, and L the love of God. Then we may say $W : F \therefore F : L$, or $W = \dfrac{F^2}{L}$."

By this he meant that in our initial state we fear God more than we love Him, and love the world infinitely more than we fear God. He believed that the creature should be more and more swallowed up by the love of God, a conviction which he made the first principle of social science.

Not all social philosophers were as keen on keeping God in society as was Hartley. As the successors of Newton found a principle by which the physical universe could be explained without God, so too the later moralists found a way of explaining the moral universe without such an appeal. Newton found a principle immanent in Nature, namely, gravitation, which for some minds dispensed with God; moralists too believed they had found a principle immanent in man which would dispense with Him. Eighteenth-century philosophy is therefore full of systems which find in man and nature the source of all morality. The principles of morality at this period were incorporated into a scheme of reason and science which was independent of religious foundations. Human nature is universally the same, hence the same rational rules should be valid everywhere, without regard for any historical perfection which revelation might bring. Not all moralists hit upon the same immanent first principle. Hutcheson, in his *System of Moral Philosophy* (1755), thought there was a "special faculty" which saw right and wrong, as the eye distinguishes between light and darkness. Adam Smith, in his *Theory of Moral Sentiments* (1759), found the first principle in self-interest, while Bentham, in his *Principles of Morals and Legislation* (1789), found his in utility.

While the spirit of the English social philosophers seemed to be a quest for some economic first principles such as that of Locke, or for a mathematical expression such as that of Hartley, the

French, on the contrary, seemed to stress more the humanitarian base. There was, however, some connecting link. Locke's sensationalism, which held that everything comes from experience, became the foundation of a conclusion concerning the equality of man, for if all that men are comes from experience, then it must be environment, and not birth, which makes them different. For the French, human equality was not so much a conclusion from the empirical order as a first principle. The suppression of human rights made men think in terms of human rights. In order to prove that the governed were as good as the governing, the theorists affirmed the equal rights of all. Thus in France, the Age of Reason became the Age of Humanitarianism. Fourier expressed the typical optimism of the French humanitarianism in an extreme form by predicting that France would one day have thirty million scientists as great as Newton, and thirty million poets as great as Shakespeare. He was the H. G. Wells of his day. The making of happy, learned men and good citizens resolved itself then merely into a matter of education and political environment. Helvétius believed that by education one could effect a kingdom of sagacious and virtuous citizens. As he himself put it, it was "the good lawmaker who makes the good citizen." [24] These ideas of the equality of men and the moral power of government to make them wise, together with the ideas of Rousseau, later formed the basis of certain statements in the American Declaration of Independence. The French Declaration of the Rights of Man, for example, stated that "all men are born free and equal." Jefferson wrote in the Declaration of Independence "all men are created equal."

The argument of Locke, it will be recalled, was that the aim of government is to protect property, that whenever any government invades the privileges of property, the people have a right to overthrow that government and establish another. Samuel Adams, who called Locke "one of the greatest men who ever wrote," in 1765 based his argument for some kind of American independence on Locke's views of the economic origin and basis of government. There are two very important consequences for government policy involved in these ideas of Locke and Adams. The first is the substitution of an economic for a spiritual basis of government; the second is the emphasis on property rights rather than personal rights. In asserting the sacredness of property, Locke laid the foundations of the new philosophy of capitalism. The first duty of government for Locke was not to defend the Christian faith but to secure the rights of private property "for the sake of which men enter into society." Thus, as Lord Acton said, the English Revolution substituted for "the Divine Right of Kings, the Divine Right of Freeholders." Jefferson saw the consequences which might result from this economic first principle, and he tempered it with the influence derived from the French humanitarian doctrine of the equality of men. Jefferson was affected by not only the English economic influence, but the French humanitarian influence, which probably accounts for the fact that in drawing up the Declaration of Independence he caused the passage on slavery to be stricken out and the words "pursuit of happiness" substituted for the "property" emphasized by Locke and Samuel Adams.

Yet Thomas Jefferson has acknowledged the influence of Locke while writing the Declaration of Independence:

I turn to neither book nor pamphlet while writing. I did not consider it as any part of my charge to invent new ideas altogether and to offer any sentiments which had never been expressed before.... All its authority rests then on the harmonizing sentiments of the day, whether expressed in conversation, in letters, printed essays, or the elementary books of public right as Aristotle, Cicero, Locke, and Sidney.[25]

As C. A. and M. R. Beard stated in their work, *The Rise of American Civilization:*

English Deism was borne to France by Voltaire, where it became the creed of nearly all the skeptics who labored at the Encyclopedia, and at the new philosophy of naturalism and humanity. From various directions the doctrine came into America, spreading widely through the intellectual leaders of the American Revolution and making them doubly dangerous characters in the eyes of the Anglican Tories. When the crisis came, Jefferson, Paine, John Adams, Washington, Franklin, Madison, and many lesser lights were to be reckoned among either the Unitarians or Deists. It was not Cotton Mather's God to whom the authors of the Declaration of Independence appealed; it was to "Nature's God." From whatever source derived, the effect of both Unitarianism and Deism was to hasten the retirement of historic theology from its empire over the intellect of American leaders.[26]

William A. Dunning in his *History of Political Theories*, in speaking of the rationalist influence on government, says:

The simple principles of a rational theory of state and government were embodied in constitutional codes, where man might readily find clearly outlined the source and substance of the social and political order. Nature, universal and immutable, was the basis of these codes; liberty and equality for every individual were the imperative dictates of nature's organ, reason.[27]

LYRICISM OF RATIONALISM, IN HOMILETICS, LITERATURE, AND THE ARTS

Two things seem to be absent from all the sermons of this period: faith and poetry. But common sense remained. They contained very high abstract reasoning or this homely common sense. Nothing was taken for granted. Every preacher felt bound to give a series of truths to generate probabilities. He never advanced very far because he never felt that he was very secure away from his base. Sermons offered diagrams instead of pictures, axioms instead of appeals. The Christian was appealed to not to get drunk because it would ruin his health; not to commit murder because he would go to the gallows. Clarke and Sherlock represented the two extremes of these rationalistic preachments in English. Clarke appealed only to logic, and Sherlock, who was a lawyer in a cassock, appealed only to common sense. The religion of nature was to him like the common law of England, a traditional body of doctrine.[28]

In the field of poetry, Pope is the typical representative of the spirit of the age; his *Essay on Man* aspires to be a work of theodicy such as Leibnitz would have written. Pope, who was a Catholic and who therefore should have believed in the supernatural life, makes little or no mention of it. His *Essay* was the poetry of deism, of Clarke, Tindal, and Shaftesbury.

Other didactic poems of that period, typical of the rationalistic spirit are Thomson's "The Seasons" (1726-1730); Akenside's "Pleasures of the Imagination" (1744); and Young's "Night Thoughts" (1742). This last work was intended by the author to be a supplement to Pope's *Essay on Man*. In the poem he sets up a man of straw who denies immortality, and then through long nights spent in unloosing a battery of arguments, he makes him admit immortality. Rationalism never lends itself readily to poetry, and hence it is not surprising to find in Young such a very unpoetical but rationalistic line as: "Hence a fifth proof arises still."

In a more general way rationalism manifested itself in literature as classicism, dating roughly from Dryden (1700). The term "classicism" may not be the most accurate, but understood properly, it means that the ideals, the methods, and the characteristics of the writers of the time expressed themselves in a general searching after rationality. In one of the finest studies in English literature, Louis Cazamian speaks thus of the literature of the period:

Classical poetry, viewed as a whole, is rational in its inspiration. The themes it treats are, therefore, most often of an abstract nature; or at least the development which is given them inclines to abstraction. For the choice of terms, the quality of style, are determined by a deep preference of the mind. Creative imagination, so to say, shows here an intellectual trend. Classical poetry refuses on principle to be nurtured by the expressive force of concrete, familiar terms, which savour of the freshness of life itself.... The poetic diction of the eighteenth century, over and above the diffuse and widespread quality, becomes concentrated in stereotyped expressions which are transmitted from poet to poet. The language of poetry thus becomes conventional, in that it no longer answers to a choice, to a verbal creation, but to a mechanical art, to passive devices.[29]

What is true of poetry is true of prose and music. Thoughts become concentrated in the discussion and solution of problems. Swift, for example, can be understood only in the light of the controversies centering about philosophy and religion. Clarke, Warburton, and Butler were primarily rational in their style, though they directed their shafts against the deists, using reason to meet reason. Bernard Mandeville conceived his work in politics in the same spirit of rationalism.

J. Combarieu, in his three-volume work, *The History of Music*, writes: "The eighteenth century until the time of the French Revolution had only one great musician, Rameau, and although he is rich in concert pieces he never produced even one great symphony." [30] When Rameau was sixty-seven years of age, he attempted to do for music what Newton had done for astonomy and Wolff had done for philosophy, namely, to reduce everything to a single principle. Up until his time, writers had been content to indicate the rules for relating chords, but he attempted to discover the law which determined the formation of the chords themselves. He presented his theory in such a way, and with such a method, as to recall the *Discourses on Method* of Descartes. Rameau made a

tabula rasa of all that had been written before him on musical
theory, just as Descartes had said he would in his letter to Gassendi.
His method was technically to reduce all modes (there are eight
modes after the Greek method) in music to one, and to place all
elements under the influence of a dominant note which was the
base of a series and generator of that series, or, as he put it, "the
master of the series." Rameau also substituted tonal unity for the ancient plural modality. In a more technical way the music of this
century showed a great contempt for minor modes, "because they
were not furnished by nature," and anything that did not come
from nature was artificial and was therefore to be condemned.

The rationalistic influence manifested itself in the art of the period,
reaching even into the sacred precincts of the Academy of Arts in
Paris, which sought to formulate rules and precepts for painting.
For many years this Academy worked out tables containing the
official pedagogy, the legislative code of design, of color, and of
expression, all attempting to be as clean-cut in their method as
that of Descartes, as universal in their application as the principle of Newton. The Academy of Architecture, under the direction of Jacques Blondel, in like manner worked out even the smallest
details of proportion. It stated that the first principle of all architecture was "beauty and good taste." But just what was meant by
beauty was difficult to define. The architects sought to state it in
terms of the a priori. The artists and painters joined in the discussion,
and the meeting to decide the first principles of art was broken up.
Among the first principles suggested, all typical of the period,
were the following: "Art is a work of the reason and not of the
imagination or the sentiment." "Reason above everything." "Reason is the father of beauty." It was Minerva, the goddess of methodic
wisdom, whom the artists of the time held up as their ideal at the
meeting of the Beaux Arts. In like manner, architecture sought,
in conformity with these principles, to introduce logic into all its
conceptions; this resulted in the strict justice of proportion and
normal distribution. For this type of architecture, the surcharge of
ornaments was avoided, as well as all decorations which troubled
the beauty of the lines.

Just what the age of rationalism thought of itself is preserved
for us in a message recently discovered in the steeple knob of the

Church of St. Margaret at Gotha, in Germany, a message placed there in 1734 for posterity to read:

Our age occupies the happiest period of the eighteenth century. Emperors, kings, and princes humanely descend from their dreaded heights, despise pomp and splendor, become the fathers, friends, and confidents of their people. Religion rends its priestly garb and appears in its divine essence. Enlightenment makes great strides. Thousands of our brothers and sisters, who formerly lived in sanctified inactivity, are given back to the state. Sectarian hatred and persecution for conscience' sake are vanishing. Love of man and freedom of thought are gaining the supremacy. The arts and sciences are flourishing, and our gaze is penetrating deeply into the workshop of nature. Handicraftsmen, as well as artists, are reaching perfection; useful knowledge is growing among all classes. Here you have a faithful description of our times. Do not haughtily look down upon us if you are higher and see farther than we; recognize rather from the picture which we have drawn how bravely and energetically we labored to raise you to the position which you now hold and to support you in it. Do the same for your descendant and be happy.

Chapter II

ROMANTICISM

There is always a permanent stratum of thought in society which represents the common-sense tradition of humanity. Alongside this, and always much more conspicuous, is another spirit which is typical of the times and which looks upon the traditional spirit as obscurantist or medieval or reactionary. Hidden beneath all of the effervescence of naturalism in natural religion, natural morals, and economic politics, there is living and breathing the Christian tradition which survives today. It would seem to be the logical result for a society which became intoxicated with any excess to swing back again into this golden mean of Christian and common-sense tradition. This perhaps does happen with a very small minority, but rarely with those who are keenly bent on following the moods and fancies of the moment. With the latter group it is generally true to say that what one generation of them believes to be true, the next generation will believe to be false. In the eighteenth century modernism was equivalent to naturalism, rationalism, and deism. These movements led to a general reaction, prompted by three causes: the reaction of common sense; the reaction of the historical sciences; and the reaction of religion.

Tertullian once said that "the soul is naturally Christian." If this means anything, it means that the soul is impelled in some way to return again to truth. The mechanical rationalism of the eighteenth century was a distortion of the soul. It was an excess, like a vice. The natural tendency of men to swing away from excesses of this kind produced in them a spirit which exaggerated the elements which rationalism had left out. With rationalism the excess had been that of deductive reason. The Spirit of the Age swung to the extreme end of the pendulum: from the domination of cold reason to the domination of gushy sentimentalism. The "naturally Christian" souls of men told them that they were rational animals. The Newtonian tradition emphasized the rational, but forgot the animal side, or feelings, which have a right to be heard. Men, analyzing their own natures, quite readily understand that life is bigger than cold deductive reason and cannot be confined within its categories. The reaction of common sense was away from reason and toward feeling, toward a philosophy of romanticism. Common sense suggested only the reaction. It did not suggest the new excess of feeling. In studying the philosophy of romanticism and its contempt of reason, it is well to bear in mind that what it was refuting was not the classical reason, but rather the crude Cartesian and mechanistic substitute for it, just as Kant was not refuting the Scholastic arguments for the existence of God, but only the badly presented rationalist arguments of Wolff.

The second cause of the reaction was the development of the historical sciences. Scientific discovery and the study of anthropology revealed that economic nature was made up of a multiplicity of groups and diversified individuals, that a Newtonian uniformity did not exist throughout all nature, and that the proper study of mankind would embrace not only those things in which men are alike, but also those things in which they are different.

Discovery of new worlds also revealed that the universe is bigger than the world of physics, that there is something in society which overflows social physics, and that the individual experience is bigger and broader than the first principles of deductive mathematical sciences. The new Spirit of the Times would take into account those important elements which rationalism had left out. The method by which humanity would be studied would be not so much the analytical and the mechanical, as the genetic and the historical. The mechanical method, it was discovered, was perfectly valid for matter, but since life was extremely mobile, only the genetic element could reveal life's innermost secrets. Romanticism was the correct reaction from the purely unhistorical approach to humanity, but it is unfortunately true that this reaction went too far and dissolved the permanent elements of history into a flux of unstable and changing elements.

The third cause of the reaction was religion, which made men turn more and more away from the rational to the traditional, so that the test of institutions became not their mechanical reasonableness but their history. The human mind had felt its demands met in the preceding Spirit of the Times, but now the human heart would have its own appetites satisfied, and this meant the domination of feeling over reasoning in the domain of religion. In England, John Wesley developed a religion which expressed a reversion of scientific reasoning. He once said that he was "convinced from many experiments" that he could not study "to any degree of perfection either mathematics, arithmetic, or algebra, without being a deist, if not an atheist." He swung so far to the other extreme of religion that he disbelieved entirely in the Newtonian astronomy and doubted very much if anyone knew the distance of the sun and the moon from the earth. In France the passionate feeling took a negative form and developed into a revolutionary assault upon the established order in the Church and the State.

The product of this triple reaction against rationalism was sentimental anarchy, which manifested itself in Protestant subjectivism and Catholic quietism. The Protestant movement now bore the fruit of its individualism. In breaking away from the unity of the Christian Church in the sixteenth century, Protestantism retained many of the rites of the traditional Church, but its fundamental principle was new—the principle of individualism. This individualism expressed itself objectively and subjectively: objectively, in the individual's right to interpret Sacred Scripture for himself, without the need of any external authority; subjectively, in the individual's direct and immediate union with God, without the intermediary of altar, priest, or sacrament. But not everyone in the sixteenth century could see the full effects of individualism. In the eighteenth century they now became completely manifested in a religion of subjectivism, which is nothing more than a religion of the emotions.

On the unorthodox but Catholic side, sentimental anarchy found expression in quietistic mysticism. The ancestors of this quietism were the unorthodox mystics of the Middle Ages, and before them the neo-Platonists. In its present development, however, most of the ideas of quietistic mysticism had their germ in the Religious Revolution. Religion here was a vague sentiment in which one lost himself in God. There was no thought, no active prayer, no attempt at contemplation, no ideas, but only a passivity. One let pour over the soul a flood of sentiments and affections and feelings which were supposed to have come from God.

The effects of sentimental anarchy were twofold: in fact, the French Revolution; in idea, the philosophy of romanticism. The

French Revolution was in actuality the break from the classical and rational spirit. If sometimes its exponents spoke of Greece and Rome, it was not because of the intellectual ideals of those countries, but because of their republics. Taine wrongly contends that the French Revolution took its point of departure in abstraction and intellectual thought. According to him, the philosophy behind it was an idealistic rationalism which, surpassing all conditions of time and space, placed all men on the footing of equality. It therefore envisaged universality from the individual point of view. This, however, is hardly true, for the egalitarian thought of the French Revolution in no way sprang from the classical spirit. The ideology of which Taine speaks is an effect and not a cause. The real cause of the Revolution was to be found in the sentimental anarchy pervading Europe, in which everyone wanted to be a master and in which anything that constrained was considered wrong. The only way this individualism could work itself out was by making everyone equal. Individualism in religion, namely, private interpretation of Sacred Scripture, became an exaggerated individualism in politics.[1]

In the realm of philosophy the effect of the sentimental anarchy was the Philosophy of Romanticism, the only Spirit of the Age since Newton which was not scientific in inspiration. Romanticism, in true fact, was sparked not so much by the way a man thought as by the way a man lived, and that man was Jean Jacques Rousseau. Born in Geneva, on the 28th of June, 1712, costing the life of his mother, Jean Jacques by the age of seven was wont to spend the whole night in company with his father, a watchmaker, reading the romances and novels which his mother had left in her library. "Even at an early age," he said, "I had acquired by this dangerous method a unique understanding of my passions for my age. I never understood anything. I just felt."

In 1728, after a harsh correction by his master in trade, he went to the Catholic curé of Confignon, a short distance from Geneva, a man interested in converting young Calvinists and Protestants. This priest, Abbé de Pontverre, who furnished him with the traits of his "Vicaire Savoyard," attempted to persuade him to a less foolish and romantic existence, and perhaps with some success. "He gave me," says Jean Jacques, "the first true notions of virtue, which my own bombastic nature had only understood by its excesses."

In 1736 Rousseau admitted that he was neurotic. "My passions made me live and my passions killed me. . . . The need of love devoured me." Speaking of this period in his life, he wrote later on: "A bombardment went on inside me which for thirty years never left me. The total loss of sleep convinced me that there was little time to live." But he lived about forty years after. In 1743, as secretary to the ambassador of France, he went to Venice, where he engaged in constant quarrel with his entourage. The revolutionary spirit fermented in him in these days, so that he criticized social structures severely but could never offer any prudent reform. Two years later he met Thérèse le Vasseur, who belonged to the *petite bourgeoisie*, but who had fallen to the common level through her poverty. He entered into a common-law marriage with her, saying he would never legally marry her. But he did so in the year 1768. She bore him five children, each of which, the day after birth, was given over to charity and abandoned by the father.

The great crisis in the life of Rousseau which made him a man of letters, a publicist, and an author, came on the occasion of his visit to Diderot, who was in prison for his *Letters on the Blind*. Rousseau read an announcement in the *Mercure de France* about a question proposed by the Academy of Dijon: "Whether the Revival of Sciences and Arts has contributed to the Purification of Morals." The question answered itself in the mind of Jean Jacques almost immediately. Reading this article while seated under a tree in the woods of Vincennes, the answer to the question came to him as a sudden flash of illumination. He describes his experience in his own language:

If ever anything resembled a sudden inspiration, it was the commotion which began in me as I read this. All at once I felt myself dazzled by a thousand sparkling lights; crowds of vivid ideas thronged into my mind with a force and confusion that threw me into unspeakable agitation; I felt my head whirling in a giddiness like that of intoxication. A violent palpitation oppressed me; unable to walk for difficulty of breathing, I sank under one of the trees of the avenue, and passed half an hour there in such a condition of excitement that when I arose I saw that the front of my waistcoat was all wet with tears, though I was wholly unconscious of shedding them. Ah, if ever I could have written a quarter of what I saw and felt under that tree, with what clearness should I have brought out all the contradictions of our social system; with what simplicity I should have demonstrated that man is good naturally, and that by institutions only is he debased.[2]

Romanticism as manifested by the life and writings of Jean Jacques stands for three things: first, a hatred of reason; secondly, the primacy of sentiment; and thirdly, naturalism. One is almost embarrassed in making a choice of texts from the writings of Rousseau confirming his hatred of reason. For example, in Book III of his *Confessions*, he writes:

Two things almost disparate unite in me in a way which I cannot understand: a very ardent temperament, impetuous passions, and ideas slow to be born, and embarrassed, which ever present themselves spontaneously. One would say that my heart and my mind did not belong to the same individual....I feel everything; I see nothing. I must be in cold blood to think...This slowness of thought joined to this vivacity of feeling, I have not only in my conversation, but also in my work.

In a letter to Dom Deschamps, September 12, 1762,[3] he says: "You are very good to point out my inexactitudes in reasoning...but I do not know how to compare; I am fertile enough in propositions, but without ever seeing the consequences. Order and method are your gods; they are my furies." And again in his Discourse on the *Origin of Inequality*: "The state of reflection is a state contrary to nature. A man who meditates is a depraved animal."[4]

Something had to take the place of intelligence, and Rousseau placed sentiment in the niche vacated by that which makes man the image of God. The rationalist of the eighteenth century emphasized the universal: one law for everything. The romanticist emphasized individuality and personality in feeling. Rousseau, the inspiration of that irrational affective experience, developed a kind of "lay quietism"—"lay" because it advocated union with nature instead of union with God; "quietism" because of a passivity or policy of nonresistance to the impulses and urges of passion.

He voices the deification of feeling, the worship of the affective self, "the attempt to find the real source and spring of the religious consciousness somewhere on the line below the level at which reflective thought arises, i.e., somewhere in the pre-rational or pre-intellectual region."[5]

The third note of Rousseau's romanticism was naturalism, and on this point some clarification is necessary. The word natural for St. Thomas may be taken in a double sense: a metaphysical sense or an historical sense. Metaphysically, it may mean essence. Hence, what is natural responds to the exigencies and inclinations of this essence.

In the historical sense, it means what is primitive or original, or that which exists before development, but which may develop. Jacques Maritain says that the Scholastics were concerned primarily with the first sense and Hobbes and Spinoza with the second. Rousseau, he claims, unites them both and labels the primitive the nature of man. Nature he sees as the ante-cultural which all men must realize; [6] nature is the primitive conditions of things at which they should stop, or which they should restore to comply with their essence.

This new conception of the natural which makes the primitive state the essence of man, is really nothing but the logical consequence of the misconception of grace shared by theologians for a hundred and fifty years previous to the days of Rousseau. Luther had taught that human nature was essentially wicked and that grace could not affect it intrinsically, but only extrinsically. His followers concluded that if grace does not affect human nature intrinsically, then it is not necessary. Grace then passed out of theology in much the same way that substance is passing out of philosophy today, because of a bad definition. Philosophy was made ripe for an entirely new notion of human nature; Rousseau gave it to the world in his new conception of original sin. In the traditional conception Adam was given certain supernatural gifts of God and he became not only a creature of God, but also a child of God. These gifts the first man lost by sin. His human nature, as such, was not intrinsically corrupted, though in virtue of the loss of those gifts, his intellect was darkened and his will weakened. Rousseau constructed an entirely new anthropology. The natural state of man for Rousseau corresponds to the supernatural state of man in the garden. The fall came not through a serpent but through civilization. As Jacques Maritain puts it:

It means that man originally lived in a *purely natural* paradise of happiness and goodness, and that Nature herself will in future perform the function which grace fulfilled in the Catholic conception. It also means that such a state of happiness and goodness, of exemption from servile work and suffering, is *natural* to man, that is to say, essentially required by our nature. Not only, then, is there no original sin of which we bear the guilt at our birth and still keep the wounds, not only is there in us no seat of concupiscence and unhealthy proclivities to incline us to evil, but, further, the state of suffering and hardship is one essentially *opposed to nature* and started by civilization, and our nature demands that we should, at any cost, be freed from it. That is what the dogma of the natural Goodness amounts to.[7]

It would be false to say that reason played no part in the development of Rousseau's romanticism. Even for the most confirmed philosophers of experience and sentiment, reason plays, as it did in the case of Rousseau, a double role. Reason came to the aid of philosophy, first, in defending malice and cloaking it with sophistry. Reason also discovered new forms of malice or new pleasures in the world of sense. In a letter which Rousseau wrote to M. X. Burgoin, January 15, 1769, he says:

You ask me to beware of this interior sense. I cannot agree with you on this point and I find, on the contrary, in this intimate judgment a natural safeguard against the sophism of my reason. I feel that in this matter you confound the secret penchant of our hearts which distract us, with that dictate still more secret and more interior which brings us to the very roots of truth. This interior sentiment is that of nature itself. It is the call of nature against the sophism of reason. I believe that it never deceives us and that it is the light of our feeble understanding, even when we wish to go further than we can conceive.

This interior spirit was the master by whom he believed himself to be divinely led. His own natural goodness united him to nature as grace unites us to God; of the validity of his sentimental mysticism, Jean Jacques had no doubts. He could never be called a man who hated himself, or held a low opinion of himself. In a letter to M. Duclos, August 1, 1763, he said: "I should go distrustfully if I knew a better man than myself," and in the first letter to M. de Malesherbes, he added: "I am persuaded that of all men whom I have known in my life, no one is better than I am." And in the first book of his *Confessions*, he states: "I believe that never did an individual of our species naturally have less vanity than I have."

ROMANTICISM IN POLITICS

Rousseau applied his romantic doctrine to politics, education, and religion. His political theory has for its fundamental idea "the state of nature." In his *Discourse on Inequality* he represents the natural man as leading a rather solitary, savage, carefree but happy existence, without any needs that cannot be satisfied by pure instinct. In this natural state are to be found all the elements of true happiness, because man is independent, contented, and self-sufficient. This natural state is not only a happy one, but is also a state of substantial equality; there is no fundamental distinction between individuals, each of whom pursues his individual needs through very placid routine. But as men begin to multiply, the state of happiness and equality is interfered with. The human race becomes numerous. Intercourse of individuals and families increases, and the complexity of civilization results. "The first man who, after inclosing a piece of ground, bethought himself to say 'This is mine' and found people simple enough to believe him, was the real founder of civil society." [8]

War, murder, competition, and all the evil of social life succeeded upon this change by which civil society was instituted. It was hopeless, however, to return to the natural order; some remedy had to be found. Rousseau stated this remedy in his work entitled *The Social Contract*, maintaining that the liberty and equality characteristic of the state of nature are, in a civil state, gone. And yet, since the state of nature can no more return, a compromise must be hit upon, and this is the social pact. If man cannot return to the natural state because of the complexity of civilization, then he must have recourse to a social contract wherein the social equalities of human beings will compensate for their natural inequalities. The problem was to found a society in which all men would be free and equal. In other words, how reconcile men such as nature wants them to be and laws such as society demands? How find an association in which each one is bound up with someone else, and yet each obeys himself and rests as free as before? The answer is: constitute an organic whole without subordination of one part to another. This is the social contract or a pact concluded by the deliberate will of individuals who once lived in a state of nature but now are to live in society. However, it may be asked, where is liberty in this compact? Rousseau defines liberty in saying:

Each one who gives to all, gives himself to no one. In submitting himself to the general will, he is not submitting himself to any individual will but really obeying himself.... Each of us puts into a single mass his person in all his power under the supreme direction of the general will: and we receive as a body each member as an individual part of the whole.[9]

This means that in submitting himself to the common will, man submits himself to no one and therefore is free. Professor William

A. Dunning, of Columbia University, writing on this peculiar conception of liberty, says: "Rousseau's exposition of the spirit and effects of his contract is an amazing medley of bad logic and utter peculiarity." Equality, he declares, "is insured because each individual makes complete alienation of himself and all his rights to the community. That is to say, the individuals reduce themselves to zeros, and as such, equals."

The inspiration which came to Rousseau in the woods of Vincennes and made him flood his vest with tears, namely, that man is naturally good and it is civilization which makes him wicked, is applied to education in his work entitled *Emile*. In Book I he treats of the child in infancy, asks the mothers to nurse their own children, which most mothers did in the days of Rousseau; he dilates on the necessity of proper clothing and cold baths, and such details of the nursery. In Book II he reminds us that the child should never do anything by obedience. There should never be a command, nor should the child know that we exercise any authority over him. His disorders must never draw from us a single word of reproach. Education in the early stages is purely negative. It does not consist in inculcating virtues positively, nor in inculcating them negatively by holding up the evils of viciousness, as the Greeks did in their dramas, but in permitting the child to develop according to his "natural state," which is good. Hence the child is not to be permitted to develop a habit, and if one follows the general rule of acting contrary to reason and tradition, he can be generally sure that he is doing right. The third and fourth books treat of subjects to be taught in education and also of the awakening of passions. Here Rousseau observes that first the child must be taught to love himself more than anyone else. In Book V he speaks of the education of young girls, but on this point he is very circumspect, probably because of the popularity of Fénelon's work on this very subject. Rousseau thus wrote as an authority on education as well as on politics; he became the father of modern educational theories which express themselves in terms of self-expression, omitting entirely the training of the will and discipline from education. According to his theories, just as civilization destroyed natural goodness, so too does disciplined education destroy the natural state of man. A certain Madame Rougin wrote to him about an expected child and he answered: "It makes little difference whether the child is placed in a basket of straw or not; give him a cold bath and don't be afraid of cold"—and all this, from a man who abandoned his five children shortly after birth, and in doing so, said he felt "like a citizen of Plato's Republic." Medicine uses a high sounding and technical name for those who neglect their own families but gush over animals—zoophilists. Rousseau certainly was one; he abandoned his children, but had, we are told, a deep affection for his dog.

His theory of religion is in accord with his idea of political education. Religion must not be given to the child from without, but must be elicited from his own heart under the influence of his needs. This idea appears in *Emile*, but the greater part of the philosophy of Rousseau is found in the *Vicaire Savoyard*; this anticipates many aspects of liberal religion today, such as a total absence of doctrine and dogma, a Christianity without history, which surpasses time and space and leaves the soul free to enjoy a tête-à-tête with the Master; finally, a Christianity without redemption or repentance, from which the fact of sin has disappeared. More particularly, his religion has three qualities: it is pragmatic, skeptical, and its goal is the divinization of nature.

Rousseau's hero, the Vicaire Savoyard, was interested only in those things which concerned him immediately. For him the universe was divided into two parts: things worth knowing and things not worth knowing, or in other words, into practical truths and speculative truths. Since, according to the Vicaire, man was not made for meditation but for action, it followed that only practical truths had any value. Thus, long before William James, Rousseau was teaching in his "Vicaire" the pragmatic view that the true was the useful. The Vicaire Savoyard was also skeptical about revelation, the attitude he approved being that of "respectable doubt." The Vicaire *feels* that there is a Providence governing this world, but whether that Providence is unique or plural matters not, nor can we know definitely. Finally there is in this work the divinization of nature. In the seventeenth century, the natural had very often meant the cosmological, discoverable by reason. By Rousseau's day, the natural has become localized within man, and it is by an intuition of the heart that he enters into union with it. His religion is a kind of absorption of God unto himself. In the last analysis, the god that Rousseau worshipped was the god within Jean Jacques.

LYRICISM OF PHILOSOPHY AND RELIGION

Romanticism, as developed by Rousseau, became the new time-spirit and flooded over the banks to saturate not only the shores, but the inlands of religion, morals, politics, and literature. In each of these fields it takes on a slightly different form, yet remains always substantially the same—exaltation of the sentimental self. In the divine order, it is natural mysticism substituted for religious belief, or sentiment in the place of faith. In the moral order, it is passion divinized, the supremacy of feeling, and the primacy of concupiscence over reason. In the social order, it is glorification of the primitive; in the literary order, the emancipation of the ego and the heart and all that is most intimate in the soul.

Romanticism became a philosophy of religion much more quickly in Germany than in France, for in Germany there arose one who bridged the shores of rationalism on one hand and romanticism on the other—Immanuel Kant. Despite his cold metaphysics, even he was not wholly untouched by the romanticism of Rousseau; in fact we shall see that Rousseau was one of the influences of his life. Yet Kant was not a romanticist, if only because he was too unemotional. His moral faith seems much more rational than romantic, and at no time does he become a sentimentalist, except perhaps in his *Critique of Judgment*, where he speaks of the "esthetic judgment" as "tasting things."

On the one side, Kant had affinities with rationalism. In the year 1784 he wrote an essay on the question, "What is Aufklärung?" in which he reviewed the various tendencies of the age and manifested unmistakably his attachment to the rationalist movement. "Free thought," he writes in that essay,

is the advance of man beyond the state of voluntary immaturity. By immaturity is meant inability to use one's own understanding except under the guidance of another. The immaturity is voluntary when the cause of it is not that of intelligence, but of resolution and courage to use it without another's guidance. *Sapere aude!* Dare to use thy *own* understanding! is therefore the motto of free thought. If the question be asked, do we live in a free-thinking age, the answer is "No," but we live in an age of free thought. As things are at present, men as a whole are far from possessing or even from being able to acquire the power of making a sure and right use of their own understanding in religious matters without the guidance of others. On the other hand, we have clear indication that the field now lies open before them to which they can freely make their way, and that the hindrances to the general freedom of thought, or abandonment of the state of voluntary immaturity, are gradually becoming less. In this sense the present age is the age of free thought, or the century of Frederick The Great.

It is perfectly clear from this essay that Kant participated to the full in the Aufklärung, but that he gauged its meaning somewhat differently from his contemporaries. He was practically saying that mankind is bound to be free and enlightened, but it is not yet so, and will not become so except by "a true reform in habits of thought."

There is other evidence which attaches Kant to the rationalist tradition, for instance his acceptance of Hume's skepticism, the Dead Sea fruit of a decayed rationalism. Hume, he said, awakened him from his dogmatic slumbers. It may very well be true, however, that he never read Hume's *Treatise,* for though it was published in 1739, it was not translated into German until 1790, and Kant could read English only with great difficulty. It is probable that he came to a knowledge of Hume principally through James Beattie's *Essay on the Nature and Immutability of Truth* (1770), which was translated into German two years later. Kant mentioned Beattie's writings on several occasions. In perfect keeping with that tradition of Hume, he proved that the methods of mathematics and physics and even of mechanics are quite valid in describing a world of experience, but held them incapable of revealing to us the *real* world. That is to say, the world as it really exists is unknowable, including the world of God, the immortality of the soul, and the freedom of the will. As he puts it:

We are brought to the conclusion that we can never transcend the limits of possible experience, and therefore can never realize the object with which metaphysics, i.e., rational theology, is primarily concerned.[10] [And again] Theoretically, we do not by the strongest efforts of reason come at all nearer to the conviction of the existence of God, the reality of the Highest God and the prospect of a future life: for we possess no insight into the nature of supra-sensuous objects.[11]

On the other hand, Kant is linked up with the Romantic Movement. He was influenced by Pietism—an antidogmatic religion started off by the publication of Spener's *Pia desideria* in 1675. It was a religion of the heart, a flowering of moral life, and a protest against the rigid Protestant Scholasticism. Purity, piety, and holiness of life were its principal tenets. On the whole, it was much like the reaction produced in England in 1738 when John Wesley was converted to the "religion of the heart." Through his own mother and through his master, Schulz, Kant felt profoundly the influence of Pietism, though it is a well-known fact that he complained against certain of Schulz's exaggerations in one of his *Critiques*.

Strengthening this influence, which might be called antirational, or even sentimental and romantic, was the general discontent with rationalism and a more general leaning toward romanticism in Kant's Germany. Johann Winckelmann, for example, was preaching a return to naturalism, Lessing, a contempt of rules and conventions; the poetry of Friedrich Klopstock abandoned mythology for natural subjects; Haller drew his theatrical inspirations from nature; the poetic pantheism of Goethe found everywhere the universal revelation of a God immanent in nature. It is well known that Kant felt some of these influences. It was between 1760 and 1770 that he read Rousseau. An analysis of his work shows that from 1760 to 1768, he separated more and more from Wolffian rationalism. It was in the year 1769 or 1770 that the critical idea was born in him, and in 1788 he published his *Critique of Practical Reason*, a work which stamped him definitely as having some relation to romanticism. While it is true, he contends in this book, that reason of itself cannot prove the immortality of the soul, the freedom of the will, or the existence of God, there is, nevertheless, a nonrational way of knowing these realities which has its certainties just as well as critical reason has its certainty. If Kant was not saying so, he at least was implying that what science can neither prove nor disprove, we are justified in holding nonrationally, or by faith. His *Critique of Pure Reason* claimed that we do not need to wait for philosophers to determine man's relation to God by an elaborate reasoning process, for such a relation cannot be so determined. Our knowledge of what we ought to do is prior to any such metaphysical speculations, and yet it is grounded on reason—not the speculative but the practical reason, which really means the will.

In his *Critique of Pure Reason* Kant says:

We may call consciousness of this fundamental law a fact of reason, because we cannot reason it out from antecedent data of reason. The objective reality of the moral law cannot be proved by any deduction, by any efforts of the theoretical reason, whether speculative or empirically supported; and therefore even if we renounced the apodictic certainty, it could not be proved *a posteriori* by experience, and yet it is firmly established of itself.

This is a revolution in the field of religion and morality. Traditionally and correctly, certitude was always held to be logically prior to religious belief. Kant reversed this order, and held that religious belief is prior to certitude, for our consciousness of moral obligation rests only on itself, and the fundamental beliefs of religion are themselves in need of only such support as our moral consciousness will give them. Already in 1766 he felt this to be true:

It seems more in accordance with human nature and with the purity of morals to base the expectation of a future world on the sentiments of a well-behaved soul than contrariwise to base a good behaviour on the hope of another world. We are thus left with *moral faith*, the simplicity of which can be superior to many a subtlety of argumentation.[12]

Granting that the defense that he gave of it was rational, it nevertheless opened the doors for all kinds of sentimental approaches to the truths of religion. In Chapter 19 of his *Critique of Pure Reason*, he makes this rather disastrous confession:

From the critical point of view, the doctrine of morality and the doctrine of science may each be true in its own spheres; which could never have been shown had not criticism previously established our unavoidable ignorance of the real world, and limited all that we can know scientifically to mere phenomena. I have therefore found it necessary *to deny knowledge of God, freedom and immortality, in order to find a place for faith.*

In this important work he transferred the religious truths from the domain of knowledge to the domain of faith and the problem of their validity became a problem of their value. It was a juxtaposition of belief and reason for belief. Religious truths cannot be proved, he contended, though they may be postulates of a practical reason or of the will. Friedrich Paulsen has well expressed the juxtaposition in these words:

Kant's *Critique of Pure Reason* prepared the death-blow in asserting that reality transcends the standpoint of knowledge. From this as a consequence, religion cannot be derived from, nor demonstrated by reason. Its roots are to be sought in the will.[13]

It is precisely from his nonrational approach to God that Kant wins a place as one of the great figures in the Romantic Religious Movement in Germany, and it is in asserting this nonrational approach that he becomes a disciple of Rousseau. "Up until now," writes Harald Höffding,

faithful to the principles of the Enlightenment, he had sought for the essence and nobility of man in the understanding only; now he discovered a still deeper foundation, common to learned and lay, in which the simplest peasant might be equal with the profoundest thinker. And Rousseau's appeal to immediate feeling and immediate faith must have seemed all the more significant to Kant, since he was just on the point of undermining the proofs which had hitherto been supposed to support the assumptions on which the doctrine of natural religion was based.[14]

It was not easy for Kant as a German to break his habits. A certain significance, therefore, is to be attached to the fact that the day Rousseau's work, *Emile*, came to Königsberg, Kant upset the routine of the city by failing to take his accustomed walk. Even stronger evidence than this for the influence of Rousseau is to be found in a passage of Kant's own work, *Nachlass*.[15] Here he admits that by a study of Rousseau, he was converted from his original attitude concerning speculative truth as the chief end of human existence, to the recognition of the nonrational element in man—of the moral capacity which belongs to educated and non-educated alike, enabling them to act in accordance with the law of duty written in their own hearts.

Religion was romanticized into religious experience. In its earlier phases, religious experience was characterized by a reaction against the separation of theory and practice, a reaction which Kant had effected, and also by the assertion of some nonintellectual element. Johann Hamann, who experienced a religious crisis in England in 1759, in which he spoke of himself as one "who was taught by the malady of his passions to conceive and feel a strength which a healthy man does not possess," was one of the early exemplars of religious experience. Hamann's religious crisis begot in him the doctrine that life must be taken as a whole and that religion comes to its truths, not by abstractions, but rather by passions, for these give abstractions their wings. Johann Gottfried Herder, a true disciple of Hamann and Rousseau who abhorred everything that smacked of the Aufklärung and rationalism, likewise felt the need of some unity which would come through feeling and not through thought. Religion, he contended, is the inmost consciousness that we live as parts of the world. He did not believe that God was distinct from the world, and defended Spinoza against Jacobi. His philosophy has been summed up as the immanence of Divine activity in ourselves, preserved in some nonrational way. "We are men," he says:

and as such methinks we must learn to know God as He has really given and exhibited Himself to us. Through conceptions we receive Him as a conception, and through words as a word; through the perception of nature, through the use of our powers, through the enjoyment of our life we enjoy Him as a real existence full of power and life.

Finally, Friedrich Jacobi, who as a boy derived more pleasure in praying with his maidservant than in playing games with his comrades, continued the search for a greater religious unity by making a distinction between reason and faith, the reverberations of which we hear in Emerson and Carlyle. That faculty by which spiritual truths are perceived is *Glaube* or faith, in counterdistinction to scientific reason—*Verstand*—or understanding. "God," he held, "cannot be known. It would be better for science if there were no God. But we have a knowledge of Him, a knowledge that comes by the immediate intuition of something greater and better than ourselves, and by that intuition we find God within ourselves."

The three foregoing men are important more for their reaction against the critical philosophy of Kant than for their positive contribution to the romantic philosophy of religion. The giant now appears on the scene in the person of Friedrich Schleiermacher, the philosopher who gave sentimental religion a new rule of faith. His theory of religion is far developed in *Speeches on Religion to its Despisers*, published in 1799. That he was concerned with unifying those things which Kant had separated is evidenced by the opening of his argument, in which he dwells on the impossibility of identifying religion either with science, on the one hand, or with morals on the other, or even with a mixture of the two so as to make it "an instinct craving for a mass of metaphysical and ethical crumbs." His entire theory of religion is the very essence of romantic belief; it can be summed up in these three principles: First, religion is feeling, the immediate feeling of our dependence on the universe or the intuition of the finite and the infinite.

So far as your feeling expresses the life, and being common to you and to your universe, it constitutes your piety; your sensations and the

effects upon you of all the life surrounding you are all elements and
the sole elements of religion; there is no feeling which is not religious,
save such as indicates an unhealthy condition of life.

Secondly, all forms of religious sentiment are equally true, for
what makes the religion true is not the propositions which it adduces,
but the feelings which it inspires. Religion is the foe of creeds and
dogmas. It invites peaceful feeling and enjoyment and does not
impel to external action. "All is immediately true in religion, but
that only is immediate which has not yet passed through the stage
of idea but has grown up purely in the feeling." A natural consequence of this idea that religion is feeling and that feeling constitutes truth, was the false notion of tolerance in religion which
Schleiermacher called real piety.

Thirdly, a religion without God can be just as acceptable as one
with the concept of God. God is not the presupposition of religion.
He is the result of reflection on it. Hence our concept of God is of
little or no importance; how we think of God depends upon the
character of our feelings. The feeling of God is better than the
conception of God. The same is true of immortality. In the midst
of the finite to become one with the infinite and to be eternal in
every movement—this is the immortality of religion.

Up until this time, Protestantism had regarded certain dogmas as
essential to religion, because these dogmas were taught in Sacred
Scripture. Schleiermacher rejected these, and in this sense has become the father of "Religion without Dogmas." But he did more
than this. He found an outlet for the conflict between the deist and
the Bible. The Bible, on the Protestant theory, was the foundation
of Christianity and its certain rule of faith. With the advent of
deism, however, the veracity of Sacred Scripture became challenged.
Protestant Christianity seemed in danger of crumbling, since it was
built upon the Bible. Schleiermacher saved it, not by criticizing the
Critiques of the deist, but by establishing a new rule of faith for
Protestantism—namely, subjective experience. Protestantism had previously invoked intimate experience as the individual variant of
faith. Schleiermacher now made fundamental that experience, from
which he deduced as the sole object of faith what the survivors of
this Spirit of the Age call "religious experience." [16]

The search for some nonintellectual approach to God went on.
The justice of Kant's criticism of a rational proof was accepted as

final. Some found the substitute in intuition, others in faith, others in feeling. Fichte finds it in moral consciousness, but not in the moral consciousness of Kant. In a work which Fichte wrote in his twenty-eighth year, entitled *Aphorisms on Religion*, he denies the intellectual element in Christianity. The Christian religion thus appears to be one adapted to the heart rather than to the understanding. "It does not establish itself by demonstrations but rather fills a need." [17] In a later work, written in 1798, entitled "Concerning the Ground of Our Faith in a Divine Government of the World," published in the *Philosophischer Journal*, of which he was editor, he presses Kant's separation of belief and reason for belief to its logical and rather shameful conclusion. Reason, he contends, can never be the basis of faith.

Where is the philosopher now to look for the necessary source of his faith which he presupposes? In a supposed necessity, to argue from the existence of a constitution of the world of sense to a reasonable author of the same? By no means, for he knows too well that reasonable philosophy cannot so argue.... Starting from the world of sense there is no possible way of arriving at the conception of a moral ordering of the world.

Where, then, is the basis for faith to be found? Fichte answers, "in the moral consciousness." "Morality," he says, "can be constituted only by means of its end, not by means of logical process." Fichte breaks with Kant, who had argued from the moral order to a personal God. Fichte claims that the impersonal moral order is the only God there is, and He is known not by reason but by moral consciousness. Moral consciousness with Kant puts us in touch with a personal God. Moral consciousness with Fichte unites us with an impersonal God—for man is rooted in one divine basal life—whose love becomes conscious in man in the form of feeling. Later on Wilhelm Herrmann (developing the doctrine of his teacher Ritschl, who too held out for an unintellectual approach to God) made the proof for religion almost psychological. He dissociated himself from Kant by holding there was no such thing as a moral proof; all morality can do is to prepare us for religion and to bring us to the point where we see that only religion can save us.

As time went on, the practical reason more and more disappeared from religious experience and the feeling of Schleiermacher came into greater prominence. A. Sabatier defined religious experience for modern times by saying that the truths of the religious and moral order are not known except by a subjective act.[18] Developing this idea, Alfred Loisy asserted that religion has three moments: first, the interior revelation of God which produces the subjective piety of man, which in its turn has developed all the historical forms of religion; secondly, the interpretations of these revelations in human formulae which have diversified into creeds; thirdly, Christianity, which is the best expression today of that inner sentiment, but which is destined to evolve and give way to more perfect religion.[19] Modernism finally made these ideas extremely popular, along with their corollary, the psychology of religion.

Modern philosophy still feels the effect of the romantic approach to religion. This is an instance of how the spirit of one age overflows into another. William James, for example, writes: "I do believe that feeling is the deeper source of religion and that philosophical and theological formulas are secondary products like translations of a text into another tongue." [20] Intuition, another form of nonintellectual religion, is supposed to transcend reason and is called "the power of direct spiritual insight into the reason of things, which is acquired neither by knowledge nor by experience and which is therefore superior to both." [21] It has also been defined as a kind of sympathy by which one sets himself in the very interior of an object in order to coincide with the very reality of that object with its uniqueness and with that in it which cannot be expressed in terms of reason.[22]

Finally, there is a modern faith which is a sum of the various hypotheses that appeal because they promise to satisfy our needs. If reason cannot supply the ground of religion, something else must supply it. Kant had already distinguished between belief and reason for belief by stating there could not be a rational basis for belief in God. This distinction carried to its logical conclusion led others to think that belief practically creates its own object. The methods of science were borrowed to support religion. Science begins with hypothesis, which is a form of faith. Why not build religion on the same basis, and let beliefs fall or rise according to the durability of an hypothesis? Accordingly, some philosophers of religion hold that if the belief in the existence of God works out as a practical hypothesis in your life, then He is true for you; if not, then He is false for you.[23] Still others say that we should live "as if" God existed,[24] basing the reason for belief on something unreasonable, a fiction.

Romantic philosophy of religion developed into the philosophy of value. God was no longer regarded as a substance, but as a moral purpose and an influence. The philosophy of value is really the heritage of a denial of truth. If the human mind can never know truth, then its supreme concern must be some second-best substitute: what certain beliefs can give the individual. It was principally Albrecht Ritschl who developed this philosophy. The question for Kant and his predecessors had been: "By what means is religious faith justified?" The concern of Ritschl, on the contrary, was "What is faith and how does it affect the human soul?" It was this changed perception of the question which broke the last bond with eighteenth-century rationalism.[25]

The difference between Ritschl and his predecessors was that Ritschl made faith create the object, whereas for the others, the object created the faith. Ritschl's own definition of religion made it something extremely anthropocentric. Religion, according to Ritschl, is born of the effort of the human spirit to find the harmony between the world of nature and the inner world of personality. "In every religion what is sought, with the help of the superhuman spiritual power reverenced by man, is a solution of the contradiction in which man finds himself, as both a part of the world of nature and a spiritual personality claiming to dominate nature." [26]

"Religion," he says, "has to do with our consciousness of value and is a faith in the reality of the objects to which that consciousness introduces us. All religious affirmations, therefore, are judgments of value." Ritschl insisted on a distinction between the world of ideas and the world of facts. Hence we make two kinds of judgments, value judgments and causal judgments, and these are distinguished, he held, by the two ways in which sensation can be apprehended by the mind. First, sensations produce feelings of pleasure or pain and so become determined according to their *value* for the ego. Secondly, sensations embodied in ideas are judged in respect to their cause or other causes. The first constitute value judgments and the second causal judgments. Religion is concerned with the first and science with the second. God, Christianity, dogmas and beliefs from Ritschl's time on are considered as values instead of realities. (Kant, of course, had the germ of this idea in making

God a value judgment and not an existential one.) Religion thus became a merely practical matter instead of a field that is both practical and theoretical.

ROMANTICISM IN LITERATURE AND THE ARTS

The romanticist influence on literature manifested itself in a protest against classicism, asserting that the only true unity was the unity of feeling. Its three dominating notes were: first, intuition as the means by which we ascend from clear consciousness to the absolute; secondly, an identification of nature and consciousness; thirdly, pantheism, or an ecstatic and mystic fusion of man and nature, divinity and humanity.

In Germany, Goethe symbolized the hopelessness of resolving the conflict between the ideal and the real in the suicide of Werther. *Faust* approves the turbid flux of sense and puts one back at the beginning of experience, which is not the dawn of reason. Instead of ascending in the line of the intellect, Faust descends in the line of impulse. For Faust, *Gefühl ist alles*, and this is the very essence of romanticism. Dr. Santayana in his study of this play says that "Faust is ready to carry even into heaven itself his romantic restlessness, in order to escape from the ennui of the world." [27] It is worth remarking, however, in justice to Goethe, that at the very moment when he was infecting others with the wild delight in the new stress on feeling, he himself was striking out on a new path, for in his *Journal* in 1778, he wrote: "A more definite feeling of limitation and in consequence, of true broadening."

Romanticism took on a distinctly new form with Friedrich von Schlegel, and his brother, August W. von Schlegel, who defined the Romantic Movement as:

an indissoluble mixture. All contrarieties: nature and art, poetry and prose, seriousness and mirth, recollection and anticipation, spirituality and sensuality, terrestrial and celestial, life and death, are by it blended together in the most intimate combination. ... Feeling all in all at one and the same time. ... [28]

Friedrich von Schlegel began at one extreme as a partisan of the Greeks' classicism, and then in works like *Lucinde*, he passed over to emotionalism and finally to a great love of the Middle Ages. This new note in romanticism, love of the Middle Ages, was due to something Herder added to Rousseau, that is, the cultivation of national genius. It was another instance, as in Faust, of looking back to beginnings; medievalism thus became an important ingredient in romantic idealism. Schiller, in keeping with the spirit of his times, believed that imagination and feeling should be free. As soon as anything has a purpose, it ceases to become aesthetic, and thereby suffers a loss of dignity. His *Aesthetics Letters* betray his faith in the native goodness of man, which had been inspired in him by Rousseau.

The elements which characterized French literary romanticism were a keen analysis of the soul, grotesque disorders, love for the foreign, and the fusion of the ego and nature. In the preface to Chatterton, Victor Hugo establishes a parallel between a man of letters, a great writer, and a poet, in which the poet is genius because "he is pure passionate nature." In *Les Miserables* Hugo sets in contrast Javert, who stands for the old order based on law, and the convict Jean Valjean, who stands for the new order based on love and sympathy. In this work, as in most of the romantic writers, there is the subordination of all the other values of life to sympathy.

Madame de Staël, in her first work on *The Influence of Passions on Happiness*, writes: "Philosophy by a great act of courage, having delivered its thoughts from the yoke of passions, no longer directs them to an unique object, but enjoys each one of them separately." A friend wrote to her on May 4, 1803, telling her the impression her words had made on the world: "The fundamental and creative idea of all your work has been to show primitive, incorruptible, naïve, passionate nature in conflict with the barriers and shackles of conventional life. . . . Note that this is also the guiding idea of the author of *Werther*." Lamartine's *Jocelyn* is a supreme type of poetic romanticism, filled as it is with numerous lines on the Alps which betray a sentimental pantheism. "*Je croyais sur mon coeur sentir Dieu palpiter.*" Chauteaubriand was a Catholic Lamartine. Lamartine sang of the lakes of Savoy; Chateaubriand of the lakes of Brittany; Lamartine shed tears over Jocelyn, a priest despite himself; Chateaubriand shed tears over Atala, the virgin condemned by an oath of her mother to an eternal, involuntary celibacy.

Chateaubriand's great work, *The Genius of Christianity*, did much to effect a religious Renaissance which extends even to our own days. His argument is that Christianity comes from God because it is good. It is good because it is most poetic and favorable to the arts, because its mysteries furnish pleasure to man, and because it gives greater value to passion, which it combats. It is worth noting that in typical romantic fashion, he does not say that Christianity is good because it is true, but it is true because it is beautiful. His other work, *René*, is purely Rousseauistic—the elixir of the doctrines of Jean Jacques. Chateaubriand here adopts the style of "confession" which Jean Jacques made popular. It is not the Confession of Augustine, acknowledging faults to God with a great chastity of expression, and asking God for pardon. It is a confession to Père Souel, Chactas, and Nature. René himself was too great to adapt himself to the society of men. In common with the spirit of the times, he was athirst for the infinite. "What is finite has no value for me." The mystical something he sought was the dream woman.

I went down into the valley. I strode upon the mountain, summoning with all the force of my desire the ideal object of a future flame; I embraced this object in the winds. I thought that I heard it in the moanings of the river. All was this phantom of the imagination—both the stars in heaven and the very principle of life in the universe.

Speaking of Chateaubriand, Irving Babbitt says:

Paganism, Chateaubriand complains, by seeing in nature only certain definite forms—fauns and satyrs and nymphs—had banished from it both God and the infinite. But Christianity expelled these throning figures in turn, and restored their reverence. The true God thus became visible in His works and bestowed upon them His immensity.[29]

The fiction of René resembles La Nouvelle Héloïse—it is a combination of passion and religion, the latter making the former more piquant. The sole teacher of René, like Emile, is Nature—in accordance with the program of Rousseau.

Romanticism in England had the following characteristics:

the feeling of the past in all its diverse aspects, the thirst for the picturesque, the longing to probe the mysterious, in a word, the quest after a world of the sense that is removed from daily reality....Among all the new elements, the one which deserves the most attention is perhaps the yearning for the past; it was the more widespread feeling besides being the most pliable....

Imagination in its conception of the ideal world seeks what is fundamentally opposed to present realities; it finds its perfect realm in the fond resurrection of what has once existed; grandeur and beauty harmonize with the special charm that clings like an aroma to the quality of what has been. The essential feature of preromantic evocation lies in the backward direction of its glance.[30]

One of the historical influences in the development of preromantic literature was the religion of feeling as taught by John Wesley. Wordsworth and Coleridge found their poetry of the heart acceptable, in part because the English mind had already had its mystical sense enkindled by Methodism. Among the preromantic poets may be mentioned James Beattie, who had written an attack on Hume which was probably Kant's first approach to Hume, and who in his poetry, such as the *Minstrel*, portrays even in this didactic form, the inner life as being suffused in the atmosphere of legend. Then too, there is Burns who, while somewhat classical in style, breathes the air of romanticism: personal effusion, sensibility, a keen love of nature, a wealth of imaginative fancy, a sympathetic interest in the poor and in animals. Finally, William Blake, whose literary doctrine was the gospel of the Revolution, protested against orthodoxy, criteria, and authority (in much the same way as Burns, who poked fun at a belief in the devil and eternal damnation), while glorifying anarchic individualism, free mysticism, and spiritual revolt. At a later date, the French Revolution played its part, influencing every branch of English literature and giving it a fresh romantic zest. Revolutions always arouse souls to a high pitch of excitement and such enthusiasm is indeed favorable to a literature of feeling. In England, however, romanticism never took a patriotic form, as it did in Germany with Fichte.[31]

Wordsworth is the best exponent of poetic romanticism, seeking always to interpret the universe in personal terms. Familiar objects are exalted by his sensibility. He believed that the deepest secrets of nature must be felt, not known by intellect. In his "Tables Turned" one finds the idea:

> Sweet is the lore which Nature brings:
> Our meddling intellect
> Mis-shapes the beauteous forms of things:
> We murder to dissect.

Tennyson, in like manner, felt that everything that is, is centered in nature, even God:

> Flower in the crannied wall,
> I pluck you out of the crannies,
> I hold you there, root and all, in my hand.
> Little flower—but if I could understand
> What you are, root and all, and all in all,
> I should know what God and man is.

Romanticism took a Catholic turn in Joseph de Maistre, who preached the mystical transmission of powers to monarchs by Providential participation. In the field of history, romanticism manifested itself in a kind of subjectivism [32] in such authors as Michelet, Froude, and Carlyle, for whom history was a biography of heroic figures. In America, romanticism became transcendentalism.

Calvinism remained unchallenged in New England for years. But the spirit of revolution and free thought made itself felt about 1800. Men could no longer believe that human nature was totally depraved and that only certain elect are marked for salvation; and so arose the group called Unitarians, who denied all revelation outside of conscience and looked wholly to the moral nature within for guidance. The immediate impulse of the philosophy came from Germany and England through Coleridge and Carlyle.

Excluded from the drawing rooms and counting houses, ostracized in society and politics, Romantic philosophy slipped quietly into Boston by the door of theology and took lodgings in the best of families.... Changing its name and arraying itself in garments cut after the best Yankee fashion, the Gospel of Jean Jacques presently walked the streets of Boston and spoke from its most respectable pulpits under the guise of Unitarianism. The heretical doctrines of the excellence of human nature and the perfectibility of man were preached to Federalist congregations.[33]

At the base of it was Idealism—the reliance on ideas and the world within as the only sure evidence of the world without. Transcendentalism is the belief that within the mind are certain intuitions, or knowledge of truth and right, that *transcend* all experience. Whence they come, we know not. We can only follow "that inner light." This was principally a cult of the cultured. As a scheme of salvation it held less interest for the masses, but all adherents were deeply concerned with right and practical living.

From the religious point of view, it was an assertion of the dignity of man and a reaction against Calvinism—a loosening of the Puritan mind. In 1836 a Transcendental Club was organized in Boston, consisting of Emerson, Alcott, Thoreau, the Ripleys, Channings, Theodore Parker, James F. Clarke, George Bancroft, Hawthorne, Margaret Fuller, Elizabeth and Sophia Peabody. In 1840, *The Dial*, a quarterly magazine, became its organ.

Ralph Waldo Emerson, descendant of seven generations of clergymen, was described as "never having anything—nothing but genius." In 1832 he went to England, met Coleridge, Wordsworth, and Carlyle. Like Rousseau, he explained the gap between the real and ideal by the pernicious influence of social institutions. In his first book, *Nature*, published in 1832, he writes, "Nature always wears the colors of the spirit."

Henry David Thoreau was more interested in the finding of an arrowhead than a presidential election. He was justified, living as a recluse in Walden Pond. "I went to the woods because I wished to live deliberately, to confront only the essential facts of life, and see if I could not learn what it had to teach, and not, when I came to die, discover I had not lived." He went to jail rather than pay his tax when he felt that a tax was contributing to a government that supported slavery. When Emerson visited him in his cell and said, "Henry, why are you here?" his reply was, "Why are you not here?" [34]

Romanticism in art did not enter the scene until Charles X had mounted the throne. At this time Paris was repairing the churches destroyed during the Revolution, and no less than 219 paintings were ordered for the churches of Paris alone; most of these were romantic in spirit. For subject matter, the romantics were fond of Orientalism. The French campaign in Egypt and the conquest of Algiers offered many subjects attractive to romantic artists. French art also loved *paysage*, which was proscribed by classical art, some French romantic paintings of the countryside equaling, if not surpassing, the best Dutch paintings of the seventeenth century. Léon Delacroix claimed that the universe in which he moved came from his imagination. His images were real to him; the rest of the world was fleeting sand. The artists of the School of Paysagists lived as peasants in the forest, away from the glory of Paris, in order to be near nature. Rousseau painted oaks; Millet painted fields, cultivators, and rude peasants; Dupré and Daubigny, limpid waters; Jacque and Troyon, animals and sheep.

The beginnings of romantic music are found in Weber and Franz Schubert, the poet of intimate music so expressive of the German *Gemüth*. Most of the ideas Beethoven translated into music were subjective moods derived from intimate contact with the objective world. The *Eroica Symphony* was designed to express Beethoven's understanding of the parting, absence, and return of friends, while the *Pastoral Symphony* was the idealization of life in fields and woods. He tells us that his descriptive music is rather the outward expression of inward feeling than outward painting.

Though it is not generally known, Kant was the inspiration for much romantic music, inasmuch as his aesthetics was antirationalist and the basis of his music was feeling: *Empfindung*. Music is defined as the "art of the beautiful play of emotions." To be added to this basic idea of romanticism in music were an enthusiasm for folklore (such as one finds in Weber, Mendelssohn, Schumann, Brahms, and Chopin) and dynamism and progressive change from one mood to another (so much a characteristic of Beethoven—in contrast with Bach's exhaustion of a single idea). Revolution as a subject for musical composition—expressed by Berlioz, Liszt, and Wagner—was another romantic introduction of the period.[35]

Chapter III

MECHANISM

It must not be thought that the scientific current in which Newton moved, ceased to exist with the advent of romanticism. The very fact that the human mind is incurably bent on knowing the why and wherefore of things would have been sufficient to account for its continuance. Its existence during the age of romanticism was rather an undercurrent to the Spirit of an Age. It now comes into its own rights and creates what might properly be called the age of mechanism. The influence accounting for the emergence of the mechanical spirit was principally the general tendency on the part of human nature to react against excesses. Civilizations which are not rooted in the eternal but in time, feel the penalty of time, and to escape monotony demand a change. Humanity, being surfeited with sentiment, emotionalism, and the poetry of life, now began to hunger and yearn for reason and explanation and science. Romanticism had been looking at the *above*, the hoped-for and infinity. The reaction now turned to the *below*, facts and the finite. The metaphysics of the heart now gave way to the physics of nature; the philosophy of the inside, to the science of the outside; consciousness, to nature; and feeling, to inductive proof.[1] The reaction arose also because of the necessity of analyzing feelings, which had been pushed to the front in the days of romanticism. Philosophy wished to strip feelings of their purely arbitrary character, and hence sought to make them emerge from their individuality into the great life of society, where they might be judged socially and even statistically. This accounts, in part, for the importance given to sociology during the age of mechanism.

But the important well-spring of the new age was the reaffirmation of the Newtonian outlook. The world was now viewed not fundamentally as a conscious thing, or even a lifelike thing, as Schelling has imagined. It was more properly, as Newton conceived it, a machine with a universal law governing it. This return to the scientific outlook marked a departure from the preceding and almost antiscientific age. In 1793, for example, the French Revolutionary Government had guillotined Lavoisier and Bailly and suspended even the Academy of Sciences. The French discovered, however, that the government had need of the former members of the society because "everything was wanting for the defense of the country"; therefore in 1795 the Academy was reopened. French science began to develop principally around this Academy, whereas in Germany it centered around the universities, and in England around individuals who held no academic position whatever. It was only in the middle of the century that Oxford and Cambridge were reformed, and mathematical physics found a place in Cambridge under the inspiration of James Clark Maxwell, and biological sciences under the leadership of Sir Michael Foster.[2] When it is said that there was a revival of the Newtonian emphasis, it must not be thought that this meant a complete identity of method between the science of Newton's day and the era which is just being ushered in. Newtonian science had been deductive. It will be recalled that out of the four principles of Newton, three were deductive and only one inductive. The new scientific outlook puts far more stress on the inductive method, and adds one idea which was quite foreign to Newton, that is, the universe is not just a great machine which came full-blown from the Creator, but a machine which is capable of growing from a simple beginning to a very complex structure. The machinery was believed to evolve, and herein lies one of the great inconsistencies of the positivist theory.

The law of the conservation of energy became a scientific club to use against those who maintained the freedom of the will. If the final energy of a closed system must be the same as its initial energy, it is possible, philosophers maintained, to predicate the final state of a system without reference to its intermediate steps. Thus it was thought that science could predict to the hour, if it knew the exact collocation of two atoms, when the Cross would supplant the Crescent on the dome of St. Sophia. Other philosophical applications of this law were that matter is eternal and indestructible, hence creation is impossible; furthermore, since the amount of energy in the universe is constant and free will implies a new energy, it follows that the freedom of the will is impossible.

Not only in the field of physics, but also in the field of biology, discoveries were being made which tended more and more to break down the then universally accepted barrier between the organic and the inorganic. The physiological relations between animal heat and muscular activity were now fitted into the law of the conservation of energy. Descartes, in his works, *De Homine* and *De Formatione Foetus*, had made biology a branch of physics and popularized the mechanical interpretation of life, though he did admit the existence of a soul. The rediscovery by Priestley of the identity of chemical changes in respiration and in ordinary combustion, and Lavoisier's physical interpretation of oxidation, whether inside or outside the body, gave mechanism a new emphasis, for it did explain mechanically the production of animal heat.

By 1840 biology was established on a purely atomic basis.

For the mechanistic theory of life the essential mechanisms thus come to be located within living protoplasm.... The real assumption behind the mechanistic physiology of the last century was that the whole of the visible world of nature can be interpreted in the physico-chemical system in the sense of Newton's mechanical interpretation of the inorganic world. If the phenomena of life are natural phenomena, they must on this assumption be mechanical phenomena.[3]

The mechanical interpretation of life made itself felt not only in the field of biology, but also in physiology and psychology. Rational psychology gradually became less and less important and was finally replaced by empirical psychology in practically all countries. Herbart used it in Germany to refute idealism. Lotze used it to further a deeper discussion of the whole materialist philosophy of life. Fechner in 1860 first used the term psychophysics. The extreme form of mechanical or empirical psychology was presented by Pierre Cabanis, who suggested that the function of the brain in relation to thought should be stated as the function of all other bodily organs. This same theory was expressed by Karl Vogt, who said that the brain secretes thought as the liver secretes bile.

One of the most important of all scientific hypotheses was that of evolution. Evolution was known before the time of Darwin through Hegel's metaphysics of "becoming," and Laplace's "nebular hypothesis," and Von Baer's *History of the Development of Animals*, which inspired Herbert Spencer's definition of religion. Buffon too put forward a theory of the modification of animals by external conditions, and Erasmus Darwin taught that "from the metamorphosis of animals as from the tadpole to the frog...the changes produced by artificial cultivation as in the breeds of horses, dogs and sheep...we are led to conclude that they have been alike produced from a similar living filament." The first connected and logical theory, however, was that of Lamarck, who attributed evolution to the cumulative inheritance of modifications induced by the action of environment. Two other nineteenth-century evolutionists who defended the direct action of environment on the individual were Saint-Hilaire and Robert Chambers, whose anonymous book, *The Vestiges of Creation*, prepared minds for Darwin's theory.

It was none of these, however, who most influenced Darwin, but rather a Reverend Thomas Malthus, who in 1798 published his *Essay on Population*, in which he developed the theory that the human race tends to outrun its means of sustenance and hence can be kept within bounds only by famine and pestilence, war, and other catastrophes. Darwin himself has recorded the effect of this work on his mind.

In October 1838, [he says], I happened to read for amusement Malthus on population, and being well prepared to appreciate the struggle for existence which everywhere goes on, from long continued observation of the habits of animals and plants, it at once struck me that under these circumstances favorable variations would tend to be preserved, and unfavorable ones destroyed. The result of this would be the formation of a new species. Here then I had a theory by which to work.

On November 24, 1859, Darwin published his theory of evolution under the title *The Origin of Species*.

His particular hypothesis of natural selection was proven to be an inadequate explanation, but his theory of organic evolution has been generally accepted and is now used as a basis for theories in many fields. In 1869 Darwin's cousin, Francis Galton, applied the ideas of heredity in *The Origin of Species* to the inheritance of mental capacities among men. From a study of books of reference, Galton discovered eminent men have more eminent relatives than ordinary men taken at random from the streets. In the light of all that has happened since the publication of Darwin's book, a prophecy has been verified which Darwin himself wrote in his notebook twenty years before he published his *Origin of Species:* "My theory will lead to a complete new philosophy." And Darwin was right. But whether a philosophy *should* be built upon biological theories is quite another matter.[4]

LYRICISM OF PHILOSOPHY, RELIGION, AND LITERATURE

Many names are given to the philosophy built upon the new science, and among them we single out the philosophy of positivism and the philosophy of agnosticism. In the face of certain scientific facts, a scientist may seek to discover the realities lying beyond experience, and may end by developing a system of metaphysics. Another scientist, in the face of the same facts, may refer occasionally to an unknown reality beyond them, but will disavow all knowledge of it rather than affirm its nature. It is from this latter outlook that positivism springs. In the language of its greatest exponent, Auguste Comte, we can know nothing except physical phenomena and their laws. Thus our senses are the sources of all thoughts, and we can know nothing except from sensations and the relations of antecedents and consequences in which these phenomena stand one to another. Mental phenomena can be resolved into material phenomena, and hence there is no such thing as efficient, final, or formal causality; more ultimately, nothing can be known or discovered about the origin or purpose of the world, or even its Providential ordering. As the mind unfolds itself and examines its contents, it necessarily finds that phenomena cannot be reasonably referred to supernatural agents; to do so would be to manifest an infantile mentality.

Comte has worked out the progressive steps of the scientific method in three stages, through which, according to him, all knowledge must pass: the theological stage, the metaphysical stage, and the positivistic stage. In the theological stage, imagination plays the leading role. It posits gods and spirits as the only way to make the world comprehensible; all reasoning in this stage is anthropomorphic. If thunder strikes the world, it is because it was thrown by Zeus. The theological stage has progressed through creeds: first in the form of fetishism, according to which a god is an interior soul lodged in an object; then polytheism, in which gods are separated from things but in some way act on them; and finally monotheism, in which gods are subordinated one to the other. From this subordination springs the science of theology. In the second or metaphysical stage, the universe is no longer explained by personal beings but by abstract principles, ideas, or forces. Men still try to do what in the theological stage they did—reduce things to a single principle. There are at first many such abstract principles, such as the vegetable soul which makes things grow, and the *vis dormitiva*, causing people to sleep. These abstract principles are finally reduced to unity, just as polytheism was reduced to monotheism, and the unique principle becomes Nature, as it was with Hobbes, Holbach, and Buffon.

Finally there comes the positivistic stage with four principles. First, positivism never looks for the *why* of phenomena or the intimate nature of things, but seeks only to discover the constant relations existing between phenomena, and to reduce their laws to a minimum. Secondly, there are two methods of the positivistic science: calculus and experiment. Calculus is to be used when the question concerns consequences deducible from premises, and experiment when the question involves facts which depend on laws. Thirdly, a positivistic spirit abstains from giving its conclusions anything but a relative value; knowledge can have only a subjective influence, not an objective one. Subjective unity consists in employing the same method everywhere, and thus produces the convergence of different theories. Fourthly, the best theory is that which represents the ensemble of corresponding observations.[5]

There was an inherent contradiction in the philosophy of positivism, with its emphasis on mechanical laws on one hand and evolution on the other. (It was the attempt to solve this disparity which produced the philosophy of agnosticism.) The contradiction of positivism was between the mechanical conception of a universe rigorously determined in all of its mathematical relations, and the historic or evolutionary unfolding of that universe in the course of time. On the one side, there was the universe which could easily be foreseen through mechanical laws; and on the other, there was the universe which could not be foreseen because of the possibility of new emergents in the evolutionary process.[6]

Herbert Spencer saw that mechanism and evolution did not go together. Mechanism asserted quantity, permanence, and determi-

nation by mathematical law; evolution asserted qualitative transformation impossible to calculate mathematically. He therefore attempted to unite the two theories, make evolution fit into the
mechanical universe, to view the universe as an evolving machine.
The impossibility of naturally embracing all phenomena in such
a scheme necessarily produced agnosticism. He had to confess his
inability to make life, with all its richness, fit into a rigid mechanical
universe. His solution was to say that whatever fits in a mathematical
and scientific outlook of the universe is knowable, whereas all else is
unknowable. He thus concluded that science represented the field
of the knowable, and religion the unknowable. Agnosticism thus
came to affirm that:

there is no other form of knowledge save that of which we have the
perfect model in mathematical physics. The rich results yielded by the
quantitative method of studying natural phenomena which modern
science had opposed to the fruitless multiplication of hypothetical qualities led to overestimation of this type of knowledge: everything which
could not be comprised in this scheme, everything which from its very
nature could not be comprehended within the narrow limits of a precise
formula, was forever banned from the domain of knowledge.[7]

In the preface to his *System of Synthetic Philosophy*, Spencer
says that religion and science confront one another today as an-
tagonists. The reason for this is that religion tries to solve problems
which properly belong to science. Every religion claims to reveal
something with which it is unacquainted. Religion cannot express
the innermost nature of the world and it will never reach its perfection until it admits that the area of mystery is greater than it has
hitherto been believed to be. The mind's task is to submit to the
necessary limitations of knowledge. Religion will not seek to bring
anything comprehensible under its sway, and science will not appropriate anything that is incomprehensible.

The doctrine of agnosticism, if it can be called a doctrine, was
propagated in England with considerable vehemence by Thomas
Huxley. He became a member of the Metaphysical Society and took
part in discussions of scientific, philosophical, and theological questions. All its other members had "isms"; having none, he said he was
like a fox without a tail. Wishing a name for himself, he recalled
the existence, in the early days of the Church, of the sect of
Gnostics, who professed to know things which he was sure they

did not know. He put a prefix to the word, and called himself "Agnostic." "So," he says, "I took the earliest opportunity of parading it at our society, to show that I too had a tail, like the other foxes." He defines the agnostic principle by saying:

it is wrong for a man to say that he is certain of the objective truth of any proposition unless he can produce evidence, which logically justifies that certainty. This is what Agnosticism asserts, and in my opinion, it is all that is essential to Agnosticism. That which Agnostics deny and repudiate, as unmoral, is the contrary doctrine, that there are propositions which men ought to believe, without logically satisfactory evidence; and that reprobation ought to attach to the profession of disbelief in such inadequately supported propositions.[8]

John Tyndall agreed with Huxley in upholding the pretensions of science. He maintained that in matter is to be found "the promise and potency of all terrestrial life," and that "the nebulae and the solar system, life included, stand to each other in the relation of the germ to the finished organism." In Germany agnosticism, as a form of materialism, was expounded by Ernst Haeckel in his *Riddle of the Universe*. According to him, there are seven riddles in the universe: the origin of life; the explanation of order in nature; the origin of reason and speech; freedom of the will; the nature of matter and force; the origin of motion; and the origin of consciousness. These seven riddles can be solved in terms of two fundamental laws. The first is the law of substance or "the fundamental law of the constancy of matter and force," both matter and force being aspects of substance. (Under matter are to be grouped all corporeal forms, ponderable mass, and imponderable ether. Under the second, or the energetic aspect, is to be brought inorganic force, as well as vital, psychic, and conscious energy.) The second solvent of the riddle is "the universal law of evolution by which life emerges from psycho-chemical conditions." Life is the energy of protoplasm, the unconscious mind of psychoplasm, the consciousness of the associative centers of the brain. The mind is nothing but force.

While Comte was declaring that the highest point of all knowledge was the correlation of the physical laws of the universe, and thus relegating religion to the realm of the unscientific and the infancy of the human race, and while Spencer was saying that science belongs to the field of knowable phenomena, and religion to the field of unknowable numina, materialists like Haeckel and Huxley were proclaiming the absolute dominion of eternal iron laws throughout the universe, and by their monism shattering, to their own satisfaction, some of the central dogmas of a dualistic philosophy: the transcendence of God, the immortality of the soul, and the freedom of the will. It was the beginning of a natural religion which Haeckel proclaimed, in opposition to the other-worldliness of Christianity.

With this new natural religion was allied:

a new aesthetic cult inspired by the wealth of natural forms which modern science has disclosed to the human eye; a new education based on the teaching of science and the new "monistic" ethics credited to Herbert Spencer, in which egoism and altruism are reconciled through the development of the social instincts in successive generations of the race.[9]

If there is one word which summarizes the spirit of the new philosophy, built on the new science, it is the word "evolutionary." Darwin had shown that evolution dominated the biological order; philosophers were now prepared to make evolution dominate everything. Henry Drummond's *Ascent of Man* interpreted Darwin so as to prove that the struggle for life is balanced by a struggle for the life of others. Benjamin Kidd applied evolution to morals and sociology in his *Social Evolution,* while Karl Pearson applied it to the theory of knowledge in his *Grammar of Science,* and Grant Allen was the first to apply it to God.

The lyricism of science, so wonderfully and fearfully worked out in the days of Newton, is now with even greater emphasis revived in the days of Darwin and Spencer. The general principle behind the lyricism of science, as has been stated, is that just as soon as a new scientific theory is launched upon the world there is a group of philosophers, theologians, and artists who attempt to carry over the categories of that science into their particular fields. Just as in the days of Newton they had attempted to apply a universal first principle to the whole of nature, so now they attempt to apply the category of evolution to the whole of religion.[10] The results from the negative point of view were disastrous. First of all, it was thought that evolution dispensed with the necessity of a Creator. Even Huxley failed to distinguish between the *how* the universe evolved and the *why* there ever was a universe to evolve. Huxley tells us that Darwin's work, the *Origin of Species,* gave him a substitute doctrine for creation.

It did the immense service of freeing us forever from the dilemma. Refusing to accept the creation hypothesis, what have you to propose that can be accepted by any cautious reasoner? In 1857 I had no answer ready and I do not believe any one else had. A year later we reproached ourselves with dullness for being perplexed with such an inquiry. My reflection when I first made myself master of the central idea of the *Origin* was, "How extremely stupid not to have thought of that before." [11]

Not only did the scientific hypothesis of evolution seem to dispense with the belief in a Creator, but it also actually did much to undermine what has been known as the fundamentalist attitude toward the Sacred Scriptures. In breaking with Catholic unity in the 16th century, the Protestant rule of faith had become Scripture and Scripture alone, with no corporate body or authority behind the Scriptures to interpret them. When science, in its study of the strata of the earth, came to the conclusion that the earth was much older than six thousand years, was possibly six million years old, the Protestant rule of faith was in a very bad way. Archbishop James Ussher, holding to the Bible as the supreme rule of faith, put the date of creation at a certain hour in the afternoon of October, 4004 B.C. Immediately, there was created the impression of a conflict between Scripture and science, and particularly between the six days of creation and geological findings. This apparent conflict between religion and science never affected the Catholic position, for the Church does not hold the Old Testament to be the sole and supreme rule of faith. She is rather a living voice which antedated the New Testament, gathered it together, and even to this day is its supreme interpreter. Catholic authority never held that the six days in Genesis means six days of twenty-four hours, as the fundamentalists were asserting. But the Catholic position not being generally known, it was assumed that all religion was in conflict with science simply because certain very narrow interpretations of the Bible were in conflict with it. Not only were the doctrine of creation and the Bible seen outlawed by new scientific advances, but even the Christian religion itself. There arose a great interest in ethnic religions and the belief that Christianity was not transcendent nor different in kind from other world religions, but was a single one of the passing stages in man's spiritual evolution. The idea that present orthodox beliefs and practices were merely developments from primitive cults of the past was something which had already been suggested by Hume and Herder. It was not, however, until evolution was brought over from the field of biology to the field of religion that it ever became popular. In 1871 E. B. Tylor wrote a work on primitive culture, of which Darwin said, "It is wonderful how you trace animism from the lower races up to the religious belief of the highest races. It will make me for the future look at religion—and belief in the soul, etc.—from a new point of view." In 1890 Frazer published the first work of his *Golden Bough*, which even to this day is regarded as one of the classic works on the evolutionary theory of religion.

A modern author who holds to this antiquated idea of the last century has expressed it in these words:

The old rationalistic notion of an original natural religion everywhere the same, from which men afterward declined—a notion already attacked by Hume in the 18th century—has been finally and forever abandoned. Similarly the belief in a primitive divine revelation containing the eternal principles of religion and morality—a revelation of which the old theologians made so much—has been completely undermined. Now it is recognized that religion, like everything else, has developed from small beginnings, that fetishism and polytheism are older than monotheism, and that the latter has been due to the play and interplay of many and diverse forces. Here as everywhere else evolution leads men to look for perfection not in the past but in the future, and to measure the worth of existing principles and forms not by their agreement with the forms and principles of an earlier day, but by their fitness to promote the religious and moral progress of the race.[12]

The impression created by the lyricism of science in the field of religion was one of general discontent with everything belonging to the supernatural order, such as the distinction between sin and righteousness, nature and grace, faith and reason. Relativity was substituted for certainty in all departments of thought; finality had not been reached in any line, nor was it even certain what was to be final. Pierre Berthelot, in his *L'Histoire d'Alchimie*, said that "the world is today without mystery." Emile Du Bois-Reymond, impressed with the deterministic character of the universe, declared that the future was in the present laws of nature and could be determined by their study. Others were repeating, with the same determinist philosophy in mind, that if the nose of Cleopatra had been the least bit longer, the whole history of the world would have been changed. In 1848 Renan wrote in a manuscript which was not published until 1890, under the title, *L'Avenir de la science*, that there is nothing either in man or outside of man which can escape scientific knowledge; the only God there is, is the god of reason. "Reason, Oh, Reason, are not you the God which I search? The true God is the Athénée, wisdom immortal and sovereign science. ... As one is more or less man, one is also more or less God."

Taine in 1857, at the end of his work on French philosophers, declared that all the events of the world depended on an eternal axiom pronounced at the beginning of things; there was no such thing as liberty or freedom, and consequently no moral order. "Vices and virtues are products like vitriol and sugar. There is no supreme doctrine or law above observation." Joseph Lalande had said, "I have swept the heavens with my telescope and not found God," while others were repeating, "We have examined the brain with our microscopes and have not found the soul." Miracles were outlawed by a single argument, the major proposition of which no scientist today accepts—"The laws of nature are determined: but a miracle is a violation of the laws of nature: *ergo*, a miracle is impossible." Mackintosh in 1894 wrote his *Natural History of the Christian Religion*, the avowed purpose of which was to do away with the miraculous; and in the literary field, Matthew Arnold was saying: "The trouble with miracles is that they never happen."

In the field of religion, the two works which probably testify above all others to the unbuttoned omniscience of the lyricizers of science, and which even today enjoy repute among those who still live in the last generation of scientific thinking, are Draper's *History of the Conflict between Religion and Science*, and White's *History of the Warfare of Science and Theology in Christendom*. Draper concludes his work with these words, so typical of the spirit of the day: "Roman Christianity and science are recognized by their adherents as being absolutely incompatible. They cannot exist together. One must yield to the other. Mankind must make its choice; it cannot have both." It reminds us of what Huxley had written: "Our great antagonist, the Roman Catholic Church, the one spiritual organization which is able to resist, and must as a matter of life and death resist, the progress of science and civilization."

From the period of eminence which our own century enjoys, free as it is from the bitter prejudices of the last century, it is possible to make some just estimate of these gross exaggerations of the conflict between religion and science. Looking back upon them, Professor Alfred North Whitehead, in his history of that century, tells us that:

in the last twenty years the century closed with one of the dullest stages of thought since the time of the first crusade. It was the ego of the eighteenth century, lacking Voltaire and the reckless grace of the French aristocrats. The period was efficient, dull and half-hearted.[13]

Chapter IV

REACTION AGAINST MECHANISM

The fierceness with which the attack was waged against religion by the deterministic science of the middle of the nineteenth century produced a reaction contemporaneous with the scientific movement itself. Thought begins to move at this period a little faster than at previous times, probably because of the ease and facility with which ideas were transmitted and made accessible to the general public. The reaction against mechanism assumed three forms: religious, philosophical, and scientific.

RELIGIOUS REACTION

The religious condition of the world at this time was somewhat akin to what it had been in Kant's day. Kant, who was a Pietist, had seen his fundamental beliefs in the existence of God, the immortality of the soul, and the freedom of the will attacked by the empiricists of England, principally by Hume. Anxious to save these natural truths, Kant made the fatal mistake of accepting the critique of Hume as final and absolute. Instead of meeting Hume intellectually, he retreated, in a rather cowardly philosophical fashion, from the speculative intellect, where his battle with Hume should have been fought, and took his refuge in the practical intellect or the will. Instead of examining the value of the attacks made on his Pietism, Kant had recourse to something nonintellectual as a means of saving his faith and his religion. He made the fatal mistake of transferring religion from the region where it was rational to the depths where it was merely desirable, thus making even natural truth a matter of faith instead of reason.

In the nineteenth century, something similar occurred. The Church found itself attacked on all sides by science, which claimed to be omnipotent and omniscient. Science was bent on dissolving supernatural truths into natural myths, and substituting vain illusions for majestic facts. It had contended that God is not necessary as the creator of the world, for evolution dispenses with creation. It had also seemingly substituted science for Providence and hygiene for morality. The supernatural states were assumed to be explained by hypnosis. All world religions were thought to be of human origin, substantially alike, and founded on fear. It seemed as though reason, which was identified with science, was wholly on the side of mechanism. Certain apologists of the Church, anxious to save the natural approach to faith through reason, felt that a time had come when some other approach to faith than reason must be used. Kant, anxious to save Pietism from Hume's empiricism, had turned to the nonrational. In like manner, these apologists made their approach to faith through the nonrational—not by the road of practical reason as Kant had done, but by the equally dark alleys of tradition, dogma, and infused ideas.

Three solutions were put forward by some of the Church's philosophical children to save the foundations of reason from the attacks of science. Their solutions, though very honest, were all as cowardly as Kant's answer. Instead of going out to meet the enemy on his own ground, by using reason to fight reason and science to battle science, they retreated into dark caves of tradition and natural faith, where it was thought that science and reason could not touch them. Their three solutions were traditionalism, fideism and ontologism.

The first escape was that of traditionalism, which was sponsored by De Bonald and Lamennais.[1] De Bonald was much influenced by the German philosophers in his idea of impersonal reason, and by Condillac's argument that "language is the sign that awakens ideas in us." Lamennais was influenced by Rousseau in his dislike of reason. At first he taught that the foundation for thought is the authority of the Church, and after the Church condemned him, he took the ultimate authority away from the Vicar of Christ and assigned it to general reason. The traditionalists, in order to save the supernatural, claimed that it was grounded not in reason but in tradition. Language, they argued, could never have been invented by man, nor could the thoughts which language expressed ever have come from man alone. They must, therefore, have come from God, who intended them to be communicated by tradition and accepted by faith as the universal reason of mankind. And there was no other basis for belief than this tradition!

The sponsors of fideism were principally Bautain,[2] Ubaghs [3] and Bonnetty.[4] The ideas of Bautain are perhaps the most typical. A convert to the faith after a moral crisis, this professor of Strasbourg was anxious to save his newly discovered faith from the attacks of mechanical science. He used Kant's argument to prove that reason itself is rather a broken reed; yet he argued that first principles are necessary for thinking. The problem was to discover why we believe in them. Basic principles do not come from experience; if they did, they would not be metaphysical. They must, therefore, have been given to us by revelation, not supernatural, but natural. He accepts the principles of philosophy, as above proof, revealed. It was really an assertion that faith precedes reason, and in 1840 the Church asked Bautain to subscribe to a proposition which is rationalistic in the correct sense of the word, namely: the use of reason precedes faith, and with the help of revelation and grace leads to faith.[5] The Church in this proposition quite clearly emphasized that reason has its rights and that faith must be preceded by it; it thus indirectly indicated that the way to meet the attacks of the rationalists and scientists was not to flee from reason, but to begin to use it.

The third escape from rationalism and mechanism was that of ontologism as sponsored principally by Gioberti [6] and Rosmini, who believed that we have an immediate intuition of God and His divine ideas. Every mind has an idea of the infinite and this cannot be obtained by abstraction from finite beings, since it is not contained in them. It must therefore be innate in our mind and perceived through intuition. Thus we can account for the universality and necessity of our fundamental judgments.

As each of these philosophies came upon the stage, the supreme authority of the Church condemned them. One of the great mysteries will always be why the contemporaries of these philosophies should ever have said that the Church was the enemy of reason. The fact is that the fundamental reason why the Church condemned traditionalism, fideism, and ontologism was simply because all three refused to use reason. The Church did not oppose to them Kants or such timid philosophers. She wanted rationalists to meet rationalists, thinkers to meet thinkers, and reason to challenge reason; and that is why the Vatican Council of 1870 declared that the human reason by its own power, without the aid of faith or revelation, is able to come to a knowledge of the supreme God.

All these other solutions—sincere enough—were rightly repudiated by the Church they intended to serve. The true answer to the difficulty and the true religious solution was given by Leo XIII in *Aeterni Patris* (published in 1879). He bade the Catholic world use its reason, and use it after the fashion of someone who used it better, perhaps, than anyone else ever had: Thomas Aquinas. He did not ask the faithful merely to use Saint Thomas as an authority, for Thomas himself had said that the argument for authority in philosophy is one of the weakest of all arguments. But he did ask that the Church lay hold of the eternal immutable principles enunciated by that scholar, reconsider them in terms of modern thought and modern science, and without sacrificing a single immutable principle, verify the gospel of *nova et vetera*. Shortly after the publication of that encyclical, Leo XIII gave 150,000 francs to start the Higher Thomistic School of Philosophy at Louvain, from which radiated scholars as the first tokens of the Thomistic revival.

PHILOSOPHICAL REACTION

Philosophers, like the theologians, were hiding their heads in the sand, refusing to meet the challenge of reason by reason. The philosophical reaction produced two distinct types of solution: spiritualism and idealism. Spiritualism appealed to our intuition of a spiritual reality to save the moral, religious, and philosophical universe, and to restore purpose to it. Some spiritualists held that the world is inherently spiritual in substance and that it is guided towards an ideal end, rather than by blind mechanical laws. Gustav T. Fechner, in his anxiety to save the nonmechanical as well as the mechanical, developed a philosophy which made room for both and in which he interpreted the physical as a mask over the psychical. The physical and the psychical are not aspects of a *tertium quid*, but the psychical is the reality, and the physical the aspect. Poetical developments of this theory led Fechner into the vagaries of panpsychism.[7] Rudolph H. Lotze was just as anxious to save philosophical realities, but he refused to follow Fechner in seeing the psychical as primary. He held to a kind of dogmatic first principle, for as the foundation of thought there are "certain necessarily valid truths," and "an absolute standard of all determinations of worth." [8] Lotze in the face of the agnostics and naturalists wished to show the necessity of reason; but he was as incapable of doing this as Kant, being unable to account for his "undemonstrable but irreversible declaration of consciousness and feeling." Eduard von Hartmann, a disciple of Schopenhauer, sought to salvage philosophy from the wreck of mechanistic science by a reconciliation of Hegel with Schopenhauer. Hegel identified the real with the rational, and hence could not account for the irrational. Schopenhauer identified the real with the blind will, and hence could not account for purpose. Von Hartmann combined both in the "unconscious" which partakes of both reason and will and which underlies the development of nature in which consciousness appears. This solution of von Hartmann was just as ephemeral as all the others, and what it did was not to solve a problem but to reconcile philosophers. It had little effect in combating the philosophy of mechanism, because it saw the source of knowledge and consciousness in the unconsciousness.

While these solutions were offered in Germany, Félix Ravaisson, in France, sought to save the philosophical realities scientism was attacking by a defense of spirit, which he held to be the very essence of nature. Inanimate nature, by this theory, differed from animate nature only in its degree of spirituality and not in any basic way. Charles Renouvier tried to save philosophy by appealing to morality. He declared that there are certain categories, nine in number (relation, number, extent, duration, quality, becoming, causality, finality, and personality), which suffice for the needs of science. But over and above these things is a moral order and a God, and they are founded not on that reason which science had attacked, but on belief, which is grounded on will. In other words, science demands determinism, morality demands free will. The difference between the two is the difference between necessity and liberty. The assumption was: let science attack philosophy all it pleases, it is still saved, for philosophy resides in the will and in freedom, which are outside of the pale and province of science. Charles Sécretan declared that philosophy is built on the incomparable value of *moral being* as opposed to the determinism of science. Alfred Fouillée popularized the notion that *ideas are force*, that mechanical evolution is the outward sign of the optative process which is our own true inner force. Consciousness is at the base of things, but scientism, according to him, had isolated things from consciousness.

In England, idealism developed with great rapidity. Thomas Hill Green [9] made war against empiricism and mechanism by the then very popular fashion of an honorable retreat. He advanced the conviction that sensation or "feeling" lays the basis of knowledge, but that thought alone can supply the "combining agency" or show us the relation between things. The ultimate source of all the relational categories is the Divine Mind, Who determines nature in advance of our acquaintance with it. Francis H. Bradley [10] denied Green's "relations" and reduced the traditional conception of causes and things in themselves to mere appearances. Reality, as Bradley saw it, was sentient experience, not crude scientific data, and the ultimate criterion was self-consistency. In America Josiah Royce [11] declared that reality is not a product of sentient experience as Bradley believed, but the very object of thought. George H. Howison and others continued in the same strain of thought, emphasizing the rights of mind against the demands of experience. Other solutions made mind *impose* necessity on experience, rather than seeing the mind *discover* it. In brief, the religious and philosophical reactions were one and the same in method, namely, accepting the attacks of rationalists and mechanists and naturalists as final and absolute.

There was, however, another philosophical reaction which was more like a counterattack on mechanism than a retreat. That was the philosophy of Henri Bergson. Bergson's point of departure was an attack on the intellect. He wrongly assumed at the very beginning of his criticism that the rigid formulas of determinism were a result of the intellect's having distorted reality. The intellect, for Bergson, was synonymous with the abused reason of rationalism—an identification which was quite unjustified. But having made that identification, he proceeded to show how the intellect in conceiving ideas distorted reality by cutting it up into static generalities, whereas the essence of life is a flux and a flow. Hence the necessity of using another faculty to attain the real, one he called intuition.[12] "*On appelle intuition cette espèce de sympathie intellectuelle par laquelle on se transporte a l'interieur d'un objet pour coincider avec ce qu'il a d'unique, et par consequent d'inexprimable.*" The mechanists, working in quantity, emphasized space as its environment. Bergson emphasized the quality of sensations, and hence emphasized time. Mechanism is determinism and supposes quantity, but our psychic life is not quantitative but free. The intellect is the faculty of the quantitative, the static, the determined, the homogeneous, but intuition is the faculty of the qualitative, the dynamic, the free, the real.[18]

Bergson's system ultimately ended in a desire to sweep away not only mechanist physics but also all logic and first principles. Despite his fundamentally wrong assumption, Bergson did much to kill mechanism from the philosophical point of view, drawing from William James a word of thanks for "killing the beast intellectualism absolutely dead."

THE SCIENTIFIC REACTION

Scientists witnessing the rapid change of hypotheses, the quick birth and death of scientific theory, came to the very practical conclusion that there is no such thing as a final solution for scientific problems, at least as far as the present is concerned. Thus, by the very failure of their theories, they were led to recognize the tentative nature of science. Scientists began to study the philosophy of these changed scientific theories, and within a scientific generation had turned away completely from determinism as the popular assumption to a rather contingent philosophy of science. Scientific theories, instead of being absolute explanations of phenomena, were now believed to be only hypothetical descriptions, their value merely problematic. Practical instances of the rapid change in scientific theories are to be found in biology and physics, to mention only two of the sciences. Darwin, in his *Origin of Species*, propounded the theory of natural selection to account for variations, a theory which Herbert Spencer dignified with the title of "the survival of the fittest." In 1907 Vernon Kellogg published his work, *Darwinism Today*, in which he showed that at least a dozen schools had already arisen within the school of Darwin himself. There was no scientific agreement amongst the Darwinians themselves as to what theory best explained the facts. Haeckel at this time offered the theory that the embryological history of the individual is the summarized history of the race, a theory which enjoyed great popularity at the time, but which Kellogg remarked "is chiefly conspicuous now as a theory on which to hang innumerable exceptions." [14]

Some years later August Weismann [15] explained the same facts Darwin had interpreted by a quite antithetical theory. He stated that inheritance of acquired characteristics was an impossibility; the environment could not possibly effect the changes Darwin had supposed. He sought the reason for the changes of species, not in the environment, but in what he called intercellular selection, which was based on a theory of "ids" and other elements of the germ cells. Hans Driesch, in a very short time, completely demolished this theory, and already the battleground of evolution was strewn with the corpses of dead and forgotten theories. Later on the writings of the Augustinian monk, Mendel, were discovered. Mendel, in contrast to Darwin, who used the world as a laboratory, was quite satisfied with the confines of the monastery garden. Working with peas, Mendel developed an entirely new theory to explain mutations, the account of which he published in a local scientific journal which lay buried for forty years until it was rediscovered in 1900, and popularized through Professor Bateson of Cambridge University. Bateson rejected the foregoing theories which held that new varieties were produced through minute variations. He contended that large variations occur, that discontinuous mutations are by no means rare and that some are transmitted in perfect form to their offspring. In effect, while older theories of evolution adhered to the idea of slow and small mutations, Bateson contended that there were large and sometimes rapid mutations. His new theory differed from Darwinism mainly in this: Darwin accounted for evolution by *addition;* Bateson accounted for evolution by *subtraction.* According to Bateson, evolution takes place by the gradual loss of factors which had previously inhibited certain tendencies. The sudden drop of an inhibiting characteristic would account for the mutation.

In the field of evolution alone, within the course of fifty years, there have been many contradictory solutions offered. Scientists who have lived through this period have learned to hold them lightly. While the facts might be certain enough, the theories to explain them were not at all certain.

In dim outline evolution is evident enough. From the facts it is a conclusion which inevitably follows. But that particular and essential bit of the theory of evolution which is concerned with the origin and nature of *species* remains utterly mysterious.[16]

Very much the same transformation has taken place within the domain of biology. In the middle of the last century and for some time after, when Huxley's *Elementary Physiology* was being widely read, the generally accepted theory concerning life was that it could be interpreted wholly as a physical-chemical system, in much the same way in which Newton had interpreted the inorganic world. Huxley was sedulous at gathering a huge mass of facts in the animal and human order which could be accounted for on mechanical grounds, but he often ignored other facts which contradicted that interpretation.

Claude Bernard, in his experiments, departed from Huxley's mechanical interpretation and revealed an organic co-ordination in life rather than a mere physico-chemical or mechanical co-ordination. A machine could never restore one of its parts if it had lost it, but certain things could restore some of their members after loss. A little later on there arose the vitalistic theory,[17] which held that some nonspecial and nonmechanical elements alone can account for the co-ordination and unification of the physico-chemical elements which enter into an organism. Various names were given to that nonmechanical unifying power, Driesch calling it "entelechy"; C. M. Williams, "genetic energy"; John S. Henslow, "the property of self-adaption"; Edward Cope, "bathmic force"; B. Moore, "biotic energy"; and William McDougall, "soul." All these interpretations represented a complete departure from the Newtonian mechanical conception of a generation or so before. Scientists seem to be in agreement today that the mechanical explanation alone will not account for life. J. S. Haldane, in his Gifford lectures, maintains that:

the actual development of ordinary physiological investigation has carried physiological knowledge to a point where the mechanistic speculation of the last century no longer affords any prospect of understanding life....

It seems to me that once for all we must formally take up the position that for biology the Newtonian philosophy is an impossible basis.[18]

While refusing to accept the mechanical theory of life, he does not believe that the vitalistic theory itself is sufficient. "However conscious physiologists may be of the defects in the mechanistic physiology of the last century, they show but little tendency to return to vitalism." [19] The only reason, he believes, that the biologists retain the mechanistic theory of life is that they find the vitalistic unsatisfactory. Haldane's rather temperate position does not represent such a complete break with mechanism as does vitalism, but in any case it reveals the great transformation of biological theory that has taken place within the lifetime of a scientist.

Not only has there been shifting, and even a *volte-face*, of biological theory as regards the meaning of life, but also as regards its unfolding. The old theory of Spencer was that the simple tends to become complex, and the homogeneous to become the heterogeneous. There was no admission of breaks or "jumps" in evolution. Lloyd Morgan has seen fit to enunciate what he calls a theory of Emergent Evolution, which claims that there is something which emerges on the life level which is not in the chemical antecedents. With each substantial change of plane, taking place through a "jump," new qualities characterize the new entity.

Working in the field of biology alone, a scientist could see within the short space of a few years a shifting of opinion concerning the explanation of life, very much as the physicists could see a shifting of opinions in the interpretation of matter. It was just such changes, and occasional revolutions in scientific thinking, which helped produce the new, tentative view of what science can perform. The new philosophy of science became humble. Omniscience gave way to nescience as relativity usurped the theories of the absolute. Since scientific theories were changing so rapidly, how could anyone be certain that his scientific theory or law was final? The new science no longer claimed absolute certainty about the universe. The laws of nature were now regarded as a mere "convention" or "useful fiction," but not "true." "The positive sciences in vain pretend to *seize the reason behind things*," said Etienne Boutroux.[20] Science arrives *merely at a descriptive formula and leaves us* there. The element of contingency in science makes all certainty impossible. Aliotta credits Mach with the view that "scientific men no longer take that dogmatic attitude toward their theories which characterized positivism in its earlier form." [21] Etienne Boutroux,[22] Henri Poincaré,[23] Hugo Dingler,[24] Gilbert N. Lewis,[25] and others were all agreed that science no longer seeks absolute certitude but only a useful description of reality, generally in terms of mathematical symbols. A more recent protest against the absoluteness of the old physics was the theory of relativity, which seemed to be another proof of the contingent character of the universe. Mechanism spoke of absolute time. Einstein showed time and space vary so that light always travels relatively to any observer with the same measured velocity. Time and space are not absolute, but merely relative to the observer.

The Quantum Theory had its first simple expression in Max Planck's theory, which "hardly went beyond suggesting that the course of nature proceeded by tiny jumps and jerks like the hand of a clock." [26] The atom, it seems, has various possible states, and it may hop from one of these to another. The atom, like an old engine, has a degree of "play" or "loose-jointedness" about it. But at the present time, there are no known facts that make it possible to predict which hop the atom is going to take. If scientists locate its position, they lose its velocity; if they find its velocity, they lose its position. The atoms have something like "free will." This lack of determinism in nature was a further confirmation of the contingency of science. [27]

LYRICISM OF SCIENCE IN PHILOSOPHY

Science asserted that its theories were contingent, its formulas fictions, and that it knew no such thing as certitude. Philosophy followed this trend and produced pragmatism. Science was well within its rights in asserting that its theories were contingent, but it is quite another matter for philosophy to say that there is no such thing as truth. Yet that is precisely what pragmatism attempted, hoping to make science *swallow* philosophy. The ideas adopted by Mach in his analysis of experience are found in William James' radical empiricism. Poincaré's idea that the value of a scientific formula is determined by its instrumental efficacy is to be found in John Dewey. The idea that the scientist chooses the theory which is most "commodious" was philosophized by Schiller into humanism, which made man the measure of truth. Science proceeded hypothetically and tested a theory by working with facts "as if" that theory were true. Hans Vaihinger made "the Philosophy of As If" out of it: live as if there is a God, and God becomes true for you.

Miracles, which were formerly declared impossible by mechanism because they were considered a violation of the laws of nature, were now not only declared possible, but necessary. Since the universe was contingent, everything was miraculous. Every new emergent in the evolutionary process was regarded as a miracle. The Gospel miracles were thus denied by the generous gesture of making everything else miraculous.

A more modern name for pragmatism is the philosophy of relativity. Space and time are relative to the observer. Richard Burdon Haldane, following this new philosophy, wrote his *Reign of Relativity*.[28] Edward Westermarck adapted it to the field of ethics in his *Ethical Relativity;* Bertrand Russell also advanced it in the field of ethics in his *Philosophy;* Walter Lippmann interpreted it for big business and added a drop of the milk of human kindness in his *Preface to Morals*. A. C. McGiffert introduced it to the field of religion in his *Rise of Modern Religious Ideas*. Practically all the popular philosophies of the day have interpreted it and made everything relative, even the Absolute. Just how far philosophy has become intoxicated with the wine of relativity is evidenced by this statement of H. W. Carr:

The general principle of relativity now proposed by Einstein is acknowledged, however, to concern the most fundamental philosophical concepts.... The new principle is that every observer is himself the absolute, and not, as has been hitherto supposed, the relative center of the universe. There is no universe common to all observers and private to none.[29]

The Quantum Theory has also been set to philosophical music. Mechanistic science argued that the universe is determined and therefore denies free will; consequently, miracles are impossible. The Quantum Theory posits a certain amount of indeterminism in the atom, inasmuch as science cannot predict the "hops" of the atom. Philosophers whose fingers are on every new theory of science as a basis for a new philosophy, now declare that the will is free. The reason they give is that science proves the atom has "free will"! "Physics," we are told

is no longer pledged to a scheme of deterministic law. Determinism has dropped out altogether and it is at least open to doubt whether it will ever be brought back.... Science, therefore, withdraws its opposition to free will.[30]

Sir James Jeans, who knows his physics, but who evidently does not know that the proof for free will has nothing whatever to do with the Quantum Theory, declares that "science has no longer any unanswerable arguments to bring against our innate conviction of free will." [31] Sir Arthur Eddington leans to this view in his *Nature of the Physical World* and asserts that those who deny free will do so on other grounds than the scientific: "Those who assert a deterministic theory of mental activity must do so as their outcome of the mind itself, and not with the idea that they are making it more conformable with our experimental knowledge of the laws of inorganic nature." [32]

The Quantum Theory has not made concessions in the realm of philosophy without demanding its pound of flesh. It gives philosophy free will on condition that it surrender causality. Dr. James Murphy, in his introduction to Planck's book, observes that

a great deal has been written about the philosophical implications of the Quantum Theory. Some of the physicists declare categorically that the development of the Quantum Theory has led to the overthrow of the principle of causation, as an axiom in scientific research. [33]

Sir Arthur Eddington believes that just as freedom and the Quantum Theory go together, in like manner go determinism and the principle of causality. Hence when one becomes antiquated, so does the other: "The old notion of causality is no longer applicable and an indeterminacy of behavior seems to be the essential feature of phenomena in nature." [34] Sir James Jeans thinks of causality as something involving time, and since physics has revealed a new "time," it antiquates causality:

The steady flow of time, which is the essence of the cause-effect relation, is something which we superimpose onto the ascertained laws of experience out of our own experience...the theory of relativity goes some distance toward stigmatising this steady onward flow of time and the cause-effect relation as illusions. [35]

Werner Heisenberg, who did so much to further the Quantum Theory, is also of the opinion that "the invalidity of the causal law is definitely determined by quantum mechanics." [36] Now that causality has been outlawed from philosophy because the scientists could not keep track of atomic hops, we are to visualize the universe as "possessing in each of its elements only a probable connection." [37] Scientists may very well make an abstraction from the principle of causality, that is, they may decide to ignore it in their experiments—no rational mind will complain. But when the scientists deny the principle of causality on the ground that there is a new theory concerning atomic motion, they have not only forgotten that the principle of causality has not a scientific basis but a metaphysical one, but they have also forgotten the limitations of the scientific method itself! The Quantum Theory may involve the problem of the applicability or the non-applicability of the principle of causality, but it does not involve the problem of its validity.[38]

Mathematical physicists stated that time should be welded with space. Bergson made a philosophy out of time. Professor Samuel Alexander, of the University of Manchester, is the authority for the statement that "Professor Bergson in our day has been the first philosopher to take time seriously." [39] Bergson made time the very essence of the universe. Space is the environment of the intellect which distorts reality, but time is the environment or the essence of reality which only intuition can grasp. Thought takes on the spatial form, but what is expressed takes on the time form. Bergsonism began to fall into some disrepute after the popularization of the Einstein theory, but the temporalism of philosophy increased as Einstein seemed to give a new life to a philosophy born of the womb of the latest scientific theory. Professor Alexander did his share to popularize it in his two-volume work on *Space, Time and Deity*. He writes:

At the present moment the special question of the exact relation of time to space has been forced into the front, because time has recently come into its full rights in science through the mathematical physicists, in philosophy also through Professor Bergson.[40]

Professor Alfred North Whitehead, who knows mathematical physics, has been inspired by Bergson and Alexander to construct a philosophy out of space-time in his *Science and the Modern World*, *Religion in the Making*, and *Adventures of Ideas*. Professor Whitehead reminds us that the antiquated notion of substance (which to him is a "chunk of something") is based on the "Fallacy of Misplaced Concreteness." Matter is erroneously viewed as "something out there," or something "spatial." The reason for eliminating the old notion of substance is that:

the stable foundations of physics have broken up; also for the first time, physiology is asserting itself as an effective body of knowledge as distinct from a scrap-heap. The old foundations of scientific thought are becoming unintelligible. Time, space, matter, material, ether, electricity, mechanism, organism, configuration, structure, pattern, function, all require reinterpretation.[41]

Since the idea of substance and "things" was grounded on the (erroneous) spatial outlook on life, it behooves us to transform everything spatial into its real pattern, which is temporal. The idea of "pattern" or "epochal-occasion" with its temporal multiplicity and its great time-depth is to be substituted for "thing" and "substance" and "matter" with their space-depth. The result is that instead of space forms there is "formation" or "reiteration." In your own turn, you become the series of temporal repetitions just as you made of music a series of temporal successions. In other words, each of us is our states; we are history. If we would have an idea of just how this time-outlook operated, Professor Whitehead bids us return to the romantic poetry of the last century. Tennyson's line about the flower in the crannied wall: "If I knew you root and all in all, I should know what God and man is," is an example of how the new temporalist outlook on life concretizes reality. The little flower "prehends" all being; the universe is "concreted in the flower," [42] the sunshine, the rain, the moisture and everything that enters into it. It is a microcosm inclusive of the whole universe.[43]

Something of this presumed conflict between space and time, or matter and event, or common sense and scientific sense, all of which are phases of the same problem, is found expressed in John Langdon-Davies' *Science and Common Sense*. "Science cannot get on without true metaphysics," he tells us, and then he adds that "true metaphysics is mathematics." The world must make a choice between science and common sense, but if it is to show any common sense, it must banish common sense, for did not that give us the Eddington table number one, which is really not a table at all, but merely a mass of dizzy electrons? Science contradicts common sense, for reality as common sense understands it cannot be expected from science. "The layman must abandon all such associations with the word *reality* before he approaches the reality of science. . . . When the scientist speaks of reality, he means something quite different from all everyday uses." [44] He then represents the man with the new outlook saying:

For my purpose...I find the common sense things called space and time useless and misleading; I can only complete my task by substituting for them various symbols and formulae which I shall regard as referring to something it is convenient to call space-time....Further, since I call my mathematical description of the universe reality, I shall say that common-sense space and time are unreal and but shadows or emanations of the only real space-time....[45] Common sense is a useless guide to reality.[46]

And then comes the error inevitable when scientific conclusions are transferred to philosophy:

The new idea of matter...undermines the whole attitude toward the stuff of the universe out of which the Aristotelian picture was made. Our morals and religions were built out of the Aristotelian conceptions of the nature of matter and the material universe, and the abandoning of those conceptions paves the way to new morals and new religions.[47]

Time is the creator of truth, and even the explanation of every moral action: "the motive of all action is inherent in the whole past history and the whole present situation of the universe." [48] And as for God:

the childish beliefs in a personal God, in absolute good and truth and beauty, in universal purpose and benevolent design, all of them seemed perfectly rational so long as the Aristotelian scientific description of the universe seemed rational. Today they are suspended in mid-air without a support, since all that supported them has been shot from under them.[49]

Not only has philosophy identified time with history, as H. W. Carr and Benedetto Croce have done, but even history itself has accepted time as a motive of interpretation. This is particularly the case in Oswald Spengler's *Decline of the West*. The new time, of course, is not the time of common sense; but that new *lived, experienced, intuited flux* in which subject and object in some way become one, like the poet and the flower in the crannied wall. If one lives the new time, he becomes timeless. It thus becomes possible to live two events contemporaneously. Spengler proceeds on the theory that everything is a time-phenomenon—a history, and not a truth. Accordingly, he identifies time with destiny. "The destiny-idea demands depth and not intellect." "Causality is a Baroque phenomenon." "We ourselves are time." This timeless time Spengler invokes under the title of the "homology principle." The application of the homology principle to historical phenomena brings with it an entirely new connotation for the word "contemporary."

I designate as contemporary two historical facts that occur in exactly the same relative positions in their respective cultures. We might describe Pythagoras as the contemporary of Descartes. The Ionic and the Baroque, again, ran their course contemporaneously. Contemporary, too, are the building of Alexandria, of Bagdad and of Washington; classical coinage and our double-entry bookkeeping system; the first Tyrannis and the Froude; Augustus and Shih-huang-ti, Hannibal and the World War!

Temporalism is made the basis of literature by Ezra Pound in *The Spirit of Romance:* it is dawn at Jerusalem, while midnight hovers about the Pillars of Hercules. Virginia Woolf lyricized the new time physics in her novel *Orlando,* the principal character of which was born in the days of Queen Elizabeth, and died at an early age just a few years ago. The character "in a short time fulfilled many years" because he lived the new time, the passage of which depends on the content and immediacy of our experience. Gertrude Stein in her *Composition as Explanation* justifies the time-spirit in literature by insisting on the necessity of repetition, or what Whitehead calls reiteration. "In my beginning," she writes, "it was a continuous present, a beginning again, and again and again." Anita Loos seized upon this idea in her *Gentlemen Prefer Blondes:*

So while we were shopping in the afternoon, I saw Louie get Dorothy off in a corner and whisper to her quite a lot. So then I saw Robert get her off in a corner and whisper to her quite a lot. So when we got back to the Ritz, Dorothy told me why they whispered to her. So it seems that when Louie whispered to Dorothy, etc.

Miss Stein also gives the philosophy behind this literature:

I wrote a negro story called *Melanchtha.* In that there was a constant recurring and beginning, there was a marked direction in the direction of being in the present, although naturally I have been accustomed to past, present, and future, and why, because the composition forming around me was a prolonged present. A composition of a prolonged present is a natural composition in the world as it has been these thirty years. It was more and more a prolonged present. I created then a prolonged present naturally I knew nothing of a continuous present but it came naturally to me to make one, it was simple it was clear to me and nobody knows why it was done like that, I did not know myself although naturally to me it was natural.[50]

Painting incorporated temporalism as the Futurists reacted against the "static inelasticity of the Cubists." As Impressionists broke up color, so Futurists broke up form, causing it to shake and vibrate like jelly. By rhythmic repetition of arms and legs, or by elongating either, artists tried to portray the primacy of motion.

The time was not far off when philosophy would completely abandon all claim to truth, would deny an absolute, and in an orgy of relativism, like Pilate would ask: "What is Truth?" and then turn its back on it. The penalty of lyricism is heavy. Once philosophy courts the Spirit of an Age, whatever it is, and marries it, it becomes a widow in the next age. Eventually philosophy grows desperate and tired from trying to fit a particular age and therefore never pleasing the ages, and is prepared to reject reason altogether. Rationalism fades into irrationalism. Dadaism in art becomes Dadaism in philosophy, as minds in their antipathy to reason seek to escape into absolute spontaneity and license. The dark, subconscious mental confusions are thrown onto canvas as a more genuine portrayal of self than the conclusions of reason. Surrealism enthrones the psychopathic irrationalist; dream worlds are substitutes for thought worlds. Music, too, glorifies motion. Dissonance becomes a goal in itself as an evidence of the protest against ends, purposes, and reason.

To arrest this chaos attendant upon the bombing of the fortress of reason, the world becomes ready for totalitarianism, in its three colors of red, brown, and black: Communism, Nazism, and Fascism. But one cannot understand the philosophical background of these systems without understanding how irrationalism became the new Spirit of the Age.

Chapter V

IRRATIONALISM OF MODERN THOUGHT

The modern world is characterized by materialism—that contempt of reason, glorification of sentiment, myth, and skepticism which reduces man to the level of animal or nature, and denies God. It is irrational, following an age which redefined "rationalism." The Rationalist Press Association of London, which was the last survival of rationalism, in 1895 defined rationalism as "the mental attitude which unreservedly accepts the supremacy of reason and aims at establishing a system of philosophy and ethics verifiable by experience and independent of all arbitrary assumptions of authority." Rationalism, according to this definition, is a good club with which to beat religion. It is interesting that the very same year A. J. Balfour, in his *Foundations of Belief*, declared that "rationalists are not philosophers. They ignore, if they do not despise, metaphysics, and in practice eschew the search for first principles."

Balfour was more correctly interpreting the new spirit of the time than was the Rationalist Press Association, for rationalists no longer believe in the basic and fundamental principles of reason. The rationalists of yesterday are the irrationalists of today. Thomas Jefferson in the days of the early rationalists could say: "Error of opinion may be tolerated where reason is left free to combat it," but today there is no error, because there is no truth.

IRRATIONALISM IN PHILOSOPHY

William James, Henri Bergson, and Friedrich Nietzsche, among others, developed irrationalism as a complete philosophical system. Perhaps no philosopher in America was more resolutely opposed to reason than William James, who insisted that truth can never be known by logical processes, because it is essentially irrational. The world is full of facts which transcend logic, the universe itself being an aggregate of individuals which are the playthings of chance and free will. In his *Pluralistic Universe*, he writes that we must "learn to give up logic, fairly, squarely, and irrevocably, for reality, life, experience, concreteness, immediacy, use what word you will, exceeds our logic, overflows and surrounds it." Thus did James substitute for the true rationalist doctrine—truth based upon conformity with reality and logical consistency—the notion of pragmatism or the supposition that an idea is true if it works, and that goodness and badness must be judged by their effectiveness in the concrete order:

The "true" to put it very briefly is only the expedient in the way of thinking, just as the "right" is only the expedient in the way of our behaving. Expedient in almost any fashion; and expedient in the long run and on the whole, of course.... Philosophy is only a matter of passionate vision rather than of logic—logic only finding reason for the vision afterwards.

The truth of any law, according to James, whether it be that of science or mathematics, is established only by the utility of its consequences. Traditional logic, which adheres absolutely to certain basic principles and to consistency, is dismissed as having attained to certitude at the cost of novelty. But despite the fact that James contended there is no such thing as truth—"truth is ambulatory; we must make it as we go"—he nevertheless tried to find some place for religion. As Hegel laid the foundations of the State on unreason, so James excludes reason from religion, giving it no other basis than our emotional nature. "We have a right to believe any doctrine which satisfies our emotional needs." If belief in God is useful, we should accept the existence of God, at least God as a working hypothesis. If, however, it is not useful, we should reject such a belief. Whether or not we will accept the hypothesis depends not upon the requirements of reason, but upon our affective needs at the moment. Most of our thinking is wishful thinking. Since beliefs cannot be decided by reason, it is man's duty to accept them only if they respond to his subjective emotional states.

Bergson's contribution to irrationalism was both negative and positive. Negatively he denied the value of concepts, maintaining that they are "naturally unsuited for life," because they substitute a symbol for reality: "A rubric under which we write all living things"; because they solidify movement whereas life is liquid:

"out of no amount of discreteness can you manufacture the concrete"; because they break up the continuous and the successive: "they bring the mind to ease in the discontinuous, the immobile and death." Since all life is evolution, and since an eternal *devenir* is at the bottom of all things, is not intelligence itself a mere emanation of this evolution, a product of its process? To say, therefore, that intelligence can grasp evolution, is to say that the part can grasp its whole, which is absurd.

As a substitute for reason, which distorts reality, Bergson recommended intuition: "In intuition we see reality as fluid, as unfixed, before it is congealed into concepts, before even it is perceived in space and time." It enables us "to apprehend reality at its sources, as it flows, before it takes the bend, before it obeys the bias which the intellect imposes." Positively, Bergson's system is not very different from that of Hegel. They both believed in the unfolding of the universe, with this difference: Bergson refused to believe that mind, as it gropes upward for free expression, follows a logical or predetermined pattern. Against the mechanistic philosophers, as well, he denied that evolution unrolled according to a preconceived plan. Evolution for him is creative, and as it moves upward is constantly unfolding new and unpredictable forms. It never follows a fixed path nor has it a fixed goal; every moment in life is creative, hence *Creative Evolution*. When Bergson published his *Creative Evolution*, James wrote to him and said that he thanked God that he had lived to see the two greatest events in the modern world: the Russo-Japanese War and the publication of *Creative Evolution*. It was not surprising that one more thinker should arise to offer a substitute for the intellectual other than the "passional nature" of James and the "intuition" of Bergson.

A third great influence in the development of modern irrationalism was Friedrich Nietzsche, who, under the influence of Schopenhauer, affirmed the primacy of will against reason. The basic principle of Schopenhauer's philosophy was that the ultimate reality in the universe is will, not the will guided by reason, but the blind, struggling will which manifests itself in the chaos of the world we see about us. This marked a departure from the materialist belief that the ultimate can be found in matter. Nietzsche accepted this doctrine that the will is the ultimate reality; but he understood the will differently, not as Schopenhauer's desire to survive, but rather a resolve to dominate and control: the Will to Power. As Nietzsche put it: "Whenever I found a living thing, there I found the will to Power, and even in the will of the servants, there I found the will to be master." Thus, Nietzsche was not only irrational in affirming the primacy of the will against reason, but also in repudiating the rationalist end of life, namely, happiness. Nietzsche insisted that man does not seek happiness; he rather seeks to overcome obstacles. Hence, true joy (not happiness) is to be found on the battlefield, even though the battlefield eventually leads to death.

In the moral order, Nietzsche worked out the full implications of the pragmatic principle that there is no absolute standard of right or wrong, of truth or error. If there is no truth, there must be uncontrolled power alone. This "Will to Power" is not born of the will of man who has a soul, but is the result of a vitality which has its roots in the physical impulse. Working out the full implications of this moral nihilism, Nietzsche claimed that the "Will to Power" would produce a race of supermen who would create aristocratic societies of a higher worth than the societies that were born of reason. "Humanity as a mass sacrifice for the benefit of a single race of strong men—that is what would constitute progress."

IRRATIONALISM IN SOCIAL THEORY

Not only did philosophy repudiate reason by denying the validity of its deliverances and by rejecting goals and purposes, but also by enthroning emotion or blind will above it. Philosophers were aided and abetted in this irrationalism by social diagnosticians and psychologists, who stated that human behavior is determined far more by irrational and unconscious impulses or instincts than by reason. Not of great importance, except as an introduction to the subject, may be mentioned Graham Wallas. In his *Human Nature in Politics*, Wallas applied his irrationalism to politics, presenting this as a subconscious process of habits and instincts, of suggestions and imitations. Contradicting the general view, he also held that political decisions do not represent a general will resulting from clear thought and reason; they are rather the result of a confusion of impulses and prejudices. Far better known are the writings of William McDougall, who, in his *Social Psychology* and in *The Group Mind*, denied that society and the state are built upon reason, on the ground that man's activity is motivated more by passions and desires than by reason. "Mankind is only a little bit reasonable and is to a very great extent unintelligently moved in quite unreasonable ways." For the basic principles of reason offered by the rationalists, McDougall substituted certain basic instincts of mankind: the instinct of flight, the instinct of repulsion, the instinct of curiosity, the instinct of pugnacity, and the constructive instinct which is the tendency to make things "from a mud pie to a metaphysical system, or code of laws." It was only natural that McDougall should bring his irrationalism to bear against religion. Since the concepts of religion are rational, they would appear as absurd to one who affirmed the primacy of instinct as did McDougall. It was, therefore, his firm belief that many of the doctrines of Christianity are the result of the blind operation of emotions and are further confused by a false interpretation of social phenomena.

Among other irrationalists of the social school in other lands may be mentioned Gabriel Tarde. His *The Laws of Imitation* completely divorced behavior from either the reason or the will and affirmed it to be motivated by three nonrational instincts: the tendencies of imitation, of opposition, and of adaptation. The irrationalism of Emile Durkheim sought the foundations of thinking and behavior not in instincts peculiar to the individual, but rather in the group mind, which he endowed with a substantial quality. This group mind, according to Durkheim, has "collective representations which exist outside of the individual and are independent of moral, legal and logical rule." Gustave Le Bon, with Durkheim, believed in the existence of the group mind, but denied that it was necessarily superior to the individual mind, since the individual man will occasionally act rationally, but the group mind never acts rationally. Being influenced by suggestion, this collective consciousness has a tremendous emotional instability and therefore men find it impossible to live without a "logical and absurd belief," such as religion. Georges Sorel, in his *Reflections on Violence*, in keeping with the spirit of irrationalism, denied that logic or reason could ever give an insight into reality. It is only when man is dominated by irrational impulses that he is capable of great and heroic action. Sorel completely repudiates truth and sets up in its stead the myth, which is "a body of images capable of evoking sentiment instinctively." Myths, by their very nature, are irrational, but they supply an emotional drive which gives great cohesion to social action. To Christians, he said, one of these irrational myths is the coming of Christ. To the eighteenth-century idealist, a myth was the notion of equality, and to the modern world, according to Sorel, the myth is the general strike. Without presently going into their complete positions, there may also be mentioned as apostles of the irrational, Freud, Marx, and Vilfredo Pareto. All agreed in positing a nonrational foundation of human life and behavior, the first making it out to be erotic desire; the second, economic methods of production; and the third, irrational residues or basic emotions and instincts which are later rationalized.

IRRATIONALISM IN LAW

The key to the true use of reason is: "In the beginning was the Word and the Word was with God and the Word was God." Goethe turned this around: "In the beginning was the Deed." According to the Christian concept, first you have an idea, then you act; first there is the Word, then the Word is made flesh. According to irrationalism, first there is the act, then there is the justification of the act. For it, the purpose of reason is to rationalize a *fait accompli*. The essence of irrationalism is the creative power of action alone. The ideology is secondary either because history and nature are predetermined to evolve, or else because the masses are guided by instinct and "faith." Social progress and evolution are determined either by a Hegelian dialectic as Marx conceived it, or else according to invariable and inflexible *evolutionary laws*, as Comte believed: "Social movement is necessarily subject to invariant physical laws, instead of being governed by the will." [1] Engels too believed that "the natural processes are essentially subject to the laws of movement." [2]

Because, according to the irrationalist scheme, society is subject to determined laws, it is impertinent to impose on it any rational plan. The pattern emerges in the movement; it is not given to it from without. For this reason, Marx was rather impatient with those who substituted "historically created conditions of emancipation for fantastic ones." There is, of course, one text of Lenin which seems to deny this view, and that is: "Without a revolutionary theory, there can never be a revolutionary movement." [3]

But Lenin did not mean by this that reason precedes the act, but only that the proletariat must be guided by their leaders, so as to keep in the swing of the dialectic which was immanent in history. Lenin only intended that men should be taught to swim with the current rather than against it. If there is a rational element, it exists only to rationalize the irrational.

What is the substitute for the rational in modern revolution? It is what Georges Sorel has called the myth. His notion of the myth arose in answer to the question, how the masses were to be incited to direct action and violence. This cannot be done, he said, by Utopias, which exist only to be criticized, but by a myth which is a description, not of things, but a determination to act, and as such is not open to rational criticism. "A myth cannot be refuted since it is at bottom identical with the convictions of a group, being the expression of their convictions in the language of the moment." [4]

There is no point in discussing the myth's value or its truth or its correctness; being essentially irrational it has no intellectual content. It is justified by the fact that it evokes mass enthusiasms. "It is to violence that Socialism owes those high ethical values by which it brings salvation into the world." [5] The particular myth which he advocated was the myth of the general strike. According to Bakunin, thanks to the myth, whatever it be, "the desire for destruction becomes a creative desire."

Irrationalism has two other social consequences: violence and atheism. When a man loses his reason, he becomes violent, because reason is the faculty which gives us purpose, goals, ends, and ideals. It is the principle which establishes the targets of life, and when it is repudiated, life loses all sacredness and inviolability. The loss of purpose is the beginning of the violence. A boiler has a purpose: the retention of steam at a given pressure for the purposes of heat and power. The boiler received its purpose from a human reason—the mind of an engineer. The moment, however, the boiler loses the purposes imposed upon it by human reason, it explodes. The moment society loses the purpose given it by the Eternal Reason of God, it revolts. Such is the origin of violence. One difference between present and past violence is this: violence in the past was based upon an affirmation—men loved something so much they resorted to violence to attain it. Today, violence is grounded, not on an affirmation, but on a negation. Men are violent, not because they love, but because they hate. They are "anti" something, whatever it may be, and they confuse their hatred of a person with the justice of their own cause.

Violence in the past ended either with the attainment of a purpose, with exhaustion, or with a return to the past. But today, since violence is secondary to an ideology, it never ends. It is used to maintain a new aristocracy in power—not the aristocracy of blood, or ideas, or wealth, but the new élite of power. This new aristocracy does not care what cause it promotes as long as it can maintain its privileged position. Revolution alone remains; only its tempo changes.[6] Periods of explosion follow periods of seeming order, because the enemy can be best attacked when he believes he is at peace. Violence is silenced only to create terror; violence is released to achieve terror. The world thus is made to live in a state of permanent revolution, where revolution exists for the sake of revolution.

Atheism is another consequence of irrationalism. Irrationality is essentially a denial of causes and purposes, and atheism likewise refuses to consider the ultimates. A Supreme Intelligence made the world rational; to deny this leaves no guarantee for the deliverances of human reason, no standard by which they may be judged, no power to account for their presence. The difference between the old and the new atheism is that the first was individual, while the second is organized. There is a verse in the Psalms which reads: "The fool hath said in his heart, 'There is no God.' " This has sometimes been interpreted as meaning that the fool's mind or intelligence told him there is a God; it was his feelings and baser passions which made him wish there were no God. But Pius XI revealed a still deeper meaning in the verse, namely, "The fool hath said *in his heart*, 'There is no God,' " because he did "not dare or did not think it opportune to reveal too openly his impious mind." He was an atheist only "in the secret of his heart."

Today, on the contrary, atheism has already spread through large masses of the people. Well organized, it works its way into the common schools; it appears in theaters ... it has formed its own economic and military systems.... It is a lamentable fact that millions of men, under the impression that they are struggling for existence, grasp at such theories to the utter subversion of truth, and cry out against God and

Religion. Nor are these assaults directed only against the Catholic Religion, but against all who still recognize God as Creator of heaven and earth, and as absolute Lord of all things.[7]

Atheism is of two kinds; either of the intellect or the will. When the intellect abandons God it creates an idol or a god of its own. In modern times it has been the religion of race for a revolutionary class; and for some intellectuals, trained beyond their intelligence until they have become intelligentsia, God is "science," or "progress," or "democracy." When the will abandons God, atheism becomes arbitrary self-will or the will to power. A human will in the person of a dictator substitutes himself for the will of God, and through violence, cruelty, and propaganda makes his will the absolute which must be obeyed at all costs. This atheism of the will exists in attenuated form in those whose god is their own will or fancy. Deification of power is the result of the will's alienation from God, as self-deification is the result of the reason's alienation.

The irrational attitude manifests itself also in domestic law. Law, for sound jurisprudence, is an ordinance of reason; for the irrational modern legalist, it is a dictate of the will—the will of the strongest in the community when that force assumes authority. There are a few variations on this theme. One school contends that law is the realization of human interests, and the principal task of law is to reconcile these conflicting interests with the least possible friction. The conflict results not from their quality but their *quantity*. The sole criterion of interest is "the received ideals of any given place or time." [8] The economic theory of law has been formulated under the inspiration of Marxism, and holds that law is an instrument of power. What that power is will depend upon the economic class which is dominant at the moment. At one period there will be class transmission of power through the capitalists, and at another moment class transmission of power through labor. It follows, therefore, that the law that served one class will fall into disuse when another class assumes power.[9] The great defect of this irrationalism in law is that it abandons all standards of justice through surrender to class interests.

As one theory makes law dependent on the moods of the times, and the other on the moods of the dominant economic class, so there is a third school which makes law dependent on *psychological moods*. This theory asserts that what comes first in law is not the reason, but an emotion, and what we call law is only a rationalization of an "emotional hunch." In the beginning was the flesh and the flesh became the Word. The judge makes his decisions on the basis of emotionalism and psychological factors, principally behavioristic, and then seeks about for arguments to sustain his feelings.

According to the school of *positivism*, there is no valid distinction between what ought to be and what is. Law is concerned only with the *is*, not the *ought*. The oughtness of law, derived from dependence on the Eternal Reason, is abandoned in order that law may be independent of ethics and philosophy and have a hegemony of its own. Positivistic law has its roots in the thinking of John Austin, who over a hundred years ago in England, following Hobbes, taught that law is the command of the sovereign, and that there is nothing beyond his decision according to which the law should regulate itself. Austin defined the sovereign as that person whom society was in the *custom* or habit of obeying.[10] This custom has no ethical foundation; it is merely a *fact*, for custom acts *ex proprio vigore*. The law is whatever the sovereign adopts as his will. One of the first expositions of legal positivism in this country was done by George Gray in his *Nature and Sources of Law*, published in 1907. Gray, living in a democracy, had to find another source of law than a sovereign, for whom he substituted the judge. Law is a rule "laid down by the courts." The standard and the criterion of the rightness of law is in the field of fact rather than in the field of *concept* and standard. This factual theory of law has become known as the Realist School of Law, of which Justice Holmes was the first protagonist.[11]

Of the extreme to which irrationalism can lead minds, Alexander Meiklejohn is an example. He dismisses the divine foundation of reason and society with the fling that

...its claim to validity is now negligible ... that presupposition is being abandoned. We know no "cosmic" principles of intelligence. We know no "divine" standards or ends.... It requires courage and honesty and love of truth to enable a man to discard a belief upon which his whole pattern of life, as well as that of the community, has been established.[12]

As Sorel and Hitler and Mussolini and Lenin appealed to various myths to sustain mass enthusiasms, Dr. Meiklejohn appeals to myths to sustain civilization. In keeping with the myth theory, he does not evaluate his theory objectively or historically, but only asks whether it can subjectively keep things going. "If God then doesn't exist, if the assertions about Him are myths, then the very presence of those myths is a fact of supreme importance for our knowledge of mankind." [13]

IRRATIONALISM IN RELIGION

Religious irrationalism is manifested by the denial of a rational approach to God and the denial of a personal, transcendent Deity. Since it is assumed in many circles that the only valid knowledge is the scientific, there are not wanting philosophers who conclude that there are no principles of thought valid enough to lift us beyond this world of experience to the transcendent cause of the universe and therefore to the knowledge of God. Bertrand Russell, for example, declares there is no such thing as unity and coherence in the universe, and hence no antecedent intelligence. It is in vain that one searches for a coherent principle in the universe.

Academic philosophers, ever since the time of Parmenides, have believed that the world is a unity. This view has been taken over from them by clergymen and journalists, and its acceptance has been considered the touchstone of wisdom. The most fundamental of my intellectual beliefs is that this is rubbish. I think the universe is all spots and jumps, without unity, without continuity, without coherence or orderliness or any of the properties that governesses love. Indeed, there is little but prejudice and habit to be said for the view that there is a world at all. [14]

One, therefore, is not surprised when this writer denies the principle of causality and denies that we can ever know anything beyond experience.

Indeed, strictly speaking, we can know only our experience in the present moment... if we cannot infer the existence of other people, or even of our own past, how much less can we infer God, or anything else that theologians desire.... Are we not to infer from this that the world was made by a Creator? Certainly not, if we are to adhere to the canons of valid scientific inference. There is no reason whatever why the universe should not have begun spontaneously, except that it seems odd that it should do so; but there is no law of nature to the effect that things which seem odd to us must not happen. To infer a Creator is to infer a cause, and causal inferences are only admissible in science when they proceed from observed causal laws. Creation out of nothing is an occurrence which has not been observed. There is, therefore, no better reason to suppose that it was uncaused; either equally contradicts the causal laws that we can observe.[15]

This rejection of metaphysics finds its echo in the position of Professor Whitehead, who writes:

Any proof which commences with the consideration of the actual world cannot rise above the actuality of this world. It can only discover all the factors disclosed in the world as experienced. In other words, it may discover an immanent God, but not a God wholly transcendent.[16]

And this rejection of the transcendental property of first principles is the fruit and heritage of the traditions of Hume, Kant, and Bergson. Hume had asserted that the principle of causality was nothing but a mental habit, acquired by the association of cause and effect. Kant had made the principle a form of the mind, wholly divorced from an empirical basis, and incapable in itself of giving us any knowledge of God. Finally, Bergson had contended that the first principle of the mind assumed a static universe, whereas, in reality, it is a flux, and that what is true at one time may be false at another.

Professor Philipp Frank, in his *Das Kausalgesetz und seine Grenzen*, pleads for the law of causality in philosophy, but like most of his contemporaries limits it to the empirical order. Propositions, he holds, are of two kinds. They are either about our use of words, and are tautologies, or they are statements about concrete existents, and all existents are experiences. The law of causality claims to be of the latter kind, but our experiences, the author concludes, provide no proof for or against the law of causality. And it is meaningless, he holds, to ask whether it applies to a real world, distinct from our experiences. It is meaningless because the statement that such a world exists, is itself meaningless. None the less, experience justifies our faith in causal laws.

Naturally, some substitute must be offered with the rejection of such a fundamental first principle as that of causality. The substitute generally offered today is the principle of relatedness: that is, philosophy is not interested in knowing the efficient cause of phenomena, but merely how their aspects coalesce and fuse into some kind of organic unity. A. E. Eddington, in order to throw this new outlook into relief, makes a distinction between causation and causality:

Primary physics postulates a strictly causal scheme, but the causality is a symmetrical relation and not the one-way relation of cause and effect. Secondary physics can distinguish cause and effect but its foundation does not rest on a causal scheme and it is indifferent as to whether or not strict causality prevails.... For convenience I shall call the relation of effect to cause, causation, and the symmetrical relation which does not distinguish between cause and effect, causality. In primary physics causality has completely replaced causation. Ideally, the whole world, past and future, is connected into a deterministic scheme by relations of causality. Up till very recently it was universally held that such a deterministic scheme must exist (possibly subject to suspension by super-natural agencies outside the scope of physics); we may therefore call this the "orthodox" view. It was, of course, recognized that we were only acquainted with part of the structure of this causal scheme, but it was the settled aim of the theoretical physics to discover the whole. This replacement in orthodox science of causation by causality is important.[17]

Or, in the words of H. A. Overstreet:

When we come forward to modern days, we discover a far clearer sense of what the cosmic order is. The sciences—mathematics, physics, chemistry, biology, psychology—have been progressively triumphant efforts to discover how matters hang together in the universe, what the basic correctedness really is.... Reality is relatedness. Our task is to discover that relatedness, or, where it still lies within the limbo of possibility, to bring it into being.[18]

Since the limit of human knowledge is the scientific and experimental, and since the human reason is unable to rise to a knowledge of the metaphysical objective truths and principles, it is contended by modern philosophy that God can be known only by the non-rational method (will to believe, hypothesis, and religious experience),[19] which is not objective and transcendent, but subjective and immanent. No term which the philosophy of religion uses, therefore, will be applicable to God as He is in Himself; it will only be an extrinsic denomination, or symbolic in its character. The Idea of God, and not God, becomes of primary importance.[20]

The conclusions of these contemporary writers merely reflect the doctrines of Kant, whose transcendental idealism (which confessed its inability to reach transcendent reality) stands at the fountain-head of the subjectivist trend in modern philosophy of religion. Since he maintained the inability of the mind to know realities which surpass sense experience, Kant was obliged to have recourse to the affective side of human nature to safeguard the truths of religion. Yet he was unable to defend these verities satisfactorily against skeptical critics who arose even in his own lifetime. During his last years, as we learn from the pages of his *Opus Postumum*, the sage of Königsberg frankly admitted that God was only an *ens rationis*, the product of our own reason:

God is not a thing existing outside of me, but my own thought. It is absurd to ask whether God is.... There is a God, namely, in the idea of the moral-practical reason.[21]

The notion of God is a necessary one, but there corresponds to it no objective reality. We satisfy the demands of our moral life and ethical aspirations, and therefore this concept is extremely useful. But it is a matter of supreme indifference to the self-legislating subject whether a real God exists independent of his thought. Man, on the Kantian view, is an autonomous god, sufficient unto himself.

THE NATURE OF THE GOD WHO IS KNOWN IRRATIONALLY

God is not transcendent to the world process, but immanent in it. This conclusion is the logical development of the assumption that reason is not the proper approach to God. Hence, there can be no Reason *outside* and transcendent to the universe. If knowledge is of the sensible order alone and is not objectively valid, then a double kind of theism results: the scientific theism which ends in a mathematical deity or cosmic God, and the nonscientific humanistic theism which ends in the finite God. With very few exceptions, both these theisms assume that God is immanent in the world, either as its mathematical harmony, or as a finite force struggling not so much with algebraic formulas, as with the problem of evil. Scientific theism proposes a God interpreted in terms of the categories of the empirical sciences and particularly in terms of physics. Today most minds are more convinced by what scientists say about God, than by what philosophers say about Him.[22] In order to understand the cosmic gods of the new science, it is necessary to recall some of the conclusions of the new physics.

In recent years materialism has been practically destroyed by the new mathematical physics which has reduced matter to electrical behavior. The new discoveries concerning the atom, coupled with the new hypothesis of relativity, have invalidated the concept of a material thing, insofar as this concept was derived from nature. Tables and chairs are now described as:

mostly emptiness, in which are scattered numerous electrical charges rushing about with great speed; but their combined bulk amounts to less than a billionth of the bulk of the table itself.[23]

The whole physical universe in turn is represented as composed of electrical impulses, or waves of light, the difference between matter and light itself being that the first is bottled and the second is not.[24] If, however, one wishes to translate this outlook on the universe into terms of the theory of relativity, then a material being becomes something which endures in time long enough to be measured. Formerly, time did not enter into measurements, but according to the present belief of science, constancy in measurement implies constancy in duration. Instead of things having three dimensions, there is now to be added a fourth, namely, time, and the union of the three spatial dimensions and the one time dimension constitutes the four dimensional spatio-temporal continuum.

If what we call a thing, for instance, a table, is no longer a thing, but a name for the relation between events, or "epochal occasions," [25] then there arises a great gulf between the concrete world about us and the mathematical conception of it as seen by the modern physicist; there is a world of difference between the table which I touch, and the table which the scientist knows as made up of events or epochal occasions in a spatio-temporal continuum. The table is "concrete," but "event" is abstract and is used as a convenient word to represent a term in a series mathematically conceived.[26] This divergence between the ordinary world of sense experience in which things are "substantial" and the scientific world in which there are no things, but only fields of influences and potentials, may be set in relief by a few conclusions drawn from modern physics:

1. Sensible qualities, such as color and noise, are in a certain sense supplied by the mind.[27]

2. The conclusions of physics are not about real things but abstracted aspects of them.

3. The selection of these abstracted aspects is determined, in part at least, by the physicist. There is no reason to believe that anything

corresponding to these abstracted aspects should exist outside of
the physicist's mind.

4. Physicists deal not with a real but with a symbolic world.
These symbols do not bring us in touch with reality. They have
meaning only in terms of each other.[28]

What is it that bridges the gulf between the abstract and the concrete? What makes one applicable to the other? How does the
knowledge of the one enable the prediction of the other? The
general answer is: God. But the cosmic gods of the physicists are
not all the same. The first cosmic god is the one born of the brain
of Alfred North Whitehead. He holds that God is the "Principle
of Concretion" or the "harmony of epochal occasions," who makes
some things happen and other things not happen among the multitude of alternative possibilities which the abstract logic of pure
forms eternally affords. God, in other words, is the one who makes
the adjustment between the mathematical world of the scientist and
the ordinary world of sensible experience. One might imagine, for
example, that in the infinite abstract possibilities of the universe the
time had come for a giraffe to have the "epochal occasion" of a
long neck. There had to be something to determine that the giraffe
would have in the concrete, a long neck instead of a long nose. The
one who determined the realization or concretion is God. To put
it in more technical language, Whitehead argues that the universe
is not made up only of possibilities but also of actualities. In order
that actualities may enter into the universe, there must be some
limitation of possibilities, that is, one thing is introduced to the
exclusion of another thing. This Principle of Limitation, which
carves the actual universe out of infinite possibilities, is God. But
this Principle of Limitation is irrational, because there is no way of
discovering why those possibilities should have been realized, rather
than any others. Hence, God is "Ultimate Irrationality." [29]

From another point of view, the unit in Whitehead is "event."
The universe consists of events and their correlations. An "event"
or "epochal occasion" is what the ordinary man means by "thing,"
although it is not inert or static, but dynamic and progressive.
"Events" are always coming into being and then perishing and giving
rise to other events. Each little "event" in the world organizes itself
without God, simply because it is its nature to do so. But Whitehead
calls on God to help correlate one event with other events, just

as Newton called on God to explain why eccentric and concentric planets did not collide, and why the fixed stars did not fall. Since each event is selfish, these combinations would be mutually destructive, unless there was some organizing power to regulate their relations one with another. The one who relates and interlocks "epochal occasions" with one another and telescopes the past into the present and produces "togetherness," or what the rest of men normally call order, is God.

But is God outside this process, transcendent to it, and omnipotent? Whitehead answers in the negative. Why be concerned with what makes the stream flow? Observation does not tell us the reason *why* it flows; it only tells us *that* it flows. God then, is not outside the stream, but in it as the mutual adjustment of all epochal occasions, enabling them to fulfill their interaction instead of destroying themselves.

This may be an unfair presentation, in our own words, of God seen as the "harmony of epochal occasions." Perhaps we should allow Professor Whitehead to explain his ideas himself:

The phrase, "Prime Mover" warns us that Aristotle's thought was enmeshed in the details of an erroneous physics and an erroneous cosmology.... Today we repudiate the Aristotelian physics and the Aristotelian cosmology, so that the exact form of the above argument manifestly fails.... In the place of Aristotle's God as the Prime Mover, we require God as the principle of concretion.... God is the ultimate limitation and His existence is the ultimate irrationality. For no reason can be given for just that limitation which it stands in His nature to impose. God is not concrete, but He is the ground for concrete actuality. No reason can be given for the actuality of God, because that nature is the ground of rationality.

According to this argument, the fact that there is a process of actual occasions, and the fact that the occasions are the emergence of values which require such limitation, both require that the course of events should have developed amid an antecedent limitation composed of conditions, particularization, and standards of value. Thus, as a further element in the metaphysical situation, there is required a principle of limitation. Some particular *how* is necessary, and some particularisation in the *what* of matter of fact is necessary. The only alternative to this admission is to deny the reality of actual occasions. Their apparent irrational limitation must be taken as a proof of illusion and we must look for reality behind the scene. If we reject this alternative behind the scene, we must provide a ground for limitation which stands among the attributes of the substantial activity. This attribute provides the limitation for which no reason can be given; for all reason flows from it.[30]

There is something in these ideas, and those mentioned in *Religion in the Making* (footnote 30), which smacks of the common-sense Aristotelian conception that the universe is made up of a determinable element (matter), and a determining element (form), and the source of both, or God; but this is only seeming. The two philosophies are poles apart, for Professor Whitehead quite clearly denies that God is transcendent to the world:

Any proof which commences with the consideration of the character of the actual world cannot rise above the actuality of this world. It can only discover all the factors disclosed in the world as experienced. In other words, it may discover an immanent God, but not a God wholly transcendent.

God is not the ultimate reality. If there is any reality at all, it is advance into novelty: "Neither God, nor the World, reaches static completion. Both are in the grip of the ultimate metaphysical ground, the creative advance into novelty." [31] The process into novelty then is not due to God: it is truer to say that God is due to it. This outlook on the universe which considers God as "organic" with the universe, or as the purely nonmathematical element in reality, has inspired Professor Henry Nelson Wieman,[32] of the University of Chicago, to try to make clear that which his precursor, Professor Whitehead, has succeeded in making vague.

God, who is organic with the universe, Professor Wieman defines as ". . . that interaction between individuals, groups and ages which generates and promotes the greatest mutuality of good.[33] God as an "interaction" is not much clearer than Whitehead's God Who is a "Principle of Concretion." Evidently Wieman's God results from the attempt to interpret everything in the light of the new physics; which asks us to define every object as an interaction—even God. This interaction, however, is not personal,[34] nor is He in perfect existence. Like the God of Whitehead, He is "partly in existence and partly in possibility." [35] A normal mind finds it difficult to conceive just how one would pray to an interaction, or how one could regard his Beloved as a "dear psycho-physical organism," but Dr. Wieman assures us that the Beloved "is a psycho-physical organism just the same, and it is very important for me to know the fact." [36]

SIR JAMES JEANS

Sir James Jeans idealizes his physics into the discovery of God by the following steps:

The universe is more easily analyzable into mathematical concepts than into concepts from any other science.

Our efforts to interpret nature in terms of the concepts of pure mathematics have so far proved brilliantly successful. It would now seem to be beyond dispute that in some way nature is more closely allied to the concepts of pure mathematics than to those of biology and engineering.[37]

This is because the physicist is concerned not with the nature of material things but only with the relations between their aspects. In this sense, physics deals with abstractions or selected aspects of reality. Ether, for example, is "abstraction" and ether waves are only "this quality of abstraction in an acute form." [38]

The above quotation also proves that our mathematical knowledge has been, as it were, spun out of our minds. We have not deduced it by studying the workings of nature. Finding mathematical principles to be true in our own mind, we apply them to things in the outside world. Taking Plato's example of the shadow and the cave, Jeans says:

When scientists study the world of phenomena, the shadow which nature throws on the wall of our cave, they do not find these shadows totally unintelligible, and neither do they seem to represent unknown or unfamiliar objects. Rather, it seems to me, we can recognize chess players outside in the sunshine who appear to be very well acquainted with the rules of the game *as we have formulated them in our cave*. To drop our metaphor, nature seems very conversant with the rules of pure mathematics, as our mathematicians have formulated them in their studies, out of their own inner consciousness and without drawing to any appreciable extent on the experience of the outer world. By "pure mathematics" is meant those departments of mathematics which are creations of pure thought, of reason operating solely within her own sphere, as contrasted with "applied mathematics" which reasons about the external world, after first taking some supposed property of the external world as its raw material.[39]

The surprising fact is that the universe compared to which we are so insignificant seems to run according to the rules which we have drawn up. We draw up our rules for the universe, and then when we go to the universe we find it running according to our rules. There is only one way to account for this fact, according to Jeans, and that is that both our minds and the external world originate in the constructive operations of the same mind. That is why they both work together. There is kinship between the universe and the designing mind, but since the universe is mathematical, it follows that the power behind the universe is mathematical. Suppose, says Sir James Jeans, a deaf musician were confronted for the first time with a pianola:

Although he could hear nothing, he would immediately recognize this succession of numbers (1, 5, 8, 13) as the intervals of the common chord, while other successions of less frequent occurrence would suggest other musical chords. In this way he would recognize a kinship between his own thoughts and the thoughts which had resulted in the making of the pianola; he would say that it had come into existence through the thought of a musician.[40]

In like manner, the universe is mathematical, and since mathematics have their origin in our mind, both have the same origin in the brain of a mathematical thinker. Hence, "the universe appears to have been designed by a pure mathematician." [41]

It now remains to inquire into the nature of God who is a Mathematician. There are moments when the universe, whose phenomena we know, but not its unbelievable nature, is described as "a pure thought." [42] God does not work in time and space; He works with them and they are therefore the products of His thinking. The implication is again slipped in that a universe which is a creation of thought must be itself a thought. Bertrand Russell says of this theory that Jeans

...reverts explicitly to the theory of Bishop Berkeley according to which the only things that exist are thoughts, and the quasi-permanence which we observe in the external world is due to the fact that God keeps on thinking about things for quite a long time. Material objects, for example, do not cease to exist when no human being is looking at them, because God is looking at them all the time, or rather because they are thoughts in His mind all the time.[43]

This is correct, says Jeans, for the apparent objectivity of things is due to "this subsisting in the mind of some eternal spirit." [44] The immanence of the world in God and God in the world thus becomes complete.

A. S. EDDINGTON

According to Professor Eddington, there are two kinds of knowledge, scientific and intuitional. The first kind gives us knowledge only about symbols with which science is concerned; the second gives us knowledge about ourselves, about humor, and about God.

We have two kinds of knowledge which I call symbolic knowledge and intimate knowledge. I do not know whether it would be correct to say that reasoning is only applicable to symbolic knowledge, but the more customary forms of reasoning have been developed for symbolic knowledge only. The intimate knowledge will not submit to codification and analysis; or, rather, when we attempt to analyse it, the intimacy is lost and it is replaced by symbolism.[45]

Despite the fact that he is a scientist, Professor Eddington says the world is meant not only to be analyzed but also to be lived in. Here is where the mystic fits into the world.

...there are regions of the human spirit untrammeled by the world of physics. In the mystic sense of creation around us, in the expression of art, in the yearning towards God, the soul grows upward and finds the fulfillment of something implanted in its nature.[46]

The approach to God, however, is not intellectual for "we cannot pretend to offer proofs." [47]

In science we sometimes have convictions as to the right solution of a problem which we cherish but cannot justify; we are influenced by some innate sense of the fitness of things. So too, there may come to us convictions in the spiritual sphere which our nature bids us hold to. I have given an example of one such conviction which is rarely if ever disputed—that surrender to the mystic influence of a scene of natural beauty is right and proper for a human spirit, although it would have been deemed an unpardonable eccentricity in the "observer" contemplated in earlier chapters. Religious conviction is often described in somewhat analogous terms as a surrender; it is not to be enforced by argument on those who do not feel its claim in their own nature.[48]

Eddington's answer to the all important question: "Is there a God?" is in perfect keeping with his anti-intellectualism:

The heart of the question is commonly put in the form "Does God really exist?" It is difficult to set aside this question without being suspected of quibbling. But I venture to put it aside because it raises so many unprofitable side issues, and at the end it scarcely reaches deep enough into religious experience.[49]

Is this God personal or not? Professor Eddington, with characteristic vagueness, seems to imply the affirmative:

My impression of psychology asserts that the word "person" might be
considered vague enough as it stands.... Force, energy, dimensions belong
to the world of physics.... After exhausting physical methods we returned to the inmost recesses of consciousness, to the voice that pro-
claims our personality. We have to build up the spiritual world out of
the symbols taken from our own personality, as we build the scientific
world out of the symbols of the mathematician. I think, therefore, we
are not wrong in embodying the significance of the spiritual world to
ourselves, in the feeling of a personal relationship, for our whole approach to it is bound up with those aspects of consciousness in which
personality is centered.[50]

Whether God, Who corresponds to a term "vague enough" to be
a person, is perfect or finite, identified with the world or separated
from it; whether He is objective or subjective, Professor Eddington
does not tell us. He has sensed this difficulty and in an article on
"Science and Religion," he tries to make himself clear on the question of the objectivity or subjectivity of God, but remains to the
end unclear.

"Is God an objective Reality?" Before attempting to answer, it would
be necessary to catechise the questioner as to what meaning—if any—he
associates with the word objective. I do not think that it is possible to
make the same hard and fast distinction between subjective and objective
that we used to make. The theory of relativity has taught us that the
subjective element in our experience of the physical universe is far
stronger than we had previously suspected. It is true that in relativity
theory we continue our attempt to reach purely objective truth. But
what results? A world so abstract that only a mathematical symbol could
inhabit it. In the other great modern development of physics—the
quantum theory—we have, if I am not mistaken, abandoned the aim,
and become content to analyse the physical universe into ultimate elements which are frankly subjective. If it is difficult to separate out the
subjective element in our knowledge of the external world, it must be
much more difficult to distinguish it when we come to the problem
of a self-knowing consciousness, where subject and object—that which
knows and that which is known—are one and the same.[51]

This view, which fails to make a rigid distinction between the two,
leaves the question of the immanent or transcendent character of
God very much up in the air. However much one feels that the
Cosmic God of Eddington is transcendent and nonscientific, he

nevertheless seems to be a potential God like the others, who has "potentialities of self-fulfillment." [52]

Here, as elsewhere, one finds the typical modern inability to wrestle with questions until both shoulders are on the mat. The God arrived at is nondescript enough to be incapable of making demands on His creatures, and at the same time sufficiently definite to satisfy those who want the cloak of religion. The greatest advantage of this type of approach seems to be that science must recognize evidence from nonscientific sources, but the disadvantage is that the nonscientific is too often confused with the mystical, the vague, and the unstable emotional life of man.

PROFESSOR SAMUEL ALEXANDER

Another sample of the mathematical deity is presented to us by Professor Samuel Alexander, of the University of Manchester.[53] Influenced by the mathematical physical conceptions of the universe, Professor Alexander contends that the stuff from which all things are made is Space-Time, which is a motion without a body. Space and time do not exist apart from the other. Time is the soul of Space-Time and space is the body of Space-Time. By definition, God is a "variable quality," [54] and as the world goes on, deity changes with it. More accurately, God is that *quality* which is just above any level of the universe. Hence, when there were only spatio-temporal configurations in the universe, God belonged to the level of the chemicals. When chemicals came into the world, God was at the quality-level of a plant. When plants came into the world, God was at the quality level for animal, and when animals came into the world, God was at the quality level of mind. Now we are at the mind stage, and God belongs one level above, which, according to Professor Alexander, is the level of the angels. God, therefore, is the whole universe striving toward Deity. Deity is infinite only in the sense that it constantly strives after Deity, or more accurately He is "the whole universe with a nisus toward deity." [55]

Within the all-embracing stuff of Space-Time, the universe exhibits an emergency in Time of levels of finite existences, each with its characteristic empirical quality. The highest of these empirical qualities known to us is mind or consciousness. Deity is the next higher empirical quality which stands toward the lower level as deity stands towards mind.... As actual, God does not possess the quality of deity, but is the universe as tending to that quality. This nisus in the universe, though not present to sense, is yet present to reflection upon experience ... if the possessor of deity were an existent individual, he must be finite and infinite. Thus there is no actual infinite being with the quality of deity, but there is an actual infinite, the whole universe, with a nisus to deity, and this is the God of religious consciousness, though that consciousness habitually forecasts the divinity of its objects as actually realized in an individual form.[56]

The explanation of the self-improving God is continued:

Even God Himself does not as actual God possess deity attained, but only the nisus toward it.... The ordinary theism, therefore, when it postulates a human intermediary between us and a God who is conceived as endowed with deity actually attained, acts consistently in believing the intermediator to be more than man, human and divine at once purchasing consistency at the cost of interposing the conception of a miraculous person without parallel in the world.[57]

HENRI BERGSON

A quite different approach to the idea of God has been developed by Henri Bergson in his *Two Sources of Morality and Religion*, which is divided into two parts: the rejection of the theodicy of Aristotle and that of his successors, and Bergson's own peculiar mystical approach to Divinity. Bergson rejects Aristotle's argument of the unmoved Prime Mover deduced from the existence of mobility. The basis of his rejection is the traditional Bergsonian prejudice that mutability is higher than immutability: "It is always the stop which requires an explanation, and not the movement." [58] Furthermore, Bergson contends, the intelligence can seize only possibilities; it cannot touch reality. He tells us:

It is one thing for the mind to conceive the idea of being, but is quite another thing for the mind to ascertain the objective existence of that being. It is only through experience that the objective existence of such a being can be determined, hence the intellectual approach to God is futile.[59]

Having rejected the intellectual approach to God, Bergson now substitutes the appeal to experience: "It is therefore on the nature of God, immediately apprehended on the positive side, I mean the side which is perceptible to the eyes of the soul, that the philosopher must question the mystic." [60]

The mystical way is, for Bergson, the only avenue to God:

If mysticism is really what we just said it is, it must furnish us with a means of approaching, as it were experimentally, the problem of the existence of the nature of God. Indeed, we fail to see how philosophy could approach the problem in any other way. Generally speaking, we look upon the object as existing if it is perceived. Such an object is therefore presented in actual or virtual experience.[61]

What interests us particularly is the kind of God arrived at by mystical experience. To make good his rejection of Aristotle's approach to God, Bergson tells us that the mystic is not at all concerned with the metaphysical attributes of God. "The mystic believes that he sees what God is, for him there is no seeing what God is not." [62]

Since the metaphysical attributes of God are completely ignored, Bergson admits only one attribute which is the one perceived by the mystic, namely love: "God is Love and the object of love: Herein lies the whole contribution of mysticism." [63] Bergson thus completely skips the natural order and jumps even beyond the theological order into the rarest of spiritual experiences. His refusal to treat God from a philosophical point of view is due to two serious errors in his thinking: his assumption that all action necessarily implies change, and that all lack of change necessarily implies inertia. He might have found in St. Thomas the necessary distinction between action and change:

Plato ... said that the first mover moves himself; even the acts of understanding, willing and loving are called movement. Therefore, because God loves and understands Himself, in that respect it may be said that God moves Himself, not, however, as a potentiality.[64]

Prescinding from defects in the Bergsonian system, the problem is: what does the mystical soul actually perceive in its experience? Is it God or merely a creative effort? At one point, Bergson seems to suggest that mysticism is a contact "with the creative effort of which life is the manifestation. This effort is of God, if not God Himself." [65]

Does this mean that God is immanent in the universe, or is this system of Bergson's dualistic? There is no doubt that Bergson tries to make his system dualistic by making a distinction between the *élan* and its source. It is here that his position appears to be very near that which he took in *Creative Evolution*. It will be recalled that there he defined God as a center which is not a thing but a continual shooting out. The critics who level the cry of monism at this concept base their conclusions on the fact that Bergson did not sufficiently distinguish between the *élan* and its source. The same error seems to have been made in *The Two Sources*. Just as he transformed the *élan vital* of the creative evolution into the *élan d'amour*, so now he transforms this continuity of the shooting out into God, into the creative energy of love.

Bergson never gives us a very clear intimation as to whether the God of Love is distinct in the world; the one passage which most explicitly treats it rather suggests no real distinction between God and the world.

Granted the existence of a creative energy which is love, and which desires to produce from itself beings worthy to be loved, it might indeed sow space with worlds whose materiality, as the opposite of divine spirituality, would simply express the distinction between created and creating, between the multifarious notes, strung like pearls, of a symphony and the indivisible emotion from which they sprang.[66]

This would lead us to believe that there is no other distinction between God and the world than that between a symphony and its emotional reaction. If this were true, God would not be transcendent to the world, nor could he be conceived as independent of it. Thus another immanent or, if we may dare say, pantheistic God is added to the modern Pantheon.

THE FINITE GOD

In addition to the modern mathematical conception of God which makes Him organic with a spatio-temporal universe, there is another view which has become increasingly popular in recent philosophical literature and that is the idea of the finite God. The mathematical conception posits God in the universe in order to account for certain otherwise inexplicable events. The finite God is immanent, not so much in the mathematical universe as in the moral and emotional life of man. In speaking of the finite God, we include both the changing or developing finite God which was emphasized by the followers of Bergson, and also the finite God produced as a reaction against the block universe.[67] The present idea of the finite God is not the same as that which was created at the close of the First World War. In those days there was a general tendency to limit the goodness of God as being incompatible with the universal slaughter, and even before that time it was limited by the period's hatred of absolute. William James, for example, defined God as "having an environment, being in time and working out a history just like ourselves." [68]

And H. G. Wells told us:

If a figure may represent Him, it must be a figure of a beautiful youth, already wise, but hardly come to his strength. He should stand lightly on his feet in the morning time, eager to go forward, as though he had but newly arisen to a day that was still but a promise; he should bear a sword, that clean, discriminating weapon. His eyes should be as bright as swords; his lips should fall apart with eagerness for the great adventure before him, and he should be in very fresh and golden harness reflecting the rising sun. Death should still hang like mists and cloudy banks and shadows in the valley of the wide landscape about him. There should be dew upon the threads of gossamer and leaves and plants of turf at his feet.[69]

A little later on, Sir Henry Jones defined God as:

perfect in process, as a movement from splendor to splendor in a spiritual world, as an eternal achievement and never resting realization of the ideals of goodness in human history.[70]

The idea of a finite God is once more being revived and is replacing Humanism as the most living alternative to a full Theism.[71]

Among the more recent writers of the finite God may be mentioned first of all Professor E. S. Brightman, who has been most vigorous in insisting that the conception of the Absolute God should be surrendered. Briefly, his contention is that the evil in the world is apparently outside of the purpose of God and to some degree beyond His control; it suggests, therefore, a deity limited by conditions within His own nature which are not of His own creation or concern, and over which He is winning a gradual mastery.

God is a person supremely conscious, supremely valuable and supremely creative, yet limited by the free choice of other persons and by restrictions within His own nature. There is within Him, in addition to His reason and actively creative will, a passive element which enters into every one of His conscious states, as sensation, instinct and impulse enter into ours, and constitutes a problem for Him. This element we call "The Given." [72]

Thus our finite God is not one of finished perfection. This does not mean that God is ever ignorant or evil in His will, yet it does mean that He confronts within His experience genuine difficulties out of which arise the apparent defects of the physical world. On this view, God does not deliberately choose the cruelties of evolution or the sufferings of creation; they represent rather the necessary outcome of His own eternal Given nature, out of which He is always bringing a higher good. According to this view, God is not yet in perfect possession of life and truth and goodness, although He is actually on the way to possession. The perfect God is a future possibility but only after considerable struggling and striving. Furthermore, the very fact that God contains within Himself a "passive element" demarcates Him completely from the traditional notion of God as pure actuality without beginning or end. It is "the Given" in the God of Professor Brightman which constitutes the whole difficulty, for the Given is necessarily a limitation quite apart from the fact that the Given must imply a giver. Professor Brightman calls the Given a "retarding factor" and likens it to sensation in man: "Just as sensation limits the reason and will of man, with present problems which can be solved in rational terms, so the Given limits the will and the foreknowledge of God." [73]

He gives four arguments for the finite God. The first is drawn from the facts of evolution which give "evidence of frustration of design and of delay in achievement." The second is taken from the nature of consciousness: "If man is truly free, God must be finite as regards His knowledge. . . . Man's freedom is an actual limitation on the foreknowledge of God." [74] The third argument develops from a principle of dialectics, to the effect that all reality is full of contrast and opposition, and hence "God is the greatest sufferer in the universe and through this the greater victor. . . . His goodness is but the constant victory of constant effort." The final argument is drawn from religious consciousness which testifies to "Something Given which his reason and will do not create, but with which they love to deal." [75]

Professor Brightman claims that the idea of God presented by Professor William P. Montague is almost identical with his own.

In a late work entitled *Belief Unbound,* which has proven very popular with agnostics and humanists, Professor Montague sees the world as made up of:

...real obstreperous entities constituting a modified mechanism which with respect to values, is a good deal of chaos. This chaos appears to be undergoing an amelioration genuine, though painfully slow, and the leaven that works in it, and by which its evolution is wrought, is the finite God. How is this unitary and personal, yet infinite cosmic consciousness related to the finite God that is the cosmic nisus...their relation is rather that of a mind to a will—a will of finite power working within the confines of an infinitely extended and all inclusive mind.[76]

This theory places the limits of God, not so much in the purpose of His will which is regarded as good, but rather in His power. He struggles with factors within His own nature which are not of His own volition. In this way Professor Montague attempts to think out a God with a finite will and an infinite mind.

Another sample of the finite God is offered by Professor H. A. Overstreet, who takes his point of departure from the findings of science and especially from the conception of a meager or creative evolution. From there he works to the conclusion of a struggling and creative God very much like that of Professor Montague. "God is in an infinite degree the everlasting creative life that moves toward wholeness." Lest we should be tempted to think that this "cosmic *élan*" is a Mind and a Personality, he reminds us that he is not as:

...an individual set over against ourselves, but as a life in which we live and which itself lives in us.... This is far different from the traditional meaning of devoting ourselves by prayer and ceremony to a deity who is afar in the heavens. On the contrary, this God is a life within ourselves. We love this God in the degree that we love the life that is creatively uniting. This is very different from loving a Father in the heavens and at the same time, on earth, exploiting or killing our fellows. To love God is to love the process of bringing life into more vital integration. Wherever there is a passionate love of integrating, there is a passionate love of God.[77]

Professor W. M. Horton should be mentioned as another member of this group. He defines God as "That supremely worthy being by devotion to which [to whom] man may attain the most vigorous vitality and the highest degree of selfhood of which he is capable." This definition of God when tested by human experience finally comes to be interpreted as "a vast cosmic drift or trend toward harmony, fellowship and mutual aid, whereby our efforts to create a just equilibrium in human affairs are supported and sustained." Professor Horton makes it quite clear that he does not include personality or infinitude or omnipotence in his conception of God.[78]

Dr. J. S. Haldane, in his *Philosophical Basis of Biology*, shares this idea of a finite struggling God: "God is not a perfect being existing apart from the ignorance, sin and suffering of our own world, but present within and around us, sharing in our struggle." [79] In a later book he says:

...the idea of God may thus be seen to express more than the mere projection of human ideals, for that expression still carries within it the whole dualism between an alien cosmos and man's little world of interest and values.... God is not supernatural, but always natural just as ideals are natural.[80]

This work on God, somewhat suggestive of Professor Overstreet, identifies Him with cosmic reality, for Haldane says that:

...God as reality is not to be thought of apart from that reality. It is no more strange that religion should have this general term than that science should have the word "nature" or that politics should speak of the "world" or that philosophy should conceive the "cosmos." If these are "current universals," might not God also be thought a concurrent universal reality? Reality conceived as friendly, as furnishing support for man's existence and for the realization of ideals...is God.[81]

And Haldane further explains:

If we secure our idea of God by generalizing our observing and experiencing living, we see that it is everywhere marked by this double aspect: it is at once both fixed and changing like a river in its course.[82]

It is quite evident from these statements that there is a positive drift toward the finite God. Fifty years ago the philosophical problem was: "Is there a God?" The present problem seems to be: "Is God identical with the universe or is God finite?" [83]

The reason which the modern world has spurned is not the reason whose root is the Word, but the geometric, mathematical, and mechanical reason that issued from Descartes. Mechanical reason is ordered to creatures rather than to God.[84] It was masterly for controlling nature, but its success in that field only emphasized its failure in the realm of the purely human.

We are at the end of that era of philosophy which was ushered in by Descartes. The period immediately preceding him had been one in which there were abundant criticisms of both Aristotle and the formalism of Scholasticism. Etienne Gilson tells us that Descartes's ambition was to change the world—not the world of sound reason, but the world of Montaigne and the doubts he had propagated against the certitude of traditional thought. Though Descartes was dissatisfied with the philosophical training he received at La Flèche—for later on in life he asked for his notebooks to see if the courses would seem as silly as they did when he took them—he nevertheless received there the seed for his new learning from the professor of mathematics, a Father Clavius. The latter held that mathematics was good for "driving all doubts out of the minds of the students." Here was the answer to the doubt. Montaigne could doubt the value of the various schools of philosophy, but there could be no doubt about mathematics, for there were no schools or sects of mathematics.

The great inspiration for Rousseau came under an oak tree in Vincennes, Newton's came under an apple tree, while Descartes found his on November 16th, 1619, alongside a hot stove in an unknown town in Germany as he rested during a winter military campaign while serving in the army of Maximilian the Great. The illumination that came to him was first that geometry and algebra were one. And if he had discovered these two sciences to be reducible to one, why should not all sciences be reducible to one? This he believed possible. The key science that would open them all would be mathematics. This moment was important because it established a new hierarchy of learning by dethroning metaphysics and substituting mathematics in its place. From the days of Aristotle the supremacy of natural knowledge had been housed within the confines of metaphysics, its certitudes dripping down the sides of the pyramid endowing all other sciences with their ultimate sanctions. Mathematics was next in importance, and then came physics, or natural philosophy.

Descartes inverts the order and makes mathematics the entry to metaphysics; but in order to give mathematics the primacy among the sciences, he has to deny that science has a double object: namely, *what* is studied and *how* it is studied, or the object and the method. He ignored the object which science studies and concentrated only on the method. By so doing, he felt justified in making the mathematical method the universal method of all sciences, including even metaphysics. He became so obsessed with the mathematical method, that in 1630 he wrote to Mersenne that he had found a "medicine grounded on infallible demonstrations."

But the gravest danger was in enthroning mathematics as the supreme science. Not only did he thus invert the relation between ideas and things by making ideas precede things in cognition, but he reduced metaphysics to a science all of whose propositions could be deduced from clear ideas in a mathematical fashion, as they are in geometry.[85] Descartes wrote:

These long chains of simple and easy conclusions used by the geometricians for obtaining their most difficult proofs, made me think that everything within the universe of man is interlaced in the same manner and that, if only we refrain from accepting as true what may be not true, and from upsetting the order required for deducing one thing from another, there can be nothing so remote that it will not finally be reached, nor anything so hidden that it will not be discovered.

It is perhaps not without significance that on the very spot in Endegeest, Holland, where Descartes in 1642 glorified the new "reason," is now an insane asylum.

The next step in the development of irrationalism was taken by Kant. As Descartes based his metaphysics on mathematics, so Kant based his metaphysics on physics. His Pietism, with its simple principles, (the existence of God, the immortality of the soul, and the freedom of the will), was subjected to attack by Hume. What Montaigne was to Descartes, Hume was to Kant—challenges to preserve their favorite certitudes from the corrosion of doubt.

In order to protect his beliefs from skepticism, Kant sought a way to give them the same certitude that Newton had given to his science. In his *Inquiry* Kant wrote: "The true method of metaphysics is fundamentally the same as that which Newton had introduced into natural science, and which there has yielded such wonderful fruits." [86] There was a new measurement for philosophy, but within the same empirical line as Descartes. Philosophy would once more be judged by a sensible science. Metaphysics would no longer hold the lead regardless of how much Kant sought to save it. Not only did he take the Newtonian method for granted, but he assumed that the world was exactly as Newton himself had described it. Newton based his science on the absolute character of space and time, which today is repudiated by the Einsteinian science. But taking this for a foundation with solid basis, Kant argued that in regard to sensible intuition, there must also be two intuitions—an external one of space, and an internal one of time. These are two a priori forms, because they are not derived from things but impose themselves on things. Our understanding and reason also have such a priori principles, no more derived from the order of senses than are the forms of space and time. Scientific knowledge comes out of the senses and metaphysics from the mind. Thus did he keep Newton's science and his own metaphysics away from the doubts and skepticism of Hume, though really at the cost of metaphysics itself.

Both philosophies were reared on cosmologies and both lasted as long as the cosmologies endured. The cosmology and the science upon which Descartes based his philosophy lasted less than thirty years; the cosmology of Kant less than a hundred years.

Irrationalism, according to Gilson, enters its third stage with Comte. In order to preserve scientific reason, Comte based it on a new series of facts, taken from the social order. All ideas and laws being positive, because derived from social facts, could be reduced to a homogeneous system of the social cohesion of humanity. Comte thus prided himself that humanity had passed out of the theological and the metaphysical stage and was now in the final stage of wisdom, the positivistic. Comte was like Descartes and Kant inasmuch as he based the foundation of science on the empirical and non-metaphysical order. He was unlike them inasmuch as he chose not mathematics or physics but social facts as the roots of his system. Once he discovered this new science of sociology, he made it the solution of all philosophical problems. From the standpoint of reason, it made little difference which science was chosen as primary, once metaphysics was dethroned. Each of the three men lived under the great illusion that he had discovered a philosophy. Really they only discovered a false method of understanding philosophy.

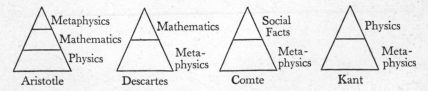

In the days when men believed in the reason whose crown was metaphysics, they believed that the specific difference between a man and an animal was reason. Upon this fact was grounded the democracy, that is, the eminent dignity of man. From this principle it followed that though it was important to know nature, it was not as important as to know the nature of man. Hence, the Greeks summarized their wisdom in "Know thyself." All the sciences were sciences about a rational creature: logic, which taught him how to reason; politics and ethics, which taught him how he ought to live; and psychology, how to understand himself.

Christianity emphasized the supremacy of reason by affirming the priority of man in the universe: "What doth it profit a man if he gain the world and lose his soul?" As the Greeks made him greater than nature, Christianity made him greater than the cosmos and all that is in it. Between material and spiritual values there was a great discrepancy, like the great chaos lying between Dives and Lazarus. Man was of such supreme importance that it was foolish to think of anything else ever being offered in exchange: "What exchange shall a man give for his soul?" This had tremendous effects; it meant that nature was subservient to man, or that man was nature's master. So long as this hierarchy was preserved, there was order. But something went wrong the day that man believed that this reasonable creature and his science of reason became secondary to nature. Philosophy became science and man became nature and one with it. Philosophy then could no longer judge science, and man could no longer claim superiority over nature.

He turned himself into a particular aspect of nature, subjected, like the rest, to the necessary law which regulates its development. A world where accomplished facts are unto themselves their own justification is ripe for the most reckless social adventures. Its dictators can wantonly play havoc with human institutions and human lives, for dictatorships are facts, and they are also unto themselves their own justification.[87]

If philosophy can no longer judge science, then science is its own justification; it can be used as well for purposes of destruction as for human betterment, and no one can pass judgment on its morality. Furthermore, if man can no longer claim superiority over nature, then there is no reason why he should not be enslaved as nature is, and such is the beginning of dictatorship. When man no longer admits to the *imago Dei* he once bore within him, he is soon reduced to the status of an instrument and is no longer treated as an inviolable person.

Cartesian reason has broken down because, though it was a fit instrument for the handling of nature, it was not equipped for understanding man. It could, and did, serve as a magnificent background of science, but it could not, and will never, serve as the foundation of philosophy. Nature will surrender its secrets to a reason that is mechanical and deterministic and geometric; man will not. He cannot be compassed within those boundaries. To attempt to do so is to make man meaningless. "Man has become an integral part of the astronomical machine, which has already been renovated and all lurking values thrown into the rubbish heap." [88]

Science cannot give us a philosophy, nor can it give us an ethics; it cannot give us a philosophy, because it immerses man in nature and avoids the important subject of his destiny. It cannot give us an ethics because science by itself is amoral. Morality comes from its ends, and science is indifferent to ends.

We are at the end of the Cartesian tradition of enthroning scientific reason in place of metaphysical reason. Nothing could better prove that we are at the fag end of that era than the tawdry scientific philosophies which have become popular in the last few decades: Hans Vaihinger, reducing philosophy to *Als-Ob,* and Eddington and Jeans who ended their treatises on physics with chapters on mysticism. Minds thus passed from a stage where they could give a reason for their faith, to one in which they could give a reason why they had no faith, until finally they reached a stage where now they no longer can give a reason for their want of faith.

There has been only one strong reaction against this skepticism issuing from irrationalism, outside of the Aristotelian tradition, and that is the philosophy of Communism. Lenin in his book *Materialism and Empirio-Criticism,* rightly contends that modern skepticism issues from Hume and Kant.

Is the source of knowledge objective reality? If you answer affirmatively then you are a materialist; if not, then you inevitably come to subjectivism, or agnosticism, irrespective of whether you deny the knowledge of the thing in itself, or the objectivity of time, space, causality (Kant), or whether you reject the idea of the thing in itself (Hume). The inconsistency of your empiricism, of your philosophy, of experience, will be in experience, the objective truth of empirical knowledge.[89]

Regardless of the weakness of Lenin's theory of knowledge, his is nevertheless holding to objective knowledge instead of subjective experiences and the personal intuitions of irrationalism. Not only did Lenin proclaim the objective against the subjective, but the absolute against the relative. That is why he has no sympathy for pragmatism.

Pragmatism extols experience only, and recognizes practice as the only criterion of truth. It points to the positivistic movement in general and leans especially upon Ostwald, Mach, Pearson, Poincaré and Duhem in their belief that science is not an "absolute copy of reality" and... in a convenient manner deduced a god for practical purposes, without any metaphysics, without leaving the grounds of experience.[90]

As Lenin sees the issue, there are only two philosophies possible. One is materialism, the other is idealism. "Idealism is merely a cunning and refined form of fideism, which, being fully armored, has great organization under its control and invariably continues to influence the masses." [91]

Casting his lot with materialism, Lenin believes he has a philosophy by which he gains some positive and dogmatic truth.

Against that absolute of materialism, skepticism has no chance whatever. And because the mass of people are today searching for a philosophy which has some definite principles, they are turning to the philosophy of Communism. Quite apart from the economic failure of this philosophy in Russia, it nevertheless has an appeal to the mind in search of an absolute. No agnostic philosophy can stand up against it. There is only one other philosophy which can meet it adequately and that is the philosophy which recognizes as the primary knowledge the science of reason, and which has had no recognition in the Western World since the days when Descartes enthroned scientific reason in its place. The era of skepticism has closed. The dawn of the day of the absolute is here, and it will be either the Absolute of Matter, which is Communism, or the Absolute of Metaphysical Reason, which is God, Whose fullest revelation in time is in the person of Christ and His historical instruction in His Body, which is the Church.

Two principal effects of rationalism are evident. The first is the exaltation of science over philosophy. Philosophers have forgotten the distinction between necessary and contingent being. Some things in the universe cannot be otherwise than they are, for ex-

ample, the part can never be greater than the whole. Certain other
things not only might not be, but might be otherwise than they are,
for example, a cow grazing in clover rather than in timothy. Because of this basic difference in being, there is a basic difference
in knowing. Necessary being cannot be experimented with; contingent being can. To know the latter you must observe it. Therefore it belongs to science. Philosophy seeks to acquire knowledge of
what *must* be, and therefore seeks to discover a reality beyond the
world process. But the modern philosopher, starting with the assumption that the only knowledge possible is experimental, concludes with agnosticism and skepticism. If there is anything beyond
the observable, it cannot be known. The great difference between
the Scholastic philosopher and the modern philosopher is that the
modern philosopher argues that you must decide on the limitations
of your knowledge before you assemble knowledge. The Scholastics,
on the contrary, maintain that one ought to go on using reason
until one reaches its limits. The modern will not take a walk down
the paths of reason until he first finds out when he must stop walking; the Scholastic walks as far as he can, and then when he can
walk no farther he picks up a ride, which is revelation. That is why
the Scholastic makes metaphysics primary, while the modern makes
epistemology primary.

A second effect of irrationalism is the shifting of the emphasis
from the universal reality or being, to the particular subject or the
ego. At first, the ego was considered as rational, particularly with
Descartes, who declared that knowledge is the knowledge of our
ego: *Cogito, ergo sum.* In order to justify this egotistic certitude he
appealed to God, for God never would have made me in such a
manner that my senses and reason would be erroneous. God was
thus "used" to validate intellectual experience. It was not long,
however, until the ego was considered not as rational, but as moral.
Kant, in order to escape Hume's criticism, sought to validate his
Pietism or belief in God, freedom, and immortality, by an appeal
to the moral sense, the practical intellect, rather than to the speculative intellect. As Descartes "used" God to guarantee the truth
of intellect, so Kant "used" God to guarantee the validity of moral
experience. Instead of man looking to God to justify human existence, God was now asked by man to prove His right to existence.
The result was that religion, which was theocentric, became an-

thropocentric. Previously, it had been argued that since God exists, man ought to be religious; now it was argued that since man is religious, God ought to be. Two conclusions follow: if man does not "feel" religious, then God does not exist, and since "feeling" is personal, religion is individual, not social or objective; religion is a private emotional experience, not a dogmatic knowledge. The answer to this irrationalism lies in the realm of metaphysics.

PART II

God and Reason

Chapter VI

THE TRANSCENDENCE OF GOD

The problem of the relation of the universe to God admits of two extreme and erroneous views, both of which have had their day of philosophical inquiry. The one extreme is deism, which divorces God from the universe. The other extreme is pantheism, which identifies God with the universe. The first admits that perhaps God made the world, but He threw it into space to be governed forever by its own inherent laws, nevermore taking an interest in it. Because God was in His heaven, it was presumed that all was right with the world; it was not considered that if God were only in His heaven and disinterested with the world, He would never have made it, and if He did, everything would be wrong with the world. Deism, as a theory of knowledge, ultimately leads to the agnostic position, and as a theory of religion, leads to the notion of an unknowable power or unknowable God.

At the other extreme, Pantheism asserts that God is one with the world, but not distinct from it. Pantheism is materialism grown sentimental, and by its very nature makes for the isolation of the soul in individual religion, and its indifference in social manifestations.

Deism, at the present time, is an unpopular philosophy and perhaps even a dead one. Pantheism is equally unpopular as a word, but not as a system, for it dominates practically all religious thinking today. Modern religious philosophers do not like to be called pantheists. They have taken over from the field of traditional thinking the word *immanence*, and have given it a new meaning. They express their belief in a God immanent in the world. One needs only to glance at some of the prevailing philosophies of religion to see how general is this new doctrine of immanence. For example, in a work entitled *Theistic Monism*, J. Evans writes: "Instead of there being two beings—God and the universe—there is but one system of energy which is at the same time God and his universe." [1]

William Browne, while disclaiming pantheism, adheres to it under the new name of immanence:

The totality of things is good, beautiful and true. That means they are aspects of the same thing. These things are abstract, but the thing itself is not abstract. It is the most concrete thing there is. It is all reality. It is the universal God.[2]

Then too, there is the outlook of John Haynes Holmes, who writes: "God is man and man is God, but both the life that is struggling and battling through to love."[3] In the same spirit is a God immanent in the common will or democracy: "To conceive of God as the common will, experimenting through the deliberations and virtues of social organizations and incarnating himself in institutions gives him concreteness and accessibility."[4]

There is also the more refined scientific view of a God immanent in the evolving universe gradually attaining some perfections, thanks to its cosmic urges, and destined finally to become perfect, providing the cosmos does its share. There is even some possibility that man himself may become God in this upward process. As Professor William P. Montague, of Columbia University, puts it "Deity may be destined never to merge into existence . . . but there is a possibility that even finite beings may in time achieve it."[5]

This idea is akin to that of Professor Alfred North Whitehead, who believes that God is organic with the world. God, according to his theory, is included or prehended in every event, a very essential part of it, and yet never wholly transcendent to it.[6]

Against these two extreme positions of deism and modern immanence, common-sense philosophy adheres to the golden mean. With deism it affirms that God is transcendent to the world, but denies that He is wholly outside of it. With pantheism, it admits that God is in the world, but rejects the theory that He is wholly absorbed by it. In other words, it claims that God is both transcendent and immanent, the one being the complement and condition of the other. Deism and pantheism each have an aspect of the truth, but err by exclusion. Reason suggests agreeing with deism that God is transcendent to the world, but dismisses the conclusion that He is wholly outside of it. With pantheism reason accepts the decision that God is in the world, but repudiates the pantheistic belief that He is wholly absorbed by it. It is our present purpose here to prove the transcendence of God as a corrective to the idea of an immanent Deity mentioned in earlier pages. Transcendence here means much more than a mere distinction of value or quality. It means a veritable separation and the real distinction between God and the World.

FIRST ARGUMENT

The first argument for the transcendence of God begins with the fact of evolution. Whether one calls it by the old name of motion, or the new name of evolution, neither senses nor reason can escape its obviousness and its universality. The evolution, or motion, of the universe may be either substantial or accidental, qualitative or quantitative, local or cosmic. The fact is, there is motion or progress or evolution in the universe. This is the starting point of modern thinking, just as it was the starting point of the proof of the existence of God for Aristotle and St. Thomas. The difference in the two positions (the old and the new) is to be sought in the interpretation of that evolution. They agree that two conditions are required for any kind of evolution, whether it be local or cosmic. First of all, that which is moved must be moved by another; secondly, the ultimate cause of that evolution is necessarily something transcendent or outside of the series of evolved things.

"Everything which is moved is moved by another." This simple principle enunciated by the Angelic Doctor has its foundation in that other principle that everything which has not the reason of its being in itself must have it in another. A square, for example, though it has the reason of being in itself, namely, its four-sidedness, still need not be red. The reason for redness must be sought outside the square. Evolution is a passage from potentiality to actuality, or from an undetermined to a determined state. For example, wood is in potency to heat before it comes in contact with fire. The fire changes that potency for heat into actual heat, or it changes the wood from an undetermined state to a determined state; in the language of grammar, it gives the subject a new predicate which it was capable of having. The relation between the two is that of potentiality to actuality; for example, that alone can be heated or illuminated which is capable of being heated or illuminated. The passage from the possibility of being heated to heat is the passage from indetermination to determination. To deny that it has need of a cause, is to say that the same thing is at one and the same time and under the same formal relation, both mover and moved or both the determined and undetermined, which is a contradiction. That which evolves certainly is not yet that which it will be. Furthermore, that which evolves is not absolutely nothing, for from nothing, nothing can come (*ex nihilio nihil fit*). Since it is not what it will be, and since it is not nothing, it follows that it must be something which it can be.

Evolution or motion or becoming is a passage from indetermination to determination, from potency to actuality. Now, that which makes it pass from a potential to an actual state should be actual. To deny this is to assert that the greater comes from the less, or being from nothingness.[7]

The first attempted escape from the argument is the subterfuge of universal dynamism which says that there is only movement, "and that movement has no need of a thing which moves." This philosophy of universal movement or motion denies that forces are in any sense a function of a thing and asserts that they constitute the sole and unique reality. Things are not in motion; things are motion. Its most popular modern expression has been given by Bergson, although he himself has but repeated the old error of Heraclitus who taught essentially the same doctrine.

The reasonable attitude is that change or motion or evolution in the world is a result of direct consciousness as distinct from reflex consciousness. The whole Bergsonian position is a confusion of *observation* and *interpretation*, or of fact, and theory imposed on fact. The fact that things do change or evolve cannot be denied, and the Thomist argument is quite independent of a theory about reality, beginning as it does with the data of common sense. The objection that things are not in motion but *are* motion, or that there is no such thing as a thing evolving, but only evolution, is a construction of mind imprisoned in reflex consciousness. As such, it does violence to common sense, which prefers to start with the direct data observable by everyone in the world whether or not he has read or even heard of either Heraclitus or Bergson.

There are several other difficulties in the way of universal dynamism. The first is to explain abiding consciousness. If everything is movement and there is nothing which underlies movement, how can we explain the abiding and permanent consciousness we have of our own identity? Our thoughts pass away, and yet we do not pass away with them, any more than the bed of a river passes away with the flowing water. We distinguish ourselves from our thoughts; we can be angry or pleased with our mental activities, and, as a matter of fact, we regard them as merely transient events through the permanent duration of our life. There are no thoughts without a thinker, no dreams without a dreamer, no volition without a will. A new mental attitude or new thought does not make a new man any more than a new suit of clothes makes a new man. There must, therefore, at least in the psychological order, be something permanent during a change of mental states. Once the important distinction between the substantial and the accidental is lost, as it always is in the philosophy of universal becoming, the mind loses its rationality and the universe its order.

Going beyond the psychological order, it is impossible to have any kind of evolution without something that evolves or a change without permanence. Just as there can never be a headache without a head, or a landslide without land, so neither can there be movement without something that moves. It is no escape from the logic of this argument to explain certain kinds of permanence—for example, the permanence of consciousness—by the metaphor of a melody. A melody is nothing but the succession of harmonious sounds, it is argued. While this is quite true, it must not be forgotten that every melody implies an abiding something which retains the successive notes, and if there were nothing to retain the successive notes, there would never be such a thing as melody. Movement is essentially a force predicated by something, it implies a subject in which it inheres, and to make the predicate the subject is not only to put an end to grammar but also to common sense.

Another fallacy underlying universal dynamism is the difficulty of accounting for movement itself. If there is nothing permanent, how can we distinguish between the point of departure and the point of arrival? And if there is no distinction between the two, why should there be any such thing as movement? If there is not something permanent in the change, how can we know we ever changed? Unless there is a fixed point, how would we know we ever progressed? How could we speak of species evolving unless we knew something of those species before, as well as after, the evolution. The only thing which will render movement intelligible is potentiality, which implies a realizable possibility in a thing, which possibility can be realized thanks to something outside itself. If there is no such thing as abiding substance, as Whitehead contends, then the change is a change of entire being and there are only continual creations.

Other important points are to be kept in mind in the unfolding of the argument from movement to evolution. The first is that in this argument neither is studied in function of *rest*, which is a mere sensible phenomenon, but in function of *being*, which belongs to the intellectual order. Rest may sometimes be inferior to movement in the sense that the point of departure may have far less value than progress to another point, but *being* is always superior to becoming for the very simple reason that that which is, is more than that which is not. It is mechanism which studies movement in relation to repose, but it is metaphysics which studies it in relation to being, and it is this latter sense which is involved in this argument.[8]

Those who object to the argument from motion imagine it to be based on the spatial metaphor of a ball at rest to which is imparted motion. On the contrary, the argument is based not on a metaphor, but on a principle that actuality must precede potentiality, or that there must be a Cause or Source from which the motion comes, or that the greater cannot come from the less. The imagination may represent the motion in terms of distance, but the *intellect* represents it in terms of actuality and potency.

The argument can take its point of departure not only in local motion or movement, which is the transfer of a body from one point in space to another point, but also in cosmic movements involving even relativities in space and time. It applies to the movement of the electron around the proton, as well as to the motion of the earth around the sun; it embraces all forms of energy, such as electrical energy in the thunderstorm, mechanical energy in the watch, and chemical energy in coal, as well as qualitative motions, such as changes in color, and quantitative changes in weight. It does not exclude instinctive movements of animals, or even the intellectual movements of man. As St. Thomas says:

...we must observe that above the intellectual soul of man we must needs suppose a superior intellect, from which the soul acquires the power of understanding. For what is such by participation, and what is mobile, and what is imperfect, always requires the pre-existence of something essentially such, immovable and perfect. Now the human soul is called intellectual by reason of a participation in intellectual power; a sign of which is that it is not wholly intellectual but only in part. Moreover, it reaches to the understanding of truth by arguing, with a certain amount of reasoning and movement. Again, it has an imperfect understanding; both because it does not understand everything, and because in those things which it does understand, it passes from potentiality to act. Therefore, there must needs be some higher intellect, by which the soul is helped to understand.... But the separate intellect, according to the teaching of our faith, is God Himself, Who is the soul's Creator, and only beatitude; as will be shown later on. (Q. 90, a. 3; ii, q. 3, a. 7). Wherefore the human soul derives its intellectual light from Him, according to Ps. 4:7, *The light of Thy countenance, O Lord, is signed upon us.*[9]

Not only is the argument independent of any particular kind of motion, but it is also independent of certain philosophical propositions concerning the number of substances. In order to make the argument effective it is not necessary to assume against pantheism a plurality of distinct substances. Whether there be one or whether there be a million is presently indifferent to the argument. It is quite sufficient to study existence as movement, whether that movement be peculiar to one thing or to many. As a matter of fact, the modern god who is in motion needs God to account for his motion.

The problem is not to learn how long the universe has existed, but how to explain its existence. It is sometimes argued that if the world was recently made, it was necessary to have a God as its cause; but now that we know that it was made millions of years ago, we can dispense with the necessity of a cause, for time itself is a cause. This argument is based upon the causal efficacy of time. There is no doubt that the efficiency of causes is increased with time; for example, a man who could not dig a ditch in an hour might very well be able to do it in a year, or a man who could not write a book in a day might possibly do it in a year. The fallacy of this argument, however, is that it assumes that time is the cause instead of the environment of certain causes. In each and every instance where the greater amount of time increases the efficacy of the cause, the cause is by its very nature adapted and capable of producing that effect, but an unsuitable cause will never produce that effect, regardless of how much time it be given. A hen might be given a thousand light years in which to hatch the soliloquy of

Hamlet, but in twice that time it could not produce even the first line of the soliloquy. The same is true of the universe. It makes no difference how much time one gives mechanical causes, the problem is whether or not they are capable of producing *by their very nature such and such an effect.* To assume that if you give a thing time enough it will dispense with the necessity of a first cause, is like saying that if the handle of a brush were long enough it would paint by itself, or that if the crank of an automobile were long enough it would automatically become a self-starter. The hare has need of an origin just as well as the tortoise, for the philosophical problem is not whether things are going fast or slow; it is why they go at all.

Another intellectual subterfuge resorted to by those who attempt to escape the implications of the argument from evolution is based upon the primeval stuff from which the universe evolved. It assumes that it requires a greater cause to make big things than to make little things, and that the only reason a cause was posited in the creational outlook was that all things were made at once. Now, if it be assumed, they argue, that the universe began not with many and powerful things, but with some very small and tiny speck, we could dispense with the necessity of a creator or a first cause. It is well here to re-member that the size of the original stuff of the universe has nothing whatever to do with the problem. It makes not the slightest bit of difference whether the universe began with an enormous mass of chaotic gas which broke up into detached condensations, or with just some small tiny spark, or even an original mass of protoplasm— the problem is still the same, namely, to account for its origin. Midgets have parents just as well as giants, and children just as well as men, and the cause of the offspring is judged, not by the *size* of the offspring, but by its nature. In the philosophical order, in like manner, a God is required just as much for the original spark as for a ready-made universe, for the cause is to be judged, not by the thing produced, but rather by the fact that the thing was made from nothing, and in this sense it demands an infinite creator. As St. Thomas writes:

The power of the maker is reckoned not only from the substance of the thing made, but also from the mode of its being made; for a greater heat, heats not only more, but quicker. Therefore, although to create a finite effect does not show an infinite power, yet to create it from nothing does show an infinite power.... For if a greater power is required in the agent in proportion to the distance of the potentiality from the act, it follows that the power of that which produces something from no presupposed potentiality is infinite, because there is no proportion between *no potentiality* and the potentiality presupposed by the power of a natural agent, as there is no proportion between *not being* and *being*. And because no creature has simply an infinite power, any more than it has an infinite being, as was proved above, it follows that no creature can create.[10]

As Sir James Jeans has affirmed, the total explanation of the universe is outside the universe:

Travelling as far back in time as we can, brings us not to the creation of the picture, but to its edge; the creation of the picture lies as much outside the picture as the artist is outside the canvas. On this view, discussing the creation of the universe in terms of time and space, is like trying to discover the artist and the action of painting by going to the edge of the picture. This brings us very near to those philosophical systems which regard the universe as a thought in the mind of its Creator, thereby reducing all discussion of material creation to futility.[11]

The argument for motion is also independent of the question of the eternity of the world. It is argued by some that if the world were eternal, it would therefore dispense with the necessity of God. In answer to this objection, it must first of all be kept in mind that modern science rejects the idea of the eternity of the world. But what is more important is that the eternity of the world could never dispense with the necessity of a cause. The world might very well be eternal (though from revelation we know it is not), but it would still be eternally dependent on God. The time element is quite independent of the causal element. I can imagine an eternal seashore and also an eternal footprint on that seashore, but I can understand it only on condition that I think of someone who from all eternity had left that footprint. So too with the universe. Though it might always have been, it would always have depended on someone to account for its movement, its development, and its purpose. In this connection, it is worth noting that St. Thomas said that by reason alone it was impossible to prove that the world began in time, though he did declare that by faith we know it to have actually begun in time.[12] Although God's action is eternal, it must not be assumed that the effect is eternal. As the Divine intellect determines the condition of the thing made, so it determines its place in time, without any new action of volition. A father wills to send his seven-year-old boy to college. That act of will becomes realized later in time without any new explicit volition.

As a final observation, evolution and creation are in no way and in no sense incompatible. As Sir Oliver Lodge has said, "one is the method of the other." [13] Evolution is concerned with the problem of *how* things take place, and creation with the problem of *why*. Evolution is description; creation is explanation. I may say, for example, that this watch was made by machine or that it was made by hand. In either case I would be describing *how* it was made. It would still leave room for another and more ultimate question, namely, *who* made it. So too with the universe. Whether it was made all at once or over a long period of time and by the evolution of one thing from another, never can and never does dispense with the ultimate question: who made it? In a word, evolution no more dispenses with creation than a "self-made man" dispenses with his mother. The problem of origin always remains, even after the most complete discussion of development.

It is no escape, either, to say a bird moves itself or a man moves himself, for the animal is moved by motion of wing and man by foot, that is, *by reason of its parts*. The foot which moves is subject to another order and demands in its turn an external mover or source for its movement.[14] The problem here is whether it is moved *by reason of itself*. The conclusion of the first part of the argument then is this: anything which is moved is moved by another. The movement understood here is not transference of energy in the physical sense, or change of position, but rather involves the relation of potentiality to actuality. That which becomes or evolves is not yet what it will *be*, but there is possibility of its becoming something else; for example, the child is capable of learning. Becoming or evolution is, therefore, a transition from potentiality to actuality, from indetermination to determination. Potency does not bring itself into act. There must therefore be an extrinsic actualization to realize the potentiality of the thing. Being is never determined and undetermined at the same time and under the same formal relation. It becomes determined under one relation because it was determined under another. Every change, therefore, comes from something different from itself. Or, as St. Thomas puts it: "Nothing is moved except in so far as it is potentially capable of receiving such motion; only in so far as anything is actually in motion does it move anything else."

THE SECOND FACT ABOUT EVOLUTION

Not only is there evolution in the world, but evolution produces new emergents, in which there is a correlation of antecedent and consequent, which brings up the question asked by Lloyd Morgan in his *Emergent Evolution:* "What makes emergents emerge?" St. Thomas in the *Contra Gentiles* makes this argument of efficient causes the appendix to his argument of motion. It is quite true that scientists may argue that science is not concerned with efficient causality, but that proves neither that it does not exist, nor that it should not be considered. Efficient causality is a metaphysical reality and not phenomenal. "This is the difference between a Divine Agent and a human natural agent, that the natural agent is the cause only of the motion, while the Divine Agent is the cause of the being." [15]

This argument adds to the argument of evolution the necessary co-operation of things in the production of an effect. The emergent or the "novelty" of the evolutionary process is conditioned upon countless antecedents. The sun, the earth, the moisture, and dozens of influences co-operated in the production of the meanest weed that grows. The flower in the crannied wall subsumes within it all the flowers that were ever its ancestors, as well as the prehistoric sun. Chemicals were involved in the evolution of plants, and plants in the evolution of animals; there has been an intrinsic dependence, one on the other. As St. Thomas says: "There is therefore a certain order of efficient causes. It is not possible for anything to be the efficient cause of itself, because in such a case it would have to exist before it actually exists, which is an impossibility."

This argument of emergence is quite distinct from the mathematical concept of sequences and coexistences of phenomena. From the point of view of mathematics, there is no necessity to investigate the cause of phenomena. But philosophy does make such a demand. As E. I. Watkin expresses the idea:

What science seeks to discover is not the process itself by which event succeeds event, but its mathematical pattern ... the fact that the sciences make only a restricted use of the principle of sufficient ground, and, ideally at least, do not employ the principle of dynamic sufficient ground, causation in the strict sense, is no argument against the reality of causation.[16]

THE THIRD FACT ABOUT EVOLUTION

Not only is there evolution; not only do certain factors unite to produce emergents; but the process takes place in a spatio-temporal continuum, the modern way of saying in an environment stamped with contingency. Things do not exist forever: prehistoric animals no longer exist. That which characterizes things is their *temporality*, for they can be and they can not be; they come into existence and they pass away. The history of their lives is a history within the historical perspective of space-time.

It is impossible that things which are so temporalized should always exist, because whatever can be, at some time must be non-existent. If all things could be nonexistent, nothing would exist, since what is not, does not begin to be, except through something which is. The explanation of the temporality of beings must therefore be found in the extra-temporal.

St. Thomas in his *Summa Theologica* puts these three facts of evolution, producing emergents in space and time, in abstract language:

It is certain, and evident to our senses, that in the world some things are in motion. Now, whatever is in motion is put in motion by another, for nothing can be in motion except it is in potentiality to that towards which it is in motion; whereas a thing moves inasmuch as it is in act. For motion is nothing else than the reduction of something from potentiality to actuality. But nothing can be reduced from potentiality to actuality, except by something in a state of actuality. Thus, that which is actually hot, as fire, makes wood, which is potentially hot, to be actually hot, and thereby moves and changes it. Now, it is not possible that the same thing should be at once in actuality and potentiality in the same respect, but only in different respects. For what is actually hot cannot simultaneously be potentially hot; but it is simultaneously potentially cold. It is therefore impossible that in the same respect and in the same way a thing should be both mover and moved, i.e., that it should move itself. Therefore, whatever is in motion must be put in motion by another.

In the world of sense, we find there is an order of efficient causes. There is no case known (neither is it, indeed, possible) in which a thing is found to be the efficient cause of itself; for so it would be prior to itself, which is impossible. Now, in efficient causes, it is not possible to go on to infinity, because in all efficient causes following in order, the first is the cause of the intermediate cause, and the intermediate is the cause of the ultimate cause, whether the intermediate cause be several, or only one. Now, to take away the cause is to take away the effect.

We find in nature things that are possible to be and not to be, since they are found to be generated, and to corrupt, and consequently, they are possible to be and not to be.

ARGUMENT BASED ON THE FACTS

Granted these three facts developed above, reason applies the principle of the rational impossibility of an infinite series in an evolutionary or dynamic universe. The alternative position is that an infinite series is not impossible, hence, one may go back infinitely in the series of things moved without ever demanding a first cause. There is some truth in this position, and Aristotle, Leibnitz, and Kant, as well as St. Thomas, saw nothing contradictory in an infinite series of things which were *accidentally* subordinated. But since the present argument is concerned only with *essential* subordination, and with the possibility of an infinite number of real changes in real beings, not with the infinite divisibility of a continuous line, it will be well to understand the following distinctions:

1. There is essential subordination (a) when the movement of the series is simultaneous, e.g., cogwheels; (b) if each thing in motion is dependent on a mover not like itself, e.g., a chisel moved by a hand, which in turn is moved by the will.

2. There is *accidental* subordination (a) if the successive series is composed of exactly similar things, e.g., one man generated by another; (b) if there is no causal dependence.

What is repugnant is an infinite series of things which are *essentially* subordinated to one another. It is possible, for example, for an artisan to use an infinite number of hammers in the forging of a brass bowl. The fiftieth hammer does not presuppose the forty-ninth, nor is it necessary that the first hammer be in order that the second hammer operate. In this case, the hammers are accidentally subordinated one to the other, and we do not come to the first efficient cause, but only to a cause which is in a different order of being from the members of the series. But it is impossible to have an infinite series of boxcars, in which one was moved by another, for unless there was the engine there would never be the movement of the second or the third boxcar. This has been put by St. Thomas in these words:

In efficient causes it is impossible to proceed to infinity *per se*—thus, there cannot be an infinite number of causes that are *per se* required for a certain effect; for instance, that a stone be moved by a stick, the stick by the hand, and so on to infinity. But it is not impossible to proceed to infinity *accidentally* as regards efficient causes; for instance, if all the causes thus infinitely multiplied should have the order of only one cause, their multiplication being accidental; as an artificer acts by means of many hammers accidentally, because one after the other may be broken. It is accidental, therefore, that one particular hammer acts after the action of another; and likewise it is accidental to this particular man as generator to be generated by another man; for he generates as a man, and not as the son of another man. For all men generating hold one grade in efficient causes—viz., the grade of a particular generator. Hence it is not impossible for a man to be generated by man to infinity, but such a thing would be impossible if the generation of this man depended upon this man, and on an elementary body, and on the sun, and so on to infinity.[17]

In a universe in which one thing is essentially bound up with another thing, and to such an extent that modern physicists do not hesitate to apply the biological term "organic" to it, there is quite naturally a series of essential and subordinate relations; hence, one must ultimately get back to something to account for the movement of the series, for:

if that by which something is put in motion be in itself put in motion, then this also must needs be put in motion by another, and that by another again. But this cannot go on to infinity because then there would be no first mover, and consequently no other mover; seeing that subsequent movers move only inasmuch as they are put in motion by the first mover; as the staff moves only because it is put in motion by the hand. Therefore it is necessary to arrive at a first mover put into motion by no other, and this everyone understands to be God.[18]

The reasoning process here does not demand a reconsideration of the long series of things moved, as one might go back from the caboose to the engine through every freight car. It is sufficient to jump out of the series at any point and come to a mover of a different order. It makes no difference how many things moved there be in the series. Let them be multiplied as much as one wills, one will never get beyond the fact that they are all instruments or intermediary causes. Multiply them unto infinity and the instrument is complicated, but you do not make a cause. You elongate the canal, but you do not make a source. The addition of instruments does not diminish the reason of their insufficiency, for the reason of their insufficiency is in each one of them. Ten thousand idiots never make a wise man, nor will the addition of ten thousand things moved be sufficient to account for the mover. The addition of dependent things never gets rid of dependence. The insufficiency of the units in the argument is not *quantitative*, but *qualitative*. If quantitative, then addition of insufficiencies might make a sufficiency; twenty horses could pull what two could not. But if *qualitative* or *essential*, the addition of insufficiencies does not make a sufficiency, e.g., one hundred blind men do not make a blind man see. The argument then is not, Where does the world come from, but Who explains it.

There are only three terms in any evolutionary process: source, intermediary, and the end. An intellectual study of any one of the things in the series of things moved is of itself quite sufficient to bring us to the idea of a first mover or first cause, who belongs to an entirely different order than that of the intermediaries. This position is now beginning to be recognized by modern philosophers of science. As Sir James Jeans has so well stated it:

Indeed the finiteness of time and space almost compel us, of themselves, to picture the creation as an act of thought.... Time and space, which form the setting for the thought, must have come into being as part of this act. Primitive cosmologies picture a creator working in space and time, forging sun, moon and stars out of already existent raw material. Modern scientific theory compels us to think of the creator as working outside time and space, which are part of his creation, just as the artist is outside his canvas.[19]

The First Cause, therefore, is not the first in the order of time, but in the order of rational sufficiency. I arrive at a first cause only when I arrive at something sufficient to explain the series and therefore outside of it.

There is a common objection against this conclusion which runs somewhat along these lines: it is quite true that every event must have a cause, but if the principle of causation be true, why should not the First Cause have a cause? Very simply because an uncaused cause, or what is known as a first cause, alone answers to the true idea of a cause. *A secondary cause, insofar as it is secondary, is really not a cause at all.* I witness a certain event. As a rational being I am compelled to look for its cause. I attribute it to a prior cause; but I find this has itself been caused. What has happened? The cause which I have gone back to, has ceased to be a cause. It has become an effect. If I am, therefore, to continue seeking a cause, I must pass over to its explanatory antecedent. It makes no difference how often I go back. If I do not arrive at something which is an uncaused cause, the idea of cause will be just as unsatisfied at the end of my search as at the beginning. *A true cause is one to which the reason not only moves, but in which it rests, and except in a first cause the mind cannot rest. The alternative does not lie between an infinite series and a first cause, but between accepting a first cause and rejecting the idea of cause altogether.* To ask the question, Who caused God, or Who caused the first cause, is to ask that a first cause be at one and the same time a secondary cause, which is a contradiction.

St. Thomas insists that there is nothing contradictory in the conception of an infinite number of secondary causes succeeding each other in *time.* His contention was that any causal series, whether temporally finite or infinite, is contradictory, unless regarded as dependent on an ultimate cause which is *not in time* at all.[20] As Professor A. E. Taylor pointed out:

The dependence meant in the argument has nothing to do with the succession in time. What is really meant is that our knowledge of any event in Nature is not complete until we know the *full reason* for the event. So long as you know only that A is so because B is so, but you cannot tell why B is so, your knowledge is incomplete. It only becomes complete when you are in a position to say that A is so because Z is so, Z being something which has its own *raison d'être*, and therefore such that it would be useless to ask why Z is so. This at once leads to the conclusion that about any event in Nature, why that event is so, what are its conditions, the Z which is its own *raison d'être* cannot itself belong to Nature. The point of the reasoning is precisely that it is an argument from the fact that there is a "Nature" to the reality of the "Supernatural," and this point is unaffected by the question whether there ever was a beginning of time, or a time when there were no events.[21]

In this universe of evolution and coherent movement, it is impossible for one thing ever to communicate to another thing that which it does not actually possess. A clock that is wound down can never wind itself by its own power, nor can a cell which has lost its activity restore its vital process, any more than a man who has lost his eyes can restore himself to vision. If one becomes interested in the "why" to the forgetfulness of the "how," he must seek the reason for movement and evolution and their novelties in space and time. But it is not necessary that he retrace each and every detailed movement, any more than that he study each and every hen and egg, because his problem is not which is *first* in the order of time, but what is first in the order of intelligibility, which is always above time. *Intellectus supra tempus.* The point is that any causal series, whether temporarily finite or infinite, is inherently contradictory, unless regarded as depending on a cause outside of time. To see this it is sufficient to look upon the universe as a tremendous machine, or as a vast "organism" which transmits movement. Everything in the universe counteracts or balances or assists some other thing; when things and movements thus are co-ordinate, they must be derivative and secondary.

The problem then becomes to find not the secondary cause, in which science is interested, but the primary cause which concerns the philosophers, or to seek the player and not the tune. There may be a million instruments in the organic universe communicating energy, evolution, and motion, but they are all *instruments*.[22]

The evolution of the universe demands a Power or Energy Who is Himself unmoved, to account for the movement of evolution; a First Cause to explain the emergents of the evolutionary process; a Necessary Being to explain the temporal contingent character of emergents and their evolution. In these three points this Being differs from the world, not in degree, but in kind. He is transcendent to the world because He is not an instrument for the communication of antecedent energy, but a Source of Pure Actuality; because He is not a product or emergent produced by an antecedent nature, but the Cause of all emergents, all natures, and all beings; and because He is the Necessary Being outside of time and space. This Being is called God.

SECOND ARGUMENT FOR TRANSCENDENCE

God is transcendent to the world, not only because He is Actuality whereas the world is evolving, but also because He is simple whereas the world is composite. The latter argument does not begin with the order of concepts and then pass on to existence. Its starting point is concrete existing things, and it states that the finite existence implies infinite existence, not as its exemplary cause alone, but as its creative cause. The argument may be stated in psychological language as follows: there is a quest for life, truth, and love in every human heart—not for a life that endures ten years, but always; not for the truths of geography, but all truth; not for a love lasting fifty years, but always. But we find that life is mingled with death, truth with error, and love with hate. Where can we find the life, truth, and love we seek? That question can be answered by asking another question. Where is the source of light in this room to be found? Not under the table, for there light is mingled with darkness; not under the chair, for there light is mingled with shadows. If we are to find the source of light, we must go to something which does not participate in light, which has no admixture of darkness. We must go to pure light. So too, if we are to find the source of the life, truth, and love that are in the world, we must go out to pure Life, pure Truth, pure Love, and that is the definition of God.

A man would never be known as a philosopher if he made all his proofs as simple as this. In part, it is the business of philosophers to complicate the ordinary simple things of life. Proceeding to that complication, the metaphysical basis of the argument is: *there is composition in the universe.* Things share goodness, truth, beauty, and more fundamentally, being.[23] But anything that is participated, is caused.[24]

That which inheres in a thing belongs to it either in virtue of its own intrinsic nature, or in virtue of something extrinsic. Threesidedness belongs to the nature of a triangle; a triangle does not share this property with any other figure. Hence, we need never look outside of a triangle for the reason of its three-sidedness. But color does not belong to the nature of a triangle. Color may be shared by a square or a circle. Hence, because it is shared or participated, the reason of color must be sought outside of the triangle. In like manner, existence does not belong to the nature of things as three-sidedness belongs to a triangle, but rather as color belongs to a triangle. Existence is shared by others. The reason of existence must therefore be sought outside the thing which participates it. In this sense whatever is participated is caused.[25]

Existence, which belongs to every creature, cannot be caused by the nature or essence of a thing as an efficient cause, for if the thing were the cause of its own existence, it would necessarily have had to exist before giving itself existence. This is impossible. Therefore, the cause of the creatures, compounded of essence and existence, must be something transcendent to the composite elements themselves. If each thing in the world possessed existence by its own nature, there is no assignable reason why anything else should possess it. If it were characteristic of *that* thing as *that* thing, it would have it in its fullness, just as, for example, that which was characteristic of George Washington *as* George Washington was possessed by him in all its fullness and admitted of no degrees of greater or less. If one starts with diversity as a fact, and asserts that each nature is the cause of its own existence and hence does not require a transcendent cause, then one would have the difficulty of explaining how diverse causes could produce the same effect (which happens to be the most universal effect), namely existence. If the nature of a stone were the cause of its existence, and the nature of a cow were the cause of its existence, and the nature of a primrose the cause of its existence, how did these divergent natures produce the same effect?

Since existence does not belong to things by their very nature, the reason for existence must be sought extrinsically and transcendentally to the things themselves. Since things *have* being but *are* not being, it must be that all things which are diversified by the diverse participation of being, so as to be more or less perfect, are caused by one First Being, Who possesses being most perfectly. This Being we call God.

THE THIRD ARGUMENT FOR TRANSCENDENCE

The third argument for the transcendence of God is based on finality. It must be emphasized that finality is quite distinct from the two tendencies in modern thinking: the divorce of thought and things, and their spurious unity in the contemporary organic philosophy. Descartes divorced the mental and the material by making ideas the essence of mind, and extension the essence of the material. When a princess asked Descartes how the two could be reconciled, he said he had to go to Utrecht to answer some charges brought against him, and could not answer the problem. The problem—a false problem—the world has been trying to solve ever since. Leibnitz tried to reunite the divorced couple by his doctrine of pre-established harmony; George Berkeley attempted to answer the problem by the mediating activity of the human mind; the empiricists solved it by reducing mind to matter, and the idealists by reducing matter to mind. Spinoza denied the problem by asserting that there was only one substance which was God, and that God had two attributes—the attributes of the Cartesian dichotomy: thought and extension.

Thus far, the problem of the relation of mind and reality was regarded as *static*. Hegel and Darwin made it *dynamic* in the sense that Hegel put the Cartesian mind in evolution and Darwin put Cartesian matter in evolution. Hegel wrote on the development of ideas, Darwin on the development of matter. Hegel stressed the *end;* Darwin the *origin*. Rationality for Hegel is to be found in history, because the historical process is the development of the Hegelian idea. The full expression of the idea is to be sought at the end and not at the beginning. Darwin, on the contrary, suggested a type of continuity which looked to the *beginnings*. Spencer made a philosophy out of it and represented all developments as pre-formed out of an original source which evolved from homogeneity to heterogeneity.

Thus the Cartesian problem became the problem of two different kinds of continuity: the Hegelian—a continuity of inner logical structure of teleological development toward ends; and the Darwinian-Spencerian—a continuity of mechanistic unfolding from origins. Hegel said the determining factor was *ahead* in time; Darwin said it was *behind* in time.

Just as idealists and realists in the static order tore asunder that which God had joined together, so too, Hegel and Darwin tore the same reality apart in the dynamic order. Hegel distorted history and nature by reducing nature to history or matter to mind. History to him was all important, for in it the logical idea unfolded itself. Darwin distorted history and nature, or reduced history to nature, or mind to matter. Little attention was given in his scheme to the development of human history, an oversight rather typical of mechanism.

There were two transitional solutions before contemporary philosophy tried to unite them in the Spinozistic fashion. James made a negative contribution by denouncing the mechanist solution in his *Pluralistic Universe*. Bergson did the same in his *Creative Evolution*, but went a step farther than James. Bergson said the concept of evolution (Nature) is meaningless unless it involves the idea of time (History) into which new factors enter. There is more in time than bare succession. Time is creative.

The present solution of the problem is akin to that of Spinoza in its assertion that Nature and History, Matter and Mind, Origin and Ends are not distinct, one from another, but are organic. The principles of this solution, presented in the preceding chapter, are these: there is no distinction between God and nature, for God's existence is inseparable from the world. This principle vitiates the whole problem of purpose and finality by making the Governor identical with the governed. This new philosophy of the Organism refuses to call itself pantheistic, saying that God is not identical with all nature as in pantheism, but is operative as one aspect of the natural world. Hence, God is knowable only to the extent that the natural world is knowable. God is thus merely "a directive activity with a scheme which aims at constructive consistency"; [26] or "the nisus through whose activity emergents emerge and the whole course of emergent evolution is directed"; [27] Samuel Alexander says that God is the "nisus" towards deity: "It is thus always the one universe of Space-Time which is God's body, but it varies in its empirical constitution and its deity." [28] God for Professor Henry Nelson Wieman is "that interaction between individuals, groups and ages which generates and promotes the greatest possible mutuality of good." [29] Whitehead says the nature of God is "the unlimited conceptual realization of the absolute wealth of potentiality." [30]

In the consideration of finality it is important to note that the modern treatment of the question is based upon a solution of a false problem, stated statically by Descartes and dynamically by Hegel and Darwin. Finality to the modern philosopher is "creative accumulation," but it in no way involves intellectual unity or purposiveness. The modern philosopher is more concerned with progress than purpose. Spencer's scheme of evolution failed because it could not account for the emergence of mind in the cosmic stage. When a certain complexity had been reached, mind began its course as a spectator of cosmic events. Emergent Evolution was offered to correct this defect, but it does not really correct it, unless mind is extrinsic to the universe and purpose is distinguished from mere progress. The basis and ground of finality in the modern view, is immanent in the process and not transcendent to it. The modern treatment of finality puts the psychical into the physical and then proceeds to draw it out, not in the mechanistic fashion of Spencer, but by attributing to the new emergents new kinds of relatedness. End and purpose for modern philosophy is identified with *time*, that is, time in its future aspect, quite unmindful of the fact that futurity depends on end and purpose. Purpose tells us what the future will be. There is a kind of immanence of the future in the present. The future is anticipated, and in this sense, true purposiveness means future in the present. The only reason a thing has a future is because it has an end. If it had no reason for tending toward the future, it would never so tend. A man without a "future" in an extended sense, is a man without a purpose. Modern theories discuss means to an end, but not the end as the cause of the means. This is the problem. They tell us how to get to Rome, but not why we should ever start for Rome. Furthermore, instead of making the purpose determine the direction, they make the direction determine the purpose. Value for them comes from progress, instead of progress from value. Ends are immanent indeed, but to make them intelligible, transcendence is demanded.

Before touching on the argument from finality, the ground must be cleared in another area; we must exclude the two extreme errors: Chance and Necessity.

Modern physicists who philosophize on the basis of the empirical are often wont to attribute the universe to chance.[31] Mathematicians, in like manner, say the idea of "randomness" is forced on them by quantum physics, yet they do not like to commit themselves to chance as an ultimate principle. In order to understand chance, the following considerations must be kept in mind: chance is not ultimate, for by its very nature chance is an *accidental* cause of an effect not intended either by nature or by mind; or better still, it is the conjunction of independent causes.[32] Aristotle gives the example of a man who is killed by robbers because he ate salt meat. The facts are: he ate salt meat, was thirsty, and went to a fountain to drink; robbers hiding behind the fountain attacked and killed him. Three causal series here conspired to produce what is called chance: the causal relation of salt meat to thirst; thirst and the desire to drink; robbers hiding behind the fountain because it offered good opportunity for attack. Each series had its cause. When we say the man was killed by chance, we do not mean it was *uncaused*. *Casus est causa per accidens*. Chance is the accidental cause. The accidental is something which happens to things independently of their essence—a kind of *deficient or diminished being*.[33] As St Thomas expresses it:

Omne quod est per se, habet causam: quod autem est per accidens non habet causam: quia non est vere ens, cum non sit verum unum.[34]

For example, blackness has a cause; so has a saxophone player, but not a black saxophone player. The latter is an effect *per accidens*, because not reducible to a pre-existing cause from which the effect would follow by necessity. "What is accidental is properly speaking neither a being nor a unity."[35]

Chance, therefore, does not preclude or exclude preordination, for each of the causal series has its own preordained end, of which chance is their conjunction. Chance presupposes a cause that is not accidental, in other words, a necessary cause. Chance cannot be the explanation of the *origin* of things, but only of their *concurrence*. Chance, or accidental causality, does not exclude mind.

It happens sometimes that something which is lucky or chancelike as compared to *inferior* causes, if compared to some higher cause, is directly intended. For instance, if two servants are sent by their master to the same place, the meeting of the two servants in regard to themselves is by chance, but as compared to the master, who had ordered it, it is directly intended. So there are some who refused to refer to a higher cause such events which by luck or chance take place here below.[36]

God is the only Being for Whom there is no chance, because He is the sole Being Whose Infinite Intelligence imposes itself on nature.

A distinction must be made between mathematical chance and real chance. That which is mathematically possible is far from being physically possible. Mathematically it is possible that a million needles thrown into the air will fall on their points, but if tried in the concrete order, it will not be found realized, because nature does not work in the abstract. There will be certain factors determining the fall of the needles, namely, line of least resistance, the law of gravitation, and economy of motion, all of which imply order.[37]

There are, therefore, two kinds of chance: pure and limited. In the latter is an admixture of chance and order. Pure chance does not exist except in the mathematical order of the imagination. It is like a machine without friction. As machines must be constructed out of existing materials, so events must happen among things which exist, which are orderly. But impure chance alone, if we could realize all of its necessary conditions, would not explain the order in the universe, if for no other reason than the complexity of the universe. How many chances are there of ten letters being so thrown on a table as to form the word "absolutely"? There is one chance in 3,628,000. What chance is there of the twenty-six letters of the alphabet falling out in order? One chance in 620 sextillions. And what is the arrangement of letters compared with the multiplicity of things which abound in creation?

Limited chance is what modern science calls the "statistical character" of the universe, or the "appearance of laws which are born of the absence of laws." The basic assumption of the new physics is that nature is undetermined or free, and that freedom or chance produces statistical uniformity. This theory overlooks the fact that the combination of individual irregularity with collective regularity is due to order. The construction of the dice box, or the construction of the dice, for example, is not left to chance; the dice are cast out on a flat surface where they will come to rest with one side turned up. Think, then, of all that might have happened but which is prevented from happening by something in the design. There is an exclusion of unknown infinities of chances and the retention of a few. Order is here limiting chance. What is uniform is due to the order; what is incalculable is due to chance. In like manner in the statistical uniformity of nature, the uniformity is due to order, the incalculable is due to chance, or perhaps better still, to our ignorance of nature's laws. Because we do not know the laws which govern the gyrations of an atom, it does not follow that there is no law.

The logic of chance is well known to logicians and life insurance companies, for whom aggregate order prevails, notwithstanding individual disorder. But this is not the whole picture, for what is forgotten is a definite law or order among even these variations. Why is it that the absolute irregularities do not diminish and become negligible, but only the *relative* irregularities? The *absolute* variation in the length of life is not much more than a hundred years, but the relative variations are infinite.[38] Dr. W. R. Matthews has written a brilliant refutation of Hume's argument, that given the conditions of a finite number of units and an infinite time, we have the *vera causa* of the order of the world. In answer, Dr. Matthews urges three objections. He contends that the possibility of chance origin is self-contradictory, for finite units with infinite variations are really not finite units. Also the separation of time and space which Hume's argument demands, is no longer scientifically tenable. Furthermore, "units" themselves imply order and one may also inquire, Who gives the "given"?[39] It is no escape to argue that nature has evolved by chance, because evolution implies: nature and the reaction of environment. This immediately creates the complex problem: what is the source of the original nature or natures; what determined nature always to be modified by its environment; why did order evolve out of the original chaos which the argument assumes. Certainly, if the dice were loaded to produce orderly results, someone must have loaded the dice.

Necessity. The other extrinsic solution of the problem of finality is Necessity. Chance left everything to indeterminism; necessity makes everything so determined that it denies there is a *raison d'être* for anything. Birds must fly, fire must burn, and men must act as they do. It is quite true that things are determined, but this "determination to one line of action belongs to a thing not as coming from itself, but from another."[40] A bird, for example, must fly. But why? Because of the structure of its wings? Certainly. But *why* that structure? Why the structure which makes flying possible? Why those peculiar characteristics which make a thing act in a certain way and not in another? Answer that question and one has gone beyond the thing itself. In other words, in complex structures and patterns, necessity is not wholly and absolutely immanent. The reason for it must be sought outside the thing itself. Even though one granted mechanical necessity throughout the physical universe, it would not exclude a purposive designer. We may restrict our understanding of a perfectly designed machine to its operation and observe how one part fits with every other part and depends upon it, but the working of its machinery would not explain the *existence* of the machine. This could not be done without positing the prior existence of an inventor who designed it. So it is with the universe. Even grant that it is determined, there still remains the question: Who made it? Who determined it?

The natural laws which science studies are only the mechanical and orderly means by which purpose works itself out. Our understanding of any machine ultimately depends on our discovery of the purpose an inventor put into it. The question: "What is its purpose?" is the proof that we do not understand the machine, and we do not understand it because we have not grasped its plan or its finality. Machines are only concretized or materialized or mechanized ideas. But the idea requires a mind. Mechanism cannot logically exclude an Intelligent Designer; as a philosophy it is short-sighted, interested only in the factual correlation of nuts and bolts and not in the reason for their correlation. Nor is the efficient cause alone sufficient. There must also be a final cause. The efficient cause is power; the final cause is the reason for acting. The efficient cause would never put forward its power for one end rather than another unless there was a final cause. An artist has the power to paint, but he would not bring that power into being unless he had a reason for doing so. The efficient cause is the only cause in which the mechanist is interested, but he cannot ignore the final cause for the realizing principle must have a reason for its realization, otherwise it would never act *this way* rather than *that way*. When one mounts to the organic order, mechanism is found to be satisfactory as a *method*, but unsatisfactory as a *philosophy*, as most biologists today agree.[41] Science must adopt the mechanistic *method* in studying life, for by its nature the method of the biologist is experimental. But philosophically, no mechanistic law can explain the co-ordination of parts and their function with a view to the welfare of the whole. There is something in the *whole* called life, as Lloyd Morgan and Field Marshal Smuts have emphasized, which is not in its chemical and physical constituents. In other words, there is a unifying, directing, synthesizing power at work, whose purposes are definitely teleological. Each organ has a function, each function has an end, and the end is always a contribution to life as a whole. Biology takes us into a different world from that of physics, just as psychology takes us into a different world from biology. The increased purposiveness in biology and psychology demands an explanation, and one, as we shall show, that is transcendent to the organism itself.

Dialectical materialism, which asserts that the energy in the world is self-generated, is another view of Necessity. Instead of regarding matter as an inert entity receiving motion from an external agent, Marx envisaged things as necessarily determined by an immanent dialectical law. As contradiction was the immanent law of development of ideas with Hegel, so now with Marx contradiction, inherent in matter, is the source of its development. Engels said:

A purpose which is not imported into Nature by some third party acting purposively, such as the Wisdom of Providence, but *lies in the necessity of the thing itself*, constantly leads with people who are not well versed in philosophy, to the unthinking interpolation of conscious and purposive activity.[42]

If purpose is due to the material organization of the thing itself, what accounts for the material organization of the thing itself? If chance is outlawed, and Marxism does outlaw it, then how explain the determined character of things, except by a "form bestowed in created things by God, by which they have a power for a determined act in proportion to their own proper endowment, but beyond which they are powerless." [43]

The modern mathematical outlook on the universe is also incomplete, because mathematical philosophy ignores both final and efficient causes. Mathematics is never interested in either.[44] It never asks who drew that triangle, or whether an angle of forty degrees is more moral than an angle of fifteen degrees. Being disinterested in one of these two causalities, it is necessarily disinterested in the other, because the two are bound up together. The final cause, as it already has been indicated, is the reason of the efficient cause's acting. The final cause is in relation to efficient cause as form to matter, or as act to potency. Potency does not terminate in act; it is for act. Final cause is first in the order of intention, but last in the order of execution. The architect plans a house, but the house itself is the last thing to appear in a long series of actions. The two causes are intrinsically and necessarily related, and a mathematical philosophy which ignores both of them is bound to present a very incomplete picture of the universe. Spinoza used the mathematical approach and ignored final and efficient causes; Eddington and

Jeans use the same approach and also ignore them. Jeans is concerned only with formal causes, because mathematical forms are ideas. That is why his concept is of God as a mathematician. The essential fallacy of such an approach consists in making mathematics and not metaphysics the supreme science of the human mind.

The principle of finality is not an empirical principle in the sense of a vague generalization of sense experience. This principle is not perceived by experience, except accidentally, but by the intellect. It becomes accessible to all in the presentation of sense data. Just as soon as we know the meaning of the word "whole" and the meaning of the word "part," the intellect immediately sees the principle that the part cannot be greater than the whole.[45] In like manner, the principle of causality is perceived essentially by the intellect and accidentally by the senses. *Omne agens agit propter finem.* The "end" does not mean *terminus*, but "reason why"; it stands for a definite perfection of an agent; for example, the perfection of the eye is vision; the perfection of the ear is sound. The *agens* could not acquire that which was good for it unless there was a tendency in it. The eye sees, but it does not hear; the ear hears, but it does not see. It is not necessary that this tendency be understood by the faculty, or be known to it. The arrow does not know it is destined for a target. Now, if the eye sees rather than hears, if the stomach digests rather than makes boats, if the bird flies rather than writes poetry, if fire burns rather than swims, if an acorn becomes an oak rather than an elephant, it must be because this tendency is *inherent* and *intrinsic* to it, *for if it were not intrinsic to it*, then there is no reason why it should act one way rather than another. "Every agent acts for an end: otherwise one thing would not follow more than another from the action of the agent unless it were by chance." [46] The mind immediately sees the principle once it grasps the meaning of the subject and predicate of the proposition; it sees that order is not an *afterthought* superadded to things, or something applied to the lower world as anthropomorphic, but rather the condition of things, their intelligibility. An adequate cause must be invoked to explain the fitting of means to an end, for there must be a necessary proportion between effects and cause. The argument does not *suppose* that nature works and acts like man; it reaches this resemblance between the products of natural forces and products of the human mind only as a logical conclusion from the facts. The argument of finality is not anthropomorphic in the sense that it turns upon any similitude between two objects of simple apprehension—a watch and the movement of the stars—but upon an analogical comparison: the discovery of the *likeness between two* ratios, or proportionality. It is only on a proportional resemblance between a work of art and a work of nature that the argument turns. The principle of finality is analogical in its character.

Furthermore, analogy, either as a means of proof or simply as an illustration, need not be sustained in more than a single point, provided that this single point is clear, well established—resting, for instance, on a moral law or causal nexus. "As the watch is to the watchmaker so is Creation to its Creator." That is to say, there exists some *ratio* or *relation* connecting the watch and watchmaker, which exists also between the world and its Creator. Put in this way, the analogy is merely *illustrative*. To see its *illative* force, we have to alter the position of the four terms. "As the watch is to such and such specimens of Nature, so is the watchmaker to the Author of any and all of these things." No identity or likeness between the watch and the world, or between the watchmaker and the Author of the world is intended or claimed at all. All that is claimed is that there is something, not specifically, but only proportionally, common between them—a resembling relation. This proportional community of character is the pivot on which the analogy turns. None of the absurdities are intended which are constantly urged against this analogy. For instance, it is not claimed that works of nature and works of art are identical; that the process of nature and of human manufacture are specifically alike; that natural products, say a flower, and human products are one and the same. A resemblance of the proportional relations governing the two is all that is asserted. The terms compared may differ in many respects and be as divergent as a rose is from a watch.

Because the principle is analogical, the Scholastics have always distinguished ways in which finality is present in the hierarchy of creation. In man, endowed with intelligence, whose object is *being*, purposefully tending toward an end, it exists *formaliter*.[47] In animals, endowed with sense knowledge and instinct, it exists *materialiter tantum*.[48] Finally, in creatures devoid of either intellectual or sensible knowledge it exists *executive*.[49]

There are two kinds of finality: intrinsic and extrinsic. The intrinsic end is the one described in the proposition: *omne agens agit propter finem*, and is the adaptation of parts of a being for its good. Extrinsic finality is the subordination of one or many things for the good of other beings, for instance, chemicals to plants, plants to animals, animals to man. For the intrinsic end, we look into a thing as a microcosm, complete and finished and self-containing; for its extrinsic end, we view it as related to other things as a part of a macrocosm. In nature, intrinsic finality is more clear than extrinsic. There is little difficulty in determining intrinsic ends, because they are unique. The eye has the intrinsic end of vision, the ear the intrinsic end of hearing. But with extrinsic ends it is different. A thing never has one extrinsic end, but many, for it is related to a multitude of things. It is always rash to assume that because a thing is useful for another thing, that therefore it exists only for that purpose; as Hegel pointed out, it is absurd to say that cork trees were made to make champagne stoppers. Furthermore, extrinsic ends are not always easy to see—why are there snakes, or cancers? The argument of finality that we use here for the transcendence of God is concerned principally with *intrinsic* ends but secondarily with extrinsic ends.

When we say things have intrinsic ends we affirm they are unities, and thus their parts are related one to another as a whole and co-ordinated for a common issue; when we say things have extrinsic ends we merely affirm that things are not isolated and independent systems, but so adjusted as to be components of a great organic universe.

Though there is a distinction between the two ends, they are not without relation. While nature did not grow cork trees for champagne stoppers, it is still not meaningless that corks do serve such a purpose.

Though rabbits and carrots were not made just to feed man, yet the relationship between food and oxygen and protoplasm—a relationship that means not only assimilation but growth, repair and activity—amazing consequences, can hardly be explained as accidental coincidence. If the mutton and potatoes Shakespeare ate were built up in his cerebral cells in such chemico-dynamic form as to produce such a mind as a Hamlet, I hardly think we can explain such marvelous architectural consequences unless we postulate a Master Builder.[50]

Here is a correlation of the two ends and a proof that the universe is a great system with many correspondencies. St. Thomas has worked out this correlation of the two ends by indicating that the lower things in the hierarchy of the universe, all of which have their intrinsic ends, serve the extrinsic end of something above them.[51] The sunshine has an extrinsic end: the nourishment of the plant; this enables the plant to attain its intrinsic end. The subordination of various levels corresponds to subordination of ends. Thus animals have an extrinsic end which helps man to attain his intrinsic end, which is God.[52] We do not know why flowers are scented or why they have colors until we know they cannot be fructified except through insects attracted by their color and aroma.

The argument of finality, then, runs as follows: there are in the world evidences of intrinsic finality which are unintelligible without the intention of an end and the adaptation of means to an end. From many such evidences we choose the following—

If we analyze man's body from the *quantitative* point of view, we find it has about four or five pounds of nitrogen; enough hydrogen to fill a ten-gallon barrel; enough oxygen to fill almost 999 barrels; enough carbon to make 10,000 lead pencils; enough hydrogen to fill a balloon capable of lifting him to an Alpine peak; enough iron to make five carpet tacks; and enough salt to fill six ordinary saltcellars. Chemically, we know up to 100 per cent of the constituents of man's body, and yet with all our knowledge of chemistry, science has never yet produced a man! Must there not be some inherent tendencies or organizing forces which make chemical elements combine in just such a way as to produce man, and not to produce a chemical laboratory? Why did these chemicals combine at a definite time in the history of the universe and not at another? Man has not long existed, but to prepare for him, a combustion lasting millions and millions of years has been going on.

Life was probably impossible until most of the radio-active atoms had been broken down, for the experience of radium shows that radium in the bulk kills. Uranium is one of the few radio-active substances left. Hence, millions and millions of years of radiation were necessary to disrupt these radio-active atoms, to prepare such elements as carbon, nitrogen, hydrogen and sulphur, etc., which are required for protoplasm, and also to arrange them by volcano, cloud, river and sea so as to render them available for man. Can we look on this tremendous preparation for millions of years—on the nebula, on the crashing suns, on the slow destruction of lucid atoms all undoubtedly leading to life, without realizing the mystery of protoplasm, without having the vision of a Mind behind the advent of Life?[53]

Hence there is a manifest combination of extrinsic finality in the lower levels of creation which serves higher intrinsic levels as Aquinas indicated. There is not only an intrinsic unity to man, but it also appears that roots of it and of him are back in the distant past. Chance could never have produced even one man from such chemical elements; and even though it had, it could never have seen to it that man should beget a man rather than a mouse. There is only one explanation to fit the facts. Behind this tremendous co-ordination and subordination of radiation, suns, and plants, and chemicals, there is a Mind and a purpose. Some years ago, when astronomers thought they saw canals on Mars, they immediately argued that Mars was inhabited. They reasoned that a canal serves a definite end. But such an end implies intelligent foresight and adjustment of means to an end. Therefore, man lives on Mars. How much more so must we argue to a Mind and a purpose behind the body of man and the universe, a mind which makes the life of that body and universe possible.

Eduard von Hartmann, in his *Philosophy of the Unconscious*, has enumerated thirteen conditions which must be fulfilled in order that an eye may see. If left to chance there are only ten possibilities in 9,999,985 that these thirteen conditions would so realize themselves as to permit vision, and this calculation ignores the conditions necessary so that an eye be found in an organism as complicated as a body. The retina of the eye is about 1/120 of an inch thick and is made up of eight, ten, or twelve layers. The layer next to the optic nerve, containing 500,000 fibers, is itself composed of 3,000,000 rods forming a single cone. The delicacy of this mechanism can be judged by the fact that the retinal image of the full moon as seen by the naked eye, is about 1/150 of an inch in diameter; while two parallel lines 1/10 of an inch apart, such as can be seen quite easily at a distance of twelve feet, are represented on the retina with a space of less than 1/2000 of an inch between them.

Not only are all these factors so combined as to produce an eye, but there is also something which allows the eye to exercise its function. Ninety-three million miles away comes light from a sun—and there is a lens to focus these light rays into thousands of fibers and millions of brain cells! Then why is it that when the light does come to the eye the lens of the eye should be transparent and not opaque? Why should the eye be convex, the one shape capable of producing images? Why should it be held in the proper position by a ligament? Why should the ligament be controlled by a muscle so placed as to adapt the focus to objects at different distances? Why should its lens be not rigid, but compressible, possessing a quality without which all the other arrangements would be useless? Why should the surface of the cornea be continually watered? Why should the water be drained off at the inner cornea by two small channels which deliver into the cavity of the nose? Why should there be a pigment layer at the back of the retina for absorbing stray light? Why should there be the iris with its two muscles to regulate the size of the pupil? Why should there be vessels to supply the eye with blood? As Hume wrote in his *Natural History of Religion:* "The whole frame of Nature bespeaks an intelligent Author, and no rational inquirer can, after serious reflection, suspend his belief for a moment with regard to the primary principles of genuine Theism."

To these facts must be added countless others, all tending to prove the intrinsic purposiveness, as well as an extrinsic purposiveness, in the sense that things are related in a system. In the case of intrinsic finality, the future, in a certain sense, is in the present, inasmuch as it is foreseen. If the end were not foreseen and determined *ante eventum*, there could not be generally the adaptation of means to an end, but this determinism is incessant. An acorn does not produce an oak once and a whale at another time; acorns continue to produce oaks. It is this incessant determination which outlaws chance. Finally, the conjunction of all things working toward their final ends is an ensemble of beings which have a unity for the human mind. This unity the mind can study in metaphysics, the science of universal being.

The prevision of an end and adaptation of means to that end can be apprehended only by the intellect, for only an intellect can foresee and predetermine. What is last in execution is first in intention, and only the intellect can intend. Hence the cause must necessarily be intelligent.[54] The argument is cosmic in its scope: not only one such phenomenon in the universe, but the whole universe must be due to the same intelligent cause, since all are subject to the same sequence. St. Thomas, it was said, has indicated in a great cosmic sweep that the extrinsic ends of the lower levels of creation serve the intrinsic ends of the higher levels; hence, the world may be regarded as a unity. That idea which St. Thomas arrived at metaphysically has today been established scientifically. In fact, modern science so much regards the universe as a *uni*verse, that it borrows from biology a concept which describes its closely knit unity—the organism—and commonly speaks of the "organic universe."

Samuel Rogers put it this way:

> That very law which moulds a tear
> And bids it trickle from its source,—
> That law preserves the earth a sphere
> And guides the planets in their course.

The very essence of the argument is the invariable presence of *law* and *order*, however imperfectly it may be apprehended by us. The advance of science is, from the philosophical point of view, the discovery of the law and order in the universe. Science is merely reading the book of nature; it is not writing it. Sometimes scientists believe that because they discover a law of the universe no lawmaker is needed; they forget they never would have discovered the law had the law not already been there, and the law would never be there unless there was a Lawmaker, and the Lawmaker would not be there unless He were intelligent. A scientist is only an amanuensis; he is taking dictation from nature; his notebook is full of the records of *another mind*. He may not clearly understand all the dictation, but the fact that he misses a word here and there should not lead him to doubt that a mind is really the source of his knowledge. It is only because there is order and law in the universe that a scientist is able to predict. Science has merely confirmed in a striking way the unity of the universe. Because the universe is one, it follows that a single intrinsic end in a tiny detail of the universe is in some way bound up with some other detail, and on and on until the universe presents itself an organic whole, exhibiting a fundamental symmetry, constructed of the same basic elements, and governed by the same great laws. Hence, it is to *one* Mind or Intelligence that we are led in conclusion. The tiny little atom which was once considered a homogeneous jelly-like substance is now discovered to be composed of protons and electrons knit together. The atoms of the ninety-two known chemical elements differ in the number and arrangement of protons and electrons bound up within each. These electrons are so small that they measure less than a million-millionth of an inch, and they flash around their little orbits at the rate of 1400 miles per second. What is more, the revolution of the electrons around their orbits is a miniature of the revolution of the planets around the sun! The plan of the infinitely little is the plan of the infinitely great. And both are constructed of the same stuff.

Our earth and the things that live on it are inseparable from the great stellar spaces which are so vast that science can speak of them not in terms of miles, but in terms of light years (the rate light travels in a year—at the rate of over 186,000 miles per second). Our earth was born and is dependent on this great womb of stellar fire. The beauty of a rose, the curling of the petals of the sweet pea, all the glory of our gardens are dependent upon the radiation emitted millions of years before our earth existed as a separate planet. The coal we burn in our furnaces is rendering back to the universe the energy the great antediluvian forests drank in from the rays of the sun millions and millions of years ago. The waves of light and sound are likewise interrelated; the keyboard of a piano has seven octaves of sound waves, but radiation waves have about sixty-four octaves of light waves. Both are so connected that the octaves of one can be translated into the octaves of the other.[55]

Even now matter and light are recognized to be a unity. Sir James Jeans states:

Matter is bottled light; light as we understand it commonly is unbottled light. Free mass from its chains and it will release light. In the sun, for example, matter is dissolving into radiation at the rate of four million tons a second. Radiation is thus the fundamental stuff of which the universe is made. The dust we tramp under our feet and the star only discovered yesterday by the astronomer are linked together by the unity of light and the laws of radiation. Modern science has thus come back face to face with the mystery of creation and is really not closer to the mystery than was Moses when he wrote: 'God said: Let there be light and light was made.'[56]

The universe is one: it is one metaphysically because it can be grasped with unity of *being;* it is one scientifically inasmuch as it is *organic;* it is one legally in the sense that there is law and order pervading it in all its parts. Law pervades the tiniest detail of nature, from the formation of the octahedron crystal—always bounded by eight triangular planes meeting one another at twelve angles at the *invariable* angle of 109.8° and never 109 degrees—to the tremendous fiery preparations of our earthly home millions of years ago. The failure of one single tiny little detail in the slow evolution of the universe, the absence of the one electron that makes carbon, would have made life impossible. And above all else, there is the greatest mystery of all, how this infinite variety of detail reached consciousness in the mind of man.

The Intellect responsible for the purpose and adaptation of means to an end is not wholly *immanent* in the universe, but distinct from it. This should be clear first of all from considering that finality involves a prevision of the future, and this prevision cannot be wholly immanent in the thing itself, but only in a mind distinct from it. The egg is formed before it knows what organs will be necessary for its future development; even man himself in embryonic form has no prevision or clairvoyance of means necessary to attain the end. This is not denying there is a vital principle in living things, but an assertion of that principle. But this vital principle in life and determining principle in inorganic things has to be explained. Why is there an "architect" in the inside of all things, ordaining them to be certain things rather than other things? There is here a manifest relation to a future effect, but this correlation cannot be explained unless it pre-existed in the cause. When it is referred to an anterior cause and its future effect, we have not merely a relation of cause and effect, but a relation of means to an end. As Pierre Janet puts it: "The agreement of certain phenomena bound together with a future phenomenon, implies a cause in which the future phenomenon is ideally represented." [57]

But this intellect with its prevision of means to an end cannot be substantially one with the thing itself, or it would in turn have to be explained; the sufficient reason of a painting is always to be found outside the frame itself, namely, in the artist; the sufficient reason of a machine must be found in the inventor. The inventor is not substantially one with his machine, nor is the sculptor one with his marble, nor is the intelligence identical with that which he orders and foresees, otherwise all would be subject to the determinism of means to end, and would themselves have to be explained.

Furthermore, the Intelligence which is distinct from the world is not an unconscious intellect, for the foreseeing and planning and adapting of means to an end is a conscious act. Nature is, as St. Thomas explains, merely "moved by another to an end, as an arrow tends to a determinate end through being moved by the archer who directs his action to the end." [58]

As the archer is distinct from the arrow's flight to the target, so is the reason foreseeing means to an end, and predisposing them to that end, distinct from the universe.

The argument may be put in another way, so as not only to present at one and the same time the philosophy of the Organic Universe, but also to reveal its fundamental defect—the refusal to recognize an intellect distinct from the universe. The universe is organic in two ways: in its life history, which is time (dynamic order), and in space (static order). There is subordination in time (universality) and co-ordination in space (constancy). The universe is organic in time because it is not simultaneous like the pieces of a mosaic, but successive like the notes of a melody. One thing is bound up with every other thing. The flower in the crannied wall "prehends" the whole life history of the universe; one thing subordinates itself to another thing; the organic adapts itself to environment; physical and chemical constituents have a biocentric reference. But things are not only organic in time; they are also organic in space. The order of the universe lies not only in the order of detail, but also in the order of ensemble—the order of the organism. This order implies *subordination* in time, and *co-ordination* in space. The simple repetition of antecedents is not enough. Life is more than chemistry; mind is more than biology; a qualitative difference is needed in all things to build up an organic universe. The absence of one element would destroy the stability of the whole. The greater the qualitative multiplicity, the greater the unity of composition. Cut a worm in two and he does not die, but cut a man in two and he does.

Modern philosophy considers that the universe is organic and that it is a unity. Things are not independent of one another, but are related in space and time. All things in space are subject to the same sequence in time. This philosophy is incomplete inasmuch as it rests in the empirical order of space and time. Suppose now it be lifted out of the empirical order into the metaphysical order, then the unity will not be merely biological, but metaphysical. Then the universe is not merely "organic," but *one—one* in being a *universe*, a unity which has no absolute multiple, otherwise we could never think of this summation. In a word, the metaphysical unity is the unity of multiplicity in the order of *being*. *Ens et unum conventuntur*.

But unity, which is the foundation of order, is possible only on the condition of an Intelligence capable of grasping the extension of the multiple into a *unity of conception*. A mind does not understand an engine if it is incapable of grasping the relation between the ignition and the carburetor. In like manner, if the universe is one, it must be because it was conceived mentally as a *unity*, even before its division into multiplicity, just as the engine was *one* in the mind of the engineer, before it was made in all its parts. This unity of conception is not a mere *static* conception, but a grasping of details in their entirety, for the being of each thing in isolation is deficient and incapable of attaining its end in relation to the whole. The unity of conception is total and dynamic. *Omnia se invicem perambulant*.

Extension and comprehension are in inverse order. Minds with greater intelligence grasp things into a unity of one principle; other minds require many countless examples and secondary principles in order to understand.[59] That is why teachers who understand philosophy very well, have to break up the unity of a universal principle into many illustrations to make it intelligible for minds with a less comprehensive scope. Einstein's theory of relativity was written in four pages, but it would take four hundred pages to explain it to a child. If then, the universe is one, the mind that conceived it and ordered it in all its multiplied parts, and subordinated it in space and co-ordinated it in time is one, for there must be an intellect commensurate with that conception.

The Mind which grasps the universe in the unity of the concept of being, is not immersed in the universe, for if the mind which seizes the unity were itself part of that order and directed to other parts, it would itself have to be directed. A man cannot pack a suitcase and still be part of that which is packed. The Intelligence which orders the universe must be transcendent to the universe.[60]

Not only is there an Intelligence governing the universe, and not only is this Intelligence distinct from the universe, but it is always infinitely perfect. In order that the argument may have as its background modern philosophical ideas, we may begin with emergent evolution. The new emergent must have a reason for its existence and its emergence, since it cannot be explained wholly by the antecedents; but it is an axiom of common-sense philosophy that whatever exists in the effect must have existed formally and eminently in the cause. An animal, for example, has "formal" pre-existence in the parent of its species. A house, for example, has a more "eminent" pre-existence in the mind of the architect than it has in the external world, for the mind of the designer is conscious and endowed with a higher existence, which Scholastics have termed "intentional existence."

Applying this principle to the various levels or hierarchies of creation, such as the emergence of life, or the emergence of mind, it is evident that these new emergents do not have their total formal pre-existence in the antecedents. Life certainly is something more than the mere addition of chemicals. There is a new "form" or pattern which cannot be discovered in the chemical antecedents; what is true of the emergence of life, is equally true of the emergence of mind. A mind which is capable of abstracting universal ideas cannot have solely emerged from the senses, the perfection of which lies not in the direction of universality, but of particularity. Since the new emergents are not wholly and formally in the antecedents, and since nothing can come from nothing, then these emergents must have had a more eminent pre-existence in a Mind outside the emerging process. In other words, the "pattern" of all that is to emerge has its exemplary cause in a transcendent Mind.[61]

Now the question arises, how can this Mind which orders not only means to ends, and determines what emergents will issue from such and such antecedents, but also determines how extrinsic purposes of lower orders can serve intrinsic purposes of higher orders—how can such a Mind weld the universe into a single conception, unless it be Infinitely Perfect and subsistent? The Mind which governs the universe is a Mind which perceives the *raison d'être* of things. Its unity is not that of a compound. The unity of a compound may refer either to quantitative parts, such as a body, or to a metaphysical composition of act and potency, essence and existence. If God's unity were only that of a compound, then the question would arise: who united the elements into composition? Who ordered God? We cannot go back infinitely in the process, other-wise we would never have the least of the finalities of the universe. If God were totally immanent in the order of the world, then we would have to account for God. It must therefore be that the One Mind which governs the Universe is a Mind identical with His very Being, a God Whose Essence is not distinct from His Ex-istence. If God's essence were not His existence, then God's existence would be caused by something prior to itself; furthermore, a being whose essence is distinct from its existence is unnecessary; it is not its nature to be.[62]

The argument for the infinity of God is not drawn exclusively from the finiteness of the universe, but also from the nature of purpose itself. The human mind cannot rest in composition as an ultimate. Creatures are finite because compounded. God is infinite because One, and He is One because anything short of perfect unity in which Essence and Existence are identical would not be sufficient explanation. The Infinity of God is the necessary correlation of all being and all thought. If there were a single emergent in the Divine Mind, as reasonable beings, we would have to inquire what made that emergent emerge; how did it fit into the composition of God's imperfect nature; and to what end is it a means? We cannot go back infinitely in a series of dependent causes. We must come to a First Unity which is Perfect and distinct from the world, and that being we call God, Who directed all things toward the proper ends.

This perfect Being is *Life*, for life is immanent activity, and in Him is perfect activity because His mind has no object outside Himself, and because it has no need of being aroused by anything outside of self.[63] The perfect Life of God is a consequence of His perfect Intellect in which there is no potentiality, no composition of knower and thing known. In God, Being and Thought are identical. Pure Thought is Pure Being.[64]

Chapter VII

THE IMMANENCE OF GOD

God is not only transcendent to the world, He is also immanent in it. In addition to the preceding arguments for transcendence, it might also be added that creation implies transcendence, for creation made the universe an effect of the creative activity of God. But every effect must differ from a cause, because no cause can communicate its identity. If it did, it would be different by the very reason that it is a twin, as the cause was not. Because the effect does not completely equal the cause, there will be some dissimilarity. The heat of the sun is possessed by objects on the earth, but not in the same way that the sun possesses the heat.[1]

But at the same time, every being acts according to its nature. Hence, something like the cause will be found in the thing produced. There will be something like God in creation, but also something different. In every effect there is something in which an effect resembles a cause, and something in which it differs. In the statue there is the artist's idea which is produced in the marble. But there is one thing the artist did not give, and that is the marble. In creation the same is true. The world made from nothingness will always retain the stigma of its parentage. Yet the universe will be like God inasmuch as it possesses similitude of being.[2]

But the human mind is not content with the bare knowledge that God made this universe; the legitimate curiosity of the mind strives to learn just what relation God bears to His masterpiece. Is He just an architect who designs an edifice but who is not necessary for its continued existence? Or if He is not disinterested in His work once it is produced, is He transformed into His creation as water becomes transformed into steam? The question arises, *how* God is present in the universe which He has created. It is one thing to say God made the world, but it is quite another thing to inquire about the relation between His work and Himself.

There are many answers to the problem, but like all philosophical answers, they can be reduced to three: the two extremes and the mean. The extreme solutions are deism and pantheism. The answer of the virtuous mean is immanence. Deism teaches that God is aloof from the universe, and thus wholly transcendent. Pantheism teaches that God is wholly identified with the universe, and therefore wholly immanent. The traditional doctrine of immanence is that God is both immanent and transcendent, or, as an old Latin hymn puts it:

> Intra cuncta, nec inclusus;
> Extra cuncta, nec exclusus.

God is in the universe, but not shut up in it; God is outside the universe, but not excluded from it.

The fundamental error of deism is its assumption that a cause, and in particular a Supreme Cause, is disinterested in the product of His Causality. As a matter of fact, the only reason any cause acts is goodness. If it were not because of goodness of purpose of some kind, a cause would never exert itself. Once it does exert itself, it can never be indifferent to that which it has done. God therefore could never have forgotten that He made the world. Born out of Love, it will always be loved. That is why deism is impossible.

Deism implies that a Cause Who is the Good God can be disinterested in goodness; pantheism, on the other hand, makes the Love of the Good God impossible by identifying Him with the world. Love implies otherness or distinctiveness. If God is not distinct from the world, then loving God means loving the world, or worse still, the world loving itself. With the possibility of love gone, morality must disappear. A God Who is the totality of the universe cannot be ethical. He is neither good nor bad, because in the "All" which is God is both evil and goodness. To make God organic with the universe and evolving with it does not help matters. This dodge reminds one of Carlyle's remark, that the making of the universe with God in it raises the same sort of question as that which one of the Georges asked about the making of a dumpling—"how the apples got in." To have recourse to space-time as the original stuff of God and the universe, reminds one of the two shipwrecked sailors on an island who supported themselves by taking in one another's washing.

The true solution lies in the mean of these extremes which place

God wholly outside the universe or wholly inside it. God is immanent in the world, but also transcendent to it. There are three ways in which God might be immanent in the universe:

Substantially: His very substance being one with the world and part of its essence, as hydrogen and oxygen are the constituents of water. This would be pantheism.

Personally: by a hypostatic union, in which the nature of God and the nature of man would be united in the unity of the Person of God. Such is the Incarnation of Our Lord and Savior, Jesus Christ. This is immanence only in the broad sense of the term and is a problem not of philosophy but of theology.

Causally: in virtue of His Creative Act, by which God brought the world into being and by which He remains the Omnipresent Ground of all finite existence and activity. This is the true notion of the immanence of God.

The discussion of the immanence of God assumes as proven the existence of God, but goes one step beyond, not content to know merely that God is the Creator of the Universe, but rather to learn whether, in creating, He left in the world the imprint of Himself and His artistry. Some workmen produce things, but never leave the stamp of their personality upon them. Is this true of God? Other workmen, or more particularly, artists, actually "put themselves into their work," become immanent in it to such an extent that paintings like those of Rembrandt or Murillo can be identified as such; these artists "live" in the artistry of their hands. Does the Divine Artist become present in His work in such an immanent manner?

The answer is to be found by studying the causality with which God created the universe. The universe is made up of an infinite variety of things, from grains of mustard seeds to mountains, from squirming amoebae to man, from planets to flowers, and yet of each and every one of these things it can be said that "it is." However different or diverse things may be, they all participate in being. Being is therefore the single effect of the Divine Creative Act to which everything is ultimately reducible. St. Thomas, in speaking of the universe, says that it is intelligible in virtue of a threefold cause:

1. The Formal Cause, which answers the question: According to what plan was the work conceived?

2. The Final Cause, which answers the question: Why was it made?
3. The Efficient Cause which answers the question: Who made it? [8]

That is to say, in order that the universe might be, three causes had to co-operate:

1. *Scientia ut dirigens*, or the Formal Cause—Who planned the work.

2. *Voluntas ut imperans*, or the Final Cause—Who commanded it.

3. *Potentia ut exequens*, or the Efficient Cause—Who executed it.

But it must not be thought that these three causes represent three distinct and absolutely separated natures. These causes pre-exist in a substance, for a substance is the foundation of all causality. They proceed from the same substance under three different relations. The Formal Cause is the intellect of the substance from which proceeds the idea. The Final Cause is the will of the substance from which the end or purpose follows. The Efficient Cause is the power of the substance whence proceeds action. Before a sculptor can produce a statue three conditions must be fulfilled. First, he must have some idea or model according to which he will cut his marble. Secondly, he must have the desire to reproduce that model in stone; that is, he must love the idea which he has conceived. Thirdly, he must have the capacity to realize his ideal, and to fulfill his desire, that is, the power to execute. Leave one of these three conditions out, and the statue could never be produced. If the sculptor never had an idea, his capacity to carve would be in vain; if he had the capacity to be a sculptor without either ideas or the desire to exercise his power, it would profit him nothing, and if he had not the power to cut stone, he would be a dream sculptor, not a real one.

When finally the finished piece of sculpture sees the light of day, it will reveal not only the co-operation of these three causes, but also the degree of perfection to which the artist possessed them. The nobler the ideal which he conceives, the more intense the love of his idea, the more delicate his creative touch, the more perfect will be the statue, for the artist himself is *immanent* in these three ways.

Since God made the universe by a threefold causality rooted in the unity of His Nature, and since *operatio sequitur esse*, which means the artist is in his work according to the degree of perfection of his being, it will follow that God is present or immanent in the world in three ways: as the Wisdom which plans it; as the Will which commands and governs it; and as the Power which sustains it.[4]

It must not be thought that God is merely the static cause of the universe—One Who planned it, gave it laws, made it, and then let it take care of itself. God is different from an architect who plans, directs, and builds a house. The architect may die, but the house will stand without him. This is because he is only the *static* cause of the house, or the reason for its *becoming*. God, on the contrary, is not only the static cause of the house, but the dynamic cause as well. He is the cause not only of the becoming of the universe—*causa in fieri*—but also the cause of its *being—causa in esse*—because He not only, like an architect, transformed existing materials, but also brought them into being by the Fiat of His Omnipotent Will.[5]

GOD IS IMMANENT IN THE WORLD BY HIS WISDOM

All things in the world of art must have been made according to a plan. There never was a chisel touched to marble, or a brush to canvas, or a dome thrown against the vault of heaven's blue, but that some idea preceded it. In a perfect manner, everything in this world has been made according to certain ideas existing in the Mind of God from all eternity. God, being Perfect Intelligence, must be, therefore, possessed of the models, ideas, or representations of all the things He wishes to call into the light of day. Every tree, every flower, every bird, every thing has had its spiritual model in the Divine Mind. And just as the ideas of a sculptor are imitable *ad extra*, so too the ideas of all things which God possesses are likewise imitable *ad extra*.[6] These ideas, which from our point of view are multiple but really are one in the Divine Mind and identical with His Being, are called Archetypal Ideas, and in relation to immanence three conclusions [7] may be drawn.

God is present in the universe in somewhat the same manner as an artist is present in his work of art. Just as the idea the painter has of the Blessed Mother is present on his canvas, so too the ideas God has of things are present in things as exemplars.[8] These Divine Archetypal Ideas reflected in things, as the very rational plan of their being, are called forms, as in the mind they are called ideas (and sometimes forms).[9] Everything in the world has its form, which is the reason for its intelligibility, and makes it what it is. A tree is a tree in virtue of its form (not external shape, but internal participation or reflection of the Archetypal Ideas) and for that reason differs from a camel which has a different form.[10] A hint of this philosophy is given in the familiar lines of Joyce Kilmer:

> Poems are made by fools like me,
> But only God can make a tree.

Not only is God present in things as the Wisdom which planned them, but in the richness and variety of His Wisdom. Being infinite, His Wisdom reaches to the abyss of all things that are known and can be known. Quite naturally, no created thing could perfectly express the depth and variety of His knowledge, only an uncreated and single Word can express it, and that is the Logos or the Son. It was fitting that God became present by His Wisdom, not only in one thing, but in many. What one created thing failed to reveal, the other might disclose. Thus creation became like a great orchestra, with thousands of instruments blending their various notes, and yet all co-operating to produce the beautiful harmony in which Heaven and earth declare forth the Wisdom of their Omnipotent Creator.[11]

Finally, God's Wisdom participating in things is not only the reason for their being and their richness, but it also explains our own intelligibility. Why, in the ultimate analysis, do we know? We know, not because we invent, but because we discover—discover the Wisdom of God hidden in the things which He has made. Every material thing in the universe is made up of matter and form. Matter makes it individual; the form, which is the architect within, is the reflection of the Divine idea. God, as it were, wrapped up His ideas in matter, just as He has wrapped up man's soul in a body. But knowledge is impossible so long as the form or idea or the reason of intelligibility is hidden by matter. Knowledge is spiritual. If the human mind is ever to know things *rationally*, it must have a power above that of the animals, a capacity for stripping off the matter from the idea, or else penetrating through the matter with a vision akin to the X ray. This power Almighty God has given to the human mind in what has been called the "active intellect," which has the power, once it enters into sensible contact with things, to grasp their essence, or the form which makes them what they are. But since the form is the participation of the Archetypal Idea of that thing in the Divine Mind—as the cathedral is the participation of the idea in the mind of the architect—it follows that in knowing the essence or nature of things, the mind knows the likeness of the Divine ideas existing in things. Thus, in an indirect way, the Wisdom of God becomes immanent in our own minds through the intermediary of things.[12] This is the fundamental reason why things are true. Truth is a conformity between the mind and things: *adaequatio rei et intellectus*.[13] My idea of a tree is true if it conforms to the material thing before me which my senses represent to be a tree. Everything in this world is true inasmuch as it corresponds with the idea which God had in mind in making it. In this sense there is absolute truth. St. Thomas says:

God's own being is not only conformed to His intellect, but His act of understanding is the measure and cause of every other being and of every other intellect, and He is Himself His own existence and act of understanding. Whence it follows not only that Truth is in Him, but He is Truth itself, and the Sovereign and First Truth.[14]

If things are true because they correspond to the Divine Mind, likewise in a derived sense, our minds enjoy truth when they correspond to the things made according to the Ideas of God immanent in them by participation, thanks to the Creative Act.[15]

In the Divine order of things, the Immanence of God in Creation by Wisdom is meant to describe a circular process. God made things intelligently; we discover their intelligibility thanks to our own intellect, make them immanent in us by an act of understanding. By lifting ourselves up to that Supreme Truth, the Source of all gifts, we lift up the material world as well, and thus all things find their way back again to God.

GOD IS IMMANENT IN THE UNIVERSE BY HIS GOODNESS

The final cause which determines the purpose or end of anything resides in the will. Oftentimes we may say that a product reveals an unwilling worker; at other times we say that the work reveals the enthusiasm and fire of the worker. How could we ever know this unless in some way the will became immanent in the thing done?

Since Almighty God created things, not only by His Wisdom which planned them, but by His Omnipotent Will, it is to be expected that His Willingness and His Goodness are in some way to be found in His works. Being Goodness Itself and hence wanting nothing for His Perfection, God did not create on account of utility, or for purposes of increased happiness, but solely and uniquely on account of His Liberality.[16]

God is immanent in all things inasmuch as He has dynamized them with a purpose which is none other than the quest for His own goodness. Since God is Perfect Goodness, He could have no other end in creating things than that those things should share in some way in His Goodness. Made by Goodness, made for Goodness, this goal and purpose of theirs was fixed—to strive for their own perfection or completion, which is a participation in that Perfect Goodness which called them into being.[17] If the zeal, the fire, the love of an artist can be found in his work, in a much more perfect manner can the Love and the Goodness of God be found in all things. St. Thomas tells us that "God is in the stone," not substantially of course, but inasmuch as it shares in His goodness.[18]

In order to insure the attainment of its goal, or a sharing in the Divine Goodness, Almighty God has placed in each thing an immanent urge, or striving for law. An arrow is shot from the bow and speeds to the target. The arrow itself has no conception of either its direction or its goal, and yet both are immanent in it thanks to the archer. In like manner, things below man tend to their perfection unconsciously, but they do so only because God has interiorly impressed them with His Purpose,[19] which is nothing else than to become God-like, each in its own way.[20] In animate creatures this immanent urge toward God is effected by the laws of nature; in the sensible world by the laws of instinct, and in conscious man by intelligence and will.[21] These laws, being the expressions of the will of God immanent in things,[22] constitute the source of what the Scholastics have called "natural love" or the inclination of things toward their perfection which is a participation in the Goodness of God.

God is so immanent in things by His Goodness that He is more the end of every particular thing than its proximate end.[23] This means the flower tends more to God than it tends to blooming. We may go even farther and say with St. Thomas that even irrational creatures love God.[24] And yet this must not scandalize us. Any man who has a great ideal to achieve regulates all his actions, proximate desires, and immediate wishes as functions of that ideal. He therefore loves his final end, which is the ideal, more than any proximate end which might be a pleasure of the moment. Everything loves the whole more than the part (that is why we would rather lose our arm than our life), and since the whole is the Goodness of God manifested in the universe, things aspire more to Him than to their own perfection. The immediate goal of every finite creature disappears from the horizon in the face of the Perfect Good which is God. It is the whole which makes the part intelligible. If the creature did not first desire God, which is Perfect Goodness, it could never desire anything else. No one can love the unknown; no thing can strive to the unknown. If every rational being in this world consciously longs for Love and Goodness in its perfect state, and if every irrational and inanimate creature strives for Goodness in its participated state, it can only be because somehow, somewhere, Goodness and Love became immanent in some way in the universe. The very fact that we seek proves that once we must have found. Here is the real law of gravitation, by which things are not pulled down to the center of the earth earthly, but rather lifted up to the center of the heaven heavenly. The power of attraction varies not in relation to mass and distance, but according to nature and spirituality. The more spiritual the beings, the more conscious and the more strong the pull, but each in its own way is attracted—attracted to God by the Immanent Gravitational Pull of Goodness and Love: *Amor pondus meum.*

GOD IS IMMANENT IN THE UNIVERSE BY HIS POWER

God defined Himself to Moses as "I am Who Am," to indicate the very perfection of His Being. The universe can be said to *have* being, but only God can be said to *be*. Creatures are compounded of being and nonbeing, but it is the very essence of the Creator to exist. Everything acts according to its nature, but the nature of God is to be. Hence, when He wills (Final Cause) to create things (Efficient Cause) according to His eternal plans (Formal Cause), being will in some way be found stamped upon His masterpiece.

God will therefore be immanent in the world, not only by His Wisdom and His Goodness, but also by His Power which is Being or Act.

If absolute nothingness ever were, then nothing would ever be. Out of the void of nothingness this universe could never come. It makes no difference whether one starts with primeval stardust or with the completed solar system, the being which is common to all things must have had a cause. Since being is that which is most profoundly intimate in a thing, it can be accounted for only by the existence of some Perfect Being Who gave it its temporary endowment of existence.[25] St. Thomas states in this regard: "Since the very essence of God is to be, it follows that being in the created order will be properly His effect, just as to burn is properly the effect of fire." [26] The universality of being is one of the certain signs that the Being of God is immanent in the universe by virtue of His creative power.[27]

It must not be thought, however, that God is in the universe merely as the initial source of its being, for God is not merely a static cause. He is much more than the Architect of its being. An architect who not only plans his house, but actually builds it, is immanent in it by his activity, but note that the architect may die and yet the house will survive, for the architect is merely the cause of the becoming—*causa in fieri*—of the house and not the cause of its being—*causa in esse;* he has merely transformed pre-existing materials. But God did not merely juxtapose already existing primordial stuff; He is the Cause of the very beginning or the *being* of things. Things, therefore, are related to His Being as the sun's rays are to the sun. They depend on God, not only for the first moment of their being, but also for their continued being or conservation.[28] If He should withdraw that Conserving Power for just a second, they would fall back into the nothingness from which they came.[29]

God is not like an artist who touches his work through the intermediary of an instrument and then leaves it. With God there is no *action in distans*.[30] He is intimately present in all things. *Deus est in omnibus rebus, et intime.*[31] So immanent is He in the universe by His Power that, as St. Thomas reminds us, all the movements, the activities, the goings and comings of things animate and inanimate are more properly God's effect than they are the effects of secondary causes.[32]

Created things may be secondary means of this conservation, but ultimately the conservation of every being depends upon God.[33] So great is this dependence that St. Thomas does not hesitate to say:

God is the ultimate cause of any action whatsoever, inasmuch as: (a) He gives its subject the power of acting; (b) He conserves it in its being; (c) He applies it to action—in sum, operates immediately in every thing without in any way excluding the operation of the will or nature.[34]

This means that God is present everywhere, not by material contact, but by power.[35] The spatial notion that God is localized in things is therefore erroneous. God is spiritual and is not contained by things. There is no division of His Being. As the soul is entirely in every part of the body, so God is Whole in all things and in each thing.[36] In all things as the cause of all being, God is nevertheless above all things, by the excellence of His Nature.[37] Insofar as knowledge and goodness are concerned, things may be said to be more in God, than God in things, just as the tree is more in my mind when I know it, than I am in the tree. But since power is applied to external things, it is true to say that by it God is more in things.[38]

In conclusion, God may be said to be immanent in all things, not by a sharing of His Nature, for since this is spiritual it cannot be shared; not by some accidental attachment, for the world entirely depends on Him; but rather by His Causality.

First of all, there is the causality of His Being inasmuch as it is Intelligence. What are our laws of science, of psychology, of physics but designations we give to things which compel us to think in a certain way and not in another? If laws were of our making, we might have water run uphill. Do not scientists return to the experimental ground of nature to verify their hypotheses, and what is this but a recognition that they are merely finding wisdom and not causing it? If nature impels us to think in a certain way, it can only be because nature itself is rational and has within it a reflection of the Wisdom of God. In the words of Browning:

> To Know
> Rather consists in opening out a way
> Whence the imprisoned splendour may escape,
> Than in effecting entry for a light
> Supposed to be without.

And this "imprisoned splendour" is the sign that God is not only in His Heavens by Nature, but in His world by Wisdom. If 250,000,-000 atoms were stretched alongside one another, they would be no more distant than an inch, and yet each is a miniature solar system, with its proton as the sun, and its electrons as the planets. All show their law, order, and plan, which have guided them in all their agelong contributions to the structure of the universe, and declare to the scientist at the other end of the microscope that he is in the very presence of Intelligence Itself.

Next, there is the Causality of God's Being, inasmuch as it is voluntary. Why did God will to make the universe? The Archetypal Ideas He had concerning it did not constrain Him. God created the world. God is Good, and being Good He could not, as it were, contain Himself; consequently, He told the secret of His Goodness to nothingness and that was Creation. The world is the overflow of Divine Goodness. Begotten of the Goodness of God, the Goodness of God is in it. All the versatile motions and strivings of the universe are modes of procedure corresponding to the continuous activity of His Will. Because God is in things by His Love and Goodness, they all strive in part to produce the same Goodness which called them into being. That is why everything in the world tends to diffuse itself. The sun is good and diffuses itself in light and heat; the tree is good and diffuses itself in the fruit; the rose is good and diffuses itself in its perfume; animals are good and diffuse themselves in the generation of their kind. Man is good and diffuses himself in the generation of thought. Fecundity, or productiveness, is the law of the universe; things give because to them has been given. The giving is their completion, and by seeking their own perfection and goodness, they seek the Perfect Goodness which is God. That is why man finds a paradox in creatures and speaks of their "traitorous trueness, their loyal deceit." They are fickle to us and faithful to Him, because God is in them drawing all things *suaviter et fortiter* back to the Heart of His Infinite Goodness.

Finally, there is the Causality of God's Being inasmuch as it is pure act. Drawn from nothingness, we will always bear the imprint of our origin, just as a statue must necessarily be imperfect if chiseled from an imperfect block of marble. God must be in all things, sustaining them at every instant. This lesson St. Paul emphasized to the Areopagites of old: "God is not far from any of us, for in Him we live and move and have our being." In fact, God is closer to us than we are to ourselves. We are just borrowers of being, living on the momentary installments which His Bounty gives us, and not only us, but all things. There is supreme philosophy in the lines of Blake:

> To see the world in a grain of sand,
> And a heaven in a wild flower;
> Hold infinity in the palm of your hand,
> And eternity in an hour.

Why is God never represented as shouting in Revealed Scripture or in the writings of any religious people? It is because He is so near He has no need to shout; He whispers. The silence of the heavenly spheres frightened Pascal; they spoke to him of the presence of God. Who will deny that some truth of the immanence of God in created things is expressed in the lines attributed to Tennyson, "On your knees, man, here are violets."

Let it not be thought that the theory of evolution runs counter to the doctrine of the immanence of God. What is evolution, but the immanence of God expressed in dynamic terms? If there be such a thing as evolution, then I see almost an added reason for emphasizing God's immanence. Evolution from the original gas or molecule would demand three things: a Power which brought that gas or molecule into being, and which sustains it in being during its progressive unfolding; a Mind which planned the evolution of that primary matter and endowed it with internal laws; a Will which chose to bring it into being, impressed each emergent of that evolutionary process with its inner finality, and gave to the whole process its own goal and purpose—for without some purpose there would be no reason for ever evolving.

Thus whether one views the universe as made in its present state, or as evolving slowly from the simple to the complex, God must be immanent in it as *Sapientia ut dirigens; Voluntas ut imperans; Potentia ut exequens.*

Reason tells us this much, but when revelation comes to tell us more, then we begin to grasp that these three Causes are rooted in the one Nature, which is God, and each is so perfect as to be personal. The Triple Causality becomes the Trinity, Three Persons in

One God. Power—God the Father: "I believe in God, the Father Almighty." Wisdom—God the Son, the Logos, the Personal Thought of an Eternal Thinker. Will—God the Holy Ghost, the Power of Attraction, Love.[39]

PART III

The Impact of the Sciences on Religion

Chapter VIII

PHYSICAL SCIENCES AND RELIGION

Let us at this point investigate the truth of the modern idea that science is the determinant of the idea of God. It is our position that the science of physics as such has no direct bearing on either philosophy or religion. Physicists have ventured into the fields of both philosophy and religion, and contended that the new physics demands a new religion. (As Professor Whitehead has said: "Anything which suggests a new cosmology, suggests a new religion.") They argue that because there is a new physics and a new cosmology, there must be a new philosophy and a new religion. The discussion must revolve about two questions: Has there really been a revolutionary change in physics? If so, does it follow that there must be a new religion and a new philosophy to suit the new physics?

REVOLUTIONARY CHANGES IN PHYSICS

The answer to the first question is unreservedly in the affirmative. Consider the changed conception since the days of Newton of the subject of matter; absolute space and absolute time; and the new mathematical background of physics.[1]

Matter, which was once regarded as a homogeneous jelly-like substance, we know now is a very complex body built up of minute particles. Instead of describing the universe as made up of tiny billiard balls, physicists now describe it in terms of electricity. Matter, in the sense of something "substantial," has been forgotten. Sir James Jeans says that:

the tendency of modern physics is to resolve the whole material universe into waves. These waves are of two kinds: bottled-up waves, which we call matter, and unbottled waves, which we call radiation or light. These concepts reduce the whole universe into a world of light, potential or existent, so that the whole story of its creation can be told with perfect accuracy and completeness in the six words: "God said 'Let there be light.' "[2]

Newton had regarded space and time as absolute and uniform throughout the entire universe. Einstein suggests that space and time are relative to the observer and his frame of reference. There is a space-frame relative to the observer on earth and a space-frame relative to the observer on a distant star. The same is true of the time-frames. Not only are space and time relative to the observer, but they are no longer regarded as separate and distinct. Previously distances were thought of only in terms of three dimensions; length, breadth, and thickness. Hermann Minkowski demonstrated that since length changes with motion, time-interval must be considered in all measurements as much as space-distance. He added to the three dimensions of space, the dimension of time. The conjunction of the three common spatial dimensions, with the fourth dimension, time, constitute what is known as the space-time continuum.

The Newtonian theory, built upon the Euclidian straight-line geometry, stipulated that any body in motion will move in a straight line unless diverted. Newton found that the planets move not in a straight line, but in curved lines. He therefore had to posit a force to explain why their motion was not straight. His answer was gravitation. Einstein, basing his work upon the non-Euclidian geometry of Riemann and others, has shown that these properties of matter are not independent of space-time. The motion of bodies is different in different space-frames and different time-frames. The geometry of any portion of space-time depends upon the distribution of matter in that region. Einstein was able to dispense with the notion of gravitation in the Newtonian sense.

There is no escaping the conclusion that there have been revolutionary changes in modern physics. To pass on to the more important question: do these changes in physics demand a new philosophy and religion, any more than changes in medicine or art or poetry would do? Our answer to this question will be in the negative.

In order to understand the basis for this negative conclusion, the following sound principles of philosophy should be recalled: There is a hierarchy of sciences or a subordination of the various disciplines of the mind. Knowledge is not like a series of telegraph poles in a field, but like a pyramid mounting from a broad base to a refined point where there is poised the most universal of all sciences in the natural order, namely metaphysics. The division of sciences into ranks is not based solely upon the different objects which the sciences study, but is principally justified by their intellectual dependence, one on another, and presupposition of one another. Psychology, for example, is dependent in part upon physiology and biology; biology is dependent in part on chemistry; and chemistry is dependent in part on physics. This truth extends beyond mere data: no science proves its own principles. Music assumes mathematics, and mathematics assumes metaphysics.

The basis of the difference between the various sciences is the degree of abstraction involved. The mind, amidst the flux of sensible things presented to it, may limit itself to the consideration of material things and their properties, which are experimentally observable. This would give the science of physics in the broad sense of the term.[3] The mind, as regards the beginning of its knowledge, must have sensible matter, but it can conceive and act *without* it, for nothing sensible or experimental enters into the definition of a cube root. This second degree of abstraction which concerns itself only with quantity, number, and extent, quite apart from their sensible manifestation in material things, is the science of mathematics.

Finally, the mind can concern itself with things not inasmuch as they are quantitative (mathematics) but only inasmuch as they *are* or have *being*, for there are certain objects of knowledge which not only can be *conceived* without matter, but which also can *exist* without matter, such as truth. This science which concerns itself with being as being is the science of metaphysics, and belongs to the third degree of abstraction.[4] The three degrees of abstraction thus give the three supreme sciences as conceived by the Scholastic synthesis: physics, mathematics, and metaphysics.[5]

It has been suggested that in addition to the physical and mathematical theories of philosophy of science, there remains yet another which is the metaphysical. Before discussing just how metaphysical science can be applied to the experimental order, let us consider a statement of the Scholastic doctrine of metaphysics.

The basis of judging an inferior or a superior science in the hierarchy of sciences is the universality of the object which the science studies. All sciences are concerned with *being*, for that is the common element in which all knowledge bathes. Every particular science adds something to the general and almost confused idea of being. Biology adds "organism" to being; anthropology adds "human origin" to being; physics adds "material" to being, and so on for the other sciences. The one supreme science whose object is not limited to being of a particular category, but being as being, is the science of metaphysics.

It now remains to exercise these principles upon the problem at hand, namely the applicability of scientific categories to philosophy and religion. Because space-time pervades the universe, is it true to say that God is space-time; or because science is concerned with averages, that God is therefore the supreme actuary; or because the conclusions of science are conventions, that therefore there is no such thing as truth; or because space and time are relative to the observer, that therefore morals are relative?

Because the sciences are differentiated from one another by degrees of abstraction, in which a particular aspect of *being* and *reality* is studied, it follows that the method of one science cannot be the method of another. The science with the more restricted object, like physiology, cannot apply its methods or its categories to a science with a more universal object, such as metaphysics. As St. Thomas reminds us, the principles of mathematics can be applied to the natural sciences (as modern physicists today are applying mathematics to physics), but physics cannot be applied to mathematics.[6] The part may not dictate to the whole, nor the citizen to his government, nor the science of the inorganic to the science of the organic and the mental.

Every science has both a material and a formal object. The material object is what is studied; the formal object is the particular point of view under which that object is studied. The methods of sciences differ. A science which studies matter will approach it experimentally, but geometry is not studied in that way. If the method and contents of one science have any application to other sciences, it is only on the basis of analogy and not because the same method pervades all the sciences. As St. Thomas remarks, "There is no uniform method of science."[7] A hierarchy of sciences exists and the distinction between the sciences in that hierarchy is grounded upon the different degrees of abstraction. The categories of biology are not applicable to physics, except analogically; the categories of sociology are not applicable to mathematics; the predicate of the sentence "The moon is made of green cheese," cannot be applied to the subject of the sentence, "John is a man." Neither can the forms of any other sciences be applied to philosophy, except poetically. Oxygen and hydrogen, atoms and protons are not studied in the same way as justice and fortitude. We simply cannot put a man into a crucible to see if he will give off unmistakable green fumes of envy. It is one thing to say space and time are inseparable in the new outlook of science, but quite another thing to say that God is space-time. Because the universe can best be studied in terms of mathematics, it does not follow that God is a mathematician, as Jeans would have it. Because physics discovers that space and time are relative to the observer, it does not follow that ethics is relative, as Westermarck believes. Relativity is good and proper within its own domain, but it becomes absurd when it is expanded into an attempt to make *everything* relative—and says that we have four toes on one foot counted one way, and six on the other foot counted the other way.

And by what right does physics become the supreme science to tell us what morality, values, and God really are? By what right has the science which studies quantity become the authority ruling over the science of the spirit? By what logic does the scientist who tells us the nature of the atom become the scientist to tell us there is no soul? Is there no other standard for the hierarchy of sciences than that which makes the *scientia scientiarum* the one which makes the minutest physical discovery? If physics is going to dominate metaphysics, and mathematics, logic, where shall the process stop? Will the Egyptologist soon claim to be the interpreter of liturgy, and the detective the interpreter of theology, simply because both deal with mystery? "No one," writes A. E. Taylor:

would think of regarding the verdict of an archeologist or a chemist on a moot point of law as deriving any particular value from the eminence of the archeologist or the chemist in his known subject; no one would attach any weight to a Lord Chancellor's opinion about the genuineness of an alleged Rembrandt, or a disputed fragment of Simonides, because the opinion was that of the best Lord Chancellor the country ever possessed.[8]

The sciences are valid in their own sphere, but not in the whole of knowledge; they are good as far as they go, but they do not go everywhere.

According to a sound conception of science, the new physics

means only a *new physics*, but *not a new philosophy*. Since the principles of philosophy were not dependent on the old physics, they do not fall with it, and since the principles of philosophy are not based on the new physics, they do not rise with it. The principle of identity, the principles of causality and finality, the transcendental properties of being, the value of ideas, all of these remain what they are, independent of a new scientific construction. Physics is not the foundation of philosophy, but only a particularization of some of its principles—a particularization which is apt to be wrong because of the incomplete induction upon which it is based. That is why St. Thomas could repeat over and over again, in the texts we have quoted, that some day there might be a new physics and a new astronomy which would upset the old, but knowing this, he never concluded that philosophy would have to be revised for that reason. Philosophy of Nature was the application of the principles of metaphysics to observed facts and phenomena of the universe; these facts might be wrong, they might be proved false, but that did not mean that metaphysics had to *conform to a new set of observed facts*. Two and two still make four, though I observe two drops of water and two drops of water fuse into one. No one ever thought of plucking out his eye because he saw a stick bent in water.

Physics, biology, and sociology are not the ground and foundation of metaphysics; otherwise the science with a more restricted object would rule the science with a more general object. That is why St. Thomas asserts that a changed conception of empirical science does not involve a change in the metaphysics which ruled that science. Philosophy is independent of science, but independent does not mean contrary to science, nor necessarily separated from science; it is independent in respect to the difference of its *how* and its *why*, the description in terms of mathematics and the explanation in terms of causes. Abstraction reveals the different *reason of being* of the juxtaposed phenomenal qualities. That is why the Angelic Doctrine contends that there is no uniform method in science. The various sciences are separated by different abstractions, and each has its own material object and its own formal object. To overflow one into the other in such a manner as to confuse abstractions and objects would be the ruination of science.[9] *Et propter hoc peccant qui uniformiter in tribus speculativae partibus procedere nituntur.*

St. Thomas calls that tendency to make all sciences uniform in method and content a "sin," and if there be a general academic "sin" today, it is precisely that. Here we call it the "Fallacy of the Uniform Method of Science"—the fallacy of taking one science as the norm, and making it the measure, the guide, the interpreter, and the inspiration of every other science. The history of philosophy bears witness that our own generation is not the first to build a metaphysics and a religion on the data of a science to the exclusion of all other possible foundations. There is a fashion in sciences as there is in clothes. Each generation seems to have its own science which is supreme for the moment. Auguste Comte gave to the world the sociological method, which was genuinely scientific as long as it was confined to society. But the lyricizers of science would not keep it restricted to its material object; they extended it beyond its natural boundaries and applied the sociological method to religion and to God, with the result that we have today the ingenious sociological interpretation of God as "society divinized." Another generation saw the popularity of biology, which Darwin carried to new heights with new revelations of the development of the organic world. Biology is a perfectly legitimate and necessary science as long as it remains biology and confines itself to the study of living beings, but Darwin and all the other biologists could not hold lyricizers in check. Soon biology was applied not only to philosophy (as in the case of Herbert Spencer) but even to God, with the result that certain modern theologians look upon God as "the God of evolution," or, with Sir Henry Jones, as "the God who advances from life to life." Then came the new fashion—psychology. William James and Jürger Bora Meyer gave to the scientific world many interesting and important conclusions concerning the effect of sublimated ideas on our waking life. However, the fallacy of the uniform method of science got the better of some psychologists who refused to limit psychology to studying the mind and its states, but insisted on making religion and philosophy conform to its rules. Psychology then became identified with theology, and conversion was explained as an eruption of a subconscious state. Sin was explained as a "complex," and God as a "mental projection," according to Professor James Henri Leuba, or as a "sublimated libido," in the terms of the Freudians.

At the present time the fashionable science is not sociology, not

biology, not psychology, but physics. It is fashionable because the
most important scientific theories in the world today are coming
from that field. Duheim, Whitehead, Einstein, Poincaré, and Meyerson have given to the world new interpretations of the physical
universe which do seem to fit the facts better than the older theories.
The thinking world welcomes these intellectual advances, although
it must frown upon any attempt to interpret everything else in
terms of physics, a spatio-temporal continuum, or relativity. Professor Whitehead, although the deepest thinker among the physicists
themselves, is also their greatest offender and their greatest lyricizer.
After writing such a delightful scientific work as *Science and the
Modern World*, he followed it with a venture into theology in his
Religion in the Making, wherein he is set forth before the world as
an example of the truth that a man may be a really great scientist
and a lamentably poor theologian.

There is a danger that our common-sense point of view may be
open to the charge of obscurantism, because the notion is current
in the world today that religion is a controversial question, and
that science is not. To dispute the extension of physics to the domain of religion is to be "unscientific," and yet, to dispute the
sacredness of established principles of religion is to be "broad" and
"tolerant." Disagreeing with science is considered as vicious as
disagreeing with the multiplication table, but to disagree about religious fundamentals is like disagreeing about politics. The rational
point of view is not that science is unscientific, but merely that
religion as "unscientific," in the sense that physics is not the science
which best studies it. It is true, and may be said without offense, that
as theologians, some of the modern lyricists of science are good
physicists.

Why, it may again be asked, should the physics of relativity enjoy
the exclusive privilege of reinterpreting God and religion? Have
our ideas of God and religion been so closely built on a world of
"simple location" and "point" and "atom" and "event" that the
overthrow of these ideas means the overthrow of God? Because
time and space are found to be physical ultimates, does it follow
that God is Space-Time, or that Space is His Body and Time is His
Soul, as Professor Alexander would have us believe? Because the
physical universe can be better interpreted in terms of the organism
rather than those of mechanism, or in terms of "events" rather than

of location, does it follow that God is the "harmony of these events," as Professor Whitehead would have it? Why should it be the kingly privilege of the new physics, any more than of medicine or engineering, to interpret God in terms of its categories? Why should not the medical profession be entitled to revise the concept of God to conform to the insulin stage rather than the quinine stage of medicine? Why should not the Egyptologist be entitled, by the same logic, to revise our concept of God to be more in keeping with the discovery of the tomb of Tutankhamen? Because life evolves, does it follow that God evolves? Are the laws and hypotheses and categories of one science transferable indefinitely to other sciences? If the laws of psychology are not applicable to astronomy, and the laws of music not transferable to medicine, and the predicates of an amoeba not applicable to a Pantheon, why should the categories of physics, psychology, and sociology be applicable to God? There is far more reason, it is true, for applying biology to God than there is for applying chemistry or mineralogy, because the laws of biology are more universal than those of chemistry, and life is more universal than chemical elements. But the laws of organisms are no more applicable to the Deity than the laws of the chemical to the non-chemical, or the laws of the flesh to the spirit, or the laws of a protoplasm to God. There is danger that the uniform method will be carried too far. The temporal and the spatial are not the best approaches to the nontemporal and the nonspatial. We must hearken back to the wisdom of Aquinas, to learn all over again that metaphysics, and not physics, is the science which properly studies God: "*Quaedam vero sunt specuabilia quae non dependent a materia secundum esse . . . id est, divina scientia vel metaphysica.*" [10] The standpoint of religion and metaphysics is more inclusive than that of physics because being is more extensive than space-time. Man is greater than all his standpoints, and the real problem, as St. Thomas so well says, is to find the standpoint of the whole man and the whole universe from which to judge the validity of all partial and subordinate views. There is something tragic in our modern philosophy of religion, which is intoxicated by modern physics; space-time has gone to its head; whole cosmic streams of flux have swept it away from its moorings. Space-time has become a cult; time a God, and physics a Revelation. Philosophers of religion breathlessly await the latest decree of space-time physics as industrialists await the latest design in machinery. Sacred Scripture says, *"There will be no more time."* Philosophers of religion today have constructed, out of time, the universe and even God!

The above argument urged against a uniform method of science is based upon the difference in objects of the various sciences and the difference in methods by which these objects are studied. Here we pass on to a consideration of philosophy as such. As we have seen, it is our contention that since philosophy was not based entirely upon science, it need not change with every change in science. Many modern scientists turned philosophers assume that the *philosophia perennis* is based upon an antiquated cosmology, and since ancient cosmology has been repudiated, therefore the *philosophia perennis* falls with it. This is not true. A change in the science of description does not necessarily mean a change in the science of explanation. It may bring new analogies, or new difficulties, but it brings no new entity. A new cosmology brings only a new cosmology. The modern scientist does not claim to tell us what things are in their essence, for he can define things only by their properties or their behavior. Aristotle and the Scholastics built their metaphysics, ethics, and religion on principles which depended in no way upon a cosmological theory. The Scholastic belief about life being dependent upon a vital principle did not depend upon the biology of time which believed in spontaneous generation, neither did Aristotle's hylomorphism depend upon the antiquated four-element theory of cosmology. There are some things in life which do not rest on an entirely empirical basis, and he who would botanize on his mother's grave is apt to miss that great truth. In this connection Monsignor Ronald Knox correctly observes:

It is not to be disputed that the ancients did think of earth, air, fire, and water as irreducible elements, and that sometimes they built quaint superstructures of scientific belief upon these premises; St. Hilary informs us, for example, that salt is made out of fire and water. I have no notion why. But torture my brain as I will, I cannot see where our common notions of religion and ethics are based upon some form of physical speculation, rather than another. If somebody discovered tomorrow that it was all a mistake about atoms and electrons, and that after all, there was not and there could not be anything smaller than electrons, I should not find my faith in any way strengthened, or the work of Christian apologetics one tittle easier.... It is all very well to tell me that the chair I am sitting on is in reality a mass of whirling electrons, but it is I who am based on the chair, not my faith. St. Thomas never told me that it was not a mass of whirling electrons; and even if he had and I was now forced to disbelieve him, I should not therefore conclude that his speculations about the nature of God were equally inaccurate. For the life of me, I cannot see what the trouble is supposed to be about.[11]

All those philosophies which were built upon a scientific theory passed away with the scientific age. To marry the spirit of any age means to be a widow in the next. The trouble with such philosophies is that they suit only the spirit of one age, and are suitable for no other. There is historical warrant for the statement that within twenty years Professor Alexander's space-time philosophy will be just as much outdated as the mechanistic philosophy of Spencer is today. It may also very well be that some of the scientific theories mentioned in this book will be antiquated before the book is published. But a hundred years from now, some philosophers of the Great Tradition will apply the immutable principles of common sense to judge the latest lyricism of a Barnes or a Whitehead of that future day.

Relativity deserves special consideration. It is quite generally asserted that, because Einstein has proven the relativity of space-time, therefore morals, truth, and God are all relative to a point of view. This is unjustified for two reasons: morals and God are not grounded uniquely on a changing cosmology, but on the intrinsic nature of things as studied by the science of metaphysics; those who think relativity means only relativity without a corresponding absolute standard of measurement do not understand the theory itself. Relativity does not mean exclusively that space and time are relative to the observer; it also means that Einstein has given us an absolute measurement by which we can find the constants between the variety of space-frames and time-frames in the universe.

As Bertrand Russell points out, the word *relative* presumes "relative to something." There is something constant in the theory of relativity, almost something absolute, for which reason Sir Oliver Lodge says it might have been called a "fundamental theory." Though space and time are relative to the observers, there is a relation between these space-frames and time-frames. Herein lies possibly the greatest contribution of Einstein—the "absolute" character of his theory of relativity. Although observers move in different space-frames and different time-frames, there is a certain definite relation between them. If any given observer takes his space and time measurements of any pair of events and combines them in a certain way, he will get a certain result. According to Einstein's mathematical theory, the square of the space-interval minus the square of the time-interval of any particular combination of events is constant through free space. This formula holds true whether we are in motion relative to the room or relative to the moon. This does not mean that the length of the rod is the same in all cases, or that any of the measurements is the true one. It does mean, however, that two observers moving with a uniform relative velocity can arrive at the same mathematical statement of the phenomena. More generally it means that everything is not relative, in the sense that there is no unification of relations, but that there is a certain relationship of four-dimensional space which is constant for all observers, regardless of the time and space. Bertrand Russell observes:

It is a striking merit of Einstein's theory that he succeeds in expressing the laws of nature in a form which is the same for all observers, whatever their motions and whatever their systems of measurement. Einstein's theory enables us to isolate those absolute features of the world which are entirely independent of the observer. For this reason, Einstein's theory of relativity could justly be called the theory of absolutes, and if it had been so called, many popular misunderstandings of it would have been avoided.

PHYSICS, CAUSALITY, AND FREEDOM

The science of physics has not in itself any direct bearing on philosophy of religion, except when it ventures into a criticism of those principles belonging to the domain of philosophy. Physicists have done this recently by discussing the problem of causality, which is all important for philosophy because of its relevance to the proofs for the existence of God. Until the time of the new advances of modern physics, philosophy knew but three general positions concerning the nature of causality: the empirical position which contended that causality was merely a certain order experienced in the sequence of sensation. One thing follows another thing —for instance, fire when a match is struck. We have in this theory only sense perceptions which accompany movement, but no causal link. From the same sensory complexes as cause, the same or similar complexes follow as effect. Causality only seems to have an objective meaning because of its utility or because of force of habit.

A reaction against this position was the attitude of Kant, who saw that the empirical theory ended in solipsism. Desiring to give to causality the same certitude which Newton had given to science, Kant lifted it entirely out of the order of the empirical into the a priori category of the mind. It became certain, but at the cost of being subjective. The rational position is that causality is neither wholly empirical nor wholly mental, but a conjunction of both.

At the present time, the problem of causality has passed from the domain of philosophy, where it belongs, to the domain of physics.[12] Before inquiring the fate it met at the hands of the physicists, it would be well to inquire into the reason for this transfer to physics. Three reasons may be offered: First, the general anti-intellectual character of modern thought has made it impatient of metaphysics, and the equally general tendency to equate all knowledge with empirical evidence has made the world suspicious of a principle whose basis is not wholly factual. Secondly, knowing little of the traditional and common-sense philosophy concerning causality, and familiar only with the one-sided statements about causality made by two extreme schools of empiricism and idealism, modern science has felt that philosophy has failed to solve its own problems. And in the words of Max Planck: "When philosophy has failed in a given instance, we are perfectly justified in turning to science." Thirdly, the most important reason of all, philosophy today is wrongly regarded as the science of the *general* instead of the science of the rational and the *intelligible*. The supreme business of philosophy, from the modern point of view, is to synthesize the conclusions of the various sciences. By its nature it is eclectic and synthetic. Traditionally, philosophy has never been just a summary of empirical sciences, but rather an explanation of these sciences in the light of superior principles. Max Planck, who has written much on causality, labors under this confusion of the true nature of philosophy. He gives an example of two travelers visiting a country. One is interested in the general features of the landscape, the patterns of the meadows and the woodlands. The other is interested in flora, fauna, and mineral products. The first, says Planck, is general and vague, the other is particular and scientific. And so it is argued philosophy "must seek information from the special branches of

science in regard to particular features of the problem at issue."
Naturally, if philosophy is interested in the general, and science in
the definite, the particular, or "scientific," it follows that philosophy
has nothing worth while to say concerning causality. Hence the
problem has shifted to the domain of physics.

This brings us to the question: "What has science to say concerning causality?" There are two views, both closely allied, but the
latter a shade more respectful to nonphysical causality. The first
view denies that causality is a valid principle, since the Quantum
Theory proves that there is indeterminacy in the universe. Werner
Heisenberg's Principle of Indeterminacy states that an electron may
have position or it may have velocity, but both cannot be known
simultaneously. The more exact the determination of the position
of an electron, the more inexact becomes the velocity; and the more
exact its velocity, the more inexact the position. If we know where
it is, we do not know how fast it is going; if we know how fast it
is going, we do not know where it is. An electron can be seen only
when it emits light, but it emits light only when it jumps, so that
to see where it was, you have to make it go elsewhere. The conclusion is that the average result of many trials might be predicted;
and in this sense the laws of physics cannot predict an event, they
tell only the chance of its occurrence. Why then posit a law which
cannot be determined in a universe which is indetermined? Causality,
therefore, does not apply to the fundamental operations of nature.
The root of every physical law is not *causal* but *statistical*.[13] Max
Planck generalizes on the indetermined character of an electron and
concludes that "causality is by no means a necessary element in
the process of human thought."[14] The law of causality in its usual
classical formulation can no longer be applied generally, because it
has definitely been found to fail to apply in the world of atomic
phenomena.

The second scientific view of causality makes a distinction between the actual world and the physical world picture. The distinction between the two is something akin to the distinction Eddington
draws between Table 1 and Table 2 in the Introduction to his
Nature of the Physical World. This second view contends that
causality does not hold for the physical world which is given by
the sense, but is valid for the physical world picture which is a
mental picture created for the purpose of escaping from the un-

certainty which inheres in every individual measurement. The actual world is inaccurate; the second is accurate, even though directly observable quantities do not appear. Any event in the physical world picture is caused if it is predictable. The word "event" is reserved for what is going on in the physical world picture. The actual world does not allow a strict determinism; the world picture does allow a determinism, not in the strict sense of the term, but in the predictable sense.

Eddington identifies *causation* with the actual world picture and *causality* with the physical world picture.

For convenience I shall call the relation of effect to cause *causation*, and the symmetrical relation which does not distinguish between cause and effect *causality*. In primary physics causality has completely replaced causation. Ideally, the whole world past and future is connected into a deterministic scheme by relations of causality. Up till very recently it was universally held that such a determinate scheme must exist (possibly subject to suspension by supernatural agencies outside the scope of physics); we may therefore call this the "orthodox" view. It was, of course, recognised that we were only acquainted with part of the structure of this causal scheme, but it was the settled aim of theoretical physics to discover the whole.[15]

CRITICAL APPRECIATION

The science of physics has a perfect right to make an abstraction from the metaphysical principle of causality, as the biologist has a right to make an abstraction from sense knowledge, for "scientific investigation does not lead to a knowledge of the intrinsic nature of things." [16] Physics is within its province when it makes a distinction between causation and causality, and regards the former as the traditional concept, and the latter as the harmonious relation between events. Not being concerned with ultimate causes, but only with secondary and proximate causes, the science of physics must not be expected to find rigorous causality. Matter in its superficial manifestations may reveal only statistical relations and never causal ones. "Whether or not there is a causal scheme at the base of atomic phenomena, modern atomic theory is not now attempting to find it." [17]

It is quite another matter to argue that because the quantum theory reveals indeterminism, therefore the principle of causality is invalid. The electron manifests no moral sense, but we may not say that therefore there is no moral sense in the universe. The metaphysical principle of causality is not necessarily invalid because it is not found applicable in the world of electrons. What is called indeterminism may only be our ignorance of the way nature works. But even though indeterminism were proved beyond the shadow of a doubt, it would in no way affect the validity of the principle of causality in the realm of *ultimates*.

Arthur H. Compton views the problem correctly in answer to his question:

Does this mean, however, that for the proton the law of causality, that all things happen "with a cause and by necessity," is no longer valid? It means at least that no physical experiment can test this principle on an atomic scale. The philosopher may retain the idea of rigid law as applied to "things in themselves" if he so desires; but he cannot refer to experiment for its verification.[18]

And it might be added, the experiment is not necessarily a *verification* of the law, but only one of its possible applications. Because the principle is not verified in the study of electrons, it does not follow that it is untrue, any more than virtue may be said to be nonexistent because the electron does not manifest it.

The assumption behind the universal denial of the principle of causality is that causality has a wholly empirical basis. The truth is that experience is not the efficient or formal cause of our assent to the first principles; it is only the material cause,[19] the instrument which furnishes the matter. There is no question of comparing the data furnished by the senses, or of watching the succession of phenomena. Empirical science claims there is no other motive for assent to a first principle than sensible experience. On this view, a principle is at the mercy of a discovery. Traditional thought agrees with the empirical position in holding that sensible experience is necessary, but it disagrees by making that experience the condition of the principle, but not the principle itself. A window is a condition of light in a room, but it is not light.

The efficient cause of assent to first principles is the mind. This is the reasoning of Aristotle in the fifteenth chapter of his *Posterior Analytics*, in which he shows that sense-knowledge should precede a knowledge of principles. He is careful not to make sensible data the total cause of the principles. To bridge the abyss between sensible data and the universal character of first principles, he points to the action of a faculty superior to the senses. Without the intervention of this faculty, which is the intellect, it would be impossible to escape from the sensible and the particular.

The modern philosopher who would overthrow all causality because of the applications of the Quantum Theory assumes that the laws of physics are the foundation of metaphysical laws, or that the higher laws of thought are merely interpretations, generalizations, and musings on the physical laws. Rather it is the contrary that is true. God, for example, is not called good because man is good. Rather man is good because God is Goodness. An interesting proof of this statement is to be found in the Scholastic theory of spiritual gravitation. Newton's law of gravitation stated that bodies increase their speed as they get closer to the earth. The Scholastics also stated that the fall of a body became more rapid as it got closer to that which was natural for it. They, of course, gave no mathematical formulation of the law.

Quanto corpus grave magis descendit, tanto magis confortatur gravitas ejus propinquiatatem ad proprium locum; et ideo argumentatur quod si cresceret in infinitum velocitas, quod cresceret etiam in infinitum gravitas.[20] *Cujus etiam signum apparet in motibus naturalibus; nam omnis motus naturalis intensior est in fine, cum recedit a termino suae naturae non convenienti; quasi natura magis tendat in id, quod est sibi conveniens, quam fugat id, quod est sibi repugnans.*[21]

This law was universal for the Scholastics. Long before Newton thought of applying it to the solar system, they were applying it even to the ascendancy of a soul to its union with God. The "Swan Song" of a poet is his last work, not only in the sense of time, but in the sense of its perfection. His facility for writing increases as it approaches more closely the goal of poetical perfection. Nature loves the whole more than the part because the whole is its perfection. That is why the hand willingly exposes itself to save the body. In like manner, man should love God more than himself, for man naturally tends to God as his perfection.[22]

This law of gravitation was applied even to the angels. The more intense their love of God, the higher the angels in their hierarchy.[23] Applying it to the order of grace, St. Thomas writes: *"Gratia autem inclinat in modum naturae; ergo qui sunt in gratia, quanto plus accedunt ac finem, plus debet crescere."* [24]

Such a cosmic sweep of gravitation extending from spirit to matter suggests that the Newtonian expression was only a mathematical and physical expression of a law universally valid. The law of gravitation, in the universal sense, was first a spiritual law, and then a physical one, and not vice versa. Souls most deeply in love with God do not tend to God more rapidly because of the Newtonian law of gravitation. Rather, matter tends to the earth as a reflection of the higher law. In like manner, causality in the lower order is only a feeble reflexion of causality in the higher. The will is not free because the electron is indetermined. Rather, the electron is indetermined as a dim far-off echo of freedom in the moral universe.

PHYSICS AND FREEDOM

The science of physics has ventured into the field of philosophy by discussing freedom. The science of psychology, which should concern itself with the problem of freedom, has bequeathed it to the science of physics, which should not. Psychology has become more and more deterministic and behavioristic; physics has become more and more free and indetermined. Physics repudiated causality because it could not discover the position and velocity of an electron; it has welcomed freedom for the same reason. The electron passes from one orbit to another without passing through intermediate orbits; it almost seems that it ceases to exist at one moment, and then begins to exist at another. Because science never knows where the electron will jump, it can only make statistical guesses. The general conclusion is that atoms appear to be determined when we observe them in a mass of millions, but individual atoms behave as if they had "free will." Accident and caprice seem to be at the heart of the universe. It is not uncommon to hear free will justified on the basis of the uncertainty in the atom. "Physics is no longer pledged to a scheme of deterministic law. Determinism has dropped out altogether and it is at least open to doubt whether it will ever be brought back. ... Science therefore withdraws its opposition to free will." [25] "Science has no longer any unanswerable arguments to bring against our innate conviction of free will." [26] "If we wish to emancipate mind we must to some extent emancipate the material world." [27]

The problem here is similar to the problem of causality. Does

the quantum theory prove the freedom of the will? Is physics justified in applying its categories to philosophy? Because there is indeterminism in physics, does it follow that there is freedom in the
will? Must the material world be emancipated in order to make
room for the emancipation of the mind?

The Principle of Indeterminism upon which the freedom of the
will is supposed to be based, is not an established and proved principle of science. A truly scientific attitude would scruple at applying
a dubious hypothesis to the whole of the universe, inclusive of matter
and mind. Bohr claims indeterminacy to be an established principle;
Einstein, as well as Bertrand Russell, contends that it is not established. Their view is that since either the position or the velocity
may be precisely measured, each is a definite quantity, and a complete theory should make possible an exact knowledge of both.
Einstein writes:

I am entirely in agreement with our friend Planck in regard to the
stand which he has taken on this principle, but you must remember what
Planck has said and written. He admits the impossibility of applying the
causal principle to the inner processes of atomic physics under the present state of affairs; but he has set himself definitely against the thesis
that from this *Unbrauchbarkeit,* or inapplicability, we are to conclude
that the process of causation does not exist in external reality. Planck
has really not taken up any definite standpoint here. He has only contradicted the emphatic assertions of some quantum theorists and I fully
agree with him. And when you mention people who speak of such a
thing as free will in nature, it is difficult for me to find a suitable reply.
The idea is of course preposterous.... The scientist, I think, is content
to construct a perfectly harmonious picture on a mathematical pattern,
and he is quite satisfied to connect up the various parts of it through
mathematical formulas without asking whether and how far these are
a proof that the law of causation functions in the external world.[28]

The presumed basis for freedom of the will rests upon the am-
biguous use of the word "determined." Determined may mean
"caused," or it may mean "measured." When the older opponents
of freedom of the will use the term "determined," they mean
caused, or explicable in terms of physical and not spiritual antecedents. But when the modern physicists use the term, they mean
"measured." The quantum, in other words, is "indetermined" or
"free" because we cannot measure both its velocity and its position.
It should be carefully noted that freedom of the will has nothing

whatever to do with measurement, but with causation. The will is not free because it cannot be measured; it is free because its actions are not completely and absolutely physically caused. *There is absolutely nothing in the quantum theory and the principle of indeterminacy to show that any physical event is uncaused.* There is therefore no basis in physics for the freedom of the will.

It would be well if physicists would proceed with the same caution St. Thomas used in speaking of the beginning of the world. He said that it could not be proved by reason that the world began in time; it could be known only by faith. He then proceeds to warn us not to give bad physical reasons for a belief that is grounded on a higher reason or revelation, lest faith be exposed to ridicule. In like manner, as much as philosophers may welcome a return to a belief in the freedom of the will, they must be very careful not to welcome it back for poor reasons. If the only reason we have for belief in the freedom of the will is the inability to measure the jumps of the electron, then freedom of the will must vanish when we do succeed in measuring them. It is indeed curious that science, which protested so much against anthropomorphism, should itself degenerate into physicomorphism in which man's will is made to the image and likeness of an eccentric atom.

The inability to measure exactly the ultimate particles of matter does not mean there is no uniformity in nature. The statistical average means that events occur with some approximate uniformity. Unlimited variability would give no results. As Father McWilliams writes:

A little reflection will convince anyone that unlimited variability would give no results that could be averaged at all. An average allows for variations, it is true, but only for variations within certain limits. It is idle to talk of averaging phenomena whose quantitative and qualitative characters vary illimitably. Hence, to state that our physical laws are statistical averages is indeed to state that, for very fine measurements, they express only an approximate uniformity. But that is far from saying that there is no uniformity in the activity of the ultimate particles of matter. It is true that the alternative to determinism is free will, for an event is either predetermined by its antecedent conditions or it is not so predetermined. But events can be predetermined to be irregular as well as predetermined to be regular. Hence, the question of how much uniformity, or regularity, events may have is irrelevant in a discussion about whether they are predetermined. Eddington and others who insist on discussing these two totally disparate questions as identically one question have occasioned great confusion in their own minds and in the minds of their readers.[29]

The problem of the freedom of the will is not a problem of physics but a problem of philosophy, because modern physics is limited to a mathematical correlation of events. Those who would identify physics and philosophy draw their illustrations from physical science, and say that because material objects act a certain way man must act the same way. But in so deciding, the man of science is really reversing the fallacy of the savage who, finding that he himself was influenced by love and hate, fear and desire, gave to the rocks and the streams, the mountains and the flowers, a character like his own. The animism or the anthropomorphism of the primitive savage is no worse than the physicomorphism of the present-day philosophical scientist. Each shuts his eyes to one part of experience and generalizes from the other. The man of science assures us that a free spiritual being *must* act in the same way a material object would do, and hence we are swamped with illustrations of free will drawn from guns, boots, sealing wax, and ships. If one draws up a scale of motives in the order of strength, he will be wrong again, for what is strongest today may be weakest tomorrow, and what is strong for one man may be weak for another. No possible classification can be suggested to determine which is the strongest motive. Then the determinist takes refuge in declaring that a motive is the strongest which proves itself so in competition with other motives, but that is equivalent to saying that the strongest motive is the one by which he is determined.

A world of difference exists between a material object and a mind. A material object acts because of something which *has* happened to it; a conscious being, because of something in the future which *will* or at any rate *may* happen. A book falls from the table because it has been pushed, not because it is going to be pushed. It may be objected, a boy is kicked and runs. The kick is the thing *that happened*, not what was going to happen. The answer is, the boy fell because he was kicked, just as a sack of potatoes would fall if it were kicked hard enough—but the sack of potatoes, even though it had eyes to see, would not have run away. Why did the boy run? Because he was kicked? No. There is nothing in a kick to make a boy run. The boy ran lest he should be kicked again.

He was moved by something in the future. The difference between an atom and a spirit is that when an apple, for instance, falls, it is moved by forces acting on it at the time, not by forces which may be conceived to be acting on it in the near future. It may be said that the motives which influence a man's action are present to his mind. Yes, they are, but the motives are the ideas of things not present. Surely it is in the highest degree unscientific to maintain that the behavior of a material particle under the action of a fixed and definite force acting on it *must* be a complete and adequate analogy for the action of a free spirit. As G. K. Chesterton has said: "I always feel sorry for the determinist. He never can say 'Thank you' for the mustard."

Freedom, on the contrary, belongs not to physics but to philosophy, and particularly to that branch of it which deals with an immaterial faculty—the intellect.[30] St. Thomas states the argument for the freedom of the will in i, q. 83, a. 1 of the *Summa:*

Man has free will: otherwise counsels, exhortations, commands, prohibitions, rewards, and punishments would be in vain. In order to make this evident, we must observe that some things act without judgment; as a stone moves downwards; and in like manner all things which lack knowledge. And some act from judgment, but not a free judgment; as brute animals. For the sheep, seeing the wolf, judges it a thing to be shunned, from a natural and not a free judgment, because it judges, not from reason, but from natural instinct. And the same thing is to be said of any judgment of brute animals. But man acts from judgment, because by his apprehensive power he judges that something should be avoided or sought. But because this judgment, in the case of some particular act, is not from a natural instinct, but from some act of comparison in the reason, therefore he acts from free judgment and retains the power of being inclined to various things. For reason in contingent matters may follow opposite courses, as we see in dialectic syllogisms and rhetorical arguments. Now particular operations are contingent and therefore in such matters the judgment of reason may follow opposite courses, and is not determinate to one. And forasmuch as man is rational, is it necessary that man have a free will.[31]

The argument may be analyzed into the following propositions: Everything has a "form." A man is what he is because he possesses the essence of man. A stone is a stone and not a tree by virtue of its "form." A cat is a cat because he has the "form" cat, but it is a particular cat because that form has been individualized by matter. The intellect, being a spiritual faculty whose operation transcends matter, has the power of abstracting "forms" hidden in matter. The intellect has the power of becoming all things, of possessing within itself the form of "tree," or "bird," "man"—everything. But not only does it possess particular "forms"; it is also capable of knowing all "forms"—even the idea of "Truth," "Goodness," "Beauty," and not merely this truth, this beautiful thing, or this good apple. But if the mind can know all forms, even the infinite "Good," it must be free. The will is a rational appetite; it pursues an object presented to it by the intellect. But the rational will can be irresistibly drawn only by that which reason proposes as so universally attractive that it contains no dissatisfactory feature. As long as the thought of an object reveals any disagreeable aspect, the will has not that which alone can satisfy it; it can therefore reject it. Let the universal "form" of Goodness represent the infinite which alone can pull the will, as only a thousand-horse-power motor can lift an airplane of a given weight from the ground. Any *particular good* falls short of that infinite and therefore can no more necessarily pull it, than a twenty-horse-power motor can lift the airplane. During the present life no object presents itself to the intellect as so attractive as to compel the will.[32] Man can know the universal good; but the earth presents only particular goods. Hence, because of the disproportion between that which alone can "force" the will, and that which is actually presented, the will is free. If the mind can know the infinite variety of good things in the world and the good in general, and if the mind presents any of these to the will for acceptance, does it not follow that the will is not bound to choose any one of them? Who would say that an architect who has a general idea such as "house" was bound to build a house with three windows instead of thirty or sixty? Who would say that man who has a general idea of "good," and the general idea of all the good natures in the world, was bound to choose any one of them to the exclusion of the other? A stone has only one form, and hence must follow its law and fall to the ground when released from the hand. Man has many "forms" or "ideas," and hence may choose any of them.

If we had only one target to shoot at, we should not be free, but our intellect presents us with millions and millions of targets, and since no one target exhausts all the attractions of all possible targets, it follows that we are not bound to choose one rather than another.

No single target or desire can master the will in its infinite desire for the good as good, hence the will is free.

Once the freedom of the will has been established on sound intellectual principles, not subject to a theory of the atom, then physics may lend at least temporary support by affording new analogies. Suppose we set out to prove the freedom of the will to someone who did not believe in a soul, or who had no understanding of the great Scholastic system of philosophy. Then some such argument as this might be used, which though not absolutely convincing *per se* might be effective for a particular mind. We might begin by defining freedom in the broad sense of the term as the capacity to vary the emergents. It is a fact that everything in this universe is complex, even to the tiny atom with its proton and electron. Naturally the more complex a thing is, the more it may vary. There are many more combinations possible in a centipede with a hundred legs than in a stork with two, and sometimes apparently only one. If for present purposes we understand freedom as the power to vary, it is permissible to speak of "degrees" of "freedom." Water has two degrees of "freedom"—it can become steam or it can become ice. These variations or emergents are hardly sufficient, however, to merit being called "free." But when we come to man it is impossible to enumerate his degrees of freedom. Let us take the brain alone (for our modern psychologists will not let us talk about a soul). Suppose we assume that the degrees of freedom of variation alter with the number of possible correlations between the nerve cells of the brain. A certain physiologist who knows well the exact number of these nerve cells, and who also knows some higher mathematics, has estimated the possible combination of these nerve cells as expressible by 10 followed by 59 zeros. There would be, consequently, that number of degrees of freedom in the brain. Now, suppose we added to these possible correlations all the sense images, auditory images, all the thoughts, fancies, pictures, memories, and the like which solicit our will during the day—then we would have degrees of variation or choice which no man could number. Certainly, therefore, if the will is free in this broad sense of being able to choose between its material variations, how much more so is it free when you consider man endowed with a spiritual soul and therefore capable of knowing everything that is good or desirable— even the Infinite Good which is God.

THE PHILOSOPHY BEHIND MODERN PHYSICS

The philosophy of physics of the last century was frankly materialistic. The philosophy of contemporary physics is idealistic. Whitehead writes in his *Process and Reality:* "The train of thought in these lectures is Platonic . . . a series of footnotes to Plato." Bertrand Russell says: "Matter is a convenient formula for describing what happens where it isn't. . . . Matter is only an abstract mathematical characteristic of events in empty space." This gets very close to saying that matter is not material, that it is only a kind of a kink in space-time, or a system of spatio-temporal events with mathematical qualities, or "a wave of probability undulating in nothingness." The external world to modern physics is devoid of quality. Eddington says the scientist has no sense organs except one eye, and with that he looks either into a microscope or telescope. This is because color, sound and smell, are not "there." Heat is only an energy of motion of molecules, sound is only atmospheric waves, and color is a wave in an electro-magnetic spectrum. This philosophy has been known as the "Underhat philosophy" because the only events that we can know are those which take place under our own hats. As Whitehead said: "Nature gets credit which should in truth be reserved for ourselves: the rose for its scent, the nightingale for its song, the sun for its radiance."

Plato held that there were two ingredients in his philosophy: immaterial forms and a featureless medium in which these forms were manifested. Modern physics has somewhat the same two ingredients, and it is not surprising that modern physicists often revert to the example of Plato's cave to prove the idealism of their science. If you ask the physicist how he envisages the physical world, he will reply that he is concerned only with certain aspects of it, which are gained by abstraction. If you press him to explain the constituents of an electron, he will point to mathematical symbols. Then he will say that he cannot go beyond mathematical symbols for they are an ultimate. Matter, therefore, exists only insofar as the mind knows it, which is the essence of idealism.

Eddington tells us that the world has three constituents: "mental images" which are in our mind and not in the external world; "some kind of counterpart in external nature of an inscrutable character";

and "pointer readings" related to other "pointer readings." [33] Physics is a knowledge not of things of themselves, but of our responses to things through various measuring machines. The external world is less perceived than it is inferred. We construct the external world from messages which reach the brain through the nerves.[34] It is impossible to conceive of any nineteenth-century scientist completing his treatise on physics with a chapter on mysticism, but that is actually what we find in Eddington's *Nature of the Physical World*.[35]

Sir James Jeans arrives at mysticism in somewhat the same fashion. He argues that in the world there are no substances and qualities, but only relations, and the science best equipped to handle them is mathematics, which is spun out of our own mind. Having formulated mathematics, we turn to the outside world, and find that it obeys these mathematical laws which we formulated. From this he concludes that both our minds and our external worlds have originated in the constructive operations of some mind, and this mind behind the universe must therefore be mathematical; God is "The Great Mathematician." [36]

Modern physicists have appealed to Plato as their patron philosopher. Among modern philosophers, the appropriate patron would be Kant, who would authorize their contention that in this world of disorderly happenings, the mind selects only those features which fit into its ready-made characters. Eddington points out, "All through the physical world runs an unknown content which must really be the stuff of our own consciousness. Modern physics is moving in the direction of philosophical idealism."

There are many difficulties in the intuitional, idealistic, and mystical approach to reality as developed by modern philosophers, particularly regarding the reality of God. The method not only gives contrary and contradictory Gods, but even gives to the same philosopher, contrary and contradictory views. Eddington at one time speaks of mysticism as giving us a glimpse of something *objective*—"a reality transcending the narrow limits of our particular consciousness." [37] At another time he pictures this reality as *subjective* or as continuous with our own consciousness. "In this background we must find first our own personality, and then perhaps a greater personality." [38] The view becomes really only a projection of our consciousness when he says: "We see in nature what we looked for or are equipped to look for.... We have to build the spiritual world out of symbols taken from our own personality," and "in the mystical feeling the truth is apprehended from within, and is, as it should be, a part of ourselves." [39] "The physical no less than the mystical significance of the scene is not there; it is here in the mind." This is equivalent to making the world of "values," "personality," "God," and "religion," mind-created or mind-stuff. In like manner, Bergson's mysticism at one time acknowledges a God distinct from the world,[40] but at another time makes God part of the evolving world. For that reason, he rejects Aristotle for whom "immutability is rated higher than mutability." [41]

The mysticism of the scientists who have become philosophers asserts that the mind is constructive in relation to the world of science. But if the mind is constructive concerning these fields, why should we not believe it is also constructive when dealing with the world of value and of God, in which case these would be only subjective creations of the mind? This would account for the fact that the God every intuitionist and mystic arrives at, is different from that of his fellowman. If reality is a featureless flux, or élan, or mind-stuff, why should the mind project beauty into some spheres, mathematics into others, love into others, unless there be a basis in reality for these projections? Either there is a basis in reality for projecting God or there is not. If there is no basis, then our projection is an illusion. If there is a basis, then God is not just a projection or a construction of our mind. In other words, God means nothing unless reality demands Him as its explanation, meaning, and cause.

Neither Eddington nor Jeans discusses the limitations of the mystical approach to God, but Bergson does admit that "mysticism means nothing, absolutely nothing, to the man who has had no experience of it, however slight." [42] This immediately creates the query if God is to be denied to men who have not had that experience? Should not God be acceptable to all men? If God is Love, and Bergson admits this definition, why should Love deny to some the capacity to love? Only a small number of privileged souls are here held capable of union with God—the rest are condemned to doubt and to be forever the "prey of the votaries of static religion." The world is thus divided into those who are "impervious" to mysticism through no fault of their own, and the "elect" who are illumined by the interior master. Thus the ancient "Gnosis" and the less ancient Calvinism is revived, dividing men into two categories, those who know God, and those who through no fault of their own know Him not.

The anti-intellectual nature of modern mysticism makes it impossible to distinguish a mystical state from an illusion. The true way to distinguish one form of mysticism from another is by its doctrinal content, but when this is missing, how differentiate Buddhistic from Christian mysticism? Bergson says, "The complete mysticism is that of the great Christian mystics." Immediately afterwards he says, "Let us leave aside their Christianity." [43] Is not this pouring out the baby with the bath, or taking the Prince of Denmark out of Hamlet? Once the intellectual content which divides true from false mysticism is eliminated, there is left no guarantee of truth. Furthermore, none of the Christian mystics believed that they were free to interpret doctrine as they saw fit, or to ignore it completely; then upon what ground does Bergson do that which they not only refused to do, but considered impossible? Religion in his scheme becomes only an emotion, or an urge to love without *knowing* the nature of what is loved.

It is to be admitted that mysticism has the value of corroborating a proof for the existence of God arrived at rationally, but it cannot initiate that proof. The mystical approach, Bergson himself admits, is only probable. [44] Once void of its intellectual content, it can never *define* what it perceives, and definition is of the essence of knowledge; it can never *communicate* what it feels, for an emotional state is incommunicable. Finally, it cannot defend its truth, or distinguish it from the false, because it has repudiated the intellect which is the faculty of the true. The rational element in religion must be restored, if religion is to have any content, truth, or universality. Feelings, emotions, and mystical states are individual; ideas and truths are universal. The intellect will once more return to philosophy when the true critical spirit returns—that is, when philosophers see that the anti-intellectualism of the present day is a protest against a distorted view of the intellect which was held by the mechanists, but not by the traditional intellectualists of the ages.

Chapter IX

COMPARATIVE RELIGION AND PHILOSOPHY

The science of comparative religions is a valid and necessary science, with its own legitimate object and method of procedure. It is neither anti-religious nor anti-Christian. In many sciences we find the comparative method employed, as in comparative philology, comparative anatomy and comparative medicine. Comparative religion as a science proceeds along three lines: *Hierography* —or the observation of religious phenomena for the purpose of knowing and describing them. *Hierology*—adds to the observation, the discovery of phenomenal laws and shows how they explain, insofar as possible, the facts of religion. *Hierosophy*—adds to the observation and the discovery of phenomenal laws, a metaphysical approach which attempts to determine their intimate nature, fundamental laws, and value. The first registers or observes; the second classifies and furnishes an empirical explanation; the third speculates. Hence, we have observation, co-ordination, and interpretation. This, in brief, is the legitimate method of comparing religions.[1]

But sometimes comparative religion is made a philosophy; all religions are reduced to historical phenomena alive at various periods of history, none of which has absolute validity. In order that comparative religion may not degenerate into a relativist philosophy, certain basic principles must be kept clearly in mind.

THE PRINCIPLE OF DEMARCATION

The distinction between *method* and *doctrine* must be rigidly preserved. A scientist may study things through a yellow glass: that is his method of working. But if he concludes that everything is yellow, he has enunciated a doctrine. A method is only an approach to a problem; a doctrine is a solution.

The method used in the study of any group of facts depends on abstraction. For example, a physicist in seeing a man jump from a bridge abstracts the law governing falling bodies; the psychologist abstracts the mental states which prompted the act. And so one might go on enumerating many other "angles" of approach, any one of which might be legitimate. Methods are multiplied and varied, but a method is not a doctrine, sometimes for the very simple reason that the method of abstraction omits so many other important aspects that it is incapable of giving an *explanation* which covers all of the facts. A biologist may indeed study life in its physico-chemical manifestations, and a psychologist may study mind in its physiological reactions, but it would be wrong for the biologist to erect his method and his narrow abstraction into a doctrine and say that life is only a combination of chemicals. It would be wrong for the psychologist to erect his method into a doctrine and say that mind is only a combination of visceral reactions. In the field of religion, likewise, it is one thing to observe the religion of a people, and to discover empirically that there is nothing revealed in their religion, but it is quite another thing to say that revelation is impossible and hence cannot be found. It is always legitimate for natural sciences to explain phenomena in terms of secondary causes, but to deny everything which falls outside their method is to be so unscientific as to render all progress through higher sciences impossible. For example, when Renan lays down the principle that "everything in history has a human explanation," [2] he has stepped outside the methods of his own science and pronounced a doctrine intended to govern those who are more interested in fundamental and primary causes. To imagine that one can exhaust the secret of the real by a single procedure is to forget that reality, like a diamond, has many facets which are worthy of consideration. Opticians must not teach that man has no ears, nor a chiropodist that man is made up of only feet, most of which are bad, nor the historian of primitive religion that all religion is primitive and therefore closely allied to barbarism.

THE PRINCIPLE OF THE PRIMACY OF THE SPIRITUAL

The most common error in the interpretation of religious phenomena is the exclusive consideration of certain superficial resemblances or material details to the utter disregard of the spiritual and moral elements. This attitude of mind is due to the positivist prejudice which looks upon the intangible as the unreal. But such prejudice is an illusion. A critic has never interpreted a poem when he describes its meter and stress; a biologist has not explained life by enumerating all the chemicals in the human body; nor has a hierographer described religion when he notes its rites and describes them as dead formulas. The critic would have all the poems except the "soul divine," the biologist all the animal organs except life, and the historian all the externals of religion except its spirit. In religion, the whole cannot be described until one has taken account of the meaning behind the acts.

It is because men look upon the intangible as unworthy of scientific note that we have the thousand and one explanations of religion today, all of which take the analogous for the identical. Reinach, Frazer, and Wells are most conspicuous for this kind of confusion. As Morris Jastrow wrote: "The passion for hasty comparison is the characteristic of the comparative method still in infancy." [3]

What is forgotten in all these hasty comparisons is what might be called the common-sense Principle of the Primacy of the Invisible. *In every human work primacy belongs to the invisible element which is the soul of it, or the idea or the intention which inspires it.*

This principle, if kept in mind, would obviate abuses, and it is a principle very easy to justify. As a matter of fact, it is the intellect which separates man from the animal, and the intention which differentiates instinctive and reflective acts. Two men may do identical things, but the idea which inspired them may differ: dropping a coin in a collection box for example. Two facts may possess entirely different meanings, and if the facts alone were observed, and the meanings not understood, the interpretation of the facts would not be true. In religion peoples may perform a number of like ceremonies, but in one instance it may be to appease a god, and in another to worship him, but only the observer who knows that facts are intelligible through ideas, notes such a difference.

Take for example, the superficial comparisons made by H. L. Mencken between Mary, the Mother of Christ, and other women in history. This author says that the Virgin Birth of Christ had its origin in a "hundred hero cults" which also had Virgin Births. The proof, he alleges, that the Virgin Birth of Christ was built upon pagan legends is this: "It was natural that His mother should have the name of Mary, for that was the name borne by the mothers of a long line of other prophets and heroes with divine fathers, among them, Myrrha the mother of Adonis, Maya the mother of Buddha, Maia the mother of Hermes, and Maritala the mother of Krishna." [4] In other words, Mary and the Virgin Birth of the Son of God is a legend because "mothers of heroes with divine fathers" also had names which began with an *M*. This excursion into etymology is too absurd to merit a serious refutation. It is an obvious devotion to externals without any attempt to penetrate beyond literal resemblances. A study of the invisible element behind the legends and the Virgin Birth would have revealed that the resemblance between Myrrha and Mary was no closer than the resemblance between Mencken and Mercury.

Another instance of overlooking the primacy of the invisible is the oft-repeated attempt to build up a vast synthesis of "human sacrifices through the ages" to prove that Calvary is exactly the same as these sacrifices. The raw material for such a thesis has often been extracted from Frazer's *Golden Bough*.[5] But the case for the naturalness of Christianity is hardly so simple. Murder and human sacrifice may visibly be the same fact, but the idea behind each is different. One might kill aged parents to deliver them from infirmities, or to rid oneself of them. In one case, it is commiseration which inspires the act, in another it is selfishness. The great distance, to take another example, between the culinary art and the religious art is a difference of idea behind the act.[6]

The rites of communion could be the object of much confusion unless the invisible element or reason was sought. There are doubtless many external resemblances between Communion of the Eucharist and communion among primitive and pagan peoples. This is because man, being what he is, feels the need of communion with Divinity. But to confine oneself merely to the externals and ignore the spiritual element behind the act is to end in confusion worse confounded. This again is the error of H. L. Mencken when he compares the "god eating" of primitives with the cannibalism of the Polynesian savages and the eating of the buffalo by the Todas [7] of India, and all of them with the Christian communion.

There is no attempt to penetrate into the soul, or meaning, or intention of the different kinds of sacrifice; no research to distinguish a family repast which unites with an ancestor from a symbolical initiation, such as that in the cult of Mithra. Nor is there any distinction made between a cannibalism in which human eats human, and a communion in which the human communes with the Divine, so that he may live, and yet not live in himself but in God.

THE PRINCIPLE OF ORGANIC UNITY

In an organic whole, such as a living body, each cell and member must be understood in relationship to the unity. Even in the physical order chemicals in certain combinations behave differently from the way they do in other combinations. In like manner, a religion, with its liturgical, dogmatic, and ascetical codes, cannot be understood merely by a study of the parts, but only by a study of the parts in relation to the whole. To isolate details is to risk understanding the whole, just as to separate the arm from the body is to imperil understanding the function of the arm. As Bernard Bosanquet has expressed it:

A second of time may be apprehended as a part of a minute, or of a musical phrase, or of an act of forbearance, and its meaning varies accordingly.... Logical completeness or universality is not a deadening but a vitalizing quality, and thought is not a principle of reproducing reality with missions, but of organizing worlds and investing their detail with fresh significance.[8]

This principle applied to religion means that the details of a religion must be studied in relation to the whole of the religion itself, and not merely in comparison to another religion, partial or whole. A detail of the Chinese religion, for example, is the particular number of prostrations and incensations, which might seem very unimportant to an outsider, but to a believer makes a distinction between heresy and sacrilege. The abstinence from meat on Friday is a Catholic practice. Among other religions there is also abstinence from meat on certain occasions, or altogether. But it does not follow that the Catholic abstains from meat for the same reason that a Mohammedan abstains from it, or that one practice was borrowed from the other. Keeping in mind the principle of organic unity, we shall study each detail in relation to the whole. Here one immediately sees why the Catholic practice differs from all other religions: it bears a relation to the whole organic structure of Redemption. Because Christ died for the sins of the world on Friday, Catholics have seen fit to honor that day of sacrifice by abstinence from meat. Just as predicates have meaning only in relation to the subject and the verb, so too the details of religion have meaning in relation to their organic whole and the life which inspires them. It is only when we pass from partial meanings to the total view that we are free from an inner unrest and a sense of logical shortcoming. A sense of proportion, expressing itself in a scale of qualitative differences, must ever be the guide in the scale of completeness of outlook. Totality and comprehensiveness—these are the keys to understanding the impelling motives of logic.

FALSE ASSUMPTIONS UNDERLYING COMPARATIVE RELIGION

Without denying the great contributions which the science of comparative religion has made to the general fund of knowledge, it still remains true that no science has ever been so much abused and distorted by those who bear a prejudice either to natural religion in general, or to Christianity in particular. With the slipping of a few logical cogs, it is easy to reduce natural religion to a superstition and Christian religion to a syncretism of pagan cults. A few unwarranted assumptions creep into the reasoning process and religion is dissolved into a baseless fabric. Logic and common sense cannot permit these assumptions to go unchallenged, and here we set down a few of them, that have been applied either to natural religion or to the Christian religion.

The first false assumption is that the religion of the savage today represents the religion of the primitive man; hence, one can conclude from the one to the other. Such an assumption helps create the illusion that religion belongs to the infancy of the race, and not to its adult or civilized stage. It lurks behind Einstein's view that religion once was a religion of fear, then of love, but that now, in our civilized days, it will become cosmic, which means it will be a religion only in the scientific sense of communion with the universe. It seems, too, to give weight and support to Bertrand Russell's contention that "traditional religion was based upon a sense of man's impotence in the face of natural powers" [9] during the infancy of the race.

It is this absolutely unanalyzed and taken-for-granted principle which inspires Mencken's *Treatise on the Gods*, wherein he explains the origin of religion:

For many generations, perhaps for many thousands of years, he had been finding life increasingly unpleasant, for the cells of his cortex had been gradually proliferating, and the more they proliferated, the more he was afflicted by a new curse: the power to think. Having escaped his enemies and eaten his fill, he could no longer take this brutal ease under a kindly tree. The doglike beasts who were his playmates and the apes who were his sardonic cousins were far happier. Their minds were empty; they could not generalize experience; they were innocent. But man suffered under the stealthy, insidious assaults of his awakening brain, now bulging and busy like a bulb in spring. It not only caused him to remember the tree that came near falling upon him last week; it also enabled him to picture the tree that might actually fetch him tomorrow. He began to live in a world of multiplied hazards and accidents, some of them objectively real and some residing in the spooky shades of his burgeoning consciousness. Once he had been content, like his faunal inferiors, to rejoice over the danger escaped; now he was harried by a concept of danger in general, and tortured by speculations about its how and why.... There was the device of trying to halt the falling trees by appealing or protesting to the unseen but palpable powers which resided in their branches, or somewhere else aloft, and caused them to fall. This was the device of magic or religion.[10]

One of the defects of this assumption of the correspondence between the savage and primitive man is that it supposes the savages remained stationary while the rest of mankind, who outgrew religion, progressed. But why should one have evolved, and not the other? If evolution is the law of life, as such writers contend, why should it apply to one group and not to another? May it not be true that these so-called primitive men are really degenerate men, and that instead of having evolved, they rather devolved? Certainly that is true of many civilizations. The Aztec civilization is today a tattered remnant of its former glory. But whether there be evolution or devolution, there must never be a confusion of the lowest forms of humanity with the oldest, for the two are quite distinct. If we carried out this principle in other walks of life, then the supposed wisdom of grandfathers would have to give way to the superior babblings of infants.

But even if the savage peoples of our day did represent the primitive people, it still remains true that the best way to study religion is not in its poorest expression but in its highest. It is hardly scientific to say that religion is nothing but magic or totemism because primitive people were magicians or totemists, for primitive mythology at its best is a mélange of heterogeneous elements, crude superstitions and beliefs. The psychologist who wants to know the meaning of consciousness does not study it in a sensitive plant, but in a man. A biologist who confined his interests solely and uniquely to embryos and rudimentary formations, would be far less capable of understanding life in its fullness than one who studied life in its highest expressions. What is true of biology and psychology is true of religion. One is less apt to understand religion when attention is fixed on its lower forms or superstitions, than when directed to its nobler and higher manifestations. One can learn far more about art in the Louvre than one can by watching the dubious artistic creations of children in the first grade. The full-blown rose tells us more about roses and perfume than the seed, and the perfect expressions of religion tell us more about it than its early superstitions and exaggerations or even distortions.

It is quite true that the primitive forms are important in studying the evolution or unfolding of religion, just as the embryo is more important for that same purpose than the developed organism, but the order of time must not be confused with the nature of a thing. In the order of time, the imperfect does precede the perfect, but in the nature of things the perfect precedes the imperfect. In the order of time we must first be children before we can become men, but in the order of nature we must be man before we can reproduce our kind. In the order of time, therefore, certain peoples may have begun with magic and others with animism, but it is not legitimate to conclude that religion is only magic or totemism.

It has sometimes been contended that one could never decide upon the truth of religion unless he had a knowledge of its primitive forms. This assertion again confuses historical and hybrid manifestations with the highest and best expression of religion. It is no more necessary to know the imperfect forms of religion in order to decide upon the nature of religion, than it is necessary to know all the theories of antiquated astronomy in order to understand certain present certainties of that science. To say that one thing is like another thing, is to say that it is also unlike that thing. All resemblances imply differences. I may say that a man is like a monkey, but because I say that man is like a monkey, I imply that he is also unlike a monkey. Likeness never means identity, nor does resemblance mean sameness. Nor do similarities between religions mean they are all alike, or that one is just as good as another—which sometimes is meant to imply that one religion is just as bad as another.

It has been a short step for many philosophers who abuse the comparative method to argue that simply because religions are like one another, there is, therefore, no such thing as religion. That is just like saying that because hats are of different shapes, there is no such thing as a hat; some would even conclude that there is no such thing as a head, or baldness, or sunstroke.

The second false assumption is that *the Divine and True religion must be different from all other human religions. Since the Christian and non-Christian religions are not absolutely different, in all details, it is falsely concluded that the Christian religion is not Divine.*

This assumption involves the problem of whether or not there may be resemblances between religions. A full understanding of this assumption involves a recognition of the distinction between truths of the natural order, and truths of the supernatural order.[11] Natural truths are those which can be known by the unaided reason alone, for example, the existence of God. Supernatural truths, in the strict sense, are those which exceed the powers of reason and can be known only by revelation, for example, the Trinity. The problem then divides into whether or not there may be resemblances between natural truths in the Christian and pagan religions, and whether or not there may be resemblances between the Christian and pagan religions as regards supernatural or revealed truths.

As for natural truths, there may be considerable resemblance, because natural truths may be known to anyone endowed with reason. God has illumined every man coming into the world. The first principle of the practical reason and the first principle of the speculative reason are the foundation stones upon which every man may build the rational edifice of art and science, morality and philosophy. Human minds, whether pagan or Christian, unlettered or learned, have a natural curiosity that inquires into the why and the wherefore of existence, as well as the origin and purpose of all their inspirations and yearnings. The uniformity of elementary doctrines, general liturgical themes, and rudimentary practices reveal the fundamental identity of human nature in all places and at all times. Since all human beings have the same physical constitution and live in society, and are witnesses of the same phenomena of nature, except differences of climate, they are all driven to seek for causes behind these phenomena, and the laws behind their social code, and thus are they led to certain fundamental religious concepts.[12]

Pagans have natural virtues, for they have, as St. Paul tells us, the law of God graven on their hearts. Man can, without faith or grace, know the difference between good and evil, immortality, supreme happiness, and at least in a vague way, sanction and retribution, all of which are elements of religion as such, and hence common to all humanity. That is why religion is a universal phenomenon. Cicero is authority for the statement, at the close of the last century before Christ, that there is "no nation or tribe so uncultured that it does not acknowledge some sort of deity, and belief in God is inborn in all men, engraved upon their souls as it were." [13] Plutarch agrees with him:

If you travel from country to country you may find cities without walls, without sciences and arts, without kings and palaces, without riches; cities where money is unknown or not in use; cities without public buildings and theatres; but no one has ever seen or will ever see, a city without temples, gods, prayers, oaths and oracles; a city which does not seek by means of sacrifices and religious festivals to obtain favors and avert evils.[14]

In all the cities of the world there is something that corresponds to a government building, divided into various rooms occupied by city officials. The resemblances do not come from their being designed by the same architect, but from the sameness of the purpose for constructing the edifice. Destined for government, one building resembles another. In like manner, religions may have many things in common, because all are destined to satisfy certain aspirations of human nature. There are bound to be some resemblances by the mere fact that human nature, being the same, has the same general destination—the possession of beatitude and happiness.

Furthermore, human nature, feeling the weakness of its own intellectual power to attain truth, feels the need of revelation, and is predisposed to accept a prophet who claims he comes from God. Hence, the vague resemblances in all religions between the prophets, Messiases, and revelations. If God willed to send a prophet with unmistakable signs of his office, there would be some vague resemblance, at least, between him and the prophets of other world religions, because both respond to the aspirations of human nature. There would be analogy without imitation. Reason would then have to establish norms for itself to judge whether the purported revelation is true. That is why, in the science of Apologetics, rational bases for belief are studied in detail, to prove the uniqueness of Christian revelation in relation to the others.[15]

Even certain supernatural truths which are necessary for salvation could be known, through the mysterious ways of God, to peoples outside direct Jewish or Christian influence. St. Thomas says that if it were necessary to instruct them by an angel, God would send one. But apart from such an evidently miraculous way of communicating supernatural truths, there could still be certain vague similarities between a truly supernatural religion such as Christianity and pagan truths. After all, a very limited number of religious ideas is possible, and hence it would not be too much to expect that the true religion should overlap false ones. Furthermore, if God did reveal Himself to the world, it is only natural that He should encourage symbolism already familiar to men, instead of confusing them with things utterly foreign and unintelligible. St. Thomas, in speaking of God in relation to creatures, uses this analogy: "I see someone coming over a hill. I may know it is a man, without knowing it is Peter." Christian and pagan alike feel the need of deliverance from sin. The pagan may feel, as the Greek dramatists put it, that there must be some "god to accept on his own head the pangs of our own sins vicarious." He knows he needs redemption. In this sense he sees a man coming over the hill. The Christian has the same aspirations for a redeemer, but he knows definitely that the Redeemer is Christ. There is some resemblance between the pagan concept of a redeemer and the Christian. A true religion does not exclude all resemblances.

God's laws are not apart from Himself. Hence we must expect to find the true and genuinely supernatural revelation following the lines of human nature, these lines having been designed by the Creator to make a way, not only for the natural end of man's existence, but also for the supernatural end, which is the beatific vision. Because revealed, supernatural truth, in the strict sense, exceeds the nature, powers, and exigencies of reason, it does not follow that revelation is contrary to reason. Reason must first of all be able to establish for itself the reasonableness of the revelation—that it comes from God and is therefore worthy of acceptance.[16] Furthermore, the human reason, inasmuch as it is capable of knowing universal goodness and the reason of being, is in immediate relation to the universal principle of being, which is God.[17] Hence, the revelation will be more fittingly given to a reasonable being than to a stone or an animal.[18] There is in reason a potential aptitude for revelation should God choose to make it. Revelation does not demand a complete break with reason, either on the part of the subject who receives the revelation, or on the part of God Who gives it. It follows that when God prepares the climax of His Providence, He will bring into it all the common characteristic lines along which human thought has groped for the divine. The human mind is teachable. But if human reason teaches, why should not the Divine Reason Who made it also teach?

To apply these general principles to Redemption, it follows that since reason feels the need of deliverance, it may grope toward a religion with a Redeemer. When God reveals the great central truth of Redemption, reason can then see the fitness of the yearning for a Redeemer. In reading the *Golden Bough*, one reads of parallels between the Redeemer of Christianity and the dying gods of paganism. If one assumes the true religion breaks with reason, which discovered the natural truths of paganism, then it would seem that Christianity borrowed the idea of Redemption. But if one realizes that faith is the perfection of reason, that reason may dimly yearn for that which faith supplies, then one sees that the resemblances of the dying gods of paganism to the Christian doctrine of Redemption are, in a certain sense, a proof of the human craving for a Redeemer. There is evidently something in both which starts with first principles common to all men. Redemption is a harsh note indeed when struck on the crude instruments of the primitive savage or corrupted pagan. But when Christianity, thanks to a revelation, strikes the harmony of Redemption on the great organ of supernatural truth, then the savage and pagan mind can say in the analogy of St. Thomas: I know I needed Redemption. Now I know that the Redeemer is Christ. Hence there could exist superficial resemblances of doctrine, culture, and liturgy between Christianity and paganism, without prejudice to the Christian faith. In fact the Christian faith, while insisting it is unique, does leave place for just such resemblances.

The third false assumption is that *the resemblances between Christian and other world religions, are possible only through plagiarism, or borrowing, or imitation.* What seems to add color to this assumption is the fact that Christianity, with the exception of Islamism, is the last of the world religions in point of time, and is assumed to be a reproduction or copy of all others.

In answer to the question whether Christianity can be Divine if it borrows from other religions, a distinction must be made between *complete* and *partial* borrowing. If the borrowing is complete and Christianity in its entirety is nothing but syncretism of pagan practices and beliefs, then certainly, Christianity is not divine. But no one has ever charged Christianity with complete borrowing, for there are some elements in Christianity which are absolutely original.

Two elements must be original in order to escape the charge of complete borrowing and full imitation. First, there are the historical facts which serve as a basis of religion. If the Gospels were proved copies of previous documents, if the miracles worked were in imitation of those worked previously, if the prophecies were mere repetitions of what had been known among other religions and if Christ never existed but was only a literary creation of later ages, then Christianity could not escape the charge of being an imitation. But none of these facts can be established. Secondly to be considered are the doctrines proper to Christianity. There is uniqueness here, as there is in the historical basis. If the doctrines of the Eucharist, the Mystical Body, the Trinity, Sanctifying Grace were borrowings from other religions, then Christianity could not claim to be unique in history. But such is not the case.

If the borrowings are *partial*, and pertain to rites, ceremonies, and even philosophical notions, these matter but little, for these are, as we have seen, the common property of mankind. At least it is dangerous to speak of parentage, or borrowing, or plagiarism, when the elements themselves have no special characteristics. Each time the same factors are found, it is not necessary to look for origins in another religion, when these factors can be accounted for by reason.

Simply because all people have a conception of paradise, or a hell, or an immortality, it does not follow that one has borrowed from the other. The moral sense common to the human race, and the appetite for happiness are sufficient to account for it. Genuflections, incensations, sacrifices, consecrations—all of these human nature can invent without borrowing, for they fit into the psychological make-up of man. There might be a borrowing of philosophical concepts without any prejudice to the Christian religion. Philosophy is not the property of any race or religion, but the common property of thinking men. As a matter of fact, the Church does use many of the concepts of pagan philosophy. St. Augustine, one of the great lights of the Church, was a follower of Plato. St. Thomas was a follower of Aristotle.

The term philosophy here is not used in the sense of an opinion, for in the last analysis, there is only one truth. In the course of history, this great tradition of common sense and truth may receive different emphasis at different times, but in its essence it remains the same. Philosophical resemblances between Christianity and paganism are not prejudicial to the cause of Christianity, first of all, because philosophy is concerned only with natural truths, and Christianity with the supernatural, and secondly, because the introduction to Christianity is sound reason.

The argument from resemblances is not as simple as it sounds. In discussing the principle of organic unity, it was stated that things act differently in composition with other things. Even though every doctrine of Christianity were founded on other religions (which is not true), the problem would still be to explain how they happen to coalesce into an organic whole, and also how these various doctrines are changed by being part of this new whole, with its new spirit and its new soul.

All resemblances imply differences. That is why the Scholastic doctrine of God says that created things tell us about God in a twofold way: by affirmation and by negation. This doctrine speaks of the communicable attributes of God, such as Truth and Love, and the incommunicable, which are not shared by creation, such as infinity and aseity.

From the days of pragmatism, it has been popular to argue that since there has been a succession of philosophical systems, theories, and opinions, therefore there is no such thing as truth. In reference to religions, the pragmatist maintains that because of their variety there is really no such thing as religion. This is like reasoning that because in the days of Columbus some said the world was round, and others that it was flat, that Columbus should have concluded that there is no world.

It is extremely easy to fall into the error of saying that the same elements in religion demand the same causes, by emphasizing only the likeness of elements, but not their difference. But as one penetrates below the superficial resemblances between Christianity and other world religions, one sees radical and fundamental differences. The remarkable thing is that being so much like other religions, the Christian religion should be so very different. Here the logic turns against the naturalists, and instead of asserting "the same effects require the same causes" one could oppose the argument by saying "different effects, therefore, different causes." To ignore the differences behind the resemblances and to say that Christianity was produced by the same cause as other world religions is a trick of bad logic, akin to saying that because the thousands of paintings in the Louvre are similar, inasmuch as they all contain red, white, and blue colors, therefore, they were all painted by the same artist.

Resemblances do not prove borrowing or plagiarism, because the resemblances may be due to other causes than those of imitation. A classic example of muddle-headed reasoning which ignores this common-sense reflection on resemblances is afforded by Professor Whitehead, who says:

Athenaeus tells us that among the Persians, it was the religious duty of the King, once a year, at some stated festival in honour of Mithras, to appear in the Temple intoxicated. A relic of the religious awe of intoxication is the use of wine in the communion service.[19]

The implication here is that since wine is used in both Mithraism and Christianity, there is a relation of dependence one on the other. But the author fails to see that though wine is used in both instances, in one case, it is for the purpose of intoxication, and in the other, for the purpose of consecration. To see no difference in wine when it is used for intoxication and when it is used for consecration, means that a man is blind enough not to see any difference in a rope when it is employed to hold up a man's trousers, and when it is used to hold up his neck.

There are, for example, many resemblances between the Buddhist monks and the Franciscans as regards celibacy, hospitality, and the spirit of poverty, but it is certain that when St. Francis founded his order, Buddhism was unknown in the West, and when Franciscans met Buddhist monks in Asia, they never suspected any connection between their respective religions.[20]

G. K. Chesterton has given an example of how those who argue from the resemblances of religions are forced to impossible conclusions:

Comparative religion is very comparative indeed. That is, it is so much a matter of degree and distance and difference that it is only comparatively successful when it tries to compare. When we come to look at it closely we find it comparing things that are really quite incomparable. We are accustomed to see a table or catalogue of the world's great religions in parallel columns, until we fancy they are really parallel.... To compare the Christian and Confucian religions is like comparing a theist with an English squire, or asking whether a man is a believer in immortality or a hundred-per-cent American. Confucianism may be a civilization, but it is not a religion.

In truth the Church is too unique to prove herself unique. For most popular and easy proof is by parallel; and here there is no parallel. It is not easy, therefore, to expose the fallacy by which a false classification is created to swamp a unique thing, when it really is a unique thing. And there is nowhere else exactly the same fact, so there is nowhere else exactly the same fallacy. But I will take the nearest thing I can find to such a solitary social phenomenon, in order to show how it is thus swamped and assimilated. I imagine most of us would agree that there is something unusual and unique about the position of the Jews. There is nothing that is quite in the same sense an international nation; an ancient culture scattered in different countries but still distinct and indestructible. Now this business is like an attempt to make a list of Nomadic nations in order to soften the strange solitude of the Jew. It would be easy enough to do it, by the same process of putting a plausible approximation first, and then tailing off into totally different things thrown in somehow to make up the list. Thus in the new list of nomadic nations the Jews would be followed by the Gypsies; who at least are really nomadic if they are not really national. Then the professor of the new science of Comparative Nomadics could pass easily on to something different; even if it was very different. He could remark on the wandering adventure of the English who had scattered their colonies over so many seas; and call them nomads. It is quite true that a great many Englishmen seem to be strangely restless in England. It is quite true that not all of them have left their country for their country's good. The moment we mention the wandering empire of the English, we must add the strange exiled empire of the Irish. For it is a curious fact, to be noted in our imperial literature, that the same ubiquity and unrest which is a proof of English enterprise and triumph is a proof of Irish futility and failure. Then the professor of Nomadism would look round thoughtfully and remember that there was great talk recently of German waiters, German barbers, German clerks, Germans naturalising themselves in England and the United States and the South American republics. The Germans would go down as the fifth nomadic race; the words Wanderlust and Folk-Wandering would come in very useful here. For there really have been historians who explained the Crusades by suggesting that the Germans were found wandering (as the police say) in what happened to be the neighborhood of Palestine. Then the professor, feeling he was now near the end, would make a last leap in desperation. He would recall the fact that the French army had captured nearly every capital in Europe, that it marched across countless conquered lands under Charlemagne or Napoleon; and that would be wanderlust and that would be the note of a nomadic race. Thus he would have his six nomadic nations all compact and complete, and would feel that the Jew was no longer a sort of mysterious and even mystical exception. But people with more common sense would probably realise that he had only extended nomadism by extending the meaning of nomadism; and that he had extended that until it really had no meaning at all. It is quite true the French soldier has made some of the finest marches in all military history. But it is equally true, and far more self-evident, that if the French peasant is not a rooted reality, there is no such thing as a rooted reality in the world; or in other words, if he is a nomad there is nobody who is not a nomad.

Now that is the sort of trick that has been tried in the case of comparative religion and the world's religious founders all standing respectable in a row. It seeks to classify Jesus as the other would classify the Jews, by inventing a new class for the purpose and filling up the rest of it with stop-gaps and second-rate copies. I do not mean that these other things are not often great things in their own real character and class. Confucianism and Buddhism are great things, but it is not true to call them Churches; just as the French and English are great peoples, but it is nonsense to call them nomads. There are some points of resemblance between Christendom and its imitation in Islam; for that matter there are some points of resemblance between Jews and Gypsies. But after that the lists are made up of anything that comes to hand; of anything that can be put in the same catalogue without being in the same category.[21]

Furthermore, the argument of resemblances mistakes the meaning of originality. Originality does not consist essentially in the production of things absolutely new, but it may mean the surpassing of the common measure of the intellect by utilizing pre-existing materials in a new way.[22]

When a people loses its power of keen thinking, it very soon loses this conception of originality, and passes over to the mistaken idea of equating the original with the unorthodox. An unorthodox thinker is often mistaken for an "original thinker." Novelty and originality are unfortunately too often identified. It would be "novel" if I said that two and two make five. It would be commonplace to say that two and two make four, but if the latter could be said in such a way and in a language that no one would ever forget, it would be both original and orthodox.

Even a natural religion is original when it is able to take in the parcel of truths discovered by philosophical schools, and by a stroke of genius, or by the infusion of a new spirit, produce an ensemble which will not be a mosaic without unity, but a system whose general co-ordination composes a truly new and perfect harmony. It is the idea which gives human works their value, and they can be made *new* if we inform them with a new thought, or develop them into a new synthesis. The point is that the utilization of pre-existing elements leaves intact the question of originality. When one has determined the dogmatic or ritual dependencies of one cult on another, one is not excused from further inquiring whether the borrowed parts, co-ordinated in a different synthesis, have not been vivified by a new thought. If they have, then there is originality, and a new cause must be sought for them in the direction of the new idea which informed and infused them. This is what is meant by the principle of organic unity.

Even suppose one could find that many of the liturgical elements, rites, and forms of worship which are found in Christianity, are actually to be found in Buddhism, would such similarities prove that Christianity was produced by these elements? It would no more prove it, than it would prove that a human body was produced by certain chemicals simply because the chemicals to be found in the human body are also to be found in a laboratory. The mixing of the chemicals will not produce a human body, because in addition to these elements there is a principle of unity which holds these elements together, and produces an entirely new synthesis, namely, a soul. Likewise, in the field of religion, the problem is not so much to find the same elements, but to discover the principle which unified these elements and made them, by that very fact, a totally new and different thing. It is quite true that the Mussulman adores a unique God, that the Brahman believes in a trinity, that the Buddhist venerates relics, and praises chastity, that the Egyptian believes in a judgment after death: it is equally true that the Christian religion contains all these doctrines and practices. But this does not mean that Christianity is a mélange of all these cults, and that there is nothing in it except what is common to all world religions. There is something else in addition to the elements, namely, the living unity which co-ordinates and synthesizes them.

The fourth false assumption declares that the supernatural is impossible, or at least indemonstrable. Hence comparative religions and the history of religions should be studied apart from all intervention of God.

This principle comes from that group which Jastrow describes in his *Study of Religion* "with decided prejudice against religion, which disqualifies them from judging religious phenomena calmly and dispassionately." Salomon Reinach, for example, in his *Orpheus*, allows his contempt for the supernatural to lead him to the denial of religion as "an ensemble of scruples which prevent the free exercise of our faculties." A priori denial of the supernatural is outside the scope of comparative religion, which is a science of observation and comparison. The supernatural belongs to an entirely different set of facts. Religions may be studied comparatively quite apart from their supernatural character, but it is one thing to abstract the supernatural character from religion and quite another thing to deny the supernatural. A chemical analysis of holy water will show that it is composed of the same elements as ordinary water, yet this does not disprove the existence of holy water. Its existence belongs to another order of facts.

It is an extremely unscientific approach to begin all discussion of Christianity with a denial of its supernatural character. Christianity presents itself *as supernatural*, and must be investigated as such. It would be quite unscientific when face to face with a person who said he was British to begin with the assumption that there are no British. It is equally unwarranted to begin a discussion of Christianity, which claims to be a supernatural religion, by asserting the supernatural to be impossible. This, of course, does not forbid a philosopher from abstracting from the supernatural character of Christianity for the purposes of comparison.

Furthermore, the possibility of a supernatural order is not absurd, particularly on the modern premise of the progressive character of the universe. Every order is *super-natural* (in the broad sense of the term) in relation to the order below it. Plants are *super-natural* to chemicals and may elevate them to their biological level by intussusception. Animals are *super-natural* to plants and may lift them up to their higher level by assimilation and sense knowledge. Men are *super-natural* to animals and may endow them with a higher existence by knowing them intelligently. No man has a right to say there is no higher life above him, any more than the rose has a right to say there is no life above it. More than that, human reason can prove the existence of a Perfect Life, Truth, and Love which is God. Granted this higher life, what is there to prevent God from elevating man to a newer and higher life than his own? As a creature, man is made, but as a supernatural child, he is begotten. We make things which are unlike us, for example, a radio; we beget what is like us—a son. The supernatural order in the strict sense is in the latter category, for by it we become children of God. Man would be less entitled to participate in that higher life of God than a plant or animal would have a right to share the life of man; in fact, it would exceed the natures, powers, and exigencies of man, and, in the strict sense of the term, would be supernatural.

The fifth false assumption is that the development of humanity follows the general laws of evolution. Starting with humble and poor origins, religions evolved little by little, until the religions of the present day emerged, but they still retain traces of their humble origins. This generic treatment of religion has been simplified by tracing every stage of the process to the operation of purely natural causes.

Despite the fact that biological evolution is just an hypothesis and not an established principle, there have not been wanting those who, having accepted evolution as true and established in the biological domain, have expanded it to embrace the realms of religion as well. There is, of course, no intrinsic connection between the two. Simply because animals or plants evolve, it does not follow that religions evolve; simply because there may have been an advance from the crude organic forms to the more highly developed, it does not follow that there has been an evolution of religion from polytheism to monotheism, or that magic or animism preceded religion. Such a process of reasoning sins by the transposition of ideas, concepts, and categories from one genus or one science, to another genus or another science. It was the excessive devotion to the evolutionary assumption which so long retarded historians from recognizing primitive monotheism. "To have admitted," says Radin:

> among primitive peoples the existence of monotheism in any form would have been equivalent to abandoning the whole doctrine of the evolutionary stages. And this they were not prepared to do, nor did the facts at the time definitely warrant it. However, twenty-five years have elapsed since Long wrote his book and his intuitive insight has been abundantly corroborated. The ethnologists were quite wrong. Accurate data obtained by trained specialists have replaced his rather vague examples. That many primitive peoples have a belief in a supreme creator no one today seriously denies.[23]

The theory of evolution of religion found one of its earliest and most complete expressions in the writings of Herbert Spencer, who stretched the evolutionary hypothesis to such extremes that it covered everything from an amoeba to a sacrifice. Spencer had little difficulty applying his theory to the more abstract sciences, such as ethics, but when he came to the social sciences and the social aspects of religion, he was compelled to rely more and more upon facts. He solved the difficulty by delegating the labor of gathering facts to assistants, who really did nothing more than find illustrations for the prearranged stages according to which Spencer believed that religion had evolved.[24] It was not long until the Darwinian method applied to religion became almost universal. It was a very simple theory; as some one has said, "flattering to the vanity of the white man and his civilization, which, in the evolutionary scheme, appeared as the crowning achievement of man's earthly career." Writers like J. G. Frazer (*The Golden Bough*), E. S. Hartland (*Myth and Ritual*), A. E. Crawley (*The Mystic Rose*), A. Réville (*Histoire des Religions*), W. Wundt (*Elements of Folk-Psychology*), and dozens of others soon dominated the field, and made it appear that evolution in religion was an established fact.

The method they used was to study available primitive civilizations, which they looked upon as almost identical with the extinct cultures of the past. Noting that these primitive cultures in America,

Africa, Australia, and the South Seas differed in the *degree* of development, they assumed that they had passed through the same stages that ancestral cultures had undergone. A chain of suppositions became transformed, with a few facts from Australia, "the godmother of evolutionism," into a quasi-historic record of effects beginning with some crude religion, and ending with the Christian religion of today. A. A. Goldenweiser wrote:

The facts were secured by a sort of literary kidnapping. They were torn forcibly from their historic homes to figure in evolutionary dissertations as cultural waifs, deprived of their local associations and chronological antecedents. When thus severed from the soil of historic reality, facts could be made to speak any tongue, to serve any dogma. What right, then, had the evolutionist to corral facts of such heterogeneous provenience and doubtful pedigree into quasi-chronological series, and call them stages? If an Indian stage 2, was made to reach down to an Australian stage 1 and reach up to an African stage 3, this could obviously be done only if cultural development in the three tribes was posited as uniform. But was not uniformity of cultural change one of the evolutionary tenets, the justice of which was first to be demonstrated by the comparative procedure? Thus, instead of providing proof of evolution the evolutionist was merely chasing his own tail.[25]

The evolution hypothesis of religion is now discredited. "Most of us," writes Radin:

have been influenced by the tenets of orthodox ethnology, and this was largely an enthusiastic and quite uncritical attempt to apply the Darwinian theory of evolution to the facts of social experience. Many ethnologists, sociologists and psychologists still persist in this endeavor. No progress will ever be achieved, however, until scholars rid themselves, once and for all, of the curious notion that everything possesses an evolutionary history.[26]

The story of the downfall of the evolutionary theory begins with the attack made on the particular stages constructed by the evolutionists. Evidence was brought forward that animism was not the essence of religion, or even co-extensive with it, and that the belief in a Supreme Being was older than had originally been believed. Totemism, as the foundation of religion, was discredited by showing that it was not a simple thing, but a mélange of psychological complexes, peculiar only to certain social forms, and not the essence of religion itself. With the advances made in the study of art and pottery, the principle of the uniformity of evolution fell into disrepute, for it was discovered that decorative symbolism was not a result of copying anterior designs, but rather a derivative of the nature of the material used, or the technique. The three stages of evolutionary pre-history, the stone, the bronze, and the iron ages, were no longer considered historically true, for it was discovered that iron was not universally known, and in Negro Africa the stage of iron followed that of stone, but there was no bronze age.

Another famous triad of the evolutionary theory—the hunting, the pastoral, and the agricultural ages—was found to be at complete variance with facts. In some places the hunting stage never preceded the agricultural, whereas, in others, agricultural and pastoral life were pursued on an equally wide scale. The evolutionary theory of marriage—as suggested by J. F. McLennan,[27] and L. H. Morgan [28] —which traces it from unbridled promiscuity, through group marriage, on to monogamy, was completely wrecked by E. A. Westermarck,[29] who said it was "the most unscientific that had ever been advanced in the whole domain of sociological speculation." Soon little remained of the uniformity of culture development.

Stages became so confused as to resemble a network rather than a ladder, and the pre-history of culture once more appeared as a set of problems, many of them barely broached, rather than as an orderly series of solutions available for use as a background of historic study.[30]

If the evolutionary theory were true, and if the various cultures were determined according to rigid laws of development, then to know humanity in one of its parts would mean to know humanity in its entirety. But when divergences were found, historians of religion had to look for other influences at work besides the purely deterministic law of evolution. The deathblow to the evolution theory in comparative study came with the knowledge and the importance of diffusion in the construction of the various cultures.

The theory of diffusion itself, when further elaborated, became a powerful foe of the simplicist evolutionary scheme. The evolutionist knew of diffusion but generally disregarded it in his theories. This could evidently be done only if the validity of the evolutionary scheme was taken for granted. But as soon as the scheme itself became subject to critical scrutiny, cultural features derived through historic contact at once acquired full right of citizenship in history. It was shown, moreover, that far from being rare and exceptional, cultural diffusion was a constant and omnipresent process characteristic of modern as well as primitive civilizations. Now, when a cultural feature borrowed from a neighboring tribe makes its appearance in a civilization and is accepted and assimilated, it thereby becomes part and parcel of that civilization, and must henceforth be included among the factors responsible for further changes. Each case of diffusion, therefore, complicates the cultural situation and makes it increasingly difficult to interpret its development in terms of inner forces alone. Thus the acceptance of the phenomena of diffusion at their face value is in itself sufficient to negate the evolutionary scheme in its original form.[31]

SOCIOLOGICAL EXPLANATION OF RELIGION

The sociological explanation of religion is that man is by birth a-religious and amoral, and that it is society which creates in man his religious and moral outlook. "Religion is the system of beliefs and practices relative to sacred things." The essence of religion is the idea of the *sacred*, as set off in contrast from the *profane*. The sacred comes from society, and the profane from the individual. Religion, then, is primarily social, for it originated in society, and its purposes are directed to collective ends, as contrasted to all forms of egoism. This explanation of religion implies a knowledge of the sociological outlook on society. Society is not, according to this theory, a collection of individuals. It is, *sui juris*, above individuals, and independent of them. Hence, sociological facts are irreducible to individual facts. The collectivity thinks, acts, and feels differently from the individuals who compose it.

There is an element of truth in the sociological explanation of religion, for religion has its foundation in the real, and in a social fact, and does depend on social traditions. It is not wholly an individual matter, as the psychological explanation would have us believe. Yet the sociological explanation of religion is fundamentally and philosophically wrong in its outlook on society. The postulate of the sociological explanation is that society is a different entity from the individuals which compose it. The analogy it uses is that the human life is a different thing from the chemical, and so is society different from the individual. The reasoning process runs in this fashion: "A composition differs specifically from its elements. But society is a composition. Therefore, it is different from its elements." The fault in logic here is to forget that society is made up of homogeneous elements, and not heterogeneous ones. The members of society are not different as gold, silver, brass, and lead are different, for in such a case, the composition would be different from the elements. Rather the members of society are homogeneous, like soldiers: a soldier added to a soldier makes an army, but not a cannon ball. The army is different from the soldiers, not in *kind* but only in *manner of being*. In like respect, society is not a new entity, but a new manner of being. It is not just a mere collection of individuals such as the bricks of a house, but a co-ordination with mutual co-operation.

The unity formed by a state is a unity of co-ordination, and not that of simple unity. Each element of the social whole has its activity, which is not that of the whole; but the whole itself has also, and as such, an action which is proper to it. Thanks to that, society differs from a whole wherein one finds unity of composition, or of continuity, for here the parts do not act separately from the ensemble, e.g., two kinds of operations: (1) the operation of the parts of the whole, namely, soldiers of an army, (2) operation of the whole, namely, the whole army in battle.[32]

If society is not a thing totally different in kind from the individuals, it follows that it cannot produce a religion apart from the individuals. Religion may be, and is, a social phenomenon, but that is because it is already a phenomenon of the individuals. Society, therefore, could not be the source of religion while the individuals which make it up were the sources of the profane.

The recognition of the sacred as a religious element is important, but the sociological theory does not account for it. The social sanction is not the kind of sanction religion claims, and as a matter of fact, a social sanction is no more sacred than a personal one. Religion in this theory is reduced to a kind of social illusion. If one grants the existence of a supernatural world which is the seat of sacredness, then society might have some sacred relations as it does in the Christian outlook. But society is just an extension of the herd instinct, in the sociological theory, and since nothing can give what it has not, the sacred in this theory must remain an illusion.

One of the difficulties in substituting society for God, is that any human society, even at its best, is too often undiscriminating in its judgments, and sometimes too ignorant and cruel, to serve as an object of worship. It likewise fails to take into account the fact that great heroes, saints, and sometimes scholars are those who opposed public opinion in the name of conscience and moral insight. Public opinion and social judgments are sometimes wrong. It was public opinion that crucified Christ.

Not only does the theory fail to account for individual rebellion against social estimates on the grounds of morality, but it also fails to take into account the equally obvious fact that as a man grows in spirituality, he often more and more detaches himself from society. Hermits, monastics, contemplatives are so many examples of those who abandoned society as the sacred developed in them. If society were sacred, as the theory assumes, then they should have striven more and more to unite themselves with it. The strong individual, retiring quality of much spirituality is a proof that man does not, *de facto*, regard society either as sacred, or as god.

Society, looking inward, can become just as self-centered as an individual looking inward. No human society can prosper by ·concentrating all its attention on its own welfare. Like a ship it must anchor outside itself.

The best things human society enjoys at this moment are the results of efforts which have *not* had the welfare of society for their object; while of the worst evils, not a few can be directly traced to its corporate selfishness—to its lack of reverence for anything but itself. Social selfishness in morality, like institutional selfishness in religion, acts as a deadly stranglehold on the spirit of man.... Of the goods possessed by society, the best are religion, philosophy, science, art. These are not the products of the entire human class consciousness, absorbingly concentrated on the welfare of society. The human class consciousness is fatal to them. They flourish only in minds which have risen above it.[33]

Unless society goes out beyond its illusory sacred to something really sacred, it can expect to end in nothing but selfishness, which is death.

PSYCHOLOGICAL EXPLANATION OF RELIGION

There are exaggerations in the psychology of religion just as there are in the sociology of religion. The latter sins by sometimes making society the total foundation of religion, while the former sins by sometimes making the individual the total foundation of religion. Three errors of method may vitiate the psychological approach, and make of it a philosophy instead of a psychology.

In a grouping of religious facts for the purposes of psychological investigation, there is apt to be a confusion of the normal with the exceptional. Such is very definitely the error of method of most psychologists who rely on autobiographies, biographies, and the observation of others. It is particularly the fault of William James in his *Varieties of Religious Experience*. In discussing conversions, he groups together a man who was converted from drunkenness to temperance, with another who was converted from Judaism to Catholicism.[34] And in his treatment of mysticism, James records a "mystical state" under chloroform, with a mystical experience of Saint John of the Cross.[35] When one is thus putting on an equal plane and common ground exaggerations and normalities, perversions and health, the results are bound to be misleading. It is just like saying that the human body could be studied as thoroughly by pathology as by physiology. The extravagance of any subject of human interest cannot be put on the same basis as the normal, and the confusion of the two can end only in a welter of sentimentality, never in science.

> ... The gods approve
> The depth, and not the tumult, of the soul.

The very title which James gave his collection of facts, namely, *The Varieties of Religious Experience*, is an evidence of the confusion which results from his combination of abnormalities and morbidities.

Indeed, we may even say that James relied more upon the exceptional than the normal, as if the normal itself were too commonplace—a usual mistake among investigators. This is, says Dr. Uren:

the fundamental defect of James. James appears to pass by the normal religious life in order to treat of the religious experiences of extraordinary persons who have figured in religious history. One rises from the perusal of his fascinating volume with the impression that none other than the extremely vicious or the extremely neurotic can have a religious experience which is worth notice. All James' varieties of religious experience and types of conversion have either bottomed the abyss of vicious degradation or have been morbid psychopaths in their psychological make-up. Stanley Hall asserts that "many, if not the most, of these experiences are the yellow literature of religious psychology," and that some of James' cases are positively "teratological." These strictures are perhaps too harsh, but James' work certainly lends itself to such criticism, for the *Varieties* is entirely based on the religious experiences of extraordinary religious subjects.

James attempts to evaluate religion by taking as his standard extreme cases in religious history. He never seems to differentiate the typical from the aberrational, and exceptional cases are conceived as characteristic of the religious life. Is this a sound procedure? Let us take an analogy from the realm of Art. There are fanatical persons in the artistic world who have delighted to violate the received canons of Art. These persons depict figures on canvas as a multiplicity of cubes, as wheeling of these fanatics—the futurists, the cubists, and the vorticists. Now if we desired a right conception of art in general, would we go to these masses of pigment, or as a complex of vortices. There are three types freaks for our standard? If freaks are not to be considered as normative in art, can they be regarded as normative in religion? [36]

This brings us to another point in a psychology of religion: its necessarily incomplete character. The empirical grouping of psychological facts does not tell us what religion is, any more than the grouping of moral facts tells us what morality is. Simply because psychology has described the empirical side of religion, it does not follow that religion is purely empirical and psychological. There is a certain type of mentality which confuses description with explanation, and feels that because we are now learning the law of things, therefore they could not possibly be made by God. We are really only readers of a great book, whether it be nature or mind. Because we are proofreaders, we must not mistake proofreading for authorship, as Professor Leuba does.

If there were extra-human sources of knowledge and superhuman sources of human power, their existence should, it seems, have become increasingly evident. Yet the converse is apparently true; the supernatural world of the savage has become a natural world to civilized man; the miraculous of yesterday is the explicable of today. In religious lives accessible to psychological investigation, nothing requiring the admission of superhuman influences has been found. There is nothing, for example, in the life of the great Spanish mystic whose celebrity is being renewed by contemporary psychologists—not a desire, not a feeling, not a thought, not a vision, not an illumination—that can seriously make us look to transcendent causes.[37]

Thouless comments on this passage and writes:

...It is impossible to pretend that our knowledge of psychological laws is so complete that we can honestly say that it provides us with an explanation of the desires, thoughts, feelings, etc. of anybody....It makes the unproved assumption that religion would be convicted of falsity if it could be expressed in terms of known psychological laws.[38]

Psychology does describe the elements of religion, but it can never exclude the philosophical or the more properly religious explanation. An illustration has been given by Professor Pratt of how a religious explanation may be the true one, although psychological investigation is powerless to prove it. He supposes the human race is living in perpetual sunlight, but that most men are blind. One who can see will, upon opening his eyes, be receiving light sensations. One of the blind psychologists could apply the method of single difference to demonstrate that the opening of the eyes was the cause of the light sensation, and hence, no reference was needed to the sun or to anything else. If the seer insisted that he saw the sun, the psychologist could challenge him to see light with his eyes shut, or to fail to see it with them open, or to point out a single element in his experience not accounted for by the psychological formula.[39] The psychological element may always be the concomitant of religion, but it does not follow that it is its complete or total cause.

To the credit of the psychology of religion it must be said that not all believe in the omniscience of psychological investigations. The psychologist works like any other scientist within limits; but there are limits. "Nothing that the psychology of religion can say should prevent the religious man, who wishes to be perfectly loyal to logic and loyal to truth, from seeing in his own spiritual experience the genuine influences of a living God." [40]

The subconscious is a particular phase of the psychological explanation. It is valid in those instances where there is a continuity between the subconscious and the conscious. The subconscious or unconscious love of Christ may be the incomplete psychological reason for a conversion to the conscious love of Christ, but it can hardly be the explanation where the subconscious hatred of Christ becomes the conscious love of Christ. It is here precisely where psychological explanations of the conversion of St. Paul fail to satisfy reason. C. G. Jung, in his treatment of this subject, in order to explain Paul psychologically, completely distorts the facts of his conversion and says: "St. Paul had already been a Christian for a long time, but unconsciously." [41] Now it is just the contrary which is true. St. Paul, at the very moment of his conversion, was "breathing out threatenings against the Lord," and was en route to perform an act of persecution.

His conversion, and thousands of others, can hardly be said to be the mere eruptions into consciousness of what was already unconscious, for here the problem is to explain how the subconscious hatred became conscious love. The subconscious and the conscious are traveling in different directions, and it is not likely that one will run into the other. Hence the necessity of positing some other non-psychological factor to account for the conversion, and in the conversion of St. Paul, it was certainly none other than the grace of God.

The subconscious explanation of religion, which eliminates all other factors of explanation, fails furthermore to leave room for the rational elements of religion. Subconscious elements may play a role in religious life, but certainly they play a less important one than the rational. The very fact that highly developed religions have creeds and dogmas, beliefs and liturgies, proves that the rational has been far more formative in religion than the subconscious. The hand of the past, the subconscious, does not so heavily weigh upon us as to make null and void our present ratiocinations about the universe and our relation to its Supreme Cause. Exaggerated psychological explanations make subconscious cerebration the reason of a conscious act. But the question here arises as to what sets the unconscious in motion, for nothing is moved unless it is moved by another. It may very well be that reason itself supplies the momentum. But whatever be its excitant, the fact still remains that the subconscious cannot account for the presence of the rational or intellectual content of religion.

The subconscious theory omits not only the intellectual element in religion, but also the voluntary. If conversion, for example, were merely a question of the eruption of the subconscious mind, how explain the fact that the convert always takes account of motives? There is a kind of "duality" in the prospective convert, in which motives are weighed and reasons are given. Finally, when the choice is made, the convert gives himself over to the light, he recognizes nothing as blind impulsion. Even where the conversions are sudden, they differ from pathological cases by the circumstances in which they take place, namely, a light concerning the nothingness of life, and the greatness of God. Says Arthur Chandler:

Psychology has a very important and interesting work to do in explaining the mechanism which the mind employs in forming ideas; in expounding the part taken in this work by feeling, perception, memory and attention; in dealing with the circumstances in which experiences are forgotten, and the methods by which they can be recalled, and similar investigations. In other words, it is concerned with the way in which the mind actually works in the formation of ideas and convictions, whether in the sphere of religion or art or science or philosophy. But the question of the validity and truth of the ideas themselves lies beyond its province. Speaking of religion, Dr. Oman says, "the reality or unreality of its objects can no more be determined purely psychologically in religion than, say, in commerce. For psychology an object is real when it is regarded as existing outside the mind; and the determination of whether it is actually real or not is a matter of evidence and not of psychology." Psychology can explain how we form an idea of God; but whether there is a God or not, and whether our ideas on the subject are valid or not, is a question to be dealt with by the united witness of theology and its various departments, and of philosophy and history.[42]

RELIGIOUS EXPERIENCE

Religious experience may be understood to mean one of two things. It may be a nonintellectual approach to God in which feeling is primary. Or it may be an intellectual approach in which there is a confused intellectual reasoning process which is primary; an affective or emotional response; and a reflex intellectual state. If by religious experience is meant the former, then religious experience is an invalid approach to God, if the latter, then religious experience is a legitimate approach to God.

William James was one of the earlier defenders of the nonintellectual approach to God, maintaining the view that "feeling is the deeper source of religion and that philosophic and theological formulas are secondary products, like translations of a text into another language." [43] Karl Otto, in his work, *The Holy*, also describes a primary religious feeling or emotion which is unlike all other feelings and which is directed to the Holy. Jung speaks of the religious instinct as something which feeds upon the incestuous libido of the infantile period.[44] Thouless defines religious experience as "the *feeling element* in religious consciousness, its feelings which lead to religious belief, or are the effects of religious behaviour." [45] Such views are heritages of the older order of Schleiermacher, for whom religion was the spontaneous feeling of man's dependence on the universe.

The following reasons may be adduced against the emotional and nonintellectual approach to God:

This approach is based upon bad psychology, *i.e.*, that the emotion about, precedes the idea of, God. The idea should precede the emotion. A husband is not dead because the wife weeps, but the wife weeps because the husband is dead. The emotion is not the cause of the idea, it is its reaction and consequence. "The affective state begins when the intellectual operation is finished," says St. Thomas.[46] Emotion never creates, but presupposes knowledge. It can add strength to knowledge and supply it content, but it can never originate it.

Secondly, we must ask how the affective state puts one in contact with God, since one had no rational knowledge of God beforehand? In the second kind of religious experience, where the intellectual element is primary, reason has proved God. But why should an emotion which is organic and physical, end in the spiritual and the divine? Why does it not put us in contact with the moon and stars instead of God? Why is there connaturality between the two? Reason can answer this question, but emotion cannot.

Whence comes the sense of "something being there"? Does it come from ourselves? If so, God is nothing but our feeling. Does it come from experience? But experience cannot produce or create an object; it can only approve or disapprove its reality. Does it come from God? But if so, why does God reveal Himself in such contrary and contradictory views to different persons? Why is He a "principle of concretion" to a Whitehead, a "Given" to a Brightman, a "nisus" for an Alexander, a "Mathematician" for a Jeans, a "youth in the morning sun" for a Wells, the "cosmic drift toward harmony" for a Horton? The answer is, the only God attained by a purely affective approach is a subjective God, born of one's own feelings. Hence there is a different God "felt" during a headache than during a climb up the mountains, and a different God "experienced" by a mathematician than by a novelist. It is precisely because affective states vary from man to man that we have as many gods as we have feelings. In every case, man worships at the shrine his own feelings have made. St. Thomas says, as taste depends upon a certain disposition of the tongue, so will God follow the disposition of the one "experimenting." God will vary from man to man, and from experience to experience, which means there is no God except the one man makes to his own feelings and experiences. Feeling good does not mean being good, and "feeling" God does not mean discovering His existence. To appeal to emotions on questions where reason is relevant, is to end in illusion and subjectivism.

The term "religious experience" has generally been applied to the affective approach to God, though there is now a greater realization that any experience which is void of the intellectual element must necessarily be illusory. For example, Dr. Thomas Hughes says that a "cognitive is involved in religious experience. There can be no religious experience without some knowledge of God. If man were absolutely certain that there was no God, then there could be no religious attitude in the real sense of the term." [47] The valid type of religious experience is one which involves three elements: a confused intellectual knowledge; an emotional response; a reflex intellectual knowledge.

It will be noted that there is a distinction between *confused* and *reflex* knowledge. Confused knowledge is that by which something is known without discernment of its parts or predicates and in which it is not always easy to distinguish one object from another. *Reflex* or *distinct* knowledge, on the contrary, discerns parts and predicates and differentiates one object from another.[48] This confused knowledge might be grounded on the inclination of nature. St. Thomas writes "every creature whether rational or irrational, or even inanimate, loves God above all things according to the kind of love which can properly belong to it." [49] By natural love is here understood the inclination of a being toward its end, which in the case of man is intellectually known.

The confused knowledge also may be a desire for the perfect. Nothing finite can give rest to the intellect. There is a natural tendency in every man to transcend the temporal as is witnessed by his pursuit of ideals.[50] The mind knows that created being does not exhaust its potentialities; it desires the perfect. This does not mean the "soul desires God as He is in Himself."

More strictly, confused knowledge applies to a spontaneous kind of reasoning process, and this is what is meant by the first stage in religious experience. It is not exclusively the privilege of some men, as in the case of the mystical approach of an Alexander, a Bergson, or an Eddington; it is given to all men without exception, and hence all men can have some knowledge of God.[51] This knowledge is not dependent on education, environment, or authority. It is even more readily attainable, according to the Book of Wisdom, than the knowledge of worldly sciences. "For if they were able to know so much as to make a judgment of the world, how did they not *more easily find out* the Lord thereof?" [52] This rational, confused, spontaneous approach to God almost happens in spite of ourselves.

Closely associated with this intellectual element in religious experience is a second factor: the affective. The difference between the religious experience we are outlining and the usual modern man's view is that the latter puts the *affective* first. It is our contention that the emotional state is dependent in man on the rational, hence the rational must precede. Once given the rational, then there is an organic repercussion or the emotional element.

The confused intellectual knowledge of God is not perfect. A reflex knowledge is necessary to bring determination and completeness, and to lift the undeveloped knowledge into a knowledge which will stand analysis and criticism.[53] In the confused knowledge St. Thomas says that reason *immediately* comes to some knowledge of God as Governor of the universe.[54] But this confused knowledge does not tell us whether God Who is the Governor is one, whether a body or a soul.[55] Consequently, a more refined reasoning process is necessary to analyze the nature of the Governor, His Unity, and His Perfection, and this is done by what are commonly called the "Proofs for the Existence of God." It is therefore not valid to object that the five proofs of St. Thomas are too dry and abstract.

TRANSCENDENCE OF CHRISTIANITY

The world today is no longer deciding which of the Christian religions is true, but which of the world religions is most useful. Some even say that all these religions are passing phases of religion. Against such a position, reason argues for the transcendence of Christianity. De Broglie reminds us that:

The proof of the transcendence of Christianity is different from the proof of its Divinity. The first is independent of any idea concerning the cause of Christianity; the second implies God. The argument for the transcendence of Christianity prepares one for the proof of its Divinity, for if Christianity is transcendent, it must have a Divine or a Supreme cause.[56]

The term divinity applied to religion indicates the *cause* of its properties: the special intervention of God in its favor; but the term transcendence expresses only a quality or a character. One can recognize the merits of an individual or a society without explaining its causes. To pass from transcendence to divinity, it suffices to prove that the Author of an exception so great and marked could be none other than God. Transcendence, furthermore, does not consist in proving that Christianity is better than any other religion, but that it is *above comparison.* Transcendence is a "change of degree, order, and species." There are, for example, similar functions in the animal and in man, respiration, digestion, circulation of blood, etc., and yet man is of a different species: he is transcendent to the animal. Transcendence is superiority of such a kind that it constitutes an exception to the common laws of human activity, and therefore, implies a superior cause. Transcendence does not imply that Christianity must bear no resemblances to pagan religions, because similarities do not prove the same cause; nor that Christianity enjoys truth and all other religions are in darkness, but rather that it has historical superiority over them.

The great problems of religion are death, pain, error, and sin. A thorough-going theory of salvation must necessarily deal with release from all of them. Historically, we find that many world religions have concerned themselves mostly with one of them to the exclusion of the others, but no religion except Christianity has interested itself in all four and in a thoroughly integrated fashion so that one flowed out of the other.

Hinduism and Buddhism, for example, are concerned principally with the problem of death and the problem of pain. Hinduism has the three great doctrines of: wandering, or transmigration of souls; Karma or Works, or cause and effect, whereby the lot of a soul in this life is held to be determined by its life in a previous incarnation, and its behavior now determines its next embodiment; release, by which the soul beholds Brahma (the impersonal pervading essence) and realizes its identity with Him and thus gets free from wandering or Works.

There is no problem of sin. Why? Because reality is an illusion, a "maya." Salvation consists not in breaking with sin, but in breaking down the illusion that keeps us from thinking we are identical with Brahma.

Buddhism was originally a cult arising within Hinduism. Gautama, called to be the Buddha, felt that the Hindu teachers of his time had exhausted their wisdom, and, moved by the sight of *suffering,* he set down his four noble truths: All personal existence is bound up with suffering. All suffering is due to desire. Hence the way to remove suffering is to remove desire. Desire can be removed only by following the noble eightfold path. Thus does one attain to the *Nirvana*.

This stresses the teaching that individuality or personality is the root of the *pain* and suffering of the world. Salvation is only salvation from death, from things of sense, from the fleeting and the impermanent. There is no salvation from *sin*.

The assumption that pain or suffering is the radical evil, that the distinction between good and evil, right and wrong, is not absolute, but only an illusory projection of our egotism, is very much akin to the skeptical humanism of the Western World today, and its idea that one can abolish pain and poverty through science and without recourse to an *ethos* which sees social ills as the consequence of sin. From this point of view, secular humanism is more Buddhistic than Christian. We find it in such writers as Walter Lippmann, who believes that the objective distinction between right and wrong is only a projection of man's desires and illusions; once we rid ourselves of illusions, the sense of evil vanishes. "Evil exists only because we feel it to be painful." [57]

Then there are other world religions, such as the Egyptian, which emphasize the problem of death and immortality, but no other detail of salvation. There is also Confucianism which treats the same problem in relation to ancestors, but which in reality is more of a sociology than it is a religion. Still other moral philosophers, such as the Stoical, claimed that we do not know whether the future will ever vindicate righteousness, but that amidst the "slings and arrows of outrageous fortune" we must grit our teeth and do our duty for its own sake. The common defect of these views is their isolation from other and correlated problems. They fail to explain why we should do our duty, or what is the foundation of duty, both of which are inexplicable, unless the universe is of such a consistency as to make self-sacrifice for noble causes not only necessary but right. Shorn of an ideal, the mere doing of duty can become a high form of self-centered egotism.

There is only one religion in history which takes account of all four problems of religion and shows how one is related to the other, and that is Christianity. In its synthesis, pain and error are the result of sin. Sin can be conquered by death, and by death personality reaches its perfection in Him Who is Exemplar and Cause of Redemption. Christianity begins first with the principle that "man is made in the image and likeness of God," meaning with an intelligence and will, or simply as a free being, which chemicals and flowers are not. As a creature he is dependent on his Creator. As a free being, he is relatively independent of Him. The paradox of Christianity is that man is independent because he is dependent, as the pendulum of a clock is free to swing because it is suspended. His true freedom consists in surrender to God; his false freedom is in disowning that dependence in a false declaration of independence by which he makes himself a limited god in opposition to God—a rebellion he could not accomplish if he were not free, or if there were no God. There could never be atheism if there was not something to "atheate."

Secondly, this denial of creatureliness, this affirmation of the relative as an absolute, this denial of an image which is indelible, is the source of pain and error, self-frustration, psychoses, and neuroses, for evil is self-defeating. Man cannot be just a natural thing like a bird or an amoeba, if for no other reason than that he is self-conscious. No lily can turn back upon itself as in a mirror, but a man can. Because he is self-conscious he must always see himself as rising either to union with Life, Truth, and Love, which is God and His Perfection, or else as falling away from it into self-assertion, self-gratification, and self-indulgence. By the mere fact that he does not rise, he must fall, as a white post will eventually become a black post. A donkey can never become anything but a donkey, but a man can be either a child of God or an ass. Once he freely rejects his perfection and seeks contentment in nature alone, he finds that even nature rebels against him in its "traitorous trueness and loyal deceit" to its Maker.

The third principle in the Christian synthesis is that the error, pain, suffering, and death attendant upon an abuse of freedom can be rectified, not by man alone, and yet not without man. If God decided to reintegrate man into his fellowship by force, He would not save man but destroy him, for freedom is of the essence of man. No Nirvana-like extinction of personality is sufficient to redeem. Man must have some part in his redemption; Divinely re-creative power ought to emerge within the world and involve man. In order that redemption might not be imposed on man from without, it was fitting that the union of God and man be effected in the realm of freedom. The first sign of man's free allegiance and consent to the entering in of God as a re-creating cause within his fallen world, is the consent of the Virgin Mary: "Be it done unto me according to Thy Word." The grant of freedom is kept inviolate. A start has been made in human regeneration by an act of freedom, and from that day to this, no one ever enters into the merits of that redemption except by a free act, as Mary did.

Sin then is serious, so serious that man in justice cannot adequately atone for it. The evil of sin is revealed in its essence by what it does to the God-man—crucifying Him. Sin in its essence is anti-God. Evil can never be more mighty than when it nailed Christ to a Cross. But having been defeated by the Resurrection, it can never be victorious again. Wrongdoing is seen on Calvary, not as a breach of law, as moral philosophers would have it, but as a free rejection of Love. But at the same time, pain, suffering, error, lies, false charges, all fit into the redemptive pattern, for the victory of Christ is not merely *over* death but *through* death, for it is the victory of self-sacrifice, and self-sacrifice is never complete until life is given. "Greater love than this no man hath."

Pain, evil, error are overcome in *principle* by His death, but not yet in *fact*. They will continue to exist until the final judgment as a punishment for sin, though regenerated man in the midst of such trials can utilize them as Christ did, for his own salvation. Instead of being obstacles, they become raw material for spiritualization. No other religion in the world gives to death the value of Christianity, because others isolated it from sin. For all others, death is either unreal or a release of the spirit or the dropping away of the body, considered an obstacle to union with God. But to Christianity death is at one and the same time a penalty for sin and a condition of eternal happiness, because through death, love accomplishes self-sacrifice which issues in self-perfection in eternal life. Because it is love which saves, life must be lost before it can be won.

World religions touch on one or the other aspect of the Christian philosophy, as do modern philosophies of religion. Some concentrate on pain and deny the reality of evil; others concentrate on evil, but make it social and unrelated to personal freedom; not many of them attempt to solve the riddle of death. Few, if any, treat the subject of sin except as a "fall in the evolutionary process." The only religion which makes a synthesis of all these problems, then shows how one has resulted from the other, and how each of them can be used instrumentally in victory, is Christianity. It does not give us a picture of defeat *followed* by victory, of pain *followed* by joy, or death *followed* by life, but as the *conversion* of one into the other. "Your sorrow shall be turned into joy." Defeat *becomes* victory, sin becomes a *felix culpa;* death becomes eternal life, and "the sufferings of this life are not worthy to be compared with the joy which is to come."

No religion except Christianity gives meaning, not only to the joys of life, but also to its sorrows. As Dean Inge observed, "Nor is there any religion or philosophy except Christianity which has really drawn the sting of the world's evil." [58] It was uniquely fitted to do so, because its "Lord of Glory" was also a "Man of Sorrows."

Christianity is also transcendent because it heals the breach between this world and the next. Most religions take either of two worlds, but do not successfully co-ordinate both. Modern and ancient paganism and all religions of worldliness from Epicureanism to Freudianism make the world the "be all and end all here." The other type of religion sets itself up in opposition to this world, in one or another form of asceticism or detachment. The central conception of Greek asceticism is indifference to the world through the affirmation of the ego. The Hindu asceticism is the attainment of bliss through the dissolution of individual human life in a state of non-being and detachment from the material universe. The Christian religion rejects both indifference to the universe and its negation. Neither the Greek nor the Hindu way of salvation includes the world; the first is indifferent to the fate of the world, the second is indifferent to self. The Christian believes in the salvation of the soul as much as any other individual religion; it believes in the regeneration and betterment of the world as much as any social religion; but it declares that the salvation of the soul is inseparable from the salvation of the world. Unlike the Hindu, it does not renounce the cosmos; unlike the Greek, it does not renounce man's relation to it. Like the Greek it affirms the freedom of the soul; like the Hindu it glorifies a supra-temporal order. But it transcends both by accepting all being, and rejects only the evil which is attendant upon an excess or a defect of particular being.

The Christian life has a twofold task: on one hand it means self-renunciation through suffering, overcoming the "world" as a lower and distorted state of being and in that sense forsaking the world—and on the other, it means perceiving the higher, the absolutely valuable essence and purpose of the cosmic life, lovingly serving the needs of others and furthering the world's perfection.[59]

Christianity renounces the world only insofar as it is a power for evil, but it affirms the world inasmuch as it was made by God and moves toward God. In both this affirmation and renunciation, Christianity possesses both a power and an independence never before realized. If at times Christianity has been criticized for being disinterested in the world, as it was when Marx labeled it "the opium of the people," it is because Christianity has been confused with Buddhism. Christianity in its doctrine of the Sacraments gives the material world a value as a channel for the communication of the spiritual. The Incarnation starts with the assumption that the disordered elements of the material universe can be re-ordered to serve God's purposes. For that reason Christ commanded His followers to "preach the Gospel to *every creature*"—not just to every man. Christianity alone of all world religions could at once reconcile the exaltation of man above his earthliness and the payment of justice to all the interests and relations of this life.

From another point of view, Christianity, because it is outside the civilizations of the East and West, is alone capable of uniting both. Western civilization is practical. In it man does everything, God does nothing. He is at best a silent partner, whose name is used in advertising to win customers, but Who has nothing much to say about the running of the business of the universe. Eastern civilization is mystical. God does everything, man does nothing. Hence it is fatalistic, anti-materialistic, and anti-historical. Christianity reminds the West—"Without Me you can do nothing," and to the East suggests the counterbalancing truth: "I can do all things in Him Who strengthened me." Because of its position, Christianity alone is capable of building "One World" by serving as a mediator between both, as it mediates man and the universe, this world and the next. "Preach the Gospel to *all* nations."

Alexander the Great did actually try to unite in marriage the East and the West, and to give a first universal tongue for a whole civilized world in the Greek Koine, but his cosmopolitanism had little in common with Christianity, for his was established by the power of arms and Christianity by the power of love. Furthermore, his religion was a syncretism rather than a genuine theology. From a purely human point of view, he united the world religiously by supplementing the defect of one people by the advantages of the other, or by equating indifference with tolerance. But the peculiar quality of Christianity is that it flew in the face of existing religions by a rigid doctrine of intolerance. At a time when different gods of various nations were housed in the same temple, Christianity dared affirm: "Neither is there salvation in any other, for there is no other name under heaven given to man, whereby we must be saved." [60] To those who were accustomed to be initiated into several mysteries, Christianity declared: "You cannot drink the chalice of the Lord, and the chalice of devils." [61] To those who were, according to a variety of religious ideas seeking many mediations, Christianity declared: "For there is one God, and one mediator of God and men, the man Christ Jesus." [62]

Greek thought saw in Christianity immense possibilities of speculation and attempted to transform it into a philosophy, but Christianity rejected it. Christianity alone of all cosmopolitan forces would not only not stoop to conquer; it would not even conquer. Its exclusivism preserved its integrity. This was the badge of its uniqueness. The hospitality of other cults to other ideas proved their downfall. The enthusiasm for humanity as such, rather than for unity at the cost of truth, was the secret of Christianity's power. Christian love was a new moral factor in the world. At last was fulfilled the dream of Socrates, who conceived of a citizen of the world.[63] To achieve unity by ignoring dogmas, lowering morals, and being tolerant to a point of broadmindedness is one thing; to achieve unity by none of these techniques, but by intolerance for Truth wedded to Love is the unique privilege of Christianity.

A most important point concerning the transcendence of Christianity is that no other religion in the world ever had a founder who has a pre-history. No one ever knew that Buddha was coming, or Confucius, or founders of other religions, including those being inaugurated this afternoon in Los Angeles. Founders of other religions appear in full bloom on the stage of history, and make their claim about being sent by God, or even being God. Acceptance of their claims depends on credulity but not on history. Human reason does suggest that if God were going to send a messenger to this world, He would pre-announce his coming so that he might be identified when he appeared. We discovered this to be the fact in the case of Christ, but of no one else. Quite apart from any belief in inspiration, the fact is that among certain people and over a long period of time there were a series of prophecies concerning Christ, for example, that He would be of the race of Abraham (Gen. 12), of Isaac (Gen. 26), of Jacob (Gen. 28); that He would come when Judah should have lost the scepter (Gen. 49), before the destruction of the second Temple (Aggeus 2), after sixty-nine weeks of years (Dan. 9); that He would be born of a Virgin (Isa. 7), in the village of Bethlehem (Mic. 5); that He would suffer in silence and be reputed with the wicked for His burial (Isa. 53), would be pierced with a lance (Zach. 12), but not a bone of his body would be broken (Exod. 12); that His hands and feet would be pierced (Ps. 21), and His sepulcher would come from a rich man (Isa. 53), that He would rise on the third day (Osee 6), and would be triumphant on Olivet (Zach. 14); would be a King universal in time (Isa. 9), and universal in place (Zach. 9), and would be not only the hope of the people from which He came, but also the desired of nations (Gen. 49).

The probability against these and many other prophecies being fulfilled is greater than the probability of any one fact taken separately. If twenty facts were predicted and if the probability of each of these facts were one tenth for two facts taken together, the probability would be one one-hundredth for three, one one-thousandth; and for twenty $\frac{1}{100,000,000,000,000,000,000}$. Edersheim in his *Life and Times of Jesus the Messias* enumerates 456 texts of the Old Testament which the Rabbis interpreted as referring to the Messias. From an historical point of view alone, here is uniqueness which sets Christ apart from all other founders of world religions. And once the fulfillment of these prophecies did historically take place in the person of Christ, not only did all prophecies cease in Israel, but there was discontinuance of sacrifices (a fact foretold by Daniel) when the true Paschal Lamb was sacrificed.

Christianity is the only religion in the world which is identified with history both in the advent of its Founder and in the repercussions of its Founder on subsequent civilizations. To such an extent is this true, that even those who would deny that Christ ever existed have to date their denial as 1940 or 1950 or 1960 years after the birth of Christ. Reason and history alike demand that the claims of one Person above all be investigated, and that is He Who in His own village could pick up an eight-hundred-year-old prophecy concerning Himself and then say: "This day is fulfilled this scripture in your ears" (Luke 4:21), and then to those who boasted of Abraham as their father, could go back to eternal beginning and say: "Before Abraham was made, I am" (John 8:58).

This brings us to another point of transcendence in relation to those other religions which have a personal, though not a pre-announced, founder, such as Gautama for Buddhism, Zoroaster for the Persian religion, and Mohammed for Islam. In each of these, the doctrine is always distinct from the person; the ideal is abstract, though communicated by a Founder. In Christianity alone does one find the identification of the Person and the ideal, the historical and the absolute. "I am the Truth." Everyone else said "Here is the Truth, follow it." Christ knew and preached of no other Truth than Himself. Buddhism is not Gautama, but Christianity is Christ. And at the one and the same time He affirmed the Truth, He associated with His Person a moral innocence and righteousness: "Which of you shall convict Me of sin." The Logos or Truth of the Stoics was a pure abstraction, and of their ideal wise man, Plutarch said that "He is nowhere on earth, nor ever been seen." The Logos of Philo was a mere hypostasis, never flowing over to others, but the Logos of Christianity was "The Word made flesh Who dwelt amongst us." Ideals were always held up to men and still are, but an ideal without personification is without appeal. No one can fall in love with a theorem of geometry. Disincarnated ideas are cold. For that reason legendary figures (such as Orpheus and Osiris) were held up before the ancient world in order to reinforce precepts. Not even a Messianic era could stand up in time of crisis, and it had to give way to a Messianic person. History about the time of the birth of Christ was ripe for a Truth Who is a Person. In all other religions there were ideals, precepts, and ethics, but only in one was the ideal not an abstraction, but an exhibition in space and time of a figure who fulfilled the inexhaustible aspirations of the human heart. Christ is not just a good man, because good men do not lie. And He lied if He is not what he claimed to be: the Son of God. Either He is the Son of God Incarnate or He is the archknave of all times, but He is not "one of the moral teachers."

Chapter X

HISTORY AND RELIGION

MODERN PHILOSOPHIES OF HISTORY

The spirit of the contemporary world is irrationalism, or a contempt of reason; but the reason against which the Western world reacted in the last two or three centuries was the scientific reason of the Cartesian tradition ending in skepticism, rather than the metaphysical reason which made metaphysics, instead of mathematics or physics, the supreme science of the human mind. Naturally, if the spirit of the world is irrational, it follows that man cannot be convinced of the necessity of an Absolute Truth and the Providence of God by reason. Denying the Divine Source of reason has made the deliverances of reason untrustworthy and unbelievable. Furthermore, denying the absoluteness of truth, man has rejected any responsibility for accepting truth when presented.

Whence then will conviction come? The answer to this question lies in the recognition of the fact that the world today is passing through a crisis, or a judgment on the way it has lived and thought and acted. But the reality of a crisis is revealed principally through history. History is the revelation of catastrophe, and it is through a catastrophe that many are finding their way back again to God. History is here understood not as a bare narration of facts, but rather as a philosophy of history. It is made up of two elements: metaphysics and events, or morality and time. History has begun to displace science as the window through which the mind envisages reality, for science is only a record of *what is happening*, whereas history is a record of what matters.

Nicholas Berdyaev suggests that in any historical crisis there are three stages. The first is a period of a fully matured and crystallized civilization, which for modern Western history might well be Medieval Christendom. The second period is one of "fateful menacing disruption" of that organic unity, in which man becomes uprooted from tradition. The third period is one in which there is a further degeneration and alienation of God from fellowman, resulting in the "de-animation of history and the annihilation of its inner mysteries" in such extremes as historical materialism and other totalitarian systems.[1] Arnold J. Toynbee speaks of these three stages in the language of the Athenian drama: The first stage is Κόρος or the psychological stage of being spoiled by too much success; the second stage, Ὕβρις, is the consequent loss of mental and moral balance; the third stage, Ἄτη, is disaster and chaos.[2] Pitirim Sorokin also enumerates three stages: the ideational, idealistic, and sensate.[3]

How these, or any other stages of history, will be interpreted depends upon the particular philosophy one brings to history. Among the more important philosophies of history the following may be mentioned:

1. The Cyclic theory of history—Grecian and Oriental.
2. The Humanistic and Deistic view of history.
3. The Evolutionary theory of history.
4. The Economic theory of history.
5. The Pessimistic theory of history.
6. The Moral view of history.

THE GREEK VIEW OF HISTORY

Neither Plato nor Aristotle nor any of the great Greek thinkers seemed to attach much importance to history, and certainly none of them had a philosophy of history. Aristotle probably denied a Providence, and was satisfied with God as the Immobile Mover, but he never thought of God as ruling and guiding the destinies of history. The perfect motion for the Greeks was the movement of the heavens, which was circular, for in circular motion the beginning is the end; from this they concluded that the temporal order must also be in cycles. Not only do plants and animals go through this cycle of generation and corruption, but the cosmos and all things that are in it have their appointed numbers and revolutions and eventually begin anew.

This notion of the Great Year and the recurrent cycles was not strictly Grecian, but in a wider sense Eastern. It was common to all the great civilizations of Persia, India, China, and Babylon. In these countries it was magical and astrological, but in Greece it became philosophical when Aristotle gave it its highest expression. "For if the movement of heavens appears periodic and eternal, then it is necessary that the details of this movement, and all the effects produced by it, will be periodic and eternal." [4] "And when these cycles do return, they will appear in identical form, not once or twice, nor a few times but to infinity." [5] Upon this theory of cyclic return is founded the popularity of astrology, in which the next stage can be foretold from the stars. By making the heavens the efficient cause of earthly age, Aristotle made the movement of the heavens worth investigating for the light they might shed on human affairs. The Hellenic mind was therefore uninterested in the historical future as the achievement of a purpose related to God, but only in a harmonious cosmos whose beginning was its end. It sought an escape from the transient and mutable by taking refuge in eternal realities. Nicholas Berdyaev summarized it well: "Truth, the Divine values and the Divine harmony were revealed to Hellenic consciousness only in eternal nature. The Greeks had no knowledge of the historical progression which carries the universe towards a catastrophic event." [6]

THE HUMANISTIC VIEW OF HISTORY

The Greek view of history was cyclic and cosmic. The humanistic was human and progressive. The guarantee of progress was not God, but man. If God exists, according to the humanistic idea, He never interferes with the universe which He made. Nature is pictured as a mechanism, as a clock which God, the First Cause, wound and left to run by itself. Because it ran so well, some concluded that a Designer was superfluous, and that the universe was self-sustaining. Any purposes which appear in history, they found to have been injected by man. To have recourse to any other explanation was a sign of weakness. The humanistic theory had its roots in deism which, while abandoning all supernatural elements, nevertheless retained something of the Christian heritage in preserving a teleological concept of human life. Denying Divine purpose, deism retained human purpose. We find something of this spirit in Macaulay and the Whig school of history with their notion of "the inherent greatness of Englishmen." More recently we find this idea among humanists of today, who with a certain amount of condescending pity for those who still believe in Providence, nevertheless refuse to take refuge in such an escape.

The humanist can appreciate why sensitive souls suffer with an inferiority feeling, or gentle hearts, sick with the anguish and chaos of a ruthless civilization should flee for refuge to the security of some system of final truth. The humanist cannot flee.... In the societies of yesterday there were sick souls who needed other worldly opiates.[7]

William James believed that throwing the purposiveness of history entirely on man was necessary to make the universe interesting. Because man makes his own destiny, "Life feels like a real fight—as if there were something really wild in the universe we needed to redeem." [8]

This particular view of history stands at the extreme end of the Oriental philosophy of life. It is apt to be an error of the Eastern World to think that God does everything and man does nothing; it is apt to be the error of the Western World to believe that man does everything and God does nothing. The Oriental thus ends in Fatalism, and the Occidental in Pride. Fatalism can stand catastrophe better than Pride, for Fatalism can take a disaster in its stride, but to the proud Humanist, disaster is the negation and overthrow of his whole philosophy of life.

EVOLUTIONARY OR OPTIMISTIC THEORY OF HISTORY

History is also interpreted as being cosmically determined by inherent laws, such as the law of evolution which guarantees perfectibility to man, and inevitable progress in an ascending line. "This process must be the necessary outcome of the psychical and social nature of man: it must not be at the mercy of any external will; otherwise there would be no guarantee of its continuance and its issue and the idea of Progress would lapse into the idea of Despair." [9] The separation of Progress from Providence was prompted by the desire of the rationalist to escape the reality of God. The alternative to Providence is not Progress, but chance. Rationalism however refused to seek the foundation of Progress in chance, for that would make Progress uncertain. There would be less guarantee for it if blind accident were substituted for an external will. For that reason, rationalism set out to find some law embodying

physical necessity which would guarantee Progress. The future
was to be certain:

In that blessed day there will be no war, no crimes, no administration of
justice, as it is called, and no government. Besides this there will be
neither disease, anguish, melancholy, nor resentment. Every man will
seek with ineffable ardour the good of all. Mind will be active and eager,
and yet never disappointed.[10]

Even in the midst of the First World War, Dr. Harry Emerson
Fosdick bemoaned the ignorance of "The Age of Faith" in the
medieval centuries. He considered with surprise the things which
medieval man did not believe:

that the world would ever grow much better, that social abuses like
political tyranny and slavery could be radically changed, that man could
ever master nature by his inventions until her mighty forces were her
servants. That war could be abolished...none of these things did the
medieval folk believe.[11]

Sir Arthur Keith said in regard to Progress: "Everything living
and dead has been found to be subject to the law of evolution. The
Bible itself has not escaped.... How can man hope to escape a law
which is universal?" [12] Mr. H. G. Wells expressed the idea in this
way: "The ages of leisure and plenty are ahead.... We are visibly
moving toward an entirely literate and disciplined world.... Progress continues in spite of every human fear and folly. Men are borne
along through space and time regardless of themselves, as if to the
awakening of the greatness of Man." [13]

The evidence for this theory was not taken from history, but
from pre-history. By transplanting certain assumptions of the scientific vision of the natural world to the human order, by dwelling
on large vistas of time, progress was thought to be inevitable. By
going back into the dim beginnings of the universe, the evolutionary
historian assumed that the earliest humanlike creature was a sub-man
and the next *homo sapiens*, and concluded that man was naturally
progressive. By stressing the pre-cultural stages of man's history, the
necessity of inquiry into man as we know him in history was rejected. By making the importance of history quantitative and temporal, instead of qualitative and rational, history became nothing
more than an arbitrary selection of isolated facts showing man's

potentialities against the background of the mythical rise from the dust by his own efforts.

The net result of this emphasis on the geological and the biological in the treatment of history, was to make historians turn their backs on the history of Europe, or to treat it as a negligible factor and regrettable interlude in the imaginary drama of man's ascent from the state of beast to that of God. It completely blinded them to the fact which the World Wars have emphasized—that the history of Europe and the history of Christianity are one.

Berdyaev, in rejecting this view of history, comments:

Both from the religious and ethical points of view this positivist conception of progress is inadmissible, because by its very nature it excludes a solution to the tragic torments, conflicts and contradictions of life valid for all mankind, for all those generations who have lived and suffered. For it deliberately asserts that nothing but death and the grave awaits the vast majority of mankind and the endless succession of human generations throughout the ages, because they have lived in a tortured and imperfect state torn asunder by contradictions.

It is this fundamental moral contradiction that invalidates the doctrine of progress, turning it into a religion of death instead of resurrection and eternal life. There is no valid ground for degrading those generations whose lot has been cast among pain and imperfection beneath that whose pre-eminence has been ordained in blessedness and joy. No future perfection can expiate the sufferings of past generations. Such a sacrifice of all human destinies to the messianic consummation of the favoured race can only revolt man's moral and religious conscience. A religion of progress based on this apotheosis of a future fortunate generation is without compassion for either present or past; it addresses itself with infinite optimism to the future, with infinite pessimism to the past. It is profoundly hostile to the Christian expectation of resurrection for all mankind, for all the dead, fathers and forefathers. This Christian idea rests on the hope of an end to historical tragedy and contradiction valid for all human generations, and of resurrection in eternal life for all who have ever lived. But the nineteenth-century conception of progress admits to the messianic consummation only that unborn generations have made their sacrifice. Such a consummation, celebrated by the future elect among the graves of their ancestors, can hardly rally our enthusiasm for the religion of progress. Any such enthusiasm would be base and inappropriate.[14]

THE ECONOMIC THEORY OF HISTORY

Karl Marx's economic theory of history is the economic side of his dialectical materialism, and must therefore be prefaced by it. The idealistic background must logically be taken up first.

In April, 1841, Marx presented to the University of Jena his dissertation, "On the Difference Between the Natural Philosophy of Democritus and of Epicurus," for which he received the degree of Doctor of Philosophy. Democritus, he called the first "materialist," and Epicurus, the first "idealist." At this particular time and until 1844, Marx was a revolutionary bourgeois. Like the other young Hegelians, he clung to the dialectical method of Hegelianism as the guarantee of the progressiveness of the human race. Only after 1844 did he become a revolutionary proletarian.

There were two features in the philosophy of Hegelianism. The first feature was dialectical. Formal logic, it is said by the Hegelians, considers things as motionless, and assumes the Principle of Identity to be true. Dialectics considers them in motion. Dialectics teaches that no individual state, whether in the external world or in thought, may remain static, but that it constantly changes. Nothing is sacred, nothing is inviolable, and from this point of view dialectics is a formula of evolution. The second feature of Hegelianism is that it is idealistic, in an extreme form. According to Hegel, thought, by which he means universal thought, is autonomous. Thought is the mover and creator of reality whether it be nature or history. Hegel recognized the temporal development in history, but not in nature. Nature for Hegel moved eternally in the same groove. Hegel had a philosophy of history based on the idea of evolution. History is the slow unfolding of the idea of freedom, and institutions are the attempts of men to concretize and embody that idea historically. But each age grasps the idea only partially; its neglected aspects are supplied later by another idea which negates something in the old idea, and thus becomes constructive. Each idea has therefore positive and negative facets: love involves hate; good, evil; and freedom, slavery. Progress is thus conditioned on the contradiction of one idea by another and their absorption into a higher synthesis.

Philosophy of history was an instrument of politics, specifically, to justify the absolute Prussian state against liberalism and democracy, and to see in it the highest embodiment of the Absolute in history. Out of this dialectical idealism, Marx took the dialectic and rejected the idealism. The method he liked; the doctrine, he scorned. The method was already popularized. Ludwig Feuerbach and David Strauss had already applied it to the destruction of Christianity; Marx would apply it, under the inspiration of Proudhon, to capitalism.

The materialist side of his thought had the following background. The problem of religion was paramount at this time. While Bruno Bauer and Strauss were attempting to elucidate the origin of Christianity, Feuerbach, a pupil of Hegel, wrote on the *Essence of Christianity* (1841), a work which was frankly materialistic. "Man is what he eats," he wrote in a famous line. The thesis of Feuerbach was that Hegel's "absolute theory" was nothing but the "departing spirit of theology"; a "metaphysical spook"—a "theology made over into logic"; a "rational mysticism." Feuerbach, as Marx afterwards put it, stood Hegel on his head. He interpreted Hegel's absolute in terms of man and he interpreted man in terms of matter. Feuerbach believed, first, that God came from man. Man makes God to his image and likeness. Secondly, there is only sensible knowledge. The so-called supra-sensible is only a fantastic transformation of sense knowledge. Thought is not separable from matter.

Engels describes the repercussion of this work as follows:

Then came Feuerbach's *Essence of Christianity*. With one blow it pulverised the contradiction, in that without circumlocutions it placed materialism on the throne again. Nature exists independently of all philosophy. It is the foundation upon which we human beings, ourselves products of nature, have grown up. Nothing exists outside nature and man, and the higher beings our religious fantasies have created are only the fantastic reflection of our own essence. The spell was broken. The "system" was exploded and cast aside. And the contradiction, shown to exist only in our imagination, was dissolved. One must himself have experienced the liberating effect of this book to get an idea of it. Enthusiasm was general; we all became at once Feuerbachians.[15]

Marx, in his turn, greeted the Feuerbachians' outlook with these words:

Who has annihilated the dialectical concept, the war with God which the philosophers alone knew? Feuerbach. Who has put man in the place of the old absolute and in place of the infinite consciousness as well?

Feuerbach, no one else! Feuerbach, who completed and criticized Hegel from a Hegelian standpoint resolving the metaphysical absolute spirit into the real man standing on the fountain of nature, with the key to complete the criticism of religion—inasmuch as, at the same time, he undertook the particular Hegelian speculation, and thereby sketched the great and masterly outline of all metaphysics.

More specifically, this materialism of Marx differed from the "mechanistic" materialism of the nineteenth century in two respects: Marx attributed primacy to biology and chemistry, whereas "mechanistic" materialism attributed primacy to mechanics. Mechanistic materialism considered the world as static, while Marx regarded it as dynamic. In the Spring of 1845, in Brussels, Marx wrote in criticism of Feuerbach:

The chief defect of all hitherto existing materialism—that of Feuerbach included—is that the object, reality, sensuousness, is conceived only in the form of the *object* or *contemplation* but not as *human sensuous activity*, *practice*, not subjectively. Thus it happened that the *active* side, in opposition to materialism, was developed by idealism—but only abstractly, since, of course, idealism does not know real sensuous activity as such. Feuerbach wants sensuous objects, really differentiated from the thought-objects, but he does not conceive human activity itself as activity *through objects*. Consequently, in the *Essence of Christianity*, he regards the theoretical attitude as the only genuinely human attitude, while practice is conceived and fixed only in its dirty-Jewish form of appearance. Hence he does not grasp the significance of "revolutionary," of practical-critical, activity.[16]

Materialism is wrong because it forgets *thought*, namely, "human sensuous activity," whereas idealism was right in admitting *thought*, or "brain activity." Idealism was wrong in making thought mental, that is "only abstract." The materialists forgot thought (brains); idealists forgot matter.

The Marxist vision of materialism was like the hylozoism of the Stoics, according to which the universe is an immense animal in perpetual evolution. It thus attaches itself both to the naturalism of Epicurus and to the naturalism of the Encyclopedists. Sorel criticized Marxists on this very point, saying, "Their socialism knew nothing except what was learned from the free-thinkers." [17] This is true, for the moral and religious ideas which Marx received from Feuerbach are closely allied to the views of the Encyclopedists.

In Marx's view, Feuerbach was right in discarding idealism; he was wrong in rejecting the dialectic method. Marx united both dialectics and materialism and begot his dialectical materialism. That Marx was indebted to both Hegel and Feuerbach is evident from his early writings. In 1844, Marx edited a *Deutsch-Französiche Jahrbücher*, in which he said editorially that Germany was saved from the "metaphysical and fantastical idea of Lamennais, Proudhon, St. Simon, and Fourier" by Hegelian logic. On the other hand, in his criticism of the *Philosophy of Law* of Hegel, he showed the influence of Feuerbach by indicating how political criticism has supplanted theological criticism. In his review, at the same time, he also stated that "revolutions need a passive element, a material basis." Further influence of Feuerbach is revealed in a work of Marx written in collaboration with Engels against the "right wing Hegelians," who accepted the idealism of Hegel, as against the "left wing," which accepted only the dialectical method.

Just as they separate the soul from the body, and themselves from the world, so they separate history from natural science and industry, so they find the birthplace of history not in the gross material production on earth, but in the misty cloud formations of heaven.[18]

The difficulties Marx had with Feuerbach have already been indicated, but the philosophy of dialectic materialism was already formulated in his mind. It needed only to be applied to history. This theory in its simplest terms contends that the material conditions of life, taken as a whole, primarily determine the changes in human thought. For Providence, Marx substituted productive forces at any given time. These forces bring into being, at each new stage, institutions and ideas which, in their turn, react upon them.

His theory starts with the assumption that ideas are always shaped by the way in which men make their living. Since productive forces are the roots of all other ideas, it follows that the law, religion, politics, and education of any given period will reflect and be determined by the particular system of production which obtains at any given time. "Men make their own history," writes Marx, "but they do not do so spontaneously under conditions they themselves have chosen. On the contrary, they must make it upon terms already handed down to them and determined." (*The Eighteenth Brumaire*.) In these words he denies the influence of the human will in history and therefore all moral purpose in history.

What else does the history of ideas demonstrate except that intellectual production changes its character in proportion with the changes in material production. The governing ideas of each period are always the ideas of its governing class.[19]

In changing the modes of production, mankind changes all its social relations. The hand mill creates a society with the feudal lord; the steam mill a society with the industrial capitalist. The same men who establish social relations in conformity with their social relations.... All such ideas and categories are therefore historical and transitory products.[20]

A critical history of technology would show how little any of the inventions of the eighteenth century are the work of a single individual. Hitherto there has been no such book. Darwin has interested us in the history of Nature's technology, i.e., in the formation of the organs of plants and animals, which organs serve as instruments of production for sustaining life. Does not the history of the productive organs of man, of organs that are the material basis of all social organization, deserve equal attention? And would not such a history be easier to compile, since, as Vico says, human history differs from natural history in this, that we have made the former, but not the latter? Technology discloses man's mode of dealing with Nature—the process of production by which he sustains his life, and thereby also lays bare the mode of formation of his social relations, and of the mental conceptions that flow from them. Every history of religion, even, that fails to take account of this material basis, is uncritical. It is, in reality, much easier to discover by analysis the earthly core of the misty creations of religion, than it is, conversely, to develop from the actual relations of life the corresponding celestialized forms of those relations. The latter is the only materialistic, and therefore the only scientific method. The weak points in the abstract materialism of natural science, a materialism that excludes history and its process, are at once evident from the abstract and ideological conceptions of its spokesmen, whenever they venture beyond the bounds of their own speciality.[21]

The sum total of these relations of production constitutes the economic structure of society—the real foundation on which rise legal and political superstructures.... The mode of production in material life determines the general character of the social, political and spiritual processes of life.[22]

The second idea in the economic interpretation of history is that in every society there is a basic conflict between those who possess or control these productive forces and those who do not. Those who control them also control government, and those who do not control them are usually oppressed by that government, though not always consciously, but simply as a reaction to material environment. There thus arises in every society a conflict of classes. Compromise is possible for a time, but when it becomes impossible there is a revolution, which is always accompanied by violence. The last phase of this conflict is that between the bourgeoisie and the proletariat. "The whole history of mankind . . . has been a history of class struggles, conflicts between exploiting and exploited, ruling and oppressed classes." [23]

In 1852, Marx explained what was new in his system.

Middle-class historians long ago described the evolution of class struggles, and political economists explained the economic physiology of classes. My contribution has been to add the following theses: (1) that the existing classes are bound up with certain phases of material production; (2) that the class-struggle necessarily leads to the dictatorship of the proletariat; (3) that this dictatorship is merely the transition to the abolition of all classes, and the creation of a free and equal society." [24]

RELATION OF THIS THEORY TO MAN AND RELIGION

In his *Critique of the Philosophy of Law of Hegel*, Marx argues that the criticism of religion is the foundation of all criticism, and that religion is the opium of the people.

The basic principle of all criticism of Religion is: Man makes Religion, Religion does not make Man. And Religion is the consciousness and sentiment of himself felt by the man who has either not yet gained possession of himself, or has lost himself again.

But man is not some abstract being, squatting outside the world; Man is the world of men: State, Society. This State, this Society produce Religion, a perverted consciousness of the world, because the world is perverted. Religion is the universal theory of this actual world, its concise encyclopaedia, its "Logic" in a cheap edition, its spiritual *point d'honneur*, its enthusiasm, its moral sanction, its solemn completion, its universal justification. It is the illusory realizaton of man's being, because man's being has no actual reality. The struggle against Religion is the struggle against the world of which Religion is the spiritual deodorant.

Religious misery is, on the one side, an expression of actual misery, and on the other, a protest against that actual misery. Religion is the sob of the oppressed creature, the heart of a heartless world, the spirit of conditions utterly unspiritual. It is the laudanum of the poor.

The removal of Religion as the illusory happiness of the people means the demand of the people for their real happiness. The demand that they should give up their illusions about their condition is the demand that they should give up a condition which needs illusions. This criticism of Religion is, in germ, a criticism of the vale of misery, of which Religion is the holy mirage.

In order to understand these statements, one must go back to Marx's *Economic Philosophy*, in which he argues that religion is self-alienation; it alienates man from himself by making him subservient to God; it alienates man from himself by defending private property, thus making him subservient to an exploiter. The condition by which man will be restored to himself will be by atheism in its theoretical and practical aspects.

Atheism therefore is the starting point of the economic theory of history, because religion is self-alienation. Marx was an atheist before he was a communist. Because he was an atheist, he could see no value in the individual. Religion gives every man value because it recognizes in him a creature of God. But for Marx, man has value only because of his social relations. In the sixth thesis against Feuerbach, he wrote: "Human essence is not something inhabiting the separate individual. In its concreteness it is the totality of social relations."

Writing in the *Deutsch-Französische Jahrbücher*, in 1844, he expresses the same idea.

As the revolution in those days began with a monk, so today it must begin in the brain of a philosopher. If Protestantism is not the true solution, it was at any rate an indication of the task. It was no longer a conflict of the layman with the priest outside himself, but with his own *inner priest*, with his clerical nature.[25]

Marx is here saying that just as Protestantism did away with the priest who regarded man as supernatural, society must do away with the idea that every man is sacred because he is human.

If man is no longer a creature of God, whose creature is he? He belongs to society. Feuerbach believed that "what man declares about God he can in all truthfulness assert about himself." (*Works,* VII, 48-49.) Marx and Engels departed from Feuerbach's conception of man. Feuerbach arrives at his type of man from God, and for this reason, "man is still surrounded by a halo of theological abstraction. . . . We have to proceed from empiricism and materialism." Man, according to Marx, is tied up with nature, and nature with him. This integration with the community is the essence of the new man.

For that reason Marx had no sympathy for the "democratic conception of man"—"because it was too Christian." In 1843 he wrote that the "democratic" conception is false because it is "Christian" and asserts "that not one man alone but each man has a value as a sovereign being: man even as uncultured and unsocial, man in his casual manner of being, man as he walks and stands ... for liberal democracy that is an illusionary dream and postulate of Christianity, namely, man has a sovereign soul." [26]

In the preface to the first edition in English of *Capital*, Vol. II, p. 864, Marx reminds us that:

if I speak of individuals, *it is only insofar as they are personifications of economic categories and representatives of special class relations and interests.* Inasmuch as I conceive the development of the economic structure of society to be a natural process, I should be the last to hold the individual responsible for conditions whose creature he himself is.

This is a repudiation of individual morality and the beginning of totalitarianism. The individual proletarian has no value. This denial of the value of the individual man and therefore of democracy and Christianity, Marx also developed in the ninth thesis against Feuerbach, in which he ridiculed the "contemplative materialism of isolated individuals and of bourgeois society." Spinoza had already decided that the individual was an illusion. Marx went beyond this and said that the individual was an illusion because he was essentially social—an interplay of unconscious economic and productive forces.

Thus the fact is: Definite individuals, engaged in definite methods of production, enter upon these definite social and political relations. Empirical observation must, in each separate case, show the connection of social and political organization with production, by honest empiricism, without speculation or mysticism. Social organization and the State incessantly arise out of the life-process of definite individuals, but not from these individuals as they may appear in their own, or others' idea of them, but from themselves as they really are, that is to say, as they work and materially produce, thus from themselves as they are active under definite material limitations, pre-conditions and conditions which are independent of their free will.

The ideas which these individuals conceive are ideas either concerning their relation to Nature, or their relations to one another, or their own nature. It is evident that in all these cases these ideas are the conscious—

whether real or illusory—expression of their true relations, their production, their traffic, their social and political "behavior." The opposite supposition is only possible if a separate Spirit is assumed apart from the spirit of real, materially conditioned individuals. If the conscious expression of their real conditions by these individuals is illusory, if in their ideas they stand the reality on its head, this is again an outcome of their stunted methods of activity, and the stunted social relations which derive therefrom.[27]

Since culture is promoted principally by productive forces of an economic character, it follows, according to Marx, that religion is of no importance either in life or history, for it is simultaneously a consequence of man's exploitation—that is, it is built upon a method of production which enslaved man; and it also is a means of exploiting man, in the sense that it is the opium of the people. It owes its existence solely to certain economic conditions and therefore could not exist without them.

Men may be distinguished from animals by consciousness, religion, or anything else. They begin to differentiate themselves from animals as soon as they begin to produce their means of subsistence, a step which is conditioned by their physical organization. By producing their means of existence, men indirectly produce their material life itself. The mode in which men produce their means of existence depends in the first place on the nature of the means of existence themselves—those which they find at their disposal and have to reproduce.

This mode of production must not be considered merely from the aspect that it is the reproduction of the physical existence of individuals. It is rather, in fact, a definite form of activity of these individuals, a definite form of expressing their life, their definite mode of life. As individuals express their life, so they are. What they are therefore coincides with their production—what they produce as well as how they produce. What individuals are therefore depends on the material conditions of their production.[28]

Finally, Marx maintains, religion has no history, because it has no independence.

In direct contrast to German philosophy, which descends from heaven to earth, here the ascent is made from earth to heaven. That is to say, we do not start from what men say, imagine, conceive, nor from men as described, thought of, imagined and conceived, in order thence and thereby to reach corporeal men; we start from real, active men, and from their life-process also show the development of the ideological reflexes and echoes of this life-process. Morals, religion, metaphysics and all other ideology and the corresponding forms of consciousness thus no longer maintain the appearance of independence. They have no history, they have no development; but men, developing their material production and their material intercourse, change, along with this their real existence, also their thinking and the products of their thought. It is not consciousness that determines life, but life that determines consciousness.[29]

The economic theory of history completely rejects religion as an influence in culture, since religion itself is considered a product of a certain method of production; this theory furthermore rejects the value of individual man in history, for man has no value under Marxism unless he is a representative of a revolutionary class. The most fundamental difference between Christianity and Marxism is in their respective concepts of the value of the individual person. The idea of the sacredness of human personality is inseparable from Christianity; but it is an obstacle to Marxism, which declares that the individual finds his perfection only in a class.

Furthermore, violence is an integral part of the Marxian dialectics of history. Admittedly, Marxists might declare that Christianity in some instances was cruel; they could never say that cruelty arose out of its teachings. The Marxist principle, on the contrary, admits the necessity of force to mold the individual into an impersonal component of a class. In all ages the Christian ethics is one of loving one's neighbor; it is not an ethics derived from historically determined forces of production, which bind Marxism to a type of civilization which has lost all understanding of man's inner life. Its ethics is a class-ethics, not an ethics based on responsibility. This is Marxism's greatest error, for in a sinful world, personality rooted in responsibility to God must maintain unyielding independence against an economic society, under the penalty of losing its happiness.[30]

THE PESSIMISTIC THEORY OF HISTORY

The best exponent of the pessimistic theory of history is Oswald Spengler (1880-1936). He was born in the Harz country in the same year as Keyserling, and later studied science and mathematics at the universities of Munich, Berlin, and Halle. After a few years of teaching in a school at Hamburg, he devoted himself principally to his studies and writing. His chief work, *Der Untergang des*

Abendlandes (Vol. I, 1918; Vol. II, 1922),[81] interpreted the history of the world as a succession of "cultures," each of which passes through various stages of growth. He considered that European culture had now passed into its final stage. This work was above all else a refutation of the idea of progress, but it also inaugurated a wave of pessimism which dominated Germany at the close of the last war.

Another work of his not so well known to English readers is *Preussentum und Sozialismus* (1920), which is said to have had a much greater effect on German youth than the *Decline of the West*. This lesser work throws particular light upon the struggle involved in World War II. His thesis was that the Treaty of Versailles would mean a continuation of the war, and that the Weimar Republic—an attempt to introduce democracy into Germany—was the most senseless act in German history. Spengler compared the Weimar Revolution with the English and French revolutions of 1688 and 1789. All three revolutions, he believed, were concerned with power. The English decided that power belonged to the individual, and therefore there must be freedom of competition and enterprise among individuals. The French decided that power belongs to nobody, and they ended in confusion and revolution. The German instinct, or more correctly the Prussian instinct, believed that power belongs to the whole community, that the individual exists for the community. Spengler, therefore, advocated a form of socialism for Germany, not of the Marxist variety, but rather German Socialism, which he declared was stronger and deeper than that of Marx. Socialism was in the German blood, and the blood decides the future. According to Spengler, it is part of the Prussian tradition that the will of the individual should surrender itself to the will of the community. English and Americans worked in order to make themselves rich. The Germans worked to bring power and happiness, not to the individual, but to the nation. "Frederich William I and not Marx was in this sense the first conscious socialist."

In order that German Socialism should not be accused of being the Marxist brand, Spengler contended that the ideas of Marx were typically English. For example, he said that Marx could have derived his idea of class war only from England, where people were graded according to the wealth they possessed. In Prussia, on the contrary, men were graded on the service they rendered to the community—according to the degree of command and obedience which their activities entailed. The basis of Marx's economics was that work was something to be bought and sold, a typically English idea, but the essence of the Prussian socialism was that work was a duty to the community and no distinction was to be made on the basis of the kind of work performed. Spengler further declared that the choice the world had to make for itself in the future was between socialism and capitalism, between the State and the Parliament. In conclusion, he appealed to the youth of Germany to put his ideas into practice.

I turn to youth. I call upon all those who have marrow in their bones as blood in their veins. Educate yourselves! Become men! ... The path to power is clearly marked; the elect of the German workers together with the best representatives of the old Prussian political spirit, both of them determined to create a truly socialistic state, a democracy in the Prussian sense, firmly united by a common sense of duty, by the consciousness of their great task, by the will to obey in order to rule, by the rule to die in order to live, by the strength to make tremendous sacrifices in order to fulfill our destinies, to be what we are and what without us would be lacking altogether in the world.

His *Decline of the West* made a few real contributions: he showed that nations are not the best subjects for the study of the general laws of history, because nations are too recent a division of society. Instead he turned to "civilizations" as basic units of history, an approach which Arnold J. Toynbee has recognized in his own magnificent study. History, Spengler maintained, cannot be understood in terms of mathematical and experimental methods and sciences. With Bergson, he insisted that life must be grasped, not demonstrated. Like plants, civilizations grow, decline, and die. The whole of history is resolved into comparisons, in which he has taken the *analogia entis* from metaphysics and applied it to history—a method valid within limits.

His theory of history also has the advantage of substituting an organic, for a mechanical interpretation. Some philosophers, for example Schopenhauer, denied that history had a pattern; others, among them the evolutionists, believed it was a rigid, unilateral progress from barbarism to industrialism. Spengler rejected both views by finding birth and decay, rise and decline, as necessary elements in history. Vico saw this before Spengler, of course. However, Spengler departed from Vico's views in his study of civilizations in place of nations, and in his insistence that each particular civilization differs from every other civilization.

Spengler believed, with something of the pride of Rousseau, that he was writing not merely a philosophy of our time, but "*the* philosophy of our time." [32] It was "a new outlook on *history* and the *philosophy of destiny*—the first indeed of its kind." [33] "I am proud to call it a *German philosophy*." [34]

The work is frankly pessimistic, and Spengler recognized it as such.

> Of course the cry of "pessimism" was raised at once by those who live eternally in yesterday and read every idea that is intended for the path-finder of tomorrow only.... It is the hard reality of living that is essential, not the concept of life that the idea of idealism propounds. Those who refuse to be bluffed by enunciations will not regard this as pessimism; and the rest do not matter.[35]

This path of pessimism is further manifested in his view of man. He taught, according to Keyserling, that:

> man is a *beast of prey*, I shall say it again and again. All the paragons of virtue and the thinkers in social ethics who wish to be or rise above that, are merely beasts of prey with their teeth drawn.... When I call man a beast of prey whom do I insult, the man or the beast? For the great beasts of prey are *noble* creations in the fullest degree and are without the mendacious habits of human mortals which are due to weakness.[36]

It followed for Spengler that "as far as the goal of humanity is concerned I am a thorough and decided pessimist. For me humanity is a zoological quantity. I see no progress, no goal, no way of humanity—except in the hands of Western Philistines, who believe in progress." [37]

In addition to this declaration that man is a zoological quantity, Spengler made these other assumptions: There is no freedom in man or history—the destiny of both are predetermined. Therefore, "in historical reality there are no ideals; there are only facts. There are no reasons, no righteousness, no equity, no final goal." All truth is relative—"The real student of mankind treats no standpoint as absolutely right or absolutely wrong." In the preface to the revised edition of *The Decline of the West,* Spengler made a similar statement. "I can tnen call the essence of what I have discovered 'true'—that is *true for me*, and as I believe, true for the leading minds of the coming times; not true in itself as dissociated from the conditions imposed by blood and by history, for that is impossible." "The Western mind," Spengler believed:

is too much inclined to judge world history from the viewpoint of his own particular civilization. It is *this* that is lacking in the Western thinker, the very thinker in whom we might have expected to find it—insight into the *historically relative* character of this data, which are expressions of one *specific existence and one only;* knowledge of the necessary limits of their validity; the conviction that his "unshakeable" truths and "eternal" views are simply true for him and eternal for his world-view. ... [38] In the face of such grave problems as that of Time, or that of Marriage, it is insufficient to appeal to personal experience, or an inner voice, or reason, or the opinion of ancestors or contemporaries. These may say what is true for the questioner himself and for his time, but that is not all.[39]

The two principal influences that Spengler acknowledges are those of Goethe and Nietzsche:

and now, finally, I feel urged to name once more those to whom I owe practically everything: Goethe and Nietzsche. Goethe gave me methods, Nietzsche the questioning faculty—and if I were asked to find a formula for my relations to the latter I should say that I have made of his "out-look" an "overlook." [40]

Though he acknowledged his debt to Nietzsche, he nevertheless insisted that Nietzsche's historical horizon was too narrow, being limited solely to Western civilization. "Strictly speaking, he never once moved outside the scheme, nor did any thinker of his time." [41]

Goethe, on the contrary, was free from such possessions:

That which Goethe called *living nature* is exactly what we are calling here world history, *world-as-history*. Goethe, who as an artist portrays the life and development, always the life and development of his figures, the thing-becoming and not the thing-become, hated mathematics. For him, the world-as-mechanism stood opposed to the world-as-organism, led nature to living nature, law to form.[42]

The *purpose* of his work was negatively to show the fallacy of the idea of progress and rationalism. The Oriental pictured the world at rest; the Western World pictured it as progression. Positively, Spengler attempted to write what he called a morphology of a history of philosophy. Such an effort involves scrapping the old historical notion that history is divided into three periods; ancient, medieval, and modern. This "angular, narrow, shallow" division was the best that could be used until Spengler gave us his own, which he called "*the* philosophy of the future." The difference between his view of history and what he chooses to call all other views, may be illustrated by a series of contrasts:

The old view of history could be compared to *mathematical* law, inasmuch as all civilizations were regarded as fixed and static and dead. Spengler's view of history is *analogical*. Since the past is not something that has become, but something which is becoming, it follows that eras, epochs, situations, and persons are ever repeating themselves through the ages. For that reason historians have drawn analogies, for example, "between Napoleon and Caesar, between Florence and Athens, and Christ-primitive Christianity with modern Socialism. The Roman financial magnate of Caesar's time was the Yankee." [43]

Those who made these analogies, Spengler says, did not use them as a principle, or out of a sense of historical necessity, but simply out of inclination. What they lacked, he intends to supply, namely, "a technique of analogies." "In this region no one hitherto has set himself to work out a *method*, nor has had the slightest inkling that there is here a root, in fact that only root, from which can come a broad solution of the problems of History." [44]

Corresponding to this distinction of mathematics and analogy, is the further one of the world-as-history and the world-as-nature. The world-as-history regards events according to a scheme of causes and effects, after the fashion of natural science. The world-as-nature emphasizes the chronological aspect of history, rather than the causal aspect. "What concerns us is not what the historical facts which appear at this or that time *are, per se,* but what they signify, what they point to, by appearing....[45] Mathematics and the principle of Causality lead to a naturalistic Chronology, and the idea of Destiny to a historical ordering of the phenomenal world." [46]

Spengler furthermore distinguishes these two views of history in Bergsonian language of the logic of Space and the logic of Time. The logic of Space, he calls, "the necessity of cause and effect." The logic of Time, he calls, "organic necessity in life"; that of Destiny "is a fact of the deepest inward certainty, a fact which suffuses the whole of mythological religions and artistic thought and constitutes the essence and kernel of all history, but is unapproachable through the cognition-forms which the *Critique of Pure Reason* investigates." [47]

Another historian, Leopold Ranke, had once emphasized the equidistance of all historical events from eternity, but Spengler having rejected God in history, and enthroned time, fate, and "organic necessity," constructs another basis for his contemporaneity of fallen cultures.

The human element in history is discarded by Spengler in favor of nature. In this sense, his theory of history is like that of the Marxists and evolutionists. Probably because he rejects the primacy of human intellect and will in history for "organic necessity," he fails to see any purpose or meaning or unity in history. Just as nature passes through the various seasons of spring, summer, autumn, and winter, so too do civilizations undergo an analogous fate. Marx had equated the human with dialectical materialism, the evolutionists merged man in biology, so Spengler equates the human with the natural, or the historical with the fateful. Once this equation is assumed to be accurate, there can be no freedom in history, for freedom is of the spirit, and necessity is of nature. The task of the historian is therefore to correlate these pluralistic and diverse civilizations in terms of their "seasons," making all "spring" civilizations contemporaneous, all "summer" civilizations contemporaneous, all "autmn" civilizations contemporaneous, all "winter" civilizations contemporaneous.

For example, in considering the birth of a myth expressing a yearning for God and a fear of the world, the period of 1500-1200 B.C., when the Aryan hero tales were told, is contemporaneous with the period of 1100-800 B.C., in which Homer wrote, and with the period between the birth of Christ and the year 300 A.D., when the Gospels and the Apocalypse were written, and finally with the period of the year 900 and 1200 A.D., when flourished both Siegfried and Francis of Assisi. In referring to symbols, the pyramid temples of the years of 2900-2400 B.C. were regarded as contemporaneous with the Doric columns of 1100-500 B.C., and these in turn were contemporaneous with the basilica and cupola of the first and third centuries of the Christian era, and finally these were contemporaneous with the flying buttresses of the eleventh and thirteenth centuries.

The perpetual struggle which history involves centers around three principal cultures: the classical or Apollinian—the latter term Spengler took from Nietzsche; the Magian culture of the Arabs with its algebra, astrology, and alchemy, its mosaics and its arabesques, its caliphates and mosques; and the Faustian culture of the Western World: "Whose prime symbol is pure and limitless space, and whose 'body' is the Western Culture which blossoms forth with the birth of the Romanesque style in the tenth century in the Northern plain."

Contrasting the classical, or the Apollinian, with the Faustian culture, Spengler states:

Apollinian are: mechanical statics, the sensuous cult of the Olympian gods, the politically individual city-states of Greece, the doom of Oedipus and the phallus-symbol. Faustian are: dynamics, Catholic and Protestant dogmatics, the great dynasties of the Baroque with their cabinet diplomacy, the destiny of Lear and the Madonna-idea from Dante's Beatrice, to the last line of Faust II.[48]

The Faustian or Western culture is in decay, Spengler believed. "The last of the Faustian arts died in *Tristan*." [49] Philosophy ended with Kant. "Systematic philosophy closes with the end of the eighteenth century. Kant is followed, as Plato and Aristotle were followed, by the specifically megalopolitan, the practical, the irreligious, and the social-ethical." [50]

Ethics too, Spengler maintained, has exhausted itself and will appear only as socialism.

Ethical Socialism, prepared by Fichte, Hegel, and Humboldt, was at its zenith of passionate greatness about the middle of the nineteenth century, and at the end thereof it had reached the stage of repetitions. The twentieth century, while keeping the word *Socialism*, had replaced an ethical philosophy that only Epigoni supposed to be capable of further development, by a praxis of economic everyday questions. The ethical disposition of the West will remain "socialistic" but its theory has ceased to be a problem. And there remains the possibility of the third and last stage of Western philosophy, that of a physiognomic skepticism. The secret of the world appears successively as a knowledge problem, a valuation problem and a form problem. Kant saw ethics as an object of knowledge, the nineteenth century saw it as an object of valuation. The skeptic would deal with both simply as the historical expression of a culture.[51]

From this point the only philosophy possessed by the world will be, in the language of Schopenhauer—which Spengler quotes approvingly—"professor's philosophy by philosophy professors." The period to which our decaying Western civilization most corresponds is that of Caesar's Rome. "We are civilized, not Gothic or Rococo, people; we are directed with the hard cold facts of a *late life*, to which the parallel is to be found not in Pericles' Athens, but in Caesar's Rome." [52]

Spengler seems to imply that there is nothing for us to do in the face of this decline of the West but to submit to a destiny over which we have no control.

> A century of purely extensive effectiveness, excluding big artistic and metaphysical production—let us say frankly an irreligious time which coincides exactly with the idea of the world-city—is a time of decline. . . . But we have not *chosen* this time. We cannot help it if we are born as men of the early winter of full Civilization, instead of on the golden summit of a ripe Culture, in a Phidias or a Mozart time. Everything depends on our seeing our own position, our *destiny* clearly, on our own realizing that though we may lie to ourselves about it we cannot evade it. He who does not acknowledge this in his heart, ceases to be counted among the men of his generation, and remains either a simpleton, or a charlatan, or a pedant.[53]

This same note he strikes again at the end of his book.

> For us, however, whom a destiny has placed in this Culture and at this moment of its development—the moment when money is celebrating its last victories, and this Caesarism that is to succeed approaches with quiet, firm steps—our direction, willed and obligatory at once, is set for us within narrow limits, and on any other terms life is not worth living. We have not the freedom to reach to this or to that, but the freedom to do the necessary or to do nothing. This historic necessity *will* be accomplished with the individual or against him. "*Ducant Fata volentem, nolentem trahunt.*"[54]

Thus closes a zoological view of history wherein civilization and cultures are determined to greatness, not by will, nor by virtue, but by a blind historic necessity. In common with Marx, Spengler believed there was an inner historical necessity; but for Marx this was economic, for Spengler it was zoological. As Marx looked forward to Communism as the inevitable result of history, so Spengler looked forward to the supremacy of the German race, inspired by Prussia.

The five foregoing schools of history attempt to meet the problem of the irrational and, in some instances, the problem of catastrophe, within the field of history. What is common to all of these schools, with the exception of the Greek, is a denial, not only of the moral element in history, but also of the eternal. Even though the Greeks suggested some idea of the eternal in their cyclic theory of history, with its endless conflagrations, "deaths," and "rebirths," they nevertheless erected a great barrier between the temporal and the eternal. God to the Greeks was the great Unmoved Mover; history, on the other hand, was movement. If religion had any place in such a universe of recurrences, it was simply an escape from the destiny, or the necessity, by which the phenomenal universe was determined.

The humanitarian view of history, which we listed second, also rejects a God who is transcendent to history; rather, He must be wholly immanent in it. It secularizes all of the Christian principles and values. If there is redemption, it is within history and not beyond it; betterment comes not with grace, but through the human will as the sovereignty of man replaces the sovereignty of God. The evolutionary view of history, under the impetus of Herbert Spencer, gently shoves God aside as a motive force in history with the gloved hand of reverent agnosticism. By later evolutionary pragmatists, such as John Dewey, Emile Durkheim, and Samuel Alexander, reverent agnosticism was dropped in favor of an out-and-out optimism. Not only was God absolved from any responsibility in regard to the universe, but even man himself is absolved. As John Dewey remarked: "With responsibility for the intelligent determination of particular acts may go a joyful emancipation from the whole which sustains them, giving them their final outcome and quality." [55] The moral element was further eliminated from history by John Dewey, who regarded it as a scandal that one method should be used in the natural sciences and another in ethics. By making "social growth" the only standard of judging evolution, Dewey thus merged ethics into the realm of biology. Recognizing that the evolutionary view of history had no impelling goal other than the vague ideal of progress, some evolutionists sought to compensate for this weakness by creating an anti-Christian and atheistic basis for this progress, as Nietzsche did. However, such compensations are only accidental to this view of history.

The Marxian and Spenglerian theories of history are one with the evolutionary in their determinism and in their outlawing of a moral and religious foundation of history. In the evolutionary theory, history is biologically determined; under the Marxian, it is economically determined; and with Spengler, it is zoologically determined. It now remains to discuss the only theory which recognizes not only the sovereignty of God in history, but also the moral determinism of particular events.

THE MORAL VIEW OF HISTORY

The moral view of history can be understood in terms of four principles set in contrast to the foregoing:

Against the Greek cyclic view, and the evolutionary view, which interprets existence and history in terms of nature, determined either astronomically or biologically, philosophy affirms the principle of: *the discontinuity of nature and man.*

Against "externalistic" views of history, which account for historical and social changes primarily and principally in terms of cycles (Greek) or biology (evolutionary) or methods of production (Marxist) or Fate and Destiny (Spenglerian), philosophy affirms the principle of: *the immanence of human reason and will in history.*

Against the humanistic and deistic view of history, which attributes social change solely to the immanence of the human reason and will in history, philosophy affirms the counterbalancing principle of: *the transcendence of God to history.*

Against all views of history which attribute historical processes to the operation of law, either mechanical, economic, biological, zoological, or fatalistic, philosophy affirms the principle of: *the supremacy of person over law.*

Concerning the discontinuity of man and nature, most amoral views of history assume that man is continuous with nature, that psychology is physiology, and that all the laws of animal evolution necessarily govern human evolution. It was by no accident that Marx, who believed in economic determinism, should have asked Darwin, who believed in biological determinism, to accept the dedication of one of his books. It was not by chance that Engels attempted to prove the truth of dialectical materialism by an appeal to the symbol of a barley seed, nor that Spengler should have relied heavily on time-physics to develop his theory of contemporaneous human histories. But this assumption of the continuity of nature and man is false.

If man is an integral part either of methods of production or the experimental sciences, then what claim shall he lay to be treated any differently from an animal or a machine? Marx and Spengler willingly accepted this consequence, Marx denying that man had any value except as a member of a revolutionary class, and Spengler affirming that he was only a "beast of prey." Once man is identified with nature, there is no reason why a man should be appealed to, to accept Marxism rather than Spenglerism, any more than a machine or a beast. If history is ever to interest man, it must be specifically *human.* The confusion of the human with economic production, or with immanent zoological laws of destiny, or with evolutionary emergents is unhistorical and irrational. "While the show is going on, it may glow with subjective light and warmth, but the truth lies with the final sum, and the final sum is the zero of meaning." [56]

Man is discontinuous with nature, among other reasons, because he has an intellect and a will. Human intelligence has operations independent of the organism; the animal has no such operations. Since the mind can produce such spiritual effects as "justice," "faith," "relation," and other abstractions, it follows that the cause must be of like nature, namely, spiritual. [57]

Morality, which is impossible without freedom and a soul conscious of ends, is a break with nature. This is proved by the fact that animal nature always operates on the principle of struggle and competition and survives as such. But man functions and prospers best by means of co-operation, and in the supernatural order, by charity. It is no escape from the principle of discontinuity between man and nature to argue that whatever is higher in the scale of biological evolution is necessarily higher ethically, for how could one judge about the "ethically higher" except by a standard outside both?

The difference between sensations and ideas proves the discontinuity of nature and man. It is quite true that when the human eye is stimulated by a light, it sees, and when the ear is stimulated by sound, it hears. But it does not follow from this that man is only a machine made up of actions and reactions like the piston of a cylinder or that his behavior is essentially that of an animal. The eye, though it is adapted for vision, can suffer a twofold harm by a too powerful stimulus, such as an ultra-violet light. A very bright light will not only impair the vision, but it will also make the eye unfit for seeing other things. The ear, though adapted to sound, if it is stimulated by an excessive sound, such as an explosion, will become temporarily deaf and thus be unable to hear other sounds. Where the stimulus is too powerful, the power of sensation is killed.

Now if the nature of man as an intelligent being is the same as the nature of an animal, why is it that when a behaviorist has a bright idea, the bright idea does not follow the law that applies to bright lights? Why does not a bright idea, like the idea of "God," or of "justice," destroy the intellect as a bright light destroys the eye? Why does it not impair the intellect for further thinking, as a bright light impairs the eye for further vision? If man is only an animal, and thinking is merely a form of animal behavior, then the same law should apply to bright ideas as to bright lights. But as a matter of fact the same law does not apply. On the contrary, a bright idea, like the idea of "God," not only does not befog and benumb the mental faculties, but gives them greater clarity for the understanding of the universe and the problems of life, for in the light of that idea a thousand other confusions become clear.

Furthermore, if intellectual activity were merely a question of nerve centers and organic reactions, then fatigue should increase in direct ratio with the sublimity and intensity of the intellectual vision, just as the senses become fatigued if they are too strongly excited. The contrary, however, is the case; the contemplation of sublime truths, instead of fatiguing the intellect and putting it in a state of incapacity for further thought, excites it and equips it for further ascensions and excursions into the realm of the spiritual. If thought were just a matter of sensible reactions, then it should follow the law of all sensible reactions. But the very fact that it does not follow these, leads me to believe that there is something nonmaterial, nonglandular, and noncorporeal, which we call the soul. A man can go blind looking at the sun, but no man ever went intellectually blind looking to the Justice of the Son of God. This can only be because the eye of the mind is different in nature from the eye of the body.

St. Thomas, after the example of Aristotle, constantly uses the example of laughter to prove the difference between man and animal. Laughter is caused by seeing the unexpected relations between two judgments, and since a relation can be perceived only by something spiritual, it follows that only a man with a spiritual principle can laugh. Take, for example, this story. A visitor once said to a little girl of six, "What will you do, my dear child, when you are as big as your mother?" "Diet," answered the child. Now that is not a particularly good story, but if you will imagine the circumstances when it first happened, it can prove my point. Suppose a dog, a cat, or a canary was in the room at the same time the child made that answer. The dog and the cat and the canary would have received exactly the same auditory stimuli. They would have heard the sounds produced by twenty-nine words. Now, why is it that the dog, the cat, or the canary did not smile at hearing those words, whereas the visitor who asked the child, smiled, or had to suppress a smile so as not to embarrass the child's mother? It is because the visitor out of those twenty-nine words got thirty reactions. In other words, he got something out of them that was not in them. The visitor had to see a double meaning in the word "big": the age meaning and the size meaning.

But in order to see both meanings at one and the same time—the condition of understanding any pun—one must not only be material but also spiritual. If a box is filled with salt, it cannot be filled with pepper at one and the same time. And if the mind is filled only with matter—the auditory sensation of "big"—it cannot see the word "big" in the other sense that produces laughter.

That is where all behavioristic and mechanistic explanations of life fail. They cannot account for that wonderful madness called laughter. Nothing in lower creation ever produced anything even remotely resembling a laugh. It is not a matter of degree, with animals beginning to smile, and man breaking out into a laugh. There is something absolutely new when we come to man. The pony did not give a smile and the truck horse, a horselaugh. The early hyenas did not merely grin and the later ones laugh—though they have their mouths open. The small valleys did not begin to titter and the bigger ones rock with laughter. One never meets a smile until one comes to man, and the only reason one meets it in man is that man has a soul that can rise above matter and see the relations between things, and in particular, the incongruous ones that help to make life more amusing. It is more than a figure of speech to say that man "breaks" out into a laugh, for it is a positive break away from everything below him in creation. It is a break with the past, it is a break with matter, it is the beginning of spirit.

The fact of nonsense witnesses also to the discontinuity between man and nature. Behaviorism holds that man is nothing more than the complexes of "receptors," "conductors," and "effectors"; and that conditioned by the same stimuli, he will always react in identically the same way. In this sense man is a machine. But we never attribute nonsense to a machine, except by exaggeration. If, for example, Key 7 and Key 6 of an adding machine are stimulated and they respond with the total of 57, we do not say that the machine is "crazy," or that it has done a "nonsensical" thing. We simply say that it has "gone wrong." But if a man adds 7 and 6 so as to make 57, we say that he is guilty of mathematical nonsense. Mr. Dumb was once asked by a dandruff-remedy company for a testimonial, and he responded: "Before using your dandruff remedy I had two bald spots. Now I have only one." That statement is colossal nonsense of which no machine is capable. Now if man is only a machine, and the sum of nerve reactions, why do we attribute nonsense only to man and not to a machine? If there is no essential difference between man and an adding machine, except that man's machinery is slightly damper, how account for the nonsense in the case of man, and the attribution of loss of efficiency in the case of a machine? It can only be because a machine is mechanical and determined, and therefore must do certain things, whereas man is spiritual and free, and therefore *ought* to do certain things. It is the difference between the "must" of machinery and the "ought" which immediately takes us out of the realms of machinery and physiology.

As Professor Eddington, in his *Nature of the Physical World*, has so well stated:

Starting with aether, electrons, and other physical machinery, we cannot reach conscious man and render count of what is apprehended in his consciousness. Conceivably, we might reach a human machine interacting by reflexes with its environment; but we cannot reach rational man morally responsible to pursue the truth as to aether, electrons, or religion.... In a world of aether and electrons we might perhaps encounter nonsense; we can never encounter damn nonsense.

After all, it is not satisfactory to account for the twitchings, twistings, and squirmings of baby life as "a reaction mass as a whole," for the whole world knows, in its moments of sanity, that no matter how many jumping Mexican beans were put into a bag and shaken together, the sum of their "reaction mass as a whole" would never make them become conscious of themselves.

Another evidence of the discontinuity between nature and man is the fact that man alone can draw pictures, for art is the projection of the ideal through the real, and man also, because of his soul, is capable of ideals. Chesterton argues in his *Everlasting Man* that as man did not come out of nature, so Christ did not come out of history. As evidence for the first statement, he adduces the fact of art.

> A monkey does not draw clumsily and a man cleverly; a monkey does not begin the art of representation and a man carry it to perfection. A monkey does not do it at all; he does not begin to do it at all. A line of some kind is crossed before the first faint line can begin.

> It is the simple truth that man does differ from the brutes in kind and not in degree; and the proof of it is here; that it sounds like a truism to say that the most primitive man drew a picture of a monkey and that it sounds like a joke to say that the most intelligent monkey drew a picture of a man. Something of division and disproportion has appeared; and it is unique. Art is the signature of man.

> Monkeys did not begin pictures and men finish them; Pithecanthropus did not draw a reindeer badly and Homo Sapiens draw it well. The higher animals did not draw better and better portraits; the dog did not paint better in his best period than in his early bad manner as a jackal; the wild horse was not an Impressionist and the race horse a Post-Impressionist. All we can say of this notion of reproducing things in shadow or representative shape is that it exists nowhere in nature except in man; and that we cannot even talk about it without treating man as something separate from nature. In other words, every sane sort of history must begin with man as man, a thing standing absolute and alone. How he came there, or indeed how anything else came there, is a thing for theologians and philosophers and scientists and not for historians. But an excellent test case of this isolation and mystery is the matter of the impulse of art. This creature was truly different from all other creatures; because he was a creator as well as a creature.[58]

Since man is not one with nature, history is not identical to biology, or zoology. History is interesting, not because it is determined either dialectically or biologically, but because man is free, whereas nature is not. The method of studying man is not the method of studying inanimate nature. The two are even more distinct than the study of a nursery garden and the study of a gasoline motor. As the "Pathetic Fallacy" endows inanimate objects with life, so the "Apathetic Fallacy" locates man and his history as if man were a toad or a monkey. History is not a study of entities, it is a study of intelligible relations which are rooted in man. Philosophy thus leads to a true understanding of history. But there is much for philosophy yet to say. Once having distinguished man from nature, it next reveals why man is so important in history, namely, because of his intellect and will.

The immanence of human reason and human will in history can be demonstrated through reason. All the philosophies of history outlined above, with the exception of the Humanistic, are "externalistic" in the sense that they deny that human will and human reason are very important determinants of history. The defects of externalistic views are grounded on a false assumption taken from the mechanics of the Cartesian and Newtonian law of inertia, that if a material body is at rest it will continue so unless disturbed by another force. Once history is treated as a branch of mechanics, it follows that the disturbance of the equilibrium of any historical era must necessarily be explained by "an external force" which sets the epoch in a new direction. If society were made up of billiard balls instead of human beings with their own intimate activity of intellect and will, this interpretation of history would be sound.

A second false assumption, and one that is more modern, is derived from behavioristic psychology, which denies the existence of the human soul. In this particular case, physiology, and not physics, becomes the basis of the study of history. Instead of the "action" and the "reaction" of physics, we have the "stimulus" and "response" of psychology. Since animals generally do not give any "response" unless they are acted upon by an outside "stimulus," the externalistic views of history assume that we must look outside of man and society for the source of changes, reactions, and revolutions. If man were not specifically different from an animal, this view of social and cultural phenomena would be acceptable. But once given an immanent source of activity in man, environment and social factors and methods of production only modify or condition historical changes; they do not cause them, or explain them. The externalistic approaches do not explain historical changes. The biological view of history assumes that change is caused either by environment or by fortuitous concurrence of acquired characteristics; the Marxist theory assumes that historical change is determined by the methods of production; but neither of these explanations is complete. When such an explanation is given, we may still ask: but why should environment affect an organism, or why should a change in the method of production affect literature, art, and culture? The human mind is not satisfied by secondary explanations of great events, nor will it agree to pursue contingent causes *ad infinitum*. An infinite regress is impossible in a series of intrinsically dependent causes. Since the externalistic views of history refuse to concede any ultimate source transcendent to the whole process, they are incapable of offering an ample explanation for change.

Furthermore, the externalistic views of history cannot explain why certain factors are always immutable and others are always variable. For example, in the Marxist view of history, why should the method of production always be the determining factor? Why should religion and science and the family, art, and literature always be variable? Why some factors should be self-starters and others not, is never explained. It is amazing how often these philosophies which reject faith demand so much of it—and of an irrational kind—as the foundation of the systems.

Externalistic theories of history are logically unsound because they explain the higher forces of human life by the lower. The Spenglerian view explains man by zoology, the Marxist explains man by economics, the evolutionary theory explains man by biology, and the cyclic theory, by astronomy. The human mind refuses to accept the explanation of the higher form of existence by the lower for the simple reason that in any level of creation there is always an X factor which cannot be explained by its antecedents. Let A stand for chemicals and B for plants, and C for animals. The externalistic concept of creation argues that A plus B plus C equals man, or ABC. But man is not the sum of A plus B plus C. He contains a factor which is not in the antecedent.

There is a further inconsistency in all materialistic theories of history in the sense that they attempt to explain the more changeable by the less changeable. Man with his religion, art, culture, and literature is considered the most variable of all historical phenomena, but man in his turn is explained in part by biology, zoology, and finally by the chemical order, the least of all the variables in nature. There is practically no evolution in a chemical order, and if there be any changes, they must be measured in a span so very vast and enormous as to make them inapplicable to man, whose life history is comparatively so very brief.

The externalistic conceptions empty history of all human responsibility by attributing changes principally to material factors. Dr.

Sorokin, who has treated this problem of historical change perhaps better than anyone, writes that his views were criticized by Crane Brinton, who, denying the immanent causes of social development or decay, argued that there was no reason why Western culture should disintegrate because there were no external factors which menaced it: "There are no barbarians who can conquer the present Western sensate culture; there are no internal destructive vandals; likewise, neither Japan nor China is a real menace; nor is any other external factor likely to destroy it." Dr. Sorokin answers his critic in this way:

The argument of my critic runs like the argument of a person who criticizes the statement that a given man sooner or later will die and that it is likely (in view of his old age and internal infirmities) that such death is not far off. "Look here, Doctor! The weather is fine and therefore our friend will have neither sun stroke nor catch cold; no gangster menaces his life; the roof of his house will not fall; there is no chance for him to swallow poison; there is no epidemic now in the vicinity. Therefore, Doctor, your prognosis is all wrong." Critics never seem to have thought about an immanent principle of change which can lead in both cases—and in the case of man certainly—to the phenomena of decline and death.[59]

The complete explanation of anything must be given in terms of four causes, but the externalistic views of history have recourse to only one and the least important of all the causes—the material. The three other causes are the *formal*, or the plan according to which anything is made; the *efficient*, or the power which creates it, and the *final* cause, or the purpose for which it is made. Aristotle explains these four causes in his *Physics*:

Now that we have established these distinctions, we must proceed to consider causes, their character and number. Knowledge is the object of our inquiry, and men do not think they know a thing till they have grasped the "why" of it (which is to grasp its primary cause). So clearly we too must do this as regards both coming to be and passing away and every kind of physical change, in order that, knowing their principles, we may try to refer to these principles each of our problems.

In one sense, then (1) that out of which a thing comes to be and which persists, is called "cause," e.g., the bronze of the statue, the silver of the bowl, and the genera of which the bronze and the silver are species. In another sense (2) the form or the archetype, i.e., the statement of the essence, and its genera, are called "causes" (e.g., of the octave the relation of 2:1, and generally number), and the parts in the definition. Again (3) the primary source of the change or coming to rest; e.g., the man who gave advice is a cause, the father is cause of the child, and generally what makes of what is made and what causes change of what is changed. Again (4) in the sense of end or "that for the sake of which" a thing is done, e.g., health is the cause of walking about. ("Why is he walking about?" we say. "To be healthy," and, having said that, we think we have assigned the cause.) The same is true also of all the intermediate steps which are brought about through the action of something else as means toward the end, e.g., reduction of flesh, purging, drugs, or surgical instruments are means towards health. All these things are "for the sake of" the end, though they differ from one another in that some are activities, others instruments.[60]

The Aristotelian philosophy of the four causes applied to history means that a complete explanation is not given until consideration is given to such important problems of origins, purposes, and plans in any given era. The externalistic theories concentrate on the least important of all the causes: the material, and thereby make history irrational.

The basic defect of the externalistic approach is its denial of the specific difference between man and animal, or man and lower creation—man's power to act for deliberately chosen ends. Everything in the world acts for an end, though not everything knows that end. Inanimate creation and animals have ends imposed upon them by Almighty God; in that sense they are determined to certain ends. Man, however, in virtue of an intellect and will is capable of determining his own end.[61]

Externalistic views of history by concentrating on *material* origins have completely ignored the ends or objectives historical generation sets for itself. Nor is it an escape to say that the origins explain the ends, for the origins, according to this theory, come from matter, whereas the intention comes from mind. Liberalism is more intelligible in its goals than in its origins. The same is true for totalitarianisms. To ignore goals is to ignore history.

The Marxist might protest against being classified as "externalistic" in his ideas of history inasmuch as he does admit the existence of other factors besides historical necessity. This is true, but we are not concerned with accidental factors. Marxism furthermore debases all rational activities into tools of unconscious forces.[62]

The phantasmagorias in the brains of men are necessary supplements of . . . their material life—processes as empirically establishable and bound up with material premises. Morals, religion, metaphysics, and other ideologies corresponding to them here no longer retain a look of independence. They have no history, they have no development, but men in developing their material production and their material intercourse, *alter along with this reality of theirs, their thought and the product of their thought.* It is not consciousness which determines life, but life which determines consciousness.[63]

The externalistic concept of history fails to distinguish between transitive and immanent activity. Transitive activity is without, and immanent activity within. Biological and economic changes are seen as merely transitive activities affecting history, but history is primarily determined by the immanent activities of reason and will, of which economics, for example, is only a by-product.[64] It is obvious that the higher one goes in the hierarchy of nature, the more immanent, and the less transitive, becomes the activity. There is more immanent activity in plants than in chemicals, more in animals than in plants, more in man than in animals, more in angels than in man. In God there is no transitive activity whatsoever. Being perfect immanent activity, He is therefore Perfect Life.[65]

History is concerned principally with the immanent activity of the human intellect and will, although it may legitimately, and should, study the environmental and conditioning factors of cultural change. But history does a great injustice to man by ignoring the fact that he has within himself the principal causes of this cultural change. Such change is produced by the truths which man knows and the decisions which he makes. In a certain sense, man creates his own destiny; neither fate, nor astronomy, nor biology, nor economics determine it. The actual historic achievements have been the direct result of intellect and will, as manifested in the idea of brotherhood and community, as built up in empires, nations, and kingdoms and city states; in the revolutions against certain regimes in the name of "social justice"; in the common norms of morality to which all people subject themselves and which made Cicero wonder; and finally in the tradition of all people that there is a Golden Age identified with an innocence wherein the mind and will of man are undefiled by egotism, greed, and wrath.

A study of history reveals that the fall of civilizations and their recovery is due less to external transitive factors than to the immanent factors of intellect and will. Arnold Toynbee, in his *Study of History*, shows convincingly that external factors do not entirely explain the genesis of civilizations. Ethnic groups do not explain it (ethnic feeling in the Western World, as Toynbee states, was unknown until Protestantism began emphasizing the Old Testament).[66] The older division of people, since the advent of Christianity, was on the moral basis of Christian and heathen, a division which took account of the morality of man rather than of his blood. Even then the heathen was considered not irretrievably lost, but a potential nobleman of the Kingdom of God. The recent emphasis on the biological or blood factors in history is an indication of how far the modern mind has departed from the rational, and in doing so has become perverted.

Environment, as another external factor, fails to account for the genesis of civilizations. The belief that environment determines human culture has been advanced from the fifth century B.C., when the Hippocratian school made atmosphere, water, and landscapes the determining influences, just as moderns make biology or economics the motivating power in society. This environmental theory cannot explain why two identical elements in an environment will give birth to two distinct civilizations. On the other hand, any similarity of climate or topography may appear to be the cause of similar civilizations, when actually the similarity is the result of the *intellects and the wills* of men in those civilizations who think and choose alike.

History is not the inter-action of inhuman forces, nor is it the product of a single factor, whether it be race, or evolution, or class struggle, or fate. It is the product of complex choices and particularly of two: good and evil, God and the Devil. But though sound philosophy affirms the immanence of the human reason and the human will in history, nevertheless it does not leave them hanging in mid-air. For the final and ultimate explanation of this immanence of man is to be found outside of the universe, in God. That is why the doctrine of the immanence of reason and will in history must be complemented by the next principle which follows: the Transcendence of God.

It belongs to Divine providence, not to destroy, but to preserve the nature of things. Wherefore it moves all things in accordance with their conditions; so that from necessary causes through the Divine motion, effects follow contingently. Since, therefore, the will is an active principle, not determinate to one thing, but having an indifferent relation to many things, God so moves it, that He does not determine it of necessity to one thing, but its movement remains contingent and not necessary, except in those things to which it is moved naturally.[67]

THE TRANSCENDENCE OF GOD TO HISTORY

Against the externalistic views of history, it was necessary to affirm the primacy of human reason and human will in history and thus relegate to a secondary consideration the influences of evolution, environment, and economics. The affirmation of this principle, however, did not answer the humanistic and deistic view of history, which would account for historical and cultural changes, and particularly for unending progress, on the basis of human reason and human will, to the exclusion of God. This incomplete view of the universe demands the statement of a second and correlative principle —the transcendence of God to history.

Humanism leaves unexplained the trustworthiness of human reason and the perfect happiness sought by the human will. If human reason is only a product of lower forces or of chance, there is no basic cause for us ever to trust human reason; there is not even an explanation of why we should have reason. It is only because there is a Supreme Intelligence beyond man, that man's rational processes ever lead to truth. The Divine Logos is the only guarantee of the validity of logic. Intelligibility is hidden in the universe, otherwise the human mind, which at the beginning is a blank, would never attain to the intelligible.

Why are things intelligible in potency? St. Thomas offers this solution. In all things not generated by mere chance the form of a thing is always the end of the generation. The plant generates a plant, not a horse; the animal generates an animal like unto itself, not a vegetable. But the form cannot be the end of the process of generation, unless the likeness of the form is in some way in the generator. In nature there are two kinds of generation, in the broad sense of the term. There is first the generation which operates in virtue of a blind necessity of nature or by instinct, and there is another which operates in virtue of the intelligence. An example of the first is all biological generation in the lower orders; an example of the second is the idea of a house, which exists in the mind of the architect before the house is built. In the first, there is an assimilation of the effect to the form; in the second, the form which is conceived in the mind is reproduced in the order of actuality. The architect seeks to make the house like the form which is in his mind.

Since the world was made, not by chance, but by God, who is Intelligence Itself, it is necessary that there should be in the Divine Mind a form according to which the world is made. And this is the reason of the idea. *"Et in hoc consistit ratio ideae."* [68] This idea which exists in the mind of God, and to which all things are likened, is nothing else than the Essence of God.[69]

God knows His Essence perfectly. He knows it in every way in which it is knowable and in all its perfections. He knows His Essence not only as it is in itself, and in its necessity and eternity, but also in its participability, that is, in all the possible ways in which created beings may participate in His Being—the stone by existence, the plant by life, the animal by consciousness, man and angel by intelligence. No creature possesses being or any other perfection, except insofar as it is an imitation or a copy or a participation in the Being and the attributes of God, just as no statue exists in the world which does not imitate in some way the design and the formal idea of the artist who conceived it.[70]

Although these exemplar ideas which exist in the mind of God, and according to which the whole universe has been made, are multiple in relation to the things themselves, they really are not distinct from the Divine Essence, inasmuch as the Divine Essence, because of its infinity, may be imitated in innumerable ways.[71] The meaning of idea is *form* in the Greek. Ideas are the forms of things existing outside the things themselves. The form existing outside the thing itself may be considered in one of two ways: as "exemplar"— that is, as the principle of the making of the thing; or as "type"— that is, as principle of its cognition, inasmuch as the forms are said to be knowable in the one knowing. As "exemplars" they pertain to the practical intellect, and as "type" or "ratio" they belong to the speculative intellect as well as to the practical.[72] The Second Person of the Blessed Trinity, in the language of theology, is the "Exemplar" and "type" or "ratio" of all things. He is therefore the source of all art and all science; for what is art but a participation in the Exemplary Cause, and what is science but the participation in the Formal Cause? It is here that the transcendentals, beauty and truth, find their perfection; it is here, too, that all art and all science must look, if they would know their source.

Since the world has been made by God, who is Intelligence Itself, the Exemplary and the Formal Cause of all creation, the world is intelligible—that is, it has been made intelligibly. We do not put intelligibility into the universe; we discover it. As the statue is the imitation of the idea in the mind of the artist, so each creature is an image of an idea existing in the Divine Mind. Boethius therefore correctly is quoted by St. Thomas as saying "all forms which are in matter can be called images, inasmuch as they come from those forms which are without matter." [73] Everything, from the stone to an angel, is the realization of an idea. Eternal ideas realized in the angels make of each one a distinct species, because there is no matter to individualize them. Eternal ideas realized in the mineral, plant, animal, and man, make of each an individual, owing to the matter which is associated with the nature of each, and which is the principle of their multiplication. It cannot, therefore, be argued that everything which is intelligible must be in matter; for it is only accidental to the object to be separated from the knower in the ontological order. This follows from the principle that knowledge ultimately comes from above and not from below. There can never be an object which an idea has not preceded, but there can be ideas which have not been materialized.[74] "The idea outside of God and outside of us is thing; the thing in God and in us is idea." [75] This is also the ultimate reason why God, and not man, is the measure of things.

Natural things are midway between the knowledge of God and our knowledge; for we receive knowledge from natural things, of which God is the cause by His knowledge. Hence, as the natural objects of knowledge are prior to our knowledge, and are its measure, so the knowledge of God is prior to natural things, and is their measure; as, for instance, a house is midway between the knowledge of the builder who made it and the knowledge of the one who derives it from the house already built.[76]

We receive our knowledge from natural things, of which things God by His knowledge is Cause.[77] In each thing, therefore, there is the ratio, the principle of its intelligibility. But this principle of intelligibility is there only in potency. Coming from the mind of God into matter, it has lost its character of universality, necessity, and transcendence, which makes it the direct and immediate object of intelligence. It has fallen into extent, number, movement, and contingency. In order that:

it may revive in the mind with its proper characteristics, it is necessary that the reality, coming into our mind by sense perception in some way, make a return to its source, disincarnate itself from matter, and go in the opposite way from that which individuation by matter imposed on it. The individuation, realized by the generation of a being, is as an attraction of the idea in matter (*"agens facit formam esse in materiam"*). In order to know, there must be a contrary action, an extraction or abstraction.[78]

The profound and ultimate reason of abstraction is to render ideas intelligibly in act, as they are in the mind of God. God Who is the Source, the Alpha and the Omega of all things. "Divine wisdom is the reason of all things." [79]

The philosophy of St. Thomas gives an answer to the intelligibility of the universe, both on the part of the object and on the part of the subject. On the part of the object, because forms are *de se* communicable; on the part of the subject, because the intellect is spiritual. For those who would go still deeper into the reason of intelligibility, Scholastic philosophy gives the more profound answer that things are intelligible on the part of the object because they have been made intelligible by God; and they are intelligible on the part of the subject, thanks to the light of the active intellect given by God, which reveals the ideas according to which all things were made.

As humanism leaves unexplained the intelligibility of the universe, so does it also leave unexplained the aspiration to perfect happiness which exists in the human will. Men generally recognize that neither in their own reason, nor in their own will, nor in the times in which they live, is the secret of happiness. That is why Greek and Roman mythology put the Golden Age in the remote past, as Virgil did in his *Fourth Eclogue,* or else in the remote future as do the Utopians and evolutionists of the present day, or the Communists, who expectantly look to an order when the dialectic will no longer apply and therefore where the transcendence of Communism will be impossible. For most religions, the goal of happiness, which man seeks, is to be found neither in an individual nor collective egotism, immanent in the womb of time but transcendent to it, but in a Perfect Truth which satisfies the reason, and a Perfect Love which satisfies the will—God. As St. Thomas explained:

It is impossible for any created good to constitute man's happiness. For happiness is the perfect good, which lulls the appetite altogether; else it would not be the last end, if something yet remained to be desired. Now the object of the will, i.e., of man's appetite, is the universal good; just as the object of the intellect is the universal true. Hence it is evident that naught can lull man's will, save the universal good. This is to be found, not in any creature, but in God alone; because every creature has goodness by participation. Wherefore God alone can satisfy the will of man, according to the words of *Psalms* 102:5: Who satisfieth thy desire with good things. Therefore God alone constitutes man's happiness.[80]

Furthermore, unless there is a law outside the universe, there is no explanation for the sense of oughtness and responsibility and duty which reside in the human will. Duty is strictly that which man is bound to perform by a law which governs his life. The term *ought* is closely related to duty, and expresses an indebtedness which a man *owes* under the compulsion of some law which speaks with authority. These ideas are inseparable from bond or responsibility or accountableness which someone has to give for his conduct to someone outside himself. Man pursues these ends because they are intrinsically worthy, and also because they correspond to his own true nature; in realizing them, he is realizing the best that is in him so far as the circumstances permit. In failing to attain this end which he recognizes as perfect, man also recognizes that he has been untrue to himself. And here we find the essential element of that faculty we call conscience. Conscience reveals itself as making laws, witnessing obedience to them, and finally as passing judgment of praise and blame, innocence, and guilt. Manifestly this triple role, upon the model of which all human government is based, must have a reason for its order, but where seek it?

What is the source of the legislative role of my conscience, which bids me to do good and avoid evil, but as such does not make things right or wrong any more than the eye makes color red or white? It merely lays down the law, thus betraying that it is an intermediary between someone else and me. This law is certainly not of my own making, nor does it come from society. It does not come from myself, for no one can be his own legislator and a superior to himself. Furthermore, if the law of conscience were of my own making, I could unmake it, but I cannot do this, for it comes to me in defiance of my own will. When my will is set against hearing it, or even obeying it, it comes as a delegate with absolute right to rule over me. This means that I did not make it, but that I am only free to obey it or disobey it. Neither does it come from society, for society is merely the interpreter of the law of conscience and not its author. Human laws may sanction it and elaborate it, but they do not create it. The approval or disapproval of society did not make the right and wrong of my conscience, because sometimes conscience bids us to flaunt the laws of society, when they are inimical to the laws of God, as was the case with the martyrs who died for the faith. Furthermore, every decent man and woman on the face of the earth knows full well there are certain things which should not be done, if he or she were the only person on earth, and that right is right if nobody is right, and wrong is wrong if everybody is wrong.

If, therefore, the voice of that interior Sinai of conscience is neither from me nor from society, and if it is universal in its whisperings and articulations, so that no moral creature can wholly shake it off, it must be that behind this law there is a Lawmaker, and behind this voice there is a Person, and behind this command a Power, which we call God, Who has sealed upon every man coming into the world the light which slays darkness and illumines souls in the paths which lead to the land of peace and the homeland of the children of liberty.

Secondly, what is the source of the executive power of my conscience? I realize that my conscience is a witness in a courtroom, something, when I am guilty, which comes to me with a "thousand several tongues and every tongue brings in a different tale and every tale condemns me as a villain." Who is this witness within me who takes the stand and turns state's evidence against me? Who is this witness who cannot be bought by gold, or crushed by threats, or won by praise? Who is this great executive who accepts no excuse, but signs the law made by conscience and applies its action? Who is this witness who is always upholding the cause of truth and righteousness?

In vain do I say that it comes from society, for conscience sometimes denies the testimony of society and calls me vicious when society calls me virtuous. In vain do I say that it comes from myself, for if it did, then I could make it testify in my own defense as if it were one of those alienists who witness to the truth of the side which hires them. Since my conscience witnesses constantly to truth and righteousness, and since this fidelity is not of my own making or the creation of society, it must therefore be that behind this Truth and Righteousness there is a Piety and a Holiness; and since Piety and Holiness can belong only to a Person, I must conclude that such a Holy Person Who witnesses my actions is in some way the same God as the Power Who laid down the law of my conscience and now urges me to be faithful unto it even for eternity.

Thirdly, the sentiments of praise and blame which follow upon the judgment of conscience are meaningless unless my actions are an offense against a personal being. If men thought that they were responsible for their evil thoughts and words and actions to no one higher than themselves or their fellows, it is inconceivable that the consciousness of guilt, and the fear of punishment would have been what both heart and experience testify them to be. Prayers and penances, sacrifices and atonements would never have prevailed so widely if there were no underlying sense of the existence of One before Whom we are responsible and Whose wrath must be turned aside. Were there no God to fear, the criminal would never be so alive to his guilt and so haunted and appalled by the fear of a judgment and a justice more terrible than that of man. Cardinal Newman has observed in his *Grammar of Assent:*

Inanimate things cannot stir our affections; these are correlative with persons. If as is the case, we feel responsibility, are ashamed, are frightened at transgressing the voice of conscience, this implies that there is One to whom we are responsible, before whom we are ashamed, whose claims upon us we fear. If, on doing wrong, we feel the same tearful, broken-hearted sorrow which overwhelms us on hurting a mother; if, on doing right, we enjoy the same sunny serenity of mind, the same soothing, satisfactory delight which follows on our receiving praise from a father, we certainly have within us the image of some person, to whom our love and veneration look, in whose smile we find our happiness, for whom we yearn, towards whom we direct our pleadings, in whose anger we are troubled and waste away.... If the cause of these emotions does not belong to this visible world, the Object to which his perception is directed must be Supernatural and Divine; and thus the phenomena of conscience, as a dictate, avail to impress the imagination with the picture of a Supreme Governor, a Judge, holy, just, powerful, all-seeing, retributive.

Thus an examination of my conscience and its triple role forces me to conclude that just as the eye corresponds to things visible, the ear to things audible, reason to things intelligible, so too the law of my conscience must correspond to a Power which legislates, the witness of my conscience must correspond to a Righteousness which executes, and the praise and blame of my conscience to a Justice which judges, and since Power, Righteousness, and Justice correspond to the essential attributes of a Person, I must conclude that that Personal Power is Intelligent in order to make laws; that that Personal Righteousness is All Knowing in order to have a perfect insight into moral character; and that that Personal Justice is Supreme in order to pass sentences after His judgments. And that Wise Power, All Knowing, Righteousness, and Supreme Justice, before Whom I kneel in sorrow even when I have not broken a single law of the land, and confess with deep anguish of soul, "Against Thee have I sinned"; that Power Who calls me away from the sin which corrodes even when it does not glare, and undermines even when it does not crush; that Righteousness Who has implanted a Spiritual law of gravitation within me to draw me away from the earth, beyond the stars to Himself as the Source of Life and Truth and Love; that Justice Who has implanted in me a spark which the wings of angels fan into a flame of everlasting happiness— is the Power, the Righteousness, and Justice which is God.

Without the transcendence of God, both the rationality of the natural universe and the rationality of the human mind are left unexplained. Thus, St. Thomas wrote: "Natural law is but a participation of the eternal law mirrored in a created intellect." Or in the language of St. Augustine: "It is the reason, or the will of God, commanding the observance of the natural law and forbidding its violations. It is the order eternally perceived by God and decreed by His will which is the *ultima ratio* of the law of nature. Its genesis involves the following series: Order perceived by the Divine Intellect, decreed by the Divine Will, mirrored and created intellects, binding on created wills." As Cicero remarked in his *De Legibus:* "This law did not begin to exist when it was written, but when it was *born*, and it was born at the same time with the Divine Intellect. Wherefore, the true law, the primary law, the law which can fully command and forbid, is the ever true mind of the Supreme Being, Jupiter. . . . If the supreme law is the Divine Intellect, when introduced in man, it dwells in the mind of the wise." [81]

It is in virtue of this transcendent Supreme Being, which is God, that all men are bound together in a moral unity and strive for universal peace. Plato declared: "Poets have wisely said, when making known the essence of friendship, that it is God Who makes friends and binds them together—He then, is the true friend for us . . . all our other friends owe to Him their friendships; but He must be the friend who is the cause of all friendships." [82]

Thus far it has been suggested that humanism is unable to explain three of the essential constituents of man: his reason, his aspiration for happiness, and his will. We now pass to some intrinsic defects of humanistic views of history. Practically all of them have thought of history in terms of an ascending line of progress and perfection, as faith in advancement replaces faith in salvation. The earlier school of humanists, under the influence of the Renaissance and rationalism, attributed this progress to human will and its energies; a later school added nonhuman forces in conjunction with the reason and the will. Regardless of the source of its origin, progress was considered automatic. Divine Providence had nothing to do with progress. The earlier representatives of progress, such as Turgot and Comte, believed that man had left behind him the perfect stages of the supernatural and the metaphysical, and was now entering into the heaven of a world dominated by the scientific and the positivistic attitudes. Condorcet, in the same spirit, wrote: "Men will never retrograde, so long, at least, as the earth occupies the same place in the solar system. . . . Progress in the art of medicine will so long prolong life that death will be the exception rather than the rule." Wordsworth was so convinced of this progress that he wrote to a student: "Burn your books on chemistry and read Godwin on necessity." The greatest of all the prophets of inevitable progress was H. G. Wells, who, in his *Outline of History*, wrote an epitaph to Christianity, admitting that it was useful for a time as propaganda, but would disappear as we ushered ourselves into "one inseparable and political system." Instead, then, of Christianity being a means to progress, Wells considered it a rejection of the very condition of progress. By rejecting history, optimists had to reject also all history with which Christianity was associated and write a new history in support of their unbounded optimism.

This idea of an immanent Logos not transcendent to history or eternal, to which all progress is attributed, has many intrinsic defects. If progress is inevitable, then why should anyone make an effort to attain it? Since all progress implies working toward a goal, how do we know that we are making progress unless we have a fixed goal? Once a Divine Providence and an end transcendent to the individual and humanity is denied, there may be a continuity of process, but not necessarily a continuity of progress. Neither the facts of the present day nor the deliverances of history reveal that man is working toward a Utopia. And when progress is arrested by war, revolution, and depression, those who believe in the immanence of reason and will, alone, are unable to explain the collapse of their Utopia. For that reason the philosophers of progress in the midst of catastrophe invariably become philosophers of despair. The disillusionment in recent philosophical literature is manifested by an excessive concern with the problem of death as a fundamental problem, and that is an admission of defeat. Fiction writers are obsessed with the powerlessness of our generation to transcend its contradictions and its frustrations. D. H. Lawrence and Aldous Huxley are obvious examples. The hope of triumph has dissolved into the ashes of defeat as coldness and despair creep over Utopian man. Israel Zangwill voiced this mood in a poem:

> The nymphs are gone, the fairies flown;
> The ancient gods forever fled;
> The stars are silent overhead;
> The music of the spheres is still;
> The night is dark, the wind is chill;
> The later gods have followed Pan,
> And man is left alone with man.

It is only the Christian and moral view of history which can stand the shock of chaos and catastrophe. The Christians never expected a Utopia in this world. As Douglas Jerrold expressed it:

Precisely as archeology has verified, in the most minute detail, the historical portion of the Old Testament narrative, so the historical method applied to the facts of archeology has vindicated the Christian, Moral and Political philosophy. They show that artistic achievement precedes the organization of society for wealth, and that the period of maximum wealth is a prelude to decline, an historical vindication of the Christian esthetic, which teaches that creative art is the process of informing matter with spirit. They show us also that, with the decay of spirituality and the growth of materialism, societies fall by their own weight, an historical vindication of the doctrine of original sin. They teach us that the decline of society is invariably preceded by a departure from traditional moral standards, particularly in regard to sexual morality, an historical vindication of the Christian teaching that the family is antecedent to the State and that society has no rights against the family. Again, we learn that the age of criticism, introspection and imitation of old arts through which we are passing today is a familiar experience of civilizations, and that it carries with it always the same Nemesis; the scepticism which man turns first on his rulers and then on his gods, he turns ultimately on himself; an historical vindication of the cardinal doctrine of Christianity, that man is not sufficient for his own salvation.[83]

The futurism of the humanistic views of history gives no value to the individuals who live at the present time or to the individuals who have lived in the past, except as instruments to a future happiness in an indefinite future. It is an outrageous affront for persons who are ends in themselves, to be told they are in reality only sticks to be thrown into a great cosmic bonfire to keep it blazing for a generation yet to be born. There can be little consolation for a thousand donkeys dying of starvation to know that the thousandth-and-first donkey is to have fields of clover. Each man who is conscious of his own intrinsic worth will refuse to find ground for hope by looking forward to a peak of historical destiny conditioned by the ruins of the historical past. To regard all past generations, as well as the present, as devoid of intrinsic and personal value, is to invalidate the very ideal of progress itself by turning it into a death rather than a resurrection and a life. No future utopia, regardless of how prosperous it may be on this earth, can validate the tragedies of previous generations or expiate their suffering, unless to each person there is accorded a right to a utopia transcendent to this world. That is why the true concept of progress is conditioned upon the immortality of the soul.

This spectacle of time perpetually marching forward over the corpse of the past and present, as the scythe of time mercilessly cuts down those who are conscious of eternal longing, makes human minds recoil in a passionate prayer for continuity such as found in the Psalm:

Call me not away in the midst of my days: thy years are unto generation and generation.
In the beginning, O Lord, thou foundest the earth: and the heavens are the works of thy hands.
They shall perish but thou remainest: and all of them shall grow old like a garment:

And as a vesture thou shalt change them, and they shall be changed.
But thou art always the selfsame, and thy years shall not fail.
The children of thy servants shall continue: and their seed shall be
   directed for ever.

The fear of death which all men have is a further indication of
the instinctive acknowledgement of the transcendent goal of history.
This fear of death is born not only of the dread of extinction, or the
doubt of entering into a new dimension, but it arises also from a
consciousness that man is not certain of his own righteousness, and
therefore may be subjected to a retribution for the wrongdoings
of this life. This ethical uneasiness, born of a dim feeling of a relation
to a superior power, bears witness to the moral dimension of human
history. It is not Christianity alone which expresses this idea; the
pagans have done it as well. Virgil, for example, in his sixth book
of the *Aeneid* writes:

> When at last the life has fled,
> And left the body cold and dead,
> E'en then there passes not away
> The painful heritage of play;
> Full many a long contracted stain
> Perforce must linger deep in grain.
> So penal suffering they endure
> For ancient crime to make them pure:
> Some hang aloft in open view
> For winds to pierce them through and through,
> While others purge their guilt deep-dyed
> In burning fire of whelming tide.
> Each for himself we all sustain
> The durance of our ghostly pain.

Hamlet expressed the same idea:

> To be, or not to be: that is the question:
> Whether 'tis nobler in the mind to suffer
> The slings and arrows of outrageous fortune,
> Or to take arms against a sea of troubles,
> And by opposing end them? To die: to sleep;
> No more; and by a sleep to say we end
> The heart-ache and the thousand natural shocks
> That flesh is heir to? 'Tis a consummation
> Devoutly to be wish'd. To die, to sleep;
> To sleep: perchance to dream: ay, there's the rub;
> For in that sleep of death what dreams may come

When we have shuffled off this mortal coil,
Must give us pause; there's the respect
That makes calamity of so long life;
For who would bear the whips and scorns of time,
The oppressor's wrong, the proud man's contumely,
The pangs of despis'd love, the law's delay,
The insolence of office, and the spurns
That patient merit of the unworthy takes,
When he himself might his quietus make
With a bare bodkin? who would these fardels bear,
To grunt and sweat under a weary life,
But that the dread of something after death,
The undiscover'd country, from whose bourn
No traveller returns, puzzles the will,
And makes us rather bear those ills we have
Than fly to others that we know not of?
Thus conscience does make cowards of us all;
And thus the native hue of resolution
Is sicklied o'er with the pale cast of thought;
And enterprises of great pith and moment,
With this regard their currents turn awry,
And lose the name of action.

Transcendence of some kind is required to give meaning to history. The present alone never suffices to produce happiness. For this reason the ancients looked to the Golden Age in the past, while under the impetus of Hegel and Darwin, the present age looks to the future. Whether it be the great-grandfathers or the great-grandsons who hold the key to world peace and happiness matters little: the fact is that transcendence must be regarded as beyond the present.

The instinct for transcendence explains the Messianism of Karl Marx, who secularized it in a coming world order wherein there would be no class but the proletariat. Even here, he transcended the immanent dialectics of history, by positing a regime wherein the dialectic would no longer hold sway. This is one of the basic contradictions of Communism, for why should the dialectics intrinsic to both history and matter, end with a classless society? To save his Communist society, Marx made it transcendent to history, and yet most illogically, for his perfect society is still in history.

But transcendence within the historical process is not satisfying. The world has existed long enough to convince us that the solution of our ills is not within the present scheme of things. Only when history is interpreted in terms of a transcendental goal do its failures, as well as its triumphs, begin to have significance in the light of freedom. It is worth noting that all immanent views of history are deterministic, whereas the transcendental view is voluntaristic. Marxism does not stress the freedom of man, but the necessity of economic struggle. Christianity, on the contrary, postulates the fulfillment of history through the agency of free spirits. Because Christianity admits freedom, it alone admits Providence and denies fatality. It was not until the advent of Christianity with its goal beyond this world, that history was ever interpreted in terms of freedom. All the philosophies of India and China stressed the obliteration of personality or the surrender of the will, rather than its freedom in the face of the Divine. There is a greater dynamism in history since the beginnings of Christianity precisely because of this emphasis on freedom.

For the beginning and for the end, Christianity looks beyond history and thus gives history meaning by making it an interaction of God's initiative and freedom's response. History has a plot because there is a pattern and a standard outside time. Furthermore, the transcendence of history not only stresses freedom, but by the same token it liberates man from servitude to the material, for where the spirit is, there is liberty. Christianity distinguishes man from matter; it makes matter his servant and the vehicle for his sacraments, and thus has made possible man's great mastery over nature. Why is it that the conquest of nature never took place in the pagan world, but only began when a civilization conscious of its transcendence, overawed it with its spirit?

Why is it that science achieved this marvelous new growth, pulling itself up into a self-developing system having a momentum of its own which nobody can stop—why was this stage reached only in Europe? The far older civilizations of Egypt, China, India, even of Greece and the Alexandrian Roman world, having their own strong roots of science, bore no such flower and left no such seed. That puzzle cannot be answered by saying that the Italian, German, Polish, British beginnings of the new astronomy and physics were the work of rebellious souls who accidentally constituted a sort of hand-to-hand relay and started something quite new in the world—from scratch! And that these heroes of the new day maintained a sort of running "conflict between science and religion," the organized religion of their day! This is neither good common sense nor good history.

The probabilities are that there was a work of maternity here which has not been fully recognized, even yet. For what goes on in the womb of a civilization, in preparing a new age, has something to do with the secret knitting of ideas and feelings which escape the chronicler.

Just to hint what that knitting may have been: Is it an accident that when Bacon came to formulate the spirit of empirical science, as he saw it, he put it this way: "We cannot command Nature except by obeying her." By "obedience" he meant that disciplined, patient, honest observation, and the reporting with scrupulous truthfulness what one finds, not what one wants to find, which belong to the empirical method. To see what is there is not easy; to make a technique of seeing what is there, this is one of the immense moral achievements of the race. Thus at the very threshold of the new science lay a profound act—humility: "In order to master, we must first obey." And has this maxim a resemblance —no, I will say kinship—to that other maxim familiar to Christendom, "In order to find our lives we must lose them"—the immortal paradox which condemns self-assertion as the way to mastery in anything having to do with truth? Are they not the same maxim? And if so, is it not clear that back of science there lies a profound ethical impulse; and that back of this ethical impulse there stands a revolutionary religious discovery, kneaded for a thousand years into the moral fabric of Europe?

Medieval piety, so far as it was sincere, was a long exercise in self-denial, and of faith in the principle of self-denial even where it was languidly practiced, a current of aspiration directed upward into the metaphysical realm like the beam of a vast searchlight. Conceive this beam to swing its concentrated energies slowly downward from the vertical to the horizontal, from the metaphysical to the physical, until it lights up with the same self-denying intensity the details of nature and the human scene. Then one understands why something began to exist which was new in the world, but by the use of powers which had been slowly nursed out during the ages of contemplation.

And one also understands that if this new and fertile concern for physical nature were to repudiate its metaphysical source, it contains the possibility of making us a race of monsters through our inability to make truly human use of unlimited power.[84]

Transcendence not only explains freedom and mastery over nature, but it alone makes possible the transfiguration of this world. Transfiguration is not the same as futurism, which regards this world as becoming better and better until it is turned into an earthly paradise. Transfiguration means that through catastrophe, crisis, and final judgment, old things are made new. This new kingdom is not in time at all, but in eternity; its existence is not due to an eruption of the mundane into the heavenly, but a visitation of the spiritual into the human—a visitation morally conditioned. It is the very reverse of the Tower of Babel.

And I saw a new heaven and a new earth. For the first heaven and the first earth passed away, and the sea is no more. And I saw the holy city, New Jerusalem, coming down out of heaven from God, made ready as a bride adorned for her husband. And I heard a loud voice from the throne saying,

"Behold the dwelling of God with men,
and he will dwell with them.
And they will be his people;
and God himself will be with them as
their God.
And God will wipe away every tear from
their eyes.
And death shall be no more;
neither shall there be mourning,
nor crying, nor pain any more,
For the former things have passed away." [85]

Although this *Civitas Dei* transcends the time dimension, it is not unrelated to history, for even now history "is growing to its full stature." But before this perfection can be manifested, the present order must pass through a Calvary and a Gethsemane. This transcendent kingdom is already immanent in human history, though not identical with it; it is in history though not of it, as the soul is in the body, but with activities transcendent to it, or as the square is in the cube, though the relation is not one of part and whole.

How this transcendent Deity is immanent in a world and yet not immersed by it, has been effectively described by Toynbee:

But how in fact can God's will be done on Earth as it is in Heaven? In the technical language of Theology the omnipresence of God involves His immanence in this world and in every living soul in it, as well as His transcendent existence on supramundane planes of being. In the Christian conception of the Godhead His transcendent aspect is displayed in God the Father and His immanent aspect in God the Holy Ghost; but the distinctive and also crucial feature of the Christian Faith is the doctrine that the Godhead is not a Duality but a Trinity in Unity, and that in His aspect as God the Son the other two aspects are unified in a Person who, in virtue of this mystery, is as accessible to the human heart as He is incomprehensible to the human understanding. In the person of Christ Jesus—Very God yet also Very Man—the divine society and the mundane society have a common member who in the order of This World is born into the ranks of the Proletariat and dies the death of a malefactor, while in the order of the Other World He is the King of God's Kingdom—and a King who is God Himself and not God's less-than-divine deputy. [86]

SUPREMACY OF PERSON OVER LAW

Here person and law are set in antithesis, not because they are antithetical when correctly understood, but rather because the word "law" in many philosophies of history is understood as divorced from reason, historical processes being attributed to the operation of either mechanical, economic, biological, zoological, or fatalistic activities. Thomistic philosophy asserts that all law is rational, whether it be the law found in the infrahuman or natural order, or human law. And since the rational is ultimately inseparable from a person, it follows that the person enjoys the supremacy over law as irrationally understood by modern schools of history.

The specific difference between human action and irrational nature is that the person always grasps the end as an end. For example, food becomes a humanly perceived end only when it is apprehended as something bearing the character of the food as such. The food as such is an abstract notion and is not to be apprehended without an abstractive process which is impossible without reason.

Law is therefore: "an ordinance of reason." [87] The explanation of the cause of human law is to be found in human reason. But the explanation of irrational creatures in the physical universe acting for pre-existing ends, is not to be found in themselves. Since, however, nothing tends toward an end without reason, the cause of their activity must be sought in a reason above the human; namely, the Eternal Reason of God. This Eternal Reason of God not only explains the purposive of action of infrahuman creatures, but also is the ultimate explanation of human action itself.[88]

The natural law for St. Thomas is far broader than the natural law understood by science. First, because it includes human reason, and secondly, because the ultimate explanation of both the physical law and the rational creature is the Eternal Reason of God.

The first criticism of the historical theories which we are investigating is that they offer no explanation whatever for the existence of the law by which they explain history. It makes no difference whether the law be mechanical, economic, biological, zoological, or fatalistic, for the question still remains: why should the law tend toward these specific ends without a rational justification for that tendency? And since reason is inseparable from person, should not history be explained more in terms of the human person rather than in terms of irrational law or blind impulse?

History is, and should be, the study of persons rather than the study of law. "In all nature there is nothing more perfect than person." [89] Economics, politics, and the material universe exist for man, and not vice versa. There is a hierarchy in creation. The less noble things exist for the more noble. The human person is the peak of this pyramid of visible creation. Aristotle called man a *microcosm* and St. Thomas described him as a *"minor mundus."* [90] In man, all the other creatures of the world are in some way found. In some instances, these creatures are present physiologically, inasmuch as they enter into his physical being, but what is more important, they are within man intellectually, since he is capable of knowing all things in the visible world. The person therefore has a worth transcendent to all other things in creation. This truth of reason was confirmed by revelation: "What doth it profit a man if he gain the whole world and lose his soul?" Hence the Marxist theory of history, which places the primary emphasis on economic laws of production, and the pessimistic view of Spengler, which makes man the plaything of blind fatalistic forces, and the evolutionary view, which regards man, in the language of Harry Elmer Barnes, as only a "cosmic accident of no more importance than a cockroach," deny the primary value of the universe—the human person. It was by no accident that these views of history which made law primary should end by absorbing the individual into the collectivity. If man is merely a product of dialectic materialism or the chance emergent of cosmic evolutions, he does not exist as a being *sui generis*, or as a value which cannot be deduced from, or reduced to, anything nonhuman. Deny the difference between person and nature and there is simultaneously denied the right of history to be a science, distinct from any of the other sciences of nature, such as physics or biology. For this reason, Marx and Engels and Lenin, in order to prove their theories about society, made constant appeal either to physics—as did Marx and Lenin—or to botany, as did Engels in referring to the example of the barley seed. Spengler, in like manner, having dethroned the person as the supreme value of the individual, bases his history on the new physics of space and time. Once the supremacy of person over law is denied, the person is reduced to an individual—a part of the material universe—and thus is prepared to be absorbed into the collectivity. It is fitting for a man to say to a grocer: "I should like to buy one of your apples," but not fitting to say: "I should like to marry one of your daughters." Things are individual, but daughters are persons, and they may not be treated in the same manner. It is by no historical accident that the totalitarian philosophies of life arose at a time when the science of law was developing, rather than the science of persons. Nor is it by chance that Buddhism, which carries a belief in the supremacy of law over person to the extreme, finally ends in the absorption of personality in the Nirvana.[91]

An interesting by-product of the Thomistic view of law is that since a human person cannot always be counted on to act rationally, but occasionally may become the plaything of passing moods and passions, St. Thomas argues for the primacy of written law over personal law, a primacy which today would mean the supremacy of civil law rather than of dictatorship. The reason for his argument is not that law is unconcerned with the person, but rather that the person cannot always be counted on to be rational. Quoting Aristotle, St. Thomas said: "It is better that all things be regulated by law than left to be decided by judges." He then proceeded to give three reasons:

First, because it is easier to find a few wise men competent to frame right laws, than to find the many who would be necessary to judge aright of each single case. Secondly, because those who make laws consider long beforehand what laws to make; whereas judgment on each single case has to be pronounced as soon as it arises: and it is easier for man to see what is right, by taking many instances into consideration, than by considering one solitary fact. Thirdly, because lawgivers judge in the abstract and of future events; whereas those who sit in judgment judge of things present, towards which they are affected by love, hatred, or some kind of cupidity; wherefore their judgment is perverted.[92]

It is an interesting fact that law has been thrown into a sharper focus in history as belief in God declined. This irrational law, which eclipses the belief in a personal Deity, has presented itself in various ways. Sometimes a mathematical law supplants God, as it did in the case of Babylon when, with the discovery of the stellar cosmos, certain Chaldean mathematicians transferred their allegiance from Marduk-Bel to seven planets; the same mentality is seen in the Western man of science. Sometimes it is an economic law, as with

Marx, or a zoological law, as with Spengler, or a psychological law, as with the humanists. Polytheism seems to be coming back, but this time the gods are not of stone or silver; they are the gods of nations. The tribute paid to the cadaver of Lenin by Communists is a tawdry substitute for Deity.

History as the story of mankind is impossible on the basis of law as understood by the above mentioned schools of history, for such law favors not humanity, but only certain human beings. The evolutionary view, for example, favors those who happen to be the lucky emergents, but not the aborigines or the retarded; the Marxist view favors the proletariat, and the Spengler view those on whom destiny sets its seal. History as the study of law tends to particularism. History as the study of persons tends to universalism, and is based on the oneness of humanity.

The Athenians, who had their own particular gods for the different professions and even for the various difficulties of life, nevertheless felt obliged to have a unifying deity, whom they called the "unknown God." St. Paul seized on that idea, and explained to the Greeks that the reason for the unity of mankind was that men have all come from God. That this idea was already familiar to them, he proved by quoting a text from some of their own poets, Epimenedes, Aratus, and Cleanthes:

Then Paul stood up in the midst of the Areopagus, and said, "Men of Athens, I see that in every respect you are extremely religious. For as I was going about and observing objects of your worship, I found also an altar with this inscription: 'To the Unknown God.' What therefore you worship in ignorance, that I proclaim to you. God, who made the world and all that is in it, since he is Lord of heaven and earth, does not dwell in temples built by hands; neither is he served by human hands as though he were in need of anything, since it is he who gives to all men life and breath and all things. And from one man he has created the whole human race and made them live all over the face of the earth, determining their appointed times and the boundaries of their lands; that they should seek God, and perhaps grope after him, and find him, though he is not far from any one of us. For in him we live and move and have our being, as indeed some of your own poets have said, 'For we are also his offspring.'" [93]

But why should Paul have insisted that only a personal God can be the bond of men and therefore the bond of history? For the simple reason that the very idea of unity implies a bond outside those elements which enter into the unity. The larger the bond, the greater the unity. "The class," which is the unit of Marxist history, and the "destined race," which is the unit of Spenglerian history, are exclusive of other units. To tie up a bundle, one must be outside the bundle. Hence the importance of an Eternal Person for human brotherhood and therefore for human history, as opposed to class history, or race history, or progressive history.

Not only is Person the only foundation for human unity, it is also the only foundation for human equality. A private and a general cannot be equal to one another in an army, but they can be equal to one another in a nation. Equality implies a common denominator. Deny it and equality degenerates into identity. Deny the basis in Person and equality then becomes only equal opportunity to get ahead, which is the essence of the evolutionary view of history. Men are then likened to tadpoles, some of whom may be fortunate enough to shed their tails and croak, while others must forever be satisfied with merely the opportunity to become frogs. The equality grounded in Person does not base equality on opportunity, but on inherent dignity. Because made by a Person, every man has supreme value. Economics and politics then become only instruments for man's perfection. Men may be comrades because they belong to the same class, but men are brothers only because they have a common Father. It is that way in the family; it is that way in the world; the brotherhood of man is impossible without the Fatherhood of God.

The fullness of this concept of the Fatherhood of God did not come into being until the time of Christ. There are, however, dim adumbrations and shadowings of it in pagan times, as the very citations of St. Paul from the pagan authors prove. The poet Terence once said, *homo sum, humani nihil a me alienum puto*. The same universalism is found in the records of Cyrus, the King of Persia. The prophet Jeremias had foretold that the captivity of Babylon would not last more than seventy years and that the Jews would then return to their own country. As had been prophesied in the seventieth year of their captivity, Cyrus issued an edict that all the Jews who were in his kingdom should go back to Jerusalem and should rebuild the Temple of the Lord. In the case of Cyrus, however, this was not done without Divine inspiration and suggestion, for Isaias so recounts it.[94] In any case there was, on the part of Cyrus, a recognition of the value of a people other than his own, and in this instance of a twice-conquered people. This fore-shadowing of universalism he fortified by restoring to the Jews the sacred vessels which Nebuchadnezzar had carried away. A year after the Jews' return from captivity, the foundations of the new Temple were laid in Jerusalem. Many of the old people who remembered the former Temple wept to see that the new one did not equal the old in magnificence. But the prophet Aggeus told them that the second Temple would be more glorious than the first, because "the desired of all nations" would be seen in it and honor it with His presence. Thus does the prophet suggest that the desire of men for unity is to be achieved only in the God to whom all nations look and yearn.

This same view of history as a story of humanity rather than of a class or of those subject to law is also foreshadowed in Alexander the Great's concept of *Homonoia* or concord. St. Paul tells us that it was only with the coming of Christ that the dividing line between the Greek and barbarian was completely broken down. But Alexander, in a confused sort of way, must have understood the unity of mankind under a person. Plutarch quotes him as saying: "God is the common father of all men, but he makes the best ones particularly his own." Alexander insisted that the ruling faction of every city-state should open its gates to the exiled opponents of the contrary political party. Plutarch, in his *Life of Alexander*, tells how very much Alexander was inspired by the Persians whom he defeated. After he had avenged Xerxes' unlucky crossing of the Hellespont, he ceased to follow the common pattern of the Greeks who called the Persians tyrants and cruel and bestial. Recognizing their bravery in battle, he held up the Persians to his soldiers as worthy of the envy of the Greeks. To cultivate a spirit of universalism, Alexander took for a wife a daughter of a Persian grandee and forced others in his retinue to marry Persians also. Plutarch says in regard to this: "At Susa he married Darius's daughter of Statira, celebrated also the nuptials of his friends, bestowing the noblest of the Persian ladies upon the worthiest of them, and at the same time making it an entertainment in honor of the other Macedonians whose marriages had already taken place." Finding the tomb of Cyrus rifled by one of his own soldiers, a certain

Polymachus, Alexander ordered him to be put to death, and he restored the inscription, which read: "O man, whosoever thou art, and from wheresoever thou comest (for I know thou wilt come), I am Cyrus, the founder of the Persian Empire; do not grudge me this little earth which covers my body."

The universalism of Cyrus and Alexander was derived from the recognition of the Person of God. Had there not been what Alexander called "the common Father of all men," there would not have been such humaneness shown to the Jews by Cyrus, and to the Persians by Alexander. Law favors particularism; even the Divinely Revealed Law favored the Jews. But the harsh laws of dialectical materialism and biology favor only a class to the detriment of another class, or a race to the ignominy of another race. It is only with the advent of Christianity that the Samaritans begin to be respected and the Gentile centurions to be recognized as worthy members of the Kingdom of God.

The great social and cultural changes in history are not due to the operation of an immanent law, such as dialectical materialism or evolution, but rather to the impetus given by persons. The explanation of both the growth and the decay of civilization is to be found in the self-determination of rational beings, not in the operation of a law outside of them; conscious beings rather than unconscious forces explain the vicissitudes of mankind. As Bergson has expressed it: "It is useless to maintain that social progress takes place of itself, bit by bit, in virtue of the spiritual condition of society at a certain period of its history. It is really a leap forward which is only taken when the society has made up its mind to try an experiment; this means that the society must have allowed itself to be convinced, or at any rate allowed itself to be shaken; and the shake is always given by *somebody*." [95] Communism, for example, can be far better explained by the appearance of a Lenin in Russia than by dialectical materialism; Nazism was much more intelligible in terms of Hitler than in terms of a zoological law of the primacy of the German race. As Plato tells us:

Among the mass of mankind there is always a certain number—though a very small number—of godlike individuals whose inspiration is of priceless social value. These rare individuals are no more apt to emerge in socially progressive countries than in others; so the members of the socially progressive societies ought to be constantly on their tracks, scouring sea and land in order to discover sterling representatives of the species and to derive from them inspiration for revising the existing body of social institutions.[96]

So long as people obey laws or feel that they are under laws, they are apt to remain very passive. Nothing can so much arouse them from that passivity as a person endowed with great powers of leadership, or a creative minority who will resist the current and the drift. The transformation of a social milieu has historically taken place only through the triumphant creative will of a great genius. The more a creative individual rises above the average level of his contemporaries, the more likely he is to precipitate a social conflict. He may have more bricks thrown at him than a mediocre person would have flowers, but it is conceivable that in such abuse a transfiguration of society could take place. " 'Do not think that I came to send peace upon the earth; I have come to bring a sword, not peace. For I have come to set a man at variance with his father, and a daughter with her mother, and a daughter-in-law with her mother-in-law; and a man's enemies will be those of his own household.' " [97]

These creative individuals are generally few in number compared to the masses upon which they react. They may be, from the point of view of proportion, as minimal as the salt to the earth or as a city to a mountain, or as a candlelight to a bushel, or as leaven to the mass, but since their influence is not in proportion to their numbers but in proportion to the invisible power of their ideas, they create an effect with which mathematicians cannot calculate.

The common man is of and by himself incapable of great social or cultural advancement without the leadership furnished by the uncommon man. The ills of the world today are not due to want of sheep, but rather to the want of a shepherd. When Philip and Andrew would have sent the common men away hungry from the desert because there was no food to give them to eat, Our Lord said: "Do not send them away lest they faint on the way, for they are as sheep without a shepherd." [98] The growth of the masses or the great uncreative majority is the beginning of the fall of any nation. And by the masses here is to be understood:

a group which does not belong to any one social or economic class. It consists of all those who no longer participate in the creative life and thought of the community: all the cynical, all the hopeless, all the angry, all the frightened. These are the frustrated men and women who no longer can, or no longer will, take part in the work of carrying forward a civilization. They are always present. An increase in their number is the first warning that the world is losing its health.... It means that because of our partial failure to be true to our promises and our traditions, the old barbarian has come back into the world, ready as ever to destroy, unable as ever to create.[99]

If the common man—the masses—is to be lifted out of his uncreativeness, it will be done not by bureaucracies and social agencies or immanent laws, but only by the uncommon man. The masses will be elevated not by an individual who belongs to society, but only by one who stands outside of it. Society, no more than man, can lift itself by its own bootstraps. The masses are like broken pieces of mirror, each reflecting a different image, each with his own conceits, desires, and libidos. The creative personality who comes into the masses alone can unite these fragments into a unit so that they reflect only one image; or to change the figure, where the sheep were scattered before, there now becomes one fold, because there is only one shepherd. If there is no great resurgence of spirit in the Western World today, it is due to the fact that it has not been salted with great leadership.

A rather forceful commentary on the placidity and uncreativeness of the herd is given by Lewis Mumford:

In America we have created a new race, with healthy physiques, sometimes beautiful bodies, but empty minds: people who have accepted life as an alternation of meaningless routine with insignificant sensation. They deny because of their lack of experience that life has any other meanings or values or possibilities. At their best, these passive barbarians live on an innocent animal level: they sun-tan their bodies, sometimes at vast public bathing beaches, sometimes under a lamp. They dance, whirl, sway, in mild orgies of vacant sexuality, or they engage in more intimate felicities without a feeling, a sentiment, or an ultimate intention that a copulating cat would not equally share. They dress themselves carefully within the range of uniformity dictated by fashion. Their hair is curled by a machine; and what passes for thought or feeling is also achieved, passively, through the use of a machine: the radio or the moving picture today, or Aldous Huxley's "feelies" tomorrow.

These people eat, drink, marry, bear children and go to their grave in a state that is at best hilarious anesthesia, and at its worst is anxiety, fear, and envy, for lack of the necessary means to achieve the fashionable minimum of sensation. Without this minimum, their routine would be unbearable and their vacancy worse. Shopgirls and clerks, millionaires and mechanics share the same underlying beliefs, engage in the same practices: they have a common contempt for life on any other level than that of animal satisfaction, animal vitality. Deprive them of this, and it is not worth living. Half dead in their work: half alive outside their work. This is their destiny. Every big city counts such people by the million; even the smaller provincial centers, imitating the luxury and the style of the big centers, with their fashion shows, night clubs, road houses, organized inanities, produce their full share of people equally empty of human standards and aims.[100]

This author's conception for the need of recreating the masses is no less clear than his portrayal of their character.

Our salvation will lie in giving a major opportunity to the creative people and in cultivating more of them: people who are capable of adapting social forms to social needs as completely as an artist is capable of creating, out of the chaos of experience, a painting, a poem, or a symphony. Subjective confidence should not be the monopoly of raging paranoiacs: its normal expression is the very quality of the artist.
Without this withdrawal, the pieties of the religious too easily become platitudes; and their vision of the universe remains a tepid one. It is alone, in the wilderness or in the cell, that men remake their destiny. In the midst of the present apocalypse of violence, one cannot hope that the synthesis of cults and creeds, or cosmologies and sciences, that must ultimately be demanded for modern man will take place in time to alter the present posture of affairs. Too much must be discarded; too many stones for the new building are still unquarried.[101]

Henri Bergson is also of the same mind, contending that the upward surges of human culture have been due to great persons rather than to law.

The appearance of each one of them was like the creation of a new species, composed of one single individual, the vital impulse culminating at long intervals in one particular man, a result which could not have been obtained at one stroke by humanity as a whole. Each of these souls marked then a certain point attained by the evolution of life; and each of them was a manifestation, in an original form, of a love which seems to be the very essence of the creative effort. The creative emotion which exalted these exceptional souls, and which was an overflowing of vitality, has spread far and wide about them; enthusiasts themselves, they radiated enthusiasm which has never been completely quenched, and which can be readily fanned into flame again.... The mystic love of humanity is a very different thing. It is not the extension of an instinct, it does not originate in an idea. It is neither of the senses nor of the mind. It is of both, implicitly, and is effectively much more. For such a love lies at the very root of feeling and reason, as of all other things. Coinciding with

God's love for His handiwork, a love which has been the source of everything, it would yield up, to anyone who knew how to question it, the secret of creation. It is still more metaphysical than moral in its essence. What it wants to do, with God's help, is to complete the creation of the human species and make of humanity what it would have straightaway become, had it been able to assume its final shape without the assistance of man himself.[102]

A person, rather than a law, effects such catastrophic changes in society because persons, and not laws alone, can directly enkindle souls. Even granted that the most of humanity is made up of dried sticks, fire can still be kindled among them by a great person, who can succeed in rubbing them together. For that reason, the greatest influence on society has been exerted less by the writings of great persons than by their lives. Plato refused to write a philosophical exposition of his system because he believed real knowledge comes from an intimate personal intercourse and an intellectual communion.

I have one thing to say about all writers, past or future, who claim to understand my philosophy either as a result of oral communications received from me or from others or by the unaided light of their own genius. All such claimants stand convicted of charlatanism on my showing. At any rate there is no written work of my own on my philosophy, and there never will be. For this philosophy cannot possibly be put into words as other sciences can. The sole way of acquiring it is by strenuous intellectual communion and intimate personal intercourse, which kindle it in the soul instantaneously like a light caught from a leaping flame; and, once alight, it feeds its own flame thenceforward. Of course I know very well that the best presentation of it, oral or written, would be my own. I also know that I should be the first to be pained by a written presentation which failed to do it justice. And if I believed that an adequate popular presentation, either written or verbal, were possible, what finer life-work could I have set myself than to write something of real benefit for Mankind; something which would bring the nature of the Universe into the light of the day for all eyes to see? Unhappily, I do not consider that the study of my philosophy is good for people, with the exception of a few who are capable of discovering it for themselves with the aid of a minimum of demonstration. As for the rest, I fancy that some would be filled perversely with a misguided contempt and others with a soaring, windy expectation—in the belief that they had learnt something tremendous.[103]

St. Thomas has a similar explanation of why Christ Himself did not write.

It was fitting that Christ should not commit His doctrine to writing. First, on account of His dignity: for the more excellent the teacher, the more excellent should be his manner of teaching. Consequently it was fitting that Christ, as the most excellent of teachers, should adopt that manner of teaching whereby His doctrine is imprinted on the hearts of His hearers; wherefore it is written that "He was teaching them as one having power" (Matt. 7:29). And so it was that among the Gentiles, Pythagoras and Socrates, who were teachers of great excellence, were unwilling to write anything. For writings are ordained, as to an end, unto the imprinting of doctrine in the hearts of the hearers.

Secondly, on account of the excellence of Christ's doctrine, which cannot be expressed in writing; according to Jo. 21:25: There are also many other things which Jesus did, which, if they were written, every-one, the world itself, I think, would not be able to contain the books that should be written. Which Augustine explains by saying: "We are not to believe that in respect of space the world could not contain them ... but that by the capacity of the readers they could not be comprehended." And if Christ had committed His doctrine to writing, men would have had no deeper thought of His doctrine than that which appears on the surface of the writing.[104]

In contrast with this exclusiveness of the philosopher, the Founder of the Christian religion bade His followers to go out into the byways and highways and compel the lame and the blind and the deaf to come in that His house might be filled. In the case of Christianity, where the Person is Himself the Word, therefore Supreme Intelligence, it is interesting that it is to the masses that He makes His appeal rather than to the intellectuals. It would seem that the uncultivated and simple souls who are at a considerable distance from philosophical abstractions, are more susceptible to supreme wisdom when vested in a person. Over and over again we find the Fathers of the Church reproaching the philosophers for their inability to convert the stubborn hearts of men. As St. Ambrose put it: *Non in dialectica complacuit Deo salvum facere populum suum.*" [105] And Augustine adds: *"Nisi fideliter praecederet piscator, non humiliter sequeretur orator."* [106]

The greatest personal influence in all history was the Person Who did not give a Truth apart from Himself but identified Himself with Truth. No one ever died for a theorem in geometry, nor will anyone ever bleed to preserve the law of dialectical materialism. There can be love only where there is a Person.

CRISES IN HISTORY

The foregoing chapters indicated that the fallacy behind all materialistic views of history is that they assume that matter is the only reality, mechanical or biological law the only law, and that history is devoid of purpose. Creative or emergent evolution makes an attempt to explain the novelties which appear in the historical process, but fails to tell us why the emergents emerged, or why there should be any purpose in man today. If the universe started with unconsciousness, then it started without purpose; if the purpose arose from unconsciousness, then we have the contradiction of an unconscious purpose at the matrix of the universe. If a transcendent Divine Principle is denied in history, then the emergence of any purpose is an accident and it might just as well not have happened. But if it is accidental, then how explain the persistent order and co-ordination and subordination and interaction of elements which we find in the universe? An a-moral spark or atomic explosion at the beginning of the universe does not explain the presence of a moral law in conscience. In vain can it be argued that the moral law comes from instinct, because very often the former contradicts the latter. There is, for example, in all of us an instinct of self-preservation, but very often the moral order and a sense of duty, as for a soldier, demand that such an instinct be contradicted. History is not automatic progress in a straight line without a definite beginning or direction, for the simple reason that if progress were automatic, no one would make progress. Neither is history, as Benedetto Croce believed, a mounting spiral, in which declines occur only to be followed by a higher rise. The spiral is a comfort for the skeptical bystander of history who decides to look upon the tragic catastrophes from the outside and does not wish to participate in any of its agonies or transfigurations. The very fact that such skeptics can look upon the spectacle from the outside without ever participating in it, means not only that the spectators have not contributed to the progress of the world, but have no right to flatter themselves by telling us to be vigilant about what will happen in the future.[107]

Somewhere there is a golden mean between those wholly immanent views of history which find the destiny entirely within the time perspective, and the transcendent views which escape the time perspective by making human beings irresponsible. To the former group belong Marxism, naturalism, materialism, and to the latter, Taoism, Buddhism, and other nonhistorical religions. The golden mean is that the transcendent purpose of God is disclosed and fulfilled immanently in history. From another point of view, it is the progressive disclosure of the Divine transcendent principle in time.

There is one word around which the moral view of history may revolve and that is *crisis*, which in Greek means judgment, or a verdict of history. It is a fact that nature passes judgment. The oak is a judgment on the acorn; the headache is a judgment on our refusal to eat; the double chin is a judgment on our eating too much; ignorance is a judgment on our refusal to study. Nature acts in a certain way simply because God has implanted certain laws in the universe. Some of these laws are physical, others bio-olgical, and others moral. The transcendent God therefore is present in the universe immanently through these laws. It is His Will that these laws be obeyed for the perfection of the creatures themselves. It is with history and human freedom that we are presently concerned. History is the testing ground for human freedom and passes judgments on the way we use it. The seed of certain ideas is planted, it bears fruit either good or evil, and this fruit is a judgment on the kind of seed we planted. History is always passing verdicts on the ideas of an age. The religious revolution of the sixteenth century was a judgment on the way those who had the faith lived. The French Revolution was a judgment on the privileges of the monarchy and the denial of political equality to all citizens. World War is a judgment on the way we think and live, marry and unmarry, buy and sell; it is a judgment on our banks, our schools, our books, our economic system, our factories, our homes, our legislatures, our hearts and souls, and above all on our humanist delusion that man is naturally and progressively good, either individually or collectively.

What has God to do with these judgments? God does not will these judgments directly. He does not send a war into the world as a punishment from outside history in a purely arbitrary and extrinsic fashion because He is angry with us. From the moral viewpoint of history, wars do not follow disobedience to God's

Will as a spanking follows a disobedient boy's eating his mother's jam. God does not send the thunder as an applause because He is thrilled with the momentary pyrotechnics of the heavens. Rather He made the universe in such a way that, when there is lightning, there is thunder. The thunder is the judgment on the lightning, the effect resulting from the cause. In the physical sphere, certain diseases are judgment on squalid living, not because God plays favorites with the nice clean hygienic people, but simply because of an essential element in the universe. God made the world in such a way that when we freely set ourselves in opposition to His Will, certain consequences follow, and the calamity attendant upon the defiance of His Will, is what we call a judgment of God. Sin brings adversity in its train, and adversity is the expression of God's condemnation of evil. A wrong attitude toward nature and a wrong attitude toward fellowman or society imply a wrong attitude toward God and here, too, the consequence is inevitable.[108]

There is a difference between the Will of God and the judgment of God. The Will of God is our peace and happiness. The judgment of God is made up of our opposition to that Will. A vertical bar stands for God's will, a horizontal bar, which crosses it in sin, stands for man's will; the result is a Cross or a crisis. The Will of God is never defeated, because in doing evil we produce an effect which we do not intend. The frustration of the modern world, therefore, is a result of the collision of our wills with the Divine Will. History then becomes the sphere where fallen man works out the consequences of his severance from God. When war comes, then, it is not in the strict sense of the term a visitation from God or even an extrinsic punishment from God; it is our apostate civilization registering sentence on our thinking, on our living. Love was meant to be our consolation. When we reject it freely, love becomes our judge. We are as free to run counter to God's Will as we are free to run counter to "the law of gravitation" by throwing ourselves from a building. But in doing the latter, we kill ourselves. When society, in like manner, sets itself up in antagonism to the gospel of love, the sovereignty of God is revealed in the judgment that follows the disobedience. Without judgment, there would be no sovereignty even in our earthly courts. But God's judgment is never separable from His Mercy. When we acknowledge Him to be our Judge, He becomes our Savior. The alternative before men, therefore, is either to live under the love of God or else to live under His Justice and His Judgment. It is under the latter that the world is in the present evil hour.

There are three important principles to be kept in mind if we are to understand the moral view of history. The first is that God may sometimes use evil instruments for good purposes. It is recorded in the Old Testament that Israel had done two evils. "They have foresaken Me, the fountain of living water, and have digged to themselves cisterns, broken cisterns that can hold no water." [109] Because Israel would not repent, God said through Amos the Prophet: "I will raise up a nation against you, O house of Israel, saith the Lord the God of Hosts." [110] The particular instrument that God would choose for a judgment upon Israel would be the Assyrian who is called "the rod and staff of my anger, and my indignation is in their hands." [111] But because Assyria is the rod and ax of God's justice it must not glory in itself and think that victory is due to itself. "Shall the ax boast against him that cutteth with it: or shall the saw exalt itself against him by whom it is drawn?" [112]

So much is God the Ruler of Nations and the Lord of the Universe, that the victorious Assyria was bidden not to glory in its conquests, for God foretold that after seventy years that proud nation would fall. "Behold I will stir up the Medes against them ... and that Babylon, glorious among the kingdoms, the famous pride of the Chaldeans, shall be even as the Lord destroyed Sodom and Gomorrah." [113]

As God foretold, so it came to pass. Balthasar, the son of the conqueror, gave a feast for a thousand nobles, during which there appeared a finger writing over against the candlestick upon the surface of the wall, that God had numbered the kingdom and it had finished, that it was weighed in the balance and found wanting, and that it would be divided and given to the Medes and Persians. Cyrus came to the great walls of Babylon that night, turned aside the waters of the Euphrates, "and the vessel was broken which he was making of clay with his hands: and turning he made another vessel, and it seemed good in his eyes." [114] The judgment was punitive against the Assyrians because it ended in their desolation, it was paternal against the Jews because it ended in their restoration.

The judgments of history therefore are not pronounced by courts but revealed in the judgments and conflicts of classes and nations.

Sometimes these crises come, not in order that one particular nation may be punished or suffer the consequences of its deeds, but that an impotent good which is presently hidden in some civilization may later on be revealed. The barbarians knocking at the gates of Rome fulfilled a Divine mission. Something good was already beginning to appear in Roman civilization—the spirit of fraternity and love, which had been engendered by nascent Christianity. But this good was as yet powerless to affirm itself because it was encrusted over with the hard shell of paganism. There is life under the shell of an egg, but before that life can assert itself, the egg must be broken; so, too, in like manner, it was necessary that the shell of paganism be broken in order that the life of Christianity might assert itself. St. Jerome, living in a cave at Bethlehem, commenting on the Sacred Scriptures, did not understand the full implications of this barbarian invasion. He tells us that he shed tears when he heard of the fall of Rome. St. Augustine, more properly informed concerning the destruction of this old civilization, saw in it the historical manifestation of the City of God. As in the Person of Christ, so in the history of nations very often the verse of the Benedictus is fulfilled: "*Salutem ex inimicis nostris de manu omnium qui oderunt nos.*" It could very well be, though it awaits historical manifestation, that the purpose of Communism is in some way to liquidate a Western World which has forgotten its God. Later the gift of Faith may be received, as it was by the barbarians of Rome, and there may arise one of the greatest Christian civilizations, thriving in peace and prosperity.

A second principle in the moral view of history is that God's purposes are never defeated. God's ultimate purpose in the universe is the salvation of all men and their vocation to the glorious liberty of the children of God. The will and intention of man does not often correspond with God's Will. Like Lucifer we can defy it, and say: "I will not." And yet, though we deliberately violate God's Will, His purpose is never defeated, because in doing evil we produce an effect which we did not intend. We do not will the effect. It is willed by the very nature of the reality which we negate. Nature is on God's side not ours. That is why the cock crew when Peter denied Him. Reality always operates in favor of God. As Francis Thompson put it: "In fickleness to me and loyalty to Him, traitorous trueness and loyal deceit." My reason tells me that the purpose of a pencil is to write. I can freely use the pencil to open a tin can, but in violating that law of reason, not only do I not open the tin can, but I also destroy the pencil. We do not attain the purposes we seek by violating God's laws; but we hurt ourselves. Modern frustration is a consequence of working against the nature of things infused with God's reason. We can never be in opposition to Him without also being in opposition to ourselves. The will to power is self-defeating. In piercing God's Heart, it is our own that we slay. In the confusion of these times of delirium, God does not so much punish us as we punish ourselves. God's purposes are never defeated—in addition, there will be a last judgment whose purpose is to be the Divine Guarantee of the permanence of Truth. The truths which we now throw into the garbage heap of the world will then be taken out and reaffirmed. The stone which the builders rejected will become the head of the corner.

A third and final truth about the moral view of history is that the acceptance of judgment is one of the conditions of recovery. Mankind, individually and socially, can never be ready for mercy until it accepts the judgments it deserves. The prodigal was ready for recovery the moment he admitted his own unworthiness. The thief was ripe for the kingdom of God when he admitted that he was suffering the just punishment of his sins. The peculiar thing about the moral order of history is that just as soon as we admit judgment, we open up a new alternative, as did the prodigal, the thief, and the city of Nineveh when it did penance. For that reason Tolstoi, in full recognition of the fact that God's judgment was visited upon him, in humility said: "Can't I plug up a hole or can you not use me to wipe something?" Sometimes it requires sickness before one admits the need of a physician. We have always to admit ignorance before we can be taught, and there must be an admission of sin before there can be redemption. In that sense, even a crisis of history can become a *felix culpa*.

While the world is in the midst of crisis and judgment there is no external difference between those who are good and bad. The sun shall go down upon the good and the bad, and there shall be no final sorting before the last judgment, for we are all members of the human family. Churches and the faithful shall be destroyed when a bomb falls as well as those who are wicked. But there is this internal difference despite the external similarity. Those who recognize justice and seek mercy are chastened; those who do not recognize it are condemned. As St. Paul told the Corinthians: "But if we would judge ourselves, we should not be judged. But whilst we are judged, we are chastised by the Lord, that we be not condemned in this world." [115]

THE LORD OF HISTORY

In many discussions of Providence, its operations seem limited to nature, to caring for the birds of the air and the fishes of the sea. There is no intrinsic reason, if its correct definition is known, why Providence should be so limited. St. Thomas compares Providence to prudence, inasmuch as it implies the foreseeing of events; the attainment of goals; and the right choice of means to attain those goals.[116] Providence is distinct from creation, which implies calling a being *ex nihilo*. Providence signifies giving ordered continuance to the being which already exists. Creation is the beginning of a fact; Providence is the continuance of the fact as process and progress. St. Augustine combines both in his definition: *Quod vero Deus mundum condiderit, et de providentia ejus, qua, universum quod condidit, regit.*[117]

The point we wish to make is that treatises on Providence have too closely followed the Greek and too distantly the Hebrew. A more balanced treatise on Providence should include both approaches, so that God is the God not only of nature, but also the Lord of History. The difference between the two ideas of Providence is that the Greek view conceived of an ideal world realized in time; everything in the world was the concretion of an archetypal idea existing in the mind of God. For the Hebrew, the world is not yet the complete actualization of the transcendent purposes of God, because the purposes of God are eschatological. The Greek view was concerned with the essence of God as *Ipsum Esse*, or as the Immobile Mover; the Hebrews were concerned not only with God as He is in Himself, but also with His purposes in relation to mankind. He is the God of Abraham, of Isaac, and Jacob. The Greek view regarded religion as rational; the Hebrew as historical. Therefore to the Greek philosophers, religion was not necessarily moral, though it was intellectual and consisted in contemplating Deity. The Hebrew religion was moral, for it viewed man in relation to the transcendent purposes of God. The Hebrews added to contemplation a moral communion with God. "You worship Me with your lips, but your heart is far from Me," complained the God of the Hebrews. For the Greeks, virtue was a balance; "sin" was due to ignorance. For the Hebrews, virtue was in obedience to the Divine Will, and sin was a willful infraction of Divine law. The basic problem of Greek philosophy was that of being and becoming, but for the Hebrews, it was a reconciliation of historical experiences with a good and righteous God. The transcendent Deity of the Greeks has received most of the emphasis, and the historical or more or less immanent Deity (transcendent to the universe and to history, but immanent in His purposes) has been neglected. Of the two views of Providence, if one had to choose, certainly the Hebrew would have a greater significance for our days of crisis.

In the presentation of this neglected aspect of Providence, three major points should be emphasized: The historical background of the problem of the Lord of History in Christian times; the neglected aspect of the Lord of History in Grecian literature; the moral principles of the Lord of History.

THE CHRISTIAN CONCEPT OF THE LORD OF HISTORY

The New Testament, following the Old, clearly presents an historical dualism. In the Old Testament, the conflict was between the chosen people under God, and the Gentiles. In the New Testament, the conflict is more spiritual and becomes a struggle between the Beast and the Woman as revealed in the Apocalypse, and Christ and anti-Christ in the Gospels. St. Augustine, as the first philosopher of Christian History, translated the conflict into a struggle between the City of God and the City of Man. Leaning more to the Hebrew than to the Grecian view, he declared that the God Who created the birds of the air could not be indifferent to human affairs. He even saw the conflict of the Two Cities prefigured in the struggle of Cain and Abel, the quarrel of Romulus and Remus.[118] Dante looked back to the Augustinian ideal and forward to the humanism of the Renaissance. At the time he wrote, the Holy Roman Empire was becoming more German, the Papacy more French, and his times were disturbed by the conflict of the Guelphs, the party of the

Papacy, and the Ghibellines, the party of the Empire. Because the conflict of the Two Cities was not so evident in his days when Christianity was synonymous with Western Civilization, he was concerned more with seeing God's purposes as manifested historically in a Universal Empire—a Christian universal empire.[119] In his *De Monarchia*, Dante tries to prove the necessity of a Universal Empire; the right of Romans to imperial authority; and the direct bequeathing by God of this authority to the Empire. In defense of the position that the Roman people rightfully appropriated imperial authority, he presents four arguments: Roman authority was willed by God because of the nobility of the Romans; God aided it by miracles; God willed this empire to be victorious over all; and Christ willed to be born under it.

When the Christian unity was disrupted by the Religious Revolution, it was only natural for Christian philosophers of history to return to the idea of conflict. The Protestant view of history was based on the Bible and St. Augustine's Two Cities, but it used a different point of view. The Church with its visible hierarchical society, called by Augustine the City of God, now became the City of Satan, a harlot sitting on seven hills, drunk with the blood of saints, and intoxicating the nations with her evil enchantment. The true Church, or City of God, was the Society of the Elect who followed the Bible as against the historical Church, which now was regarded as the anti-Christ.

The Reformation was like the Renaissance in its relation to history—both wiped out the past and gave us *discontinuous history*. As the Renaissance skipped supernatural man to get to the natural man, so the Reformation skipped the Middle Ages, and got back to primitive "classical" Christianity. The result was that there was a great emphasis on Hebraic and prophetic elements as against Hellenic metaphysical elements. The Old Testament became a familiar theme.

Next history was emptied of all religious elements, beginning with Socinianism and continuing with deism and liberalism. If the "supernatural" does not intrinsically justify, then it is unnatural. Therefore abandon it. Philosophy of history thus became secularized and broke into two currents: Pessimism and Optimism, the former being principally German, the latter principally French. Pessimism was most clearly revealed in Lutheranism which taught that man was intrinsically corrupt. Socially, Lutheranism taught that since society was made up of corrupt individuals, the purpose of a state was primarily to tame and control these anarchic impulses. The sinfulness of men could be checked only by Divine ordinance of government. The secular government is the "Kingdom of God's left hand," and was instituted to amend the anarchy and conflict resulting from sin. Hence the highest possibility in the social order was not justice, but *coerced tranquillity*. This pessimism we find later on in Hobbes: "Man is essentially selfish, a wolf to his neighbor."

The other current was the optimistic, stemming more directly from the Renaissance than the German religious revolution. The Renaissance was optimistic, for it saw the realm of infinite possibilities of good in human nature, while forgetting the possibilities of evil. This optimism did not come to us in pure form, but through the Enlightenment, rationalism, and deism, which identified reason not with Logos above, but with Nature below. Out of it came the liberal notion of the natural perfectibility of man and capitalism based on the idea that a pre-established harmony in nature guarantees a just relation between economic forces, if man or state does not interfere.

The political repercussion of Optimism and Pessimism in our times expressed itself in Germany and in the West. Germany gave up the task of unifying political forces on a religious basis, and resorted to force. This became the basis of the three fascisms of red, brown, and black. In the Western world generally, the task of unifying society is seen out of focus because liberty has degenerated into license, and evil is underestimated because of false optimism. The result is a secularist view of history, stressing a Messianism without a Messias. This theory indicates that man will be reborn through natural laws, not through an Incarnation. Salvation is from man and not from God. Redemption is conceived to be within history, not outside of it. The Kingdom of God becomes the kingdom of man. The coming of the kingdom of man makes the Church superfluous, or in totalitarian countries, makes it necessary to annihilate it. The conflict of the Two Cities is eliminated by secularist historians. Evil is either denied outright or made social, that is, attributed to capitalism, ignorance, bad milk, or insufficient playgrounds. The Lord of History disappears as a Transcendent Governor.

The age of reason is passed. We are now living in the days of faith—faith in dictators, to whom men surrender their freedom in order to escape from the chaos created by its abuse. Secular civilization has conquered the world by losing its soul, and having lost its soul, it must now be prepared to lose the world. But the dualism of history still exists. In the days of Augustine, it was the material that was dying, and the spiritual that was about to emerge. Today it is the spiritual which is crushed and the material which is claiming mastery. The present struggle is for the soul of man. That is why the Lord of History, despite all denials, is still involved in the struggle.

NEGLECTED ASPECTS OF GRECIAN THOUGHT CONCERNING THE LORD OF HISTORY

Contrasting the Grecian and the Hebrew ideas of Providence, we said that the Grecian conception was primarily intellectual. There are, however, certain phases of Grecian literature which present God not only as a transcendent Being but also as a Lord of History. Before presenting these two aspects, it would be well to recall the better known philosophical tenets of the transcendent God. Socrates did indeed reach a very high pre-Christian concept of God and religion when in his discussion with Euthyphro, who was prosecuting his father for killing a slave, he forces Euthyphro to define piety as "what is dear to the gods." By further discussion, Socrates amends his definition of piety to mean "what all the gods love is pious and what they all hate is impious." [120]

For Plato the Divine Essence is an eternal idea; hence contact with God is established by contemplation. Immortality depends on assimilation into the Supreme Idea and is, in like manner, effected through contemplation. Contemplation is conditioned upon the right ordering of the "three parts" of the soul in relation to one another—the reasoning part; the higher and nobler emotions; the appetites and passions.[121]

Aristotle differed from Socrates in recognizing two different kinds of excellence: intellectual and moral.[122] The goodness of moral character for Aristotle was bound up with the goodness of the moral intellect, because the latter is the condition of the former. One must be good in order to know goodness. Happiness comes through moral excellence, and moral excellence expresses itself in activity. But the end of theoretical reason is the contemplation of God and all contemplation is Godlike because God contemplates Himself.

That perfect happiness is a contemplative activity will appear from the following considerations. We assume the gods to be above all other things blessed and happy, but what sort of actions must we assign to them?....Everyone supposes that they live and that they are active; we cannot suppose them to sleep like Endymion. Now if you take away from a living being, action and, still more, production, what is left but contemplation? Therefore the activity of God, which surpasses all others in blessedness, must be contemplative; and of human activities, therefore, that which is most akin to this must be most of the nature of happiness.[123]

Besides the moral and intellectual contemplation of Deity, which is only too well known to the philosophers, there are two other neglected facts concerning the Grecian attitude toward religion which deserve consideration: Philosophical religion proved insufficient in time of crisis. Grecian drama, more than Grecian philosophy, recognized a Lord of History.

Every now and then in history, as philosophy becomes increasingly abstract, there are those who yearn for the more simple presentations of a rule of life. The Stoics found Plato too sublime, Aristotle too abstract and theoretical. As the peace of the world began to be disturbed and times of trouble were ushered in, the Stoic coined a philosophy to face them. In a certain sense, Stoicism was more of a religion than a philosophy, being concerned with character rather than intellect. The noblest of its followers thrust themselves before God, and we find such Stoics as Epictetus writing, "Brethren, await your God. For when He gives the sign and releases you from this service then shall you go to Him." [124] Seneca reminded his followers "The mind unless it is pure and holy cannot apprehend God." [125] For the neo-Pythagoreans, philosophy became the art of curing, or a devotional guide. Men were no longer seeking to understand. The followers of this particular group were asked to abandon all theoretical research and to live in union with the gods, both superior and inferior. Appealing to Orphism, they took cognizance of the fact of sin and the necessity of purification and emphasized the Orphic doctrine in two ways: by stressing the change of souls according to moral progress; and by popularizing moral retribution in a future life. The very low stage into which philosophy had fallen in the Roman days, is manifested in the *De Natura Deorum* of Cicero, who presented philosophy as a kind of mélange of systems existing at that time. Cicero, noting the contradictions of their representations, says that philosophy gives no certain deliverance.

There are three reasons why philosophy alone proves insufficient in days of crisis. First, because it addresses itself to the intellectually elite, it becomes exclusive and has little attraction for the masses. As Horace said, *odi profanum vulgus et arceo*. Secondly, philosophy provides for the intellect out of all proportion to its provision for the other faculties of the soul. It makes man a spectator of reality rather than its maker. Finally, philosophy discourages the elite to whom it does appeal from throwing themselves into the task of converting their fellowmen. It is not apostolic, its followers have but little zeal; it cultivates but few disciples. Julian the Apostate, the philosopher, was obliged in a world becoming Christian to turn from Socrates to Diogenes, for only the latter as a legendary figure could have the appeal of the martyrs of the Church.[126]

The two principal reactions against philosophy which most attracted the people were astrology and mystery religions. Astrology was introduced from the East to supply the deficiencies of philosophy. It was assumed that there was a certain "sympathy" between man and the stars in an organic universe. If our destiny is in the heavens, we can read it there. Until the second century before Christ, astrology influenced only the lower strata of society, but after that time, it began to win adherents among the upper classes. When Rome had completely mastered the world and was beginning to lose its soul with the decline of religion, astrology came to fill the void.

The other nonphilosophical solution was that of the mystery religions, which had remarkable success, not merely because philosophy was a closed book to most people and few had the leisure to pursue it, but also because almost everyone in time of crisis was seeking deliverance from tyranny, from the slavery of passions, and even release from self. It was generally recognized that this deliverance could come only from some kind of unity with God, and the mystery religions made use of signs as material guarantees that the believers were in contact with divinities. The philosophers permitted man to contemplate God, but the mystery religions admitted very definite and vital bonds between man and God, such as revelation, divination, prophecy, and mystical union. While the philosopher was saying, "Be united to God and become immortal," mystery religions were saying, "Be happy and become divinized."

The emphatic historical turning from philosophy to mystery cults in the Grecian world probably occurred at the time of Alexander the Great, whose conquest effected a religious convergence of the East and the West. He set the nations free for international relationships and is actually quoted by Plutarch as saying that God is the common Father of all men.

There are four principal reasons for the appeal of mystery religions against philosophy. First, the mystery religions acknowledged a sense of guilt, of which mankind became more conscious as self-sufficiency gave way to a mood of pessimism in time of trouble. The necessity of self-examination, which was recommended by Socrates, began a new era by diverting investigation from the outside world to the inside, from physics to morality. Seneca tells us that Sextius, a professor of Stoicism, wrote:

Every day I plead my case before myself. When the light is extinguished, and my wife who knows my habit, keeps silence, I examine the past day, go over and weigh all my deeds and words, I hide nothing, I omit nothing. Why should I hesitate to face my shortcomings when I can say, "Take care not to repeat them, and so I forgive you today."

Epictetus commended Socrates for self-examination. Plutarch asked all men to practice it, and Marcus Aurelius' life involved searching self-investigation. It should, however, be pointed out that such an examination was for human betterment and not necessarily for closer union with God.

Mystery religions attracted also because they emphasized asceticism and restraint. The classical period of Greece would not admit a view of life with such limitations upon human action, because they could not be justified by human reason; but as the times became disturbed, men felt the idea of balance emphasized by the Greek philosophers to be inadequate, and saw the necessity of some recoil from the excesses of a naturalistic religion which believed that nothing natural was base. This asceticism was founded upon a dualism of flesh and spirit, the Grecian counterpart to the ethical dualism of the East, which saw the two hostile principles as light and darkness, good and evil. Like all forms of asceticism lacking the counterbalance of charity, it very often went to extremes and regarded every act identified with the flesh as sinful. It was a common saying of ancient asceticism that "the body is the tomb of the soul." It differed from Christian asceticism, which attempted to attain the salvation of man's whole being. The Grecian asceticism made man behave as though he were not a spirit in an animal body, but a pure spirit.

The drawing power of mystery religions rested also on man's craving for salvation. In an age when the old systems were collapsing and when property was rapidly changing ownership, men began to yearn for some kind of salvation. They spoke less of God and more of Savior as a kind of surname to certain deities. Even living rulers were afterwards lauded as gods, who saved the race when the gods of theology were asleep. It must not, however, be thought that the deliverance for which men yearned was theological. Salvation was conceived as negative, that is to say, as a deliverance from misfortune rather than a positive communion with God Himself. But it must be said in fairness to these pre-Christian people, that their deep sense of need and desire for salvation became excellent raw material for the early apostles of the Christian Church to build upon.

A fourth reason for the success of mystery religions was man's yearning for immortality. Philosophers had very often denied personal immortality. Not even Seneca was too sure of it. Writing to Lucilius, he said: "I am presently engaged in inquiring about the eternity of souls, or rather I should say, trusting. For I was ready to trust myself to the opinions of great men who avow so acceptable a theory. I was surrendering myself to this great hope when I suddenly was aroused by the receipt of your letter and the beautiful dream vanished." It was less philosophy, however, than the influence of the Eastern religions which turned men's minds to immortality. The Egyptians, who had for a thousand years brooded over the mystery of death, through their mystery religions influenced the Greeks to accept belief in immortality. Aristophanes in *The Frogs* wrote: "It was a common belief in Athens that whoever had been taught the mysteries would be deemed worthy of divine glory."

Though the mystery religions attempted to supplant the weakness of philosophy in times of trouble, nevertheless, they were incapable of bringing satisfaction to the soul because of the scandals connected with them, their want of balance between the individual and society, and their extreme emotionalism. Plato, for example, in his *Republic*, scorns popular Orphism for promising in the mysteries "eternal drunkenness, fairest meed of virtue." [127]

Because of the wickedness and sensuality very often associated with mystery religions, the early Christian writers, such as Clement of Alexandria, Origen, Epiphanius, and Hippolytus, found them easy to attack. A further weakness of the mystery religions was their inability to fit individual contact with Deity into the city-state religions of Greece and Rome, which emphasized the social aspect of religion. Finally, there was so much emotionalism in the Eastern religions that they could hardly appeal to men who still had respect for the powers of reason. Aristotle detected this defect in mystery religions when he said: "It is not necessary that the initiates learn anything but merely that they should receive impressions and be brought to a suitable frame of mind." Emotionalism was right, Socrates said, if it came from God, but the advocates of mystery religions could not tell whether or not their emotion was of divine origin. It may well be asked in our own days of crisis whether philosophy alone can give the solution. Certainly it will be of greater assistance if it becomes the handmaid to theology.

GRECIAN DRAMA

There is much more religious philosophy contained in the epics and dramas of Grecian literature than in the abstractions of the philosophers. It is indeed regrettable that in the historical survey of Grecian thought, philosophers have so much neglected the wisdom contained in the literature and the tragedies of the theaters. Plato tells us that Homer was the educator of all Greece.[128] When one surveys the two great epics attributed to Homer, one cannot help feeling that he has thrust into pre-Christian history one of the great moral and religious problems of all time. The real hero of the *Iliad* is Hector, not Achilles; the real hero of the *Odyssey* is not Odysseus but faithful Penelope, who "amongst all women was most sorrowful." Into the teeth of history Homer threw the problem of Hector, a defeated man who was made glorious, and a sorrowful woman who was made noble. It was impossible for all the Greek philosophers to understand how there could be victory in defeat, how there could be nobility in suffering. There was really no answer given to this problem until the day of Calvary, when a defeated man hanging on a Cross ultimately became the conqueror, and a *Mater Dolorosa* at the foot of the Cross became the Queen of Christendom.[129]

While the Jews had their priests and their prophets, the Greeks had not only their philosophers but also their poets and their artists, all of whom had one dominating ideal—excellence. As Simonides wrote:

> Not seeing invisible presence by eyes of men
> Is excellence, save him from whom in utmost toil,
> Heart-wracking sweat comes, at his manhood height.

Homer presents all actions as being dictated by the gods, and the ultimate cause of any event is the will of Zeus. Even the tragedy of Achilles is the fulfillment of the will of Zeus. The readers of Homer's epics must always see the plot on two levels: that of human purpose and that of divine purpose. This notion of the purpose of God, found feebly in Homer, is complemented in Hesiod by the idea of justice. What Homer was doing for the great and noble people, Hesiod was doing for the common man and for the peasants. Zeus preserves justice even though earthly judges may spurn it. Justice is made an independent deity, the daughter of Zeus, who sits beside him to complain when men do wicked things. It is interesting that Aristotle opens his *Ethics* with a quotation from Hesiod.[130]

But more than the epics, the dramas reveal the problem of the Divine Purpose. While mystery religions effected individual union with God, drama brought men together and produced a communal spirit, for it made citizens rejoice and weep over the same thing. Men were set free from individual suffering by realizing together the universal suffering of life. We are here principally concerned with the tragedies. Only twice in literary history has there been a period of great tragedy, in the Athens of Pericles and in Elizabethan England. There can never be tragedy where men's conception of life is sordid. One of the essentials of tragedy is a belief in the dignity of human life. And a further condition of all tragedy is immortality. If there is no justice beyond the grave, then tragedy is pointless. Because there is a God, because there is justice, because there is immortality, tragedy is something more than pain. As Walter

Scott said: "Never let me hear that brave blood has been shed in vain; it sends an imperious challenge down through all the generations."

Aeschylus, one of the most prominent of all the tragedians, was born in Athens around 535 B.C., and according to a legendary tradition it is said that the god Dionysius appeared to him in a dream and commanded him to write tragedies. Aeschylus, above all the dramatists, gives us an insight into philosophy because he is concerned principally with the problems of man in his ultimate destiny. In a certain sense it is not so much man that is the central problem, it is rather the destiny of man. Aeschylus held that God is holy and just and that His eternal government of the world is faultless, but he gives a heart-rending pathos to the tragedy of man who incites God's punishment by his own pride and blindness and sin. In *The Suppliants*, the theme is developed that Zeus is able to bring good out of evil. It would be very difficult for any philosopher ever to say a prayer to the Immobile Mover of Aristotle, but Aeschylus found it easy to pray to Zeus.

> O King of Kings, among the blest
> Thou highest and thou happiest,
> 　　Listen and grant our prayer,
> And, deeply loathing, thrust
> Away from us the young men's lust,
> 　　And deeply drown
> In azure waters, down and ever down,
> 　　Benches and rowers dark,
> 　　The fatal and perfidious bark! [131]
>
> Unto what other one,
> Of all the gods, should I for justice turn?
> 　　From him our race did spring;
> 　　Creator He and King,
> Ancient of days and wisdom he, and might
> 　　As bark before the wind,
> 　　So, wafted by his mind
> Moves every counsel, each device aright.
>
> 　　Beneath no stronger hand
> 　　Holds he a weak command,
> No throne doth he abase him to adore;
> 　　Swift as a word, his deed
> 　　Acts out what stands decreed
> In counsels of his heart, for evermore. [132]

In *The Persians,* which was written in the first flush of Greek victory, Aeschylus makes his audience, the victorious citizens, witness the catastrophe following their fall through pride, a catastrophe revealing the power of God. He calls up from the dead the wise old King Darius, whose late legacy of power, his heir, Xerxes, squandered in empty arrogance. His ghost foretells the heap of corpses on the battlefields of Greece, which will be a warning to posterity that mortal pride never prospers. Disaster will come because the people have lost their piety and overturned altars.

> There misery waits to crush them with the load
> Of heaviest ills, in vengeance for their proud
> And impious daring; for where'er they held
> Through Greece their march, they fear'd not to profane
> The statues of the gods; their hallow'd shrines
> Emblazed, o'erturn'd their altars, and in ruins,
> Rent from their firm foundations, to the ground
> Level'd their temples; such their frantic deeds,
> Nor less their suff'rings; greater still await them;
> For Vengeance hath not wasted all her stores;
>
> Behold this vengeance, and remember Greece,
> Remember Athens: henceforth let not pride,
> Her present state disdaining, strive to grasp
> Another's, and her treasured happiness
> Shed on the ground: such insolent attempts
> Awake the vengeance of offended Jove.[133]

In the tragedy *Seven Against Thebes,* a tragedy of vicarious redemption, Aeschylus found it necessary to explain how certain curses which were laid upon men could be reconciled with the justice of God. Eteocles is to die, but before he dies, he is to save his country from defeat and slavery. Behind a mournful account of his death we can hear the triumphant hymn in thanksgiving for deliverance. The hero, by sacrificing his doomed life for the salvation of his fellowmen, reconciles what might seem to be a senseless and needless destruction with the very highest virtue.

> But we this dead Eteocles,
> As Justice wills and Right decrees,
> Will bear unto his grave!
> For—under those enthroned on high
> And Zeus' eternal royalty—

He unto us salvation gave!
    He saved us from a foreign yoke,
    A wild assault of outland folk,
A savage, alien wave![134]

In *Prometheus Bound*, Aeschylus deals with the legend of the great Prometheus who stole fire from Zeus and made a gift of it to the human race, whom Zeus was planning to destroy. In punishment for this insubordination, Zeus bound him to a rock and there tortured him. The moral problem with which Aeschylus was dealing was that of the conflict of power and love, Zeus standing for power and Prometheus for love. It almost seems to be a struggle of God with God, and the great crime of Prometheus is that he loves men too much. "Too much thou honorest mortals." This cry of Prometheus seems to be a distant and feeble anticipation of the cry of the *Ecce Homo* on the Cross, Who had loved men so much that He would suffer for them.

        Alas!
    To what land far-off have I wandered?
    What error, O Zeus, what crime
    Is mine that thus I am yoked
    Unto misery? Why am I stung
    With frenzy that drives me unresting
    Forever? Let fires consume me;
    Let the deep earth yawning engulf me;
    Or the monstrous brood of the sea
    Devour; but O great King,
    Hark to my pleading for respite!
    I have wandered enough, I am weary,
    And still I discern no repose.[135]

In the end, power and wisdom, Prometheus and Zeus, must be reconciled in order that God may reign. It is Prometheus alone who knows the secret without which Zeus must be destroyed. In other words, power without love comes to a bad end. One would completely miss the point of the tragedy in holding that Aeschylus thought the sin of Prometheus was merely an offense against the properties of the god—the theft of fire. Rather, it involved some Greek, tragic imperfection in the benefit he had hoped to do to mankind by his wonderful gift.

We said that Aeschylus was dealing with the problem of destiny. Destiny may here be understood as heredity, as curse, as taint, as a dark drop in the red current of blood. Basically, what Aeschylus means is that in some way our ancestors' sins are ours. The retribution visited upon one man for his sin also affects the other. Individual transgressions call down the retribution of the God of Justice, not merely on the criminal, but on his family, on his friends, and on his state. It blights the coming generation and spreads its contagion and infection from wrongdoer to wrongdoer. The tradition that the Golden Age of the human race was in the past, when men enjoyed greater intimacy with God, is revealed in the lines of Agamemnon.

> Some past impiety, some grey old crime,
>   Breeds the young curse, that wantons in our ill,
> Early or late, when haps th' appointed time—
>   And out of light brings power of darkness still,
> A master-fiend, a foe, unseen, invincible;
>
> A pride accursed, that broods upon the race
>   A home in which dark Ate holds her sway—
> Sin's child and Woe's, that wears its parents' face.[136]

In order that this curse might be lifted and retribution made, there must be some outpouring of blood. If the guilty one himself cannot expiate, then it shall be done by someone else who is bound up with him.

> Zeus, the high God!—what'er be dim in doubt,
>   This can our thought track out—
> The blow that fells the sinner is of God,
>   And as he wills, the rod
> Of vengeance smiteth sore.[137]
>
> Ah woe, ah Zeus! from Zeus all things befall—
>   Zeus the high cause and finisher of all!—
> Lord of our mortal state, by him are willed
>   All things, by him fulfilled![138]
>
> Lo! sin by sin and sorrow dogg'd by sorrow—
>   And who the end can know?
> The slayer of to-day shall die tomorrow—
>   The wage of wrong is woe.
> While Time shall be, while Zeus in heaven is lord,
>   His law is fixed and stern;
> On him that wrought shall vengeance be outpoured—
>   The tides of doom return.

> The children of the curse abide within
> These halls of high estate—
> And none can wrench from off the home of sin
> The clinging grasp of fate.[139]

Though the Greek philosophers had very little to say about sin, the Greek dramatists made it the great burden of their tragedies. This hereditary taint of sin is not in one man, but in the entire human race. In *The Eumenides*, the question arises, when will this chain of crimes cease?

> Ho! clear is here the trace of him we seek:
> Follow the track of blood, the silent sign!
> Like to some hound that hunts a wounded fawn,
> We snuff along the scent of dripping gore.[140]

The answer given by Aeschylus is that this hereditary blight shall be wiped out when its penalties fall upon a righteous man. In this particular drama, Orestes had not identified himself with the bad blood of his house. When the stain came upon him, it was washed away. It is the innocent who make atonement for the guilty.

> O queen Athena, first from thy last words
> Will I a great solicitude remove.
> Not one blood-guilty am I; no foul stain
> Clings to thine image from my clinging hand;
> Whereof one potent proof I have to tell.
> Lo, the law stands—The slayer shall not plead
> Till by the hand of him who cleanses blood,
> A suckling creature's blood besprinkle him.
> Long since have I this expiation done,
> In many a home, slain beasts and running streams
> Have cleansed me. Thus I speak away that fear.[141]

The final summation of the theology of Aeschylus is that there will be no end to the evil and woe afflicting the human race until someone takes that sin upon himself vicariously and makes atonement and redemption.

As the dramatist advises in *Prometheus Bound:* "Neither look for any respite from this agony, unless some god shall appear as a voluntary successor to thy toils, and of his own free will goeth down to sunless Hades and the dark depths of Tartarus." [142]

The next great figure in Greek drama was Sophocles, who witnessed the disaster which Aeschylus had warned would happen to that city because of its pride. The glory of Marathon had passed away when Sophocles began to write. Sparta was already at the gates of Athens, and the only citadel left was that of the soul. Aeschylus was primarily concerned with explaining why God treated man as He did. Sophocles attempted to show what would be the effect on man of this treatment. Without ever explaining suffering in the world, he does, however, contend that what appears as evil will in some way contribute to the goodness of the whole. The moral law for Aeschylus is something that is certain, and from its certitude there follows the lesson that suffering may indeed have a purpose—that man may learn from its pain. For Sophocles, to know oneself is to know one's own powerlessness, but it is also to know the indestructible and conquering majesty of suffering humanity. Nobody reveals this better than Oedipus, a blind old man begging his way through the world, bearing a weight which symbolizes the suffering of all humanity.

"Then blessed be thou. May heaven prove to thee a kinder guardian than it hath to me! My children, where are ye? Come hither, hither to the hands of him whose mother was your own, the hands whose offices have wrought that your sire's once bright eyes should be such orbs as these—his, who seeing nought, knowing nought, became your father by her from whom he sprang! For you also do I weep—behold you I cannot —when I think of the bitter life in days to come which men will make you live. To what company of the citizens will ye go, to what festival, from which ye shall not return home in tears, instead of sharing in the holiday? But when ye are now come to years ripe for marriage, who shall he be, who shall be the man, my daughters, that will hazard taking unto him such reproaches as must be baneful alike to my offspring and to yours? For what misery is wanting? Your sire slew his sire, he had seed of her who bore him, and begat you at the sources of his own being! Such are the taunts that will be cast at you; and who then will wed? The man lives not, no, it cannot be, my children, but ye must wither in barren maidenhood." [143]

"Crave not to be master in all things: for the mastery which thou didst win hath not followed thee through life."

"Dwellers in our native Thebes, behold, this is Oedipus, who knew the famed riddle, and was a man most mighty; on whose fortunes what citizen did not gaze with envy? Behold into what a stormy sea of dread trouble he hath come!

Therefore, while our eyes wait to see the destined final day, we must call no one happy who is of mortal race, until he hath crossed life's border, free from pain." [144]

It is outside the scope of philosophy to explain how Christianity became the fulfillment of the yearnings of the ancient world. It is worth pointing out, however, that the universality which Alexander ushered in was never finally realized until Christianity preached the doctrine that there is neither bond nor free, Jew nor Gentile.[145] Socrates had claimed that he was a citizen of the world, and Diogenes stated that he was cosmopolitan, but the basis of Christian unity was something new, for Christianity offered supernatural love as the new moral factor of unity. More than that, in answer to the problems presented in the tragedies of Greece, the test of any religion is not its attitude to the joys and raptures of life, but its ability to give moral content to the sorrows and complexities. Christianity stood this test and brought a saving gospel to the Greek and Roman world. It was uniquely fitted to do this because from its birth it was a religion whose "Lord of Glory" had been also "the Man of Sorrows." The two centuries preceding the Christian era had been a period of uninterrupted misery. It is significant that Christianity spread most rapidly in the half-century of the great confusion of pagan society. It is significant too that every persecution strengthens the faith. Perhaps because of the sufferings throughout the Roman Empire during the days of early Christianity, many of the Fathers at that time most frequently applied the title of Physician to Christ. As Ignatius of Antioch wrote: "There is only one Physician, Christ Jesus." Tertullian calls Him, *Christum Medicatorum*. Christianity too was the crown of philosophy, because for the first time in the history of the world, there was a Person Who was greater than His teaching. Herein lay the great originality of the main secret of Christian power. Disembodied ideas make but little appeal. Christian enthusiasm, however, was awakened by the fact that for the first time in history an ideal and a personality were equated: "I am the Truth." His followers did not require merely faith in His teachings, but in Himself. Ideas must be incorporated into a person before they can ever effectively move mankind. The Stoic teachers knew that the best of their men fell very short of the ideal, and for that reason preferred to portray their ideal wise man as one who had not actually lived. The despairing question of Seneca was at last answered: *Ubi enim iustum invenies quem tot saeculis quaerimus?*

PART IV

Man and Religion

Chapter XI

MAN AS A PROBLEM

Classical philosophers might just as well face the unpalatable fact that modern man is no longer interested in metaphysics. This does not indicate in any sense at all, the invalidity of the metaphysical approach. This has, and will always have, the profoundest appeal to men who still believe in reason and universals. But metaphysics is unpopular today partly because of the irrationality of modern man. Despite the fact that he uses the word "reason," it does not follow that his reason leads him to metaphysics; for the "reason" the modern uses is not the classical reason which discovers ends and purposes and goals; it is a diminution or perversion of that reason. For historical liberalism, reason was used to discover the happiness and pleasure of the individual; for capitalism, it became a technical reason which was concerned only with the means of production and the acquisition of profit. For the totalitarians, it meant a planning reason which attempted to organize the chaos created by a capitalism and a liberalism divorced from purpose.

Now that the philosopher has perspective in which he may contrast the modern distortions of reason with the classical reason, there arises the surprising paradox that reason is strongest in days of faith, not the faith of superstition or blind credulity, but the faith which admits a life above that of reason. Rationalism was strongest in the thirteenth century. Just as our senses work better when perfected by reason, so too our reason works better when perfected by faith. A man temporarily devoid of reason, such as a drunkard, has the same senses that he had before, but they do not function as well as they did when he was under rational direction and government. What the senses are without reason, reason is without faith. Though reason can still function, it very quickly reaches the end of its rope. It follows that metaphysical reason is unpopular today because we live in a state of world confusion. Philosophy functions best in days of relative peace. As soon as a time of trouble comes, men turn to nonrational solutions, such as astrology in pre-Christian times, or to a queer kind of mysticism, such as one finds in contemporary thinkers like Aldous Huxley. Metaphysics, being the abstract universal science, has little appeal to the concrete practical man. For those who still retain a taste for metaphysics, there are some, like Berdyaev, who would substitute as the universal object, a philosophy of freedom for a philosophy of being.[1] To fill the void caused by the rejection of metaphysics, there has been substituted a worship of epistemology, which attempts to find out how much you can know before you actually start knowing. There are many philosophers in this field who have made the problem of knowledge very much like the problem of discovering how you go to sleep, forgetful that we are already asleep before we know that we are asleep. We have to wake up before we know that we were asleep, and we have to know before we can know that we knew. St. Thomas says we know the stone before we know the idea of the stone. Another reason for the contempt of the metaphysical approach to reality is the contemporary idea that philosophy is nothing more than a syncretism of the experimental sciences. This view owes its success to the material triumphs of the last century. Because science solved so many technical problems, it was felt that it could solve all other problems.

With particular relation to the subject of God and religion, regardless of how much we may stress the primacy of metaphysics, it is obvious that the contemporary mind is not concerned with going to God from nature, but from God to man. By nature here we mean not only the physical nature endowed with movement, uniformity, contingency, finality, and dependence revealed in the Five Ways of St. Thomas, but also what Aristotle called the first physics, or the science of being. Nature, in either one of these senses, will always remain the best approach to God and religion, though it may not always be the most popular. Today it is unpopular because nature seems to be turning against man, particularly since the invention of the atomic bomb. So long as men use their reason in order to discover the over-all purpose of life, nature assists them as a kind of earthly sacrament to reveal Divinity. But as soon as nature is made autonomous—as it was by Descartes, who separated man from God as a basis of rationality; and by Rousseau, who separated man from the community; and by Kant, who separated man from God as the basis of morality—then it becomes meaningless. Man can then only love nature as a lover loves his mistress, knowing that his love will not last and that tomorrow may be the last day. As a result, man finally becomes enslaved by the external world and therefore is in slavery to himself.

The Man with whom philosophy is concerned today is not the dignified man of the Renaissance who still breathed the atmosphere of Christianity, but rather a Man isolated from himself and the community and from God. His value increasingly diminished as generations of philosophers interpreted science so as to devaluate personality. The Copernican revolution was interpreted so as to remind man of his unimportance, for now the earth was no longer the center of the universe. This cosmic intimidation increased to a point where Dr. Harry Elmer Barnes declared that man was of no more significance than a cockroach. The astronomical blow against human dignity was followed by a biological blow, in which philosophers interpreted Darwinism to mean that man is not divided from the animal world and therefore has no transcendence to it. Finally came the psychological blow when Freud said, "The ego is not master in his own house." [2] Insult was added to injury as Freud declared "that man's superiority over animals may come down to his capacity for neurosis." Human freedom was denied as man was declared to be determined either biologically, as with the Darwinians, psychologically, as with the Freudians, or economically, as with the Marxists. Just as the Marxists interpreted history in terms of different techniques of production, so Freud interpreted culture and thought as the different ways in which men sought to compensate for the sacrifices they had to make while living in society.

If the modern thinker is not interested in metaphysics but only in the subject of man, then it behooves the classical philosophers to reveal the full depths of their philosophy by a revelation of the true nature of man. This will involve in some way avoiding the two extremes: pessimism, which declares man is intrinsically corrupt, and optimism, which believes that man is destined to become a kind of god. It will steer a middle course between the humanism of a Bertrand Russell, who morosely confronts the universe with his "Free Man's Worship," and the false optimism of a Swinburne, who, with one eye on ancient Greece and the other on the industrial development of Victorian England, sings "Glory to man in the highest, for man is the master of things." In preparation for the study of man as an approach to God and religion, it is well to record that since the days of the Renaissance, there have been two principal views of man: Natural or Liberal Man; and Frustrated Man.

NATURAL MAN

The Natural Man of historical liberalism had his roots in the Renaissance concept of man, a concept which in a Christian environment discovered the greatness of the pagan past. Petrarch in his work, *My Secret,* an imaginary dialogue with St. Augustine, wrote:

Few people are aware of the very definition of man, though it is scrawled on the walls and pillars of every room. This prattling of dialectitians will never come to an end; it throws up summaries and definitions like bubbles. Modern philosophers are wont to think they have done nothing if they fail to bark against Christ and his supernatural teaching.

Petrarch then put into the mouth of St. Augustine the Christian definition of a man: "When you can find a man so governed by reason that all his conduct is regulated by her, and all his appetites subject to her alone, then he may have some true and fruitful definition of a man." In what follows, Petrarch makes St. Augustine discourse on the autonomy and self-sufficient sovereignty of reason. It is interesting that St. Augustine never once quoted Sacred Scripture, but Virgil, Seneca, Horace, Cicero, and Juvenal. Though Dante quoted equally both from Christian and pagan authorities, Petrarch quoted only from the latter. As history unfolded itself, man became more and more divorced from his Christian background. Luther held that man was intrinsically corrupt, "a lost lump," to whom the merits of Christ were extrinsically imputed. There was no such thing as an internal renovation and regeneration of man, Christ's merits being merely like a cloak that was put over a sick man. The next step in the thought process was to argue that if the supernatural does not intrinsically regenerate man, then it is not natural to man. If it is not natural to man, then it ought to be eliminated. The Aufklärung movement in Germany, Pietism in France, deism in England completely eliminated the supernatural with the explanation that it was a perversion of the natural man. Rousseau then made his study of the natural man and declared that he is wicked because of civilization. Reacting from the Lutheran concept of the intrinsic corruption of man, Rousseau affirmed the natural goodness of man. Under liberalism there was formulated the doctrine of the self-sufficiency of man—a kind of brotherhood without tears.

The three tenets of the liberal concept of man were: man is naturally good and infinitely perfectible; Christianity is not the final religion; evil is ignorance, and the imperfections still remaining in this evolving universe are due to a lack of education. From these three notions, there grew a complete system of the universe based on naturalistic and positivistic thinking, which asserted that in the economic order the naturally good man ought to be free to work out his destiny as he saw fit. The result of such a policy would be the greatest good of the greatest number. Freedom was then defined as the right to do whatever you please, meaning in the economic order, the right of a man to acquire as much wealth as he pleased, without any interference from without. In politics, it was concluded that the judgment of each individual is sufficient to assure community of interests. In the international order, it was maintained that just as individual interests would produce the common good in one nation, so each nation, seeking its own good, would produce a balance of power and international peace. Education was interpreted as a form of free expression. The right of every student to elect whatever courses he desired to follow would produce a harmonious society. In religion, as in politics and economics, individual self-interpretation, it was believed, would produce a harmonious religious community. The philosopher who gave some rational substance to these ideas was Leibnitz, with his pre-established harmony, in which each individual monad was presumed to ripen according to its own inner laws and establish a harmony with every other monad. Religion then became a kind of an ambulance to take care of the wrecks of the liberal society until evolution had reached the stage where there would no longer be any poverty, ignorance, or disease. God was reinterpreted in order to dignify either man or nature, Hegel holding that man is a particle of divinity and what he needs is not redemption but an awareness of his integration into the whole. Schleiermacher, in keeping with the self-sufficiency of man, attempted to find a new rule of faith to substitute for an Infallible Church and a Bible. This he found to be religious experience, which is not dogmatic or ethical, but a feeling of dependence on the universe. "Religion is the undulation of the mind between two points, of which the world is one and your ego the other." Religion then was focused not Godward but manward.

From this point on, we meet little else in philosophy except the deification of man, the exaltation of a limited, contingent existence into an absolute, and the relegation of the Creator, as in the case of Samuel Alexander, to the role of a creature issuing from the womb of space-time. Best known among the interpreters of the Liberal Man were George Bernard Shaw and H. G. Wells. If there is any religion at all in Shaw, it might be called a religion of life-force. Shaw's man was the Liberal, Pelagian man who lives in the world of social values and needs neither faith for his intellect nor grace for his will. He accepted completely the materialistic sense of values, and even tried to justify art and literature on utilitarian grounds. As he is the greatest of all anomalies, an Irishman without the faith, certain Christian assumptions constantly crop up in Shaw's work. Though he does not believe in God definitely, nevertheless, he beats a drum at the most unexpected moments for various social causes which become his religion. Cynicism, which is always typical of the man who is without faith and yet does not find the universe solvent, made Shaw affirm that a man who was useless for society should be "liquidated." When asked which of twelve men he would save if he were Noah and there were a second flood, he answered that he would save none.

In the early writings of Wells, his hope for the man-god was based on a planned world of eugenics, mechanized labor, scientific diet, and progressive education. In his *Anticipations*, he wrote: "The nation that produces the largest proportional development of educated and intelligent engineers and agriculturalists, doctors, schoolmasters, will be the dominant nation before the year 2000." In perfect keeping with the spirit of theological liberalism, he believed "that a time is coming when men as gods will stand on earth as on a footstool and reach their hands among the stars."

FRUSTRATED MAN

The liberal concept of man which believed in the inevitable progress of humanity through science and evolution, was knocked into a cocked hat by the rapidity of wars. It was very hard to sus-

tain a belief in progress when one realized that the interval between
the Franco-Prussian War and the Napoleonic Wars was fifty-five
years, and the interval between the Franco-Prussian War and the
First World War was forty-three, and the interval between the First
and Second World Wars was twenty-one years. The growing manifestation of man's inhumanity to man in the cruelties of modern
wars also made it difficult to sustain belief in the natural goodness
of man. Freedom, interpreted as the right to do whatever you
pleased, did nothing but create a civilization torn by a conflict of
individual egotisms, a conflict which totalitarian philosophies tried
to solve by reducing the individual ego to a collective ego.

Rather typical of the disillusionment that followed the crash of
optimism was the pessimism of H. G. Wells himself, in his *Fate of
Homo Sapiens,* written at the end of his life:

There is no reason whatever to believe that the order of nature has
any greater bias in favor of man than it had in favor of an ichthyosaur.
In spite of all my disposition to brave-looking optimism, I perceive that
now the universe is bored with him, is turning a hard face to him, and
I see him being carried less and less intelligently and more and more
rapidly along the stream of fate to degradation, suffering and death.

While the Liberal Man was naturally good and progressive, the
Frustrated Man is a "fallen" man. His defects must be accounted
for, and his redemption charted. Like Rousseau, philosophers seek
to discover what has made man corrupt, and how he can enter
again the primitive Eden. If there is a fall, it is envisaged to have
taken place not in man's nature but merely in society. If man is ever
to return to the primitive state, it will be by a revolt against society
and institutions which have made him corrupt. As the Christian
would seek the redemption of man by a recovery of grace which
was lost in the Fall, the believers in the Frustrated Man would
recover it, not in a gift of God, but in nature itself. What the Christian attributes to grace, D. H. Lawrence attributes to sex. He deliberately chooses the experience of the senses to get in touch with
his dark god.

Aldous Huxley turns his satire on the impulses of the Natural
Man, an insight which leads him to depict many characters as unpleasant sensation seekers, bored, cultured women of pleasure, and
middle aged roués; he shows them as sharing an earnest desire
to escape from all the obligations of society, family, marriage, and

ordinary morality. The result is a kind of natural mysticism by which man seeks to divest himself of a love of created things.

Attempting to escape from the boredom resulting from the failure of Natural Man, Huxley, in his *Perennial Philosophy*, groups together similar points of view on the subjects of mortification, asceticism, and mysticism taken from various spiritual thinkers of history. What Our Lord said of the young man who came to him, may be said of Huxley: "He is not far from the kingdom of God."

What sex was to Lawrence, and mysticism to Huxley, brute force is to Ernest Hemingway. His characters are seldom people of intelligence. They rarely live on an intellectual plane, but on the contrary, inhabit a world of sensuous love, war, and bullfights. They exhibit few feelings except the purely animal feelings; they have little love, little remorse, but move about amid sensations of greed and lust and rape. All are doomed to failure in an attempt to be rid of their desires. The killer kills in vain, the thief loses his booty, and the lover dies. From a negative point of view Hemingway's work is a revealing description of the failure of the Natural Man, but it is weak in its remedy. Once man is divested of the sense of right and wrong, he can hardly justify himself by serving the anthills of the Totalitarian Man.

The Frustrated Man is one who has within himself some radical tension or dialectic—who is groaning for some kind of sublimation or deliverance. The Frustrated Man is the Old Testament without the New, the Fall without the Redemption, the tragedy of man without the hope of a Calvary. From a theological point of view, the concept represents the rediscovery of the doctrine of Original Sin, though the exponents of the Frustrated Man are playing only on its fringes.

Two great prophets of the Frustrated Man are Dostoevski and Nietzsche. Both of them saw that the Liberal Man was incapable of enduring, that his degeneration of liberty into license was bringing on a crisis in which the alternatives would be: either the embrace of Christ, as in Dostoevski, or the embrace of the anti-Christ, as in Nietzsche. Dostoevski's characters do not fit into the familiar category of positive and negative men and women. For them, life is a struggle, a battle between love and hate, between the readiness to help and the desire to hurt; they are less personalities than civil wars. Through this kind of character analysis Dostoevski brought to an end the optimistic humanism of the nineteenth century and became an interpreter of the present troubled and restless world. He revealed that the basic problem of the Russian soul is not atheism but dualism—the inner struggle between the City of God and the City of Satan. In this rivalry between the forces of good and evil for supremacy, Dostoevski indicated that man could reach great heights of perfection, and could also descend to the lowest depths of degradation. All this was possible because man was free. He could resist God to the very end, and there was no power in heaven or on earth that could break down his independence. Father Zossima in *The Brothers Karamazov* expresses this conviction when he says:

"Oh, there are some who remain proud and fierce even in hell in spite of the certain knowledge and contemplation of the absolute truth. They refuse forgiveness, they curse God who calls them. They cannot behold the living God without hatred, and they cry out that the God of life should be annihilated; that God should destroy Himself and His own creation. And they will burn in the fire of their own wrath forever, and yearn for death and annihilation, but they will not attain to death."

Attacking the liberalism of the nineteenth century in *The Possessed*, Dostoevski foretold that the Liberal Man, alienating himself from belief in God, would end by deifying himself, placing himself above all moral laws and attempting to make himself the Lord of Creation. This assertion of his own aseity in the face of Divinity, would end in man's subjection to dark and irrational forces which would completely destroy his personality. And of the characters in this novel, Kirilov who once boasted that, because he was self-sufficient, he could do a better work of creation than God, ultimately takes his own life. Foreseeing the conflicts of the twentieth century, Dostoevski became a prophet of totalitarianism. He foresaw a disillusioned Liberal Man, who had rebelled against God, developing a passion for social reform, but beneath the ardent longing of revolutionaries to help the socially disinherited and to dethrone the rich and establish equality, he saw yet a stronger desire to rearrange the world according to man's will, to dethrone the Creator, and to prove that man can sit on the throne of God. In 1876, in *An Author's Diary*, he wrote:

It seems to me this century will end for old Europe with something colossal, I mean with something, if not exactly like the events of the

French Revolution of the eighteenth century, nevertheless, so colossal, so irresistible and terrifying, that it would change the face of the earth, at any rate in Western Europe.

Despite his certitude that the world of the twentieth century would be populated with frustrated souls, he nevertheless believed that his own Russian people would one day find their peace and their power in religion. In the same work he writes:

Not in Communism, not in its mechanical forms, is contained the socialism of the Russian people. They believe that the final salvation and all illuminating unity is in Christ and in Him alone. This is our Russian socialism. Those who do not understand the meaning of Orthodoxy for our common people, and its final purpose, will never be able to understand.... The Russian people bear the image of Christ and love Him only.

No amount of political, economic, or social maneuvering, no international treaties or pacts, no rearrangement of property could solve the basic conflict within the soul of man. Only something outside of men could solve this conflict—Christ Himself. In *Pages from the Journal of an Author*, Dostoevski concludes:

It is absolutely evident that in mankind is lurking an evil much deeper than the socialist doctor supposed, that whatever the social organization is, evil cannot be eliminated, that the human soul will remain the same, that abnormal manifestations and sin are born in it, and finally, that the laws of the human spirit are still so little known, are still so much outside the reach of science, so mysterious, that doctors cannot be found yet to deal with them efficiently.

The other prophet of the Frustrated Man of the twentieth century, Friedrich Nietzsche, was born in the days of nationalism, Darwinism, Biblical criticism, rationalism and vacant optimism. He bade the Liberal Man to be logical and thrust aside all Liberal moral values: "Let us be done with Socrates and Christ and all other hoary moralists, for if what we believe and practice is true, then they were monstrously wrong, Christ most of all. Let us plainly then say that we are for the anti-Christ." The Frustrated Man is apprehended in Nietzsche, not so much as possessing a conflict within himself, but as being a unit in the universal conflict of Christ and anti-Christ. Nietzsche was more clear in his chants over the corpse of the Liberal Man than he was in proclaiming the nature of the Frustrated Man, for what nauseated him most was the man just released from Christianity but devoid of a positive passion. He declares: "Man is something that must be surpassed, man is a bridge and not a goal." Thus he arrives at the gospel of the Super-man: "the great blond beast." In a final intoxication of pride he writes, "If there were no God how could I endure it to be no God, therefore there are no Gods." As perverted as his philosophy was, it at least contains something of the logic that Dostoevski said the world must ultimately face—"the self-affirming man who ends in self-destruction." Nietzsche was not wide of the mark when he said that the greatest danger to the world comes not from wicked-ness, but from conventional "goodness." The frustrated world that will not have Christ must have anti-Christ.

Besides these prophets of the inevitable conflict between the forces of good and evil, we find in literature, philosophy, and the-ology countless expositions of the Frustrated Man. James Joyce attempted to deal with the Frustrated Man in a literary fashion. He believed that one method of handling the disorder within man was by the Catholic Faith, which alone, he said, would give "co-herence and purpose to life." But he rejected Catholicism and, as a substitute, he imposed a violently artificial literary form on his novels and on his characters. His solution of frustration was, there-fore, very much the same as that of totalitarianism, except that it was accomplished in the field of letters instead of in the field of politics. Because his own nonreligious solution did not satisfy him, he became blasphemous, as most men do who hate themselves for having aban-doned what they love.

T. F. Powys recognized the same imperfect and frustrated man that Joyce saw, but because he could not envisage religion as the only integration of the human soul, he became obsessed with the total depravity of man, and wrote violently, not only against his fellow creatures, but particularly against clergymen, although he himself was the son of a country clergyman. His emphasis on the sinfulness of human nature, however, shows that a few minds were becoming conscious of the new outlook on man. On the theological level, Cardinal Newman somewhat anticipated the confusions of the twentieth century by rejecting a communion with nature such as Wordsworth had advocated, and the Divine mission of heroes sug-gested by Carlyle, with rationalism and religious liberalism, mere manifestations of the pride of man. Against all these, he affirmed the Church as a "prodigious power set on earth to encounter and master a giant evil."

Miguel de Unamuno, in his *Tragic Sense of Life,* admitted with the liberals that man might be a social molecule, as Pareto asserted, or an economic atom, as Marx believed; he still contended that there was a mystery within man's soul, and that its full illumination could not be found in the perspective of space and time. "Is man's purpose," he asks, "to catalogue the universe? Is it that at last the human race will fall exhausted at the foot of a pile of libraries in order to bequeath them—to whom, for God will surely not accept them?"

The greatest inspirer of all twentieth-century philosophers of the Frustrated Man was Sören Kierkegaard who at the middle of the last century wrote in his *Journal:* "Denmark has need of a dead man. My life will cry out after my death. Some day not only my writings but my whole life will be studied and studied. I can be understood only after my death." His prophecy became true, and though he wrote a theology of the Frustrated Man, it actually was nothing but an enlargement and expansion of his own experiences. Early in life the conviction of sin was burned into his soul. Before dying, his father confided to him some guilty secret of his past life, and as a consequence, the youth resolved to give all of his powers to the defense of Christianity in what he believed to be a virtually pagan world. This obsession with evil later on became intensified when he broke off his engagement to Regina Olsen because he felt the necessity, he said, of surrendering the life of the world in order to dedicate himself to the cause of Christianity. He wrote in his *Journal:* "I was an eternity too old for her. When I left her I chose death." It would seem that she became for him the embodiment of the secular spirit he felt that he must deny if he were ever to be true to himself. In his famous work, *Either Or,* published when he was thirty, Kierkegaard brushes aside all speculation concerning the universe and addresses the reader with the question: "What kind of a life ought a man to live?" He poses this question in a Socratic fashion. The debate is left unfinished, however, and the answer remains with the reader. But the answer must be a *choice,* a decision, made "existentially," in the face of life itself and not through an abstract or logical argument. Because of this conviction, he was very impatient with Hegelianism and its harmonious unity, in which frustration and tragedy were nothing more than a passing phase of the absolute. In contrast to the vague subjectivity of Hegelian formulas, he presented the subjectivity of the individual man who is conscious of his guilt and his aloofness from the Eternal.

So obsessed was Kierkegaard with the notion of the Frustrated Man that he made little room in his theology for the social character of man or for corporate religion. He went back to the publican's category—God, me, the sinner—and founded his religion upon what he called: "The existential relation between the soul and God." Like Nietzsche, who himself lived in an age of romantic liberalism, he too criticized the Renaissance man, his works, and his pomps. The tolerance of the modern religious man, for Kierkegaard, was misplaced, because it was really a form of hypocrisy. He believed that absolute self-sacrifice cannot tolerate self-seekers, and absolute excellence cannot tolerate either mediocrity or compromise. This release from frustration by surrender to God was so sincere in Kierkegaard that he would not even spare himself: "When I want to spit, I spit at my own face." Christianity for him was severe. It evolved from the soul's inner conflicts, and what he called the troubled truth. He believed that the foundation of religion is "dread," and from dread comes despair, and from despair the sense of sin, and from the sense of sin the "instant of choice. From the choice of Christ, faith in the immortal life of the spirit, with gentleness, grace, peace and love of God follow." [3]

But there are many defects in the theology of Kierkegaard, despite its great work in recognizing the bankruptcy of the Liberal Man and its rediscovery of tension. One basic weakness is the overemphasis on subjectivity—not by a denial of objective reality, but through his assumption of the barrenness of the intellectual element in religious experience. There is no such thing for him as a spiritual truth unfused with personal experience. On every point the one question he asks is: "What does this truth signify for *my* tragically real existence?" While the connection between truth and human existence is desirable and necessary, it is not true, as Kirkegaard assumes, that the ethical and the speculative move in different directions or that the speculative abstracts from reality and the ethical sustains it. Allied with this extreme subjectivity is his contempt for the historical. He believes with Emerson that from history, faith has nothing to learn, and that to gain anything worth having,

the single soul must sink more deeply in its own inner experience—
its only fruitful source.

In spite of these limitations, Kierkegaard has challenged liberal
and modern ways of thinking with a conviction that is inclusive
and uncompromising: the naturally good man does not exist; man
is a source of conflict and tension and dialectic. While Nietzsche
was choosing the will to power and the anti-Christ as a release from
frustration, Kierkegaard was advocating surrender to God. The
fear or dread felt by men he believes to be a challenge of eternity,
the call to be spiritual. The despair of modern man results from his
refusal to accept that call.

Another theologian of the Frustrated Man is Karl Barth, who
is uncompromising in his opposition to the idea of a naturally good
man, and of a society that is naturally progressive. He believes that
both collectivities and individuals have been wrong at the root for
about two hundred years. Barth called his theology, *The Theology
of Crisis*. The derivation of the word implies "separation" or "judgment." It connotes a reorientation of thought and of life, a moral
decision in the domain of ethics and a demand made upon man by
the word of God, "a dividing, a thunder, and a judgment." In his
delineation of the Frustrated Man, Barth adheres very closely to
the Lutheran doctrine of the intrinsic corruption of human nature.
This deep pessimism about sinful man may in part be explained by
his reaction against modern humanism and optimism. Because man
is intrinsically corrupt, there is no point of contact with God. Not
even in the natural order is there an analogy of being, just as there
is no analogy of faith in the supernatural order. "I hold the *Analogia
Entis* to be the discovery of anti-Christ and consider that on that
ground alone one cannot be a Catholic." The cure of the Frustrated
Man who has a civil war raging within his soul is not evolution but
a faith in the ingression of God, or the "breaking-through" from
man to God. Salvation comes from the "Word of God" not the
Word of the Church. From a historical point of view, his theology
may be described as that of a modern Luther pitted against science
and humanism. Whatever be the solution, the fact is that Karl Barth
is dealing with a different type of man from that of the liberal
theologians of the nineteenth and early twentieth centuries. He has
not found the real man because of his pessimism and his adherence
to the doctrine of the intrinsic corruption of man, but he is far

closer to a valid anthropology than any of the optimists of the nineteenth century. Therefore, he can more correctly quote the problem which faces the Frustrated Man: "The ethical question of our
time is not how we shall effectively organize our activities, but how
the terrific loss of the substance of faith, which in the long run must
prove to be the losing of ethical energy, can be regained." [4]

Emil Brunner, in his work *The Mediator*, made the theology of
Karl Barth popular. It has been sometimes called *The Theology of
Eclipse*, for man who was left in the darkness of eclipse has only
occasional flashes of revelation. Brunner starts his anthropology with
a discussion of evil and sin, and to the frustrated manhood of the
twentieth century declares that the choice is between a God-ruled
humanism and a Godless humanism.

One of the greatest contemporary philosophers of the Frustrated
Man is Nicolas Berdyaev, who is concerned with man not so much
as he is in himself psychologically, but with man as he appears on
the stage of history. Before Berdyaev was expelled from the University of Moscow, he wrote: "The hands of universal history are
pointing to a fatal hour, that of twilight, when it is time to light
our lamps and prepare for the night." Like Nietzsche he revolted
against the moribund conventions of his time, but, like Dostoevski,
he escaped despair by finding relief in reason and the spirit.
He had no patience with the liberals and their linear theory of
progress.[5] Communism he saw not as the fulfillment of the whole
dialectic of history, but only as the last gasp of an expiring cultural
era which began with the Renaissance, and as the first clear intimation of a doom which is to overtake Modern Man in the twentieth
century. "This disintegration of the human image" will be effected
through the vast engulfing tide of impersonal collectivism. The most
important problem of the world, therefore, is the salvation of man,
a problem conditioned upon "the complex interaction of the three
principles of necessity, freedom, and transfiguring grace; the deepest
of these is grace." [6] The present crisis for him is not one of humanism but of humanity. The tension inside of man has historical
roots. First, the Renaissance meant the discovery of the "Natural
Man"—man not in the likeness of God but in the likeness of nature.
Later on, aiming at freedom of thought instead of at the freedom
of man, the Renaissance set up the separate autonomy of the intel-

lect and thereby ruined man's integral spiritual life. The French Revolution carried forward this naturalistic humanism for formulating the Natural Rights of man, thus making man merely a political animal, endowed with rights but no duties. This non-Christian humanism, which began by identifying man with nature, ended by making man a thing. Consequently, by a peculiar paradox, non-Christian humanism gradually transformed itself into the opposite, anti-humanism, for there is nothing more anti-human in the universe than to make man a thing.

It was the Russian philosophers, more than the Western philosophers, who saw clearly that the problem of the twentieth century would be the problem of man. Tolstoi, among others, rejected Western Civilization, not just because of its self-sufficiency, but because its values were false. He did not advocate a violent overthrow of the secularist institutions, but a withdrawal from them, a retreat which would lead to their disintegration. In place of these institutions, Tolstoi would erect a different kind of state, consisting of a free association of individuals pledged to love one another and to live in simple communal life without tribunals, magistrates, or police.

Alexei Khomyakov, in keeping with the philosophy of the Slavophiles, predicted that the liberal and individualistic civilization of the West, with its trust in the self-sufficiency of man, and its belief in uninterrupted progress, would one day bring ruin upon Europe. He foresaw that the growth of democratic liberalism was due to a loss of faith in the guidance of the Holy Spirit. As people became afraid of their own freedom, they replaced the rule of self-governing communities by forms of government copied from the pagan states. "A self-centered individual is powerless; he is the victim of an irreconcilable inner discord. Modern society in its decay releases every individual to the freedom of his own impotence." He foresaw that Russian philosophy would one day conquer the world, but only after it had passed through a terrible, diabolical trial. "The interests of Moscow are those of all mankind. We must remember that no one of us would survive till the end of the harvest, but that our spiritual and ascetic labors of plowing, sowing, and weeding are not for Russia's sake alone, but for the sake of the whole world." Vladimir Soloviëv, in his prophetic work *Three Conversations*, also attacked the optimism of the Western World in regard to human nature. He declared that the greatest heresies of all time were the heresy of Islamism, which reveres an inhuman God; and the heresy of the West, which deifies a godless man, under the auspices of rationalism, secularism, and modern civilization.

One of the most significant works in English on the subject of the Frustrated Man, is *God and Evil*, by C. E. M. Joad, who is tremendously impressed with the moral dialectic within man. There may not be, he declares, more evil now than in the nineteenth century, but it is more obtrusive.

> I mean the evils of cruelty, savagery, oppression, violence, egotism, aggrandizement, and lust for power. So pervasive and insistent have these evils become that it is at times difficult to avoid concluding that the Devil has been given a longer rope than usual for the tempting and corrupting of men. Insofar as evil becomes more obtrusive, it becomes correspondingly more difficult to explain it away by the various methods which have been fashionable during the last twenty years.[7]

He rejects the economic explanation of evil. He denies that evil is caused by want of money, and argues that if poverty is the root of all evil, then money ought to be the source of all power. "Evil is not *merely* a by-product of unfavourable circumstances; it is too widespread and too deep-seated to admit of any such explanation; so widespread, so deep-seated that one can only conclude that what the religions have always taught is true, and that evil is endemic in the heart of man." [8]

Another philosopher of the Frustrated Man is Reinhold Niebuhr,[9] who has made the startling "discovery" of original sin. Negatively, this meant the rejection of liberal theology and its false optimism, as he became convinced of the disparity between the relatively good man and men in mass.[10] Niebuhr reached the belief that this disparity was due to the conflict within man as a result of his duality. "The obvious fact is that man is a child of nature subject to its vicissitudes, compelled by its necessities, driven by its impulses. . . . The other less obvious fact is that man is a spirit who stands outside of nature, life, himself, his reason, and the world." [11] There then follows one of the best descriptions in contemporary literature of pride and lust as the two consequences of original sin. While psychology was stating the conflict within man in flimsy technical language, Niebuhr was investigating it historically, philosophically, and sociologically. Once he became convinced of the truth of the doctrine, liberal theology collapsed for him. "What is absurd is that modern Christianity should have accepted this modern rejection of the doctrine of original sin with such pathetic ignorance and should have spent so much energy in seeking to prove that a Christian can be just as respectable and modern as a secularist." [12] At this point Niebuhr was compelled to become a theologian, with somewhat unfortunate results, for Niebuhr is evidently not familiar with the traditional concept of original sin in Christian thought. He understands the Catholic doctrine only through the perversion of it in the last few centuries. His brilliant first volume peters out weakly into a second volume where there is a failure to understand the difference between nature and person in reference to original sin. Consequently the role of Christ in Redemption and the concept of the historical community as the prolongation of the Incarnation are likewise misunderstood. In spite of these deficiencies, Niebuhr is doing, and has done, more sound thinking on the subject than all the so-called liberal theologians put together.

Added to these solid works on the subject of man, are treatises from the psychological side, all of which describe man in terms of a tension between the lower and the higher self, or consciousness and environment. In retrospect, it is clear that modern man is not going to God from nature but from self. The self with which he starts is the frustrated self. The modern world has become conscious of evil, objectively as it manifests itself in war, and subjectively as it manifests itself in inner discord.

Prosperity killed the sense of evil at the beginning of the century as the intelligentsia argued that there was no real difference between good and evil; it depended entirely upon the individual's point of view. But the war killed moral relativism, for if right and wrong depend upon point of view, then why go to war? Stating it as simply as one can, it would seem today that men are coming to God through the devil—through a consciousness of evil. The evil of the world was often urged in other days as an objection against a belief in God, but today it is used rather as an argument in favor of God's existence. The darkness which once made men doubt the light, now causes them to see that they would never know darkness unless there was light.

It is the subject of tragedy in another form which stands in the forefront of philosophical speculation, and for which there are ultimately only two solutions. One is that of nontheistic humanism. This solution asserts that man is too noble for the universe; tragedy results from attempts to reconcile the man-god with his reiterated failures. These failures of man to realize himself are generally reducible to fatalism; man is determined by fate, as with Spengler; by biological antecedents, as in Darwinism; by the subhuman, as with psychologists; or by economic methods of production, as with Marxists. Theistic humanism, the other solution, asserts that man is not too noble for the universe, but he is too low and too base for God. All the catastrophes which come to man are consequent upon his loss of the purpose of living. That is why most moderns, to escape the disease of meaninglessness and their own intolerable subjectivity, throw themselves into the collectivity of the mass, that the zero of their individuality may be fulfilled in some vague anonymity. Just as soon as a man becomes disgusted with his personal life, he becomes a candidate for one of the other forms of totalitarianism. Because the theistic philosophy is essentially personalist and free, it follows that as God is abandoned, there is a decrease in personal responsibility and human dignity. Totalitarianism grows in direct ratio to, and in proportion with, the dehumanization of man, and it does offer some temporary satisfaction, for it gives the depersonalized man an object of devotion in place of God.

If classical philosophy is ever to bring any solace, comfort, and guidance to the modern world, it must begin to recognize the importance of the metaphysics of man. It has always been the position of theistic humanism that man is at the top of visible creation but not its God. In the true hierarchy of creation, man is for the glory of God, things are for the good of man, and money is for the distribution and production of things. With the loss of Divinity, man has become disoriented, with the result that things today are used for making money; man is considered an instrument for the production and consumption of things; and God—if He exists—is for the sake of contributing occasional moral uplift to man. Anthony of Florence, centuries ago, stated the true philosophy when he said: "Production is for man, not man for production. The object of gain is that a man may provide for himself and others according to their state. The object of providing for himself and others is that they may live virtuously. The object of virtuous life is the attainment of everlasting glory."

THE METAPHYSICS OF MAN

Before an architect prepares the plan for a building, he asks who is going to live in it. If criminals are to live in it, he will design a penitentiary; if dogs are to live in it, he will design a doghouse. Before reconstructing society, we must ask the nature of man, who is to live in it. At the end of the last century, it was assumed that society existed for the Biological Man, who had his roots in primeval swamps. The highest type of Biological Man, it was believed, would emerge as a result of the conflict in which the fittest would survive. Herbert Spencer conceived society "in relations of either antagonism or competition." In this conflict the weaker individuals are annihilated that the strong species may have the dubious immortality of propagation. More recently, there are those who would build society for the Freudian Man, for whom, not moral laws, but unconscious, irrational promptings are the guides of action—freedom, nothing but a "rationalization" of hidden forces which dominate man. Still others would build society for the Economic Man, who is dominated by the motive of profit and self-interest, sometimes veiled under the guise of free enterprise. The conflict of classes, in turn, by historic necessity, will produce a classless society. As the Freudian Man lost his freedom to the psychic forces, the Economic Man lost his to historical determinism. "When the consciousness of my lack of free will," explains a Marxist:

presents itself to me only in the form of the complete subjective and objective impossibility of acting differently from the way I am acting, and when at the same time my actions are to me the most desirable of all possible actions, then in my mind, necessity becomes identified with freedom and freedom with necessity; and then, I am unfree only in the sense that I cannot disturb this identity between freedom and necessity, I cannot oppose one to the other, I cannot feel the restraint of necessity. But such a lack of freedom is at the same time its fullest manifestation.[13]

In other words, we are free because we are not free, or because we cannot help acting unfreely. This is the logic behind the Soviet notion of freedom of the press and of speech. The error in these views of man is that they are partial, truncated, and therefore heretical, for the essence of heresy is the isolation of the part from the whole. Man is political, economic—sometimes unconscious, biological—but to equate any one of these with the nature of man is as fallacious as to describe humanity in terms of the "Blue-Serge Man," "the Tweed Man," or the "Plastic Man."

The regeneration of the world is conditioned upon understanding the whole nature of man, and upon realizing that he moves not only on one level but on three.

Here we turn to various aspects of man as presented in St. Thomas. Man is not any one of these exclusively, though some contemporary theories would isolate one from the others.

Subhuman Man. Man is a *Minor Mundus*, because he contains within himself, in some way, the whole universe: the chemical universe by assimilation, the animal kingdom by his possession of sensitive and affective powers.[14] Since all things were made for him, it follows that he ought in some way to share their natures.[15] Aristotle and St. Thomas included the word "animal" in their definitions of man. Though he has something in common with the animals, he is the most perfect of all.[16] Freudians, behaviorists, materialists, sensualists are right in describing man either in terms of atoms, or of complexes, erotic urges, and instincts, but they are wrong in making these subhuman components of man stand for the whole man. An exponent of behaviorism has said that if "*we*" really understood glandular activity, we could make men do what we pleased. But who is the "we" that discovers the glands, classifies their activities, and uses them? Intelligence is here used to glorify the nonintellectual. These myopic ways of thinking confuse philosophy, as barbarism distorts human action; they unleash the subhuman activities as the motive spring of culture. Once man believes that he is a beast, then he immediately proceeds to act as one.

Rational Man. The subhuman finds its perfection in the human, where the passions, instincts, impulses, and urges are under the domination of an intellect and will. It is these two faculties of the soul which make man human, and greater than the cosmos. Because he has a body, he can physiologically contain part of the chemical and animal order within his own organism, but because he has an intellect, he can contain the universe within himself by knowledge. He is bigger than the cosmos because he can get the heavens into his head,[17] which leaves him the greater task of getting his head into the heavens.[18] The animal can only know *this good* pasture, or *that good* water, but man can know Goodness.[19] Man is transcendent to the animals, too, because he can turn a free thought into a free action. Ice *must* be cold, but man merely *ought* to be good. The basic defect of all totalitarian systems is that they place freedom in the collectivity, not in the person.

Man is a person because he has an intellect capable of knowing truth and a will which can choose love and goodness. To this extent man is made to the image of God, for God has intelligence and freedom. But God has no instincts, complexes, or glands.[20] In all visible creation there is nothing more perfect than personality.[21] Society exists for man, not man for society.[22] Personality as such, is a break with nature and cannot be a part of anything, though anything can be associated with it. Personality does not find its full explanation within itself and hence seeks to transcend itself. All lower things exist for man, but he exists for God, Who is his self-perfection.[23] The existence of personality is unintelligible if there is no higher world toward which man ought to rise. Character in personality is victory over the subhuman forces, not in the sense of their annihilation, but in their subordination to self. Vocation, both temporal and eternal, is also inseparable from personality, since the essence of vocation is the utilization of God's gifts. Human history is nothing else but the story of how man has used his freedom and responded to his double vocation to use matter as the channel to the spiritual, and to perfect personality by progressive assimilation to Eternal Life, Eternal Truth, and Eternal Will, which is God.

Frustrated Man. The purely rational man, in the most strict sense of the term, does not exist. Midway between the realm of pure spirit and matter, God and the subhuman, he is pulled in one or the other direction. St. Thomas describes the theoretical rational man in i, q. 75, of the *Summa*, but this is not explicitly a treatise on man, for the whole first part of the *Summa* is a treatise on God. Here man is treated as a product of the creative power of God along with the angels. Man as he exists historically St. Thomas treats in the *Prima Secundae*, where there are descriptions of a series of tensions, among them, the pull of wealth, power, pleasure as against the pull of God. It is this section that the Thomists must make their point of departure for contact with the modern mind, for here is the Thomistic treatise on Frustrated Man. The description of the Frustrated Man in this particular volume is amazing, though few Thomists have realized its significance in reference to modern thought. The section opens with a description of the tensions within man, each one of which is occasioned by the attempt to satisfy the infinite urges within the limitations of the finite. Man becomes frustrated by having no over-all purpose in life but only multiple desires;[24] by the pursuit of popularity as the essence of happiness;[25] by making the end of life the acquisition of power, either economic or political;[26] by converging all human activities in expression of the sub-human and the erotic. (This is one of the principal sources of frustration because it sets in opposition the body and the soul.[27]) Man also becomes frustrated by making the goal of his life the search for truth while denying either its existence or its absoluteness.[28]

After noting that the tension is external and internal, emotional and intellectual, but basically temporal and eternal,[29] St. Thomas next analyzes the mechanics of the tension in terms of human passions.[30] Passion is something man has in common with the animal, but in man it differs from that of the animal, because in man, passion is under the rule of reason. Tension arises the moment passion is isolated from reason. Physically all passion is good and an integral part of manhood, but morally, it is what we make it. Passion is not a reflex as some modern psychologists believe, because the latter is unconscious, the first conscious. Reason should keep the passions in check; frustration results the moment any passion gains dominion over reason. Passions are divided into two categories: the acquisitive and the dispersive.[31] The acquisitive passion has to do with desire and gives rise to the tensions of joy and sorrow, depending on whether we attain or do not attain what we desire. In a society dominated by the economic motive of wealth and power, there are tremendous potentialities for exhilaration and depression, and even for a disordered mind, once the acquisitive instinct is divorced from the ultimate goal of life.[32] The dispersive passions have to do with emergencies and include such feelings as hope and despair, fear and daring, anger and hate,[33] for the emergency passions are the appetites' response to danger or to difficulty. With these, as with the acquisitive passions, the important thing is whether they are under the lord of the house, which is reason. Once the purpose of life is eliminated, once a moral norm for judging passions is denied, once there ceases to be an ideal personality, the falling away from which turns man into a kind of demon whose name is legion, frustration results.

As William Ernest Hocking so well expressed it:

Psychology in particular must recognize that feeling is essentially metaphysical, and that the whole emotional life of man is affected by that restlessness of which Augustine spoke until it has established its relations with the most Real. We would mean when we say that God is the law of normal mental life that a life lived on the plan of getting along without God, without a sense of cosmic demand, is already, whether one knows it or not, sick, off from normal, its values infected with the dry rot of mortality, intrinsically unhappy, because unreal, driven subconsciously by a need which some day it is bound to recognize and define.[34]

St. Thomas, after describing both the existence of tensions and the mechanics of tensions, next assigns the cause: the separation of man from God and the consequent separation of man from himself. The basis of unhappiness is not to be found in the subconscious, or in the blood, or in bad environment, though the effects of unhappiness are in all these departments. The principal causes of frustration are threefold: internal, external, and historical.[35] The internal causes of frustration are an excessive concentration on a passion or appetite to the exclusion of, or divorce from, the will, or to the blacking out of the intellect and the use of knowledge. Common to both is the enthronement of the ego, the exaltation of the animal over the rational, the loving of the subhuman self above all else.[36] The external cause of frustration is the demonic element in history and nature which offers us inducements to sin as a store advertises its wares.[37] The historical cause is an abuse of freedom in the historical beginnings of the human family.[38]

Classical philosophy, this brief outline suggests, is as much concerned with Frustrated Man as is modern thought, and in a far more profound way. Unfortunately, attention has not been centered on this particular treatise, but rather on other aspects which have little significance for contemporary minds. Many branches of Scholastic philosophy are directed toward an exposition of the fallacies of an antiquated deism and rationalism which no longer exist. A revitalization of the *philosophia perennis* is possible by constructing a new *regula studiorum* on the subject of man: as he is himself, as he stands in relation to the cosmos, to fellowman, to God; to the political, economic, social, and international order. This would entail new disciplines such as the philosophy of economics, the philosophy of law, the philosophy of science, the philosophy of politics, etc. In the domain of Apologetics the most important treatise today is *De Peccato Originali*. It is this subject which the modern thinker has just discovered, and all psychological theories are playing on the edges of the doctrine of original sin. The classical philosopher who would speak a language intelligible to the modern man must dig out of his treasures new things and old. His starting point is the *Prima Secundae* of St. Thomas, which we have described as the Philosophy of the Frustrated Man. All other systems of thinking today treat man on one level exclusively: scientism, in all its departments, regards man as subhuman—one with the cosmos or animals. Humanism regards man on the human level only; psychology considers him frustrated, but merely on a purely animal basis. Classical philosophy treats him on three levels—subhuman, animal, and spiritual—but sees the root of frustration in his alienation from God, and the cure of his frustration in restoration to a knowledge of, and friendship with, God.

Despite the queer eroticisms behind contemporary writing about man, it is much closer to the truth than that of the liberal of the last century who regarded man as a god. What is the recognition of the need of "the unconscious impulses being directed to the satisfaction of the demands of the ego ideal," [39] but an attempt to recognize the need of a standard or ideal to which men ought to conform? The search for a wholly integrated personality is a dim grasping for One Whom no one can accuse of sin. The conflict within man which psychology has discovered—what is it but the dim echo of what Paul describes as the conflict of the law of the mind and the law of the members? The rediscovery of sin under the name of frustration is the rediscovery of freedom, for only a free being can sin. The cohesive unity of the human race has been indirectly envisaged in what psychologists call collective unconsciousness. "I am so profoundly convinced of this homogeneity of the human psyche," writes Jung:

that I have actually embraced it in the concept of the collective conscious, as a universal and homogeneous substratum whose homogeneity extends even into a worldwide identity, in similarity of myths and fairy tales, so that a Negro in the Southern States of America dreams in the motives of Grecian mythology, and a Swiss grocer's apprentice repeats in his psychosis the vision of an Egyptian Gnostic. [40]

But while psychology has done much to rediscover man, it nevertheless suffers from the basic defect of trying to find the cause of the frustration in the person himself by probing into psychic antecedents. This would be a total explanation of frustration, if the cause were wholly in the individual. *But notice that, though different persons may be in varying degrees frustrated, it remains true that everyone is frustrated.* Therefore the cause of the frustration must not be sought in *this* human person alone, but in *human nature.*[41] This frustration in human nature consists formally in a schism from God and materially in a schism within self.[42]

In the Middle Ages, philosophers discussed the problem of man; today they discuss man as a problem. As we have suggested, St. Thomas treats the first subject in i, q. 75, of the *Summa;* man as a problem is discussed in the entire volume of *Prima Secundae.* Basically there are only two philosophies about man: the Marxist and the classical, which through Revelation becomes the Christian. The Marxists believe that man is a product of nature, not a creation of God. This view, by identifying man and nature, dehumanizes man. The classical position makes it possible for man to subdue the world, because he has a spirit that is not part of it. How a small piece of matter, such as man, can conquer the material world is difficult to conceive. Furthermore, the Marxist makes matter dialectical, an idea born of the wedding of Hegel and Feuerbach. The classical system offers a better basis for dialectics, because it admits the existence not only of matter but of spirit. There is no true dialectic in matter, but only action and reaction. Dialectic is possible only when there is something different in kind to matter. The greatest dialectic in the visible universe is the tension between free will and God, between the law of the members and the law of the mind. Marxism is not sufficiently dialectical to satisfy logic and common sense. From another point of view, the Marxist view of man is inadequate, because it cannot conceive of man as existing apart from class relationships, while classical philosophy affirms the social without destroying the person. The difficulty with integrating man to a material totality is, that since matter is determined, it follows that man loses his freedom as his subjection to society increases. The world has too many unredeemed and hostile elements in it to satisfy human aspiration. Marxism is at one and the same time a product of a bourgeois, liberal civilization and a judgment upon it. Its protests are just, but its judgments and reforms are wrong, because it has failed to recognize the primacy of personality. Its doctrine of opposites is held together by a suicidal incoherence, which is a secularization of the Christian idea of the Kingdom of God, as Hegelianism was the secularization of the idea of the Trinity. It has tried to solve the problem of Frustrated Man, but it adds frustration to frustration by annihilating man's nature and by equating original sin with private property.

The source of human frustration is schism. As St. Thomas explains:

> No sooner did man's reason turn away from God than his lower powers rebelled against his reason, and his body became subject to suffering that counteracted the life of the soul. Although these defects seem natural to man absolutely if we consider his nature from its lower side, nevertheless, if we consider Divine Providence and its dignity of the higher part of man's nature, it can be proved with sufficient probability that these defects are penal.[48]

It would seem therefore that man has injured himself by an abuse of freedom. Man is in the position of a clock whose main spring is broken. The clock cannot fix itself. A new spring must be brought in from the outside, but it must be applied from the inside. At this point, philosophy is at a loss to supply the remedy. No one can supply it but God "Who is able, not only to incite man's will to goodness, so as to reintegrate him, but also to condone the sin committed against Him, since an offense is not forgiven save by the person offended." [44] Furthermore, since not only persons are individually frustrated by their particular schisms, but the human race because of its unity, solidarity, and common origin, it follows that to deliver humanity from its common schism, it was necessary that atonement with God be made by one who was man, from whom reparation was due, and more than man—God—in order that His merits would be sufficient to atone for the schism of the whole human race.[45]

St. Thomas sees the whole of pre-Christian history as a preparation for the great Redemptive act that would overcome frustration in principle. Man, he says, can be proud either of what he knows or of what he can do. He knew what was wrong. Gentile history in its entirety and Jewish history in its pre-Law period were indications that man by his own knowledge could not save himself, for the inherent weaknesses of reason were revealed in idolatry, in the killing of the unfit, and in weird nature cults. The Jews, who were later on given the Law, were to prove that man by his own *power* could not save himself, for even with knowledge, men did wrong. When, after this long experiment in humanism, man learned that his own power and his own wisdom were insufficient, he looked to the "Power and the Wisdom of God, Who supplied man's lack of knowledge by removing his doubts and his lack of power by strengthening him against the assaults of temptation." [46]

Evil is not therefore an argument against God, but an argument for God. The opposite of evil is not goodness, but a particular good, as "blindness is not universal non-being, but a particular kind of non-being, namely, the privation of sight." Most apt of all the texts in St. Thomas is the one in which he cites the:

error of those who though observing the presence of evil in the world, say that there is no God. Thus Boethius introduces a philosopher who asks: "*If there be a God, whence comes evil?*" He should have argued: "*If there is evil, there is God.*" For there would be no evil if the order of good were removed, the privation of which is evil: and there would be no such order, if there were no God. [47]

At this point philosophy ends and theology begins. But until theology takes over, philosophers have a double task, which is incumbent on those who enjoy the classical tradition and those who are outside of it, but are still making considerable contributions to the progress of human thinking. Each group has something to learn from the others. The modern philosopher must correct his ignorance concerning classical philosophy. The Thomists know contemporary ideas, but modern philosophers know practically nothing about the *Philosophia Perennis*. Bergson, for example, could profitably have learned from a single article in St. Thomas the difference between reason and intellect, and saved himself the necessity of trying to invent for man a faculty corresponding to the instinct of bees. Similarly, Whitehead, perhaps, would not have found it necessary to write a book calling "substances" examples of "misplaced concreteness," had he studied closely the classical definition of substance. A professor of architecture would hardly be equipped to teach if he ignored the development of both Norman and Gothic, nor can a philosopher handle the problems of modern times unless he knows something about the organized thinking of common sense which is outside the moods of the times.

Classical philosophers, on the other hand, can learn something from the moderns, especially that the problems of the twentieth century are not the problems of the eighteenth. Endless theses on the criteriology of Locke and Kant and Hume, refutations of their agnosticisms have only an historical interest. What Karl Marx wrote in his *Thesis on Feuerbach* is worth recording: "Philosophers invent theories of the world; we must change it." By this he meant that thinking has some relation to action, or that we should be not only hearers of the word, but doers also. Many of the present textbooks in classical philosophy fail to equip the student for handling the philosophical problems of the world except in abstract isolation and on condition that the modern with whom he argues uses the same terms. There need not be a change of truth, for that would deny the reality of truth, but there can be a change of emphasis. The problems which modern philosophy presents do suggest some neglected aspects of truth. The problem of man is not one of these, but man as a problem is. The task is to shift, *not the primacy* of, but the stress on, man as he finds himself "jangled, out of tune and harsh." In other words, rationalism is dead; therefore, why exhume it in order to re-inter it? Irrationalism is stalking the earth, why not recognize it, diagnose it, heal it, then rationalize it, and bring it, in all of its forms, back to that *Ipsum Esse*, Who on Sinai defined Himself for philosophers as "I am Who am," and Who, later on, inspired St. John to define Him for theologians as Love: "*Deus est caritas.*"

Notes

CHAPTER I

[1] *Progress and Religion,* p. 10.

[2] Professor Alfred North Whitehead states: "In the age of Galileo, Descartes, Spinoza, Newton and Leibnitz, mathematics was an influence of the first magnitude in the formation of philosophical ideas....The seventeenth century had finally produced a scheme of scientific thought framed by mathematicians, for the use of mathematicians. The great characteristic of the mathematical mind is its capacity for dealing with *abstractions;* and for eliciting from them clear-cut demonstrative trains of reasoning, entirely satisfactory as long as it is those abstractions which you want to think about....Thereby philosophy has been ruined." *Science and the Modern World,* pp. 44, 81, 82.

[3] *Mathematical Principles of Natural Philosophy,* tr. Motte.

[4] *Ibid.,* II, 160.

[5] Newton laid down a fourth rule, however, which was to serve as a limitation of the others: "In experimental philosophy we are to look upon the propositions collected by general induction from phenomena as accurately or very nearly true, notwithstanding any contrary hypotheses that may be imagined, till such time as other phenomena occur, by which they may be made either more accurate or liable to exceptions. This rule we must follow, that the argument of induction may not be evaded by hypotheses." This means that there is no guarantee against exceptions even in the application of the rational principles set down in the first three rules.

[6] Edwin A. Burtt, *Metaphysical Foundations of Modern Physical Science,* p. 223.

[7] Anthony Collins (1676-1729), in his *Essay Concerning the Use of Reason in Propositions the Evidence Whereof Depends upon Human Testimony,* laid down the principles which guided him in his denial of the supernatural. Collins was a particular and intimate friend of Locke, and a lover of his philosophy. It was only natural for him to take as his rule the postulate that assent to any proposition depends upon the evidence with which it presents itself to the human mind. From this he deduces *more geometrico* two conclusions concerning Sacred Scriptures: everything in Sacred Scripture which interpreted literally shocks our sense, should be interpreted allegorically; all expressions which are not in accord with our manner of looking upon God, should be rejected as interpolations. His belief was that Sacred Scripture is not inspired, and because it is not, there is a lack of correspondence between any prophecy contained therein and its fulfillment. Then, in 1713, he declared that since men have fallen into a multitude of errors, the best attitude to take is that of atheism, for atheism is better than superstition.

Thomas Woolston (1670-1733) applied the allegorical interpretation to miracles, after the fashion of Collins, and by the same token banished miracles from religion. In 1705 he published *The Old Apology for the Truth of the*

Christian Religion Against the Jews and Gentiles Revived. Woolston gave as the reason for dissension among the sects the fact that the Scriptures have been interpreted literally instead of allegorically. He considered Moses an allegorical person, the changing of water into wine, symbolic.

[8] In 1730 Matthew Tindal (1657-1733) published *Christianity as Old as Creation, or the Gospel of a Republication of the Religion of Nature,* which was a denial of the supernatural and revelation. The only true religion, according to Tindal, is natural religion, and it is this religion Our Lord came to promulgate on earth. Such is the reason of the title: *Republication.* Revelation is an unnecessary duplication of natural religion. The two differ not in kind but in degree, i.e., in the manner of their communication. They are, as he puts it, "like two talkers who exactly answer one another." The unassisted reason of man can come to the knowledge of all the truths of revelation. Reason must of necessity be sufficient for man.

Four years after the death of Tindal, his disciple, Thomas Morgan, made war on the Old Testament and declared that Jehovah was merely a local god of the Hebrews, and that the Old Testament miracles were myths. Thomas Chubb (1679-1746) attacked the New Testament—miracles he explained naturally; diabolical possessions were merely natural maladies. The Bible he considered no more inspired than the Koran.

David Hume (1711-1776), applying his empirical principles, eliminated the supernatural from religion by declaring that religion was originally polytheistic and that only by evolution did it become monotheistic. It was the personification of natural forces that led to belief in gods. Hume did not deny miracles, but, in his *Essay on Miracles,* put forward the view that a supposed supernatural event proves only the existence of a previously unknown law of nature. From another point of view, he held that miracles were incapable of being proved. "No testimony is sufficient to establish a miracle, unless the testimony be of such a kind, that its falsehood would be more miraculous than the fact which it endeavors to establish."

[9] Victor Cousin, *Histoire Générale de la Philosophie,* pp. 526-527.

[10] Voltaire à D'Alembert, 15 sept., 1761, *Oeuvres,* X, 575, 607.

[11] *Oeuvres,* 15 sept., 1761, XI, 218.

[12] *Miracle, Dictionnaire Philosophique.*

[13] Voltaire, *op. cit.,* XI, 650. A good refutation of Voltaire is to be found in L'Abbé Guenee, *Lettres de quelques Juifs;* Nonnotte, *Les Erreurs de M. de Voltaire;* and Larcher, *La Philosophie de L'Histoire.*

[14] Friedrich Nicolai (1733-1811) was the principal collaborator with Lessing in the work of fostering religious indifference. He was the German Diderot in the sense that he began the publication of a Universal Library, which appeared at the rate of eighteen volumes a year. He explained the Bible throughout according to reason. Rationalist interpretations of the Life of Christ were formulated by Johann J. Hess in his *History of the Last Three Years of the Life of Jesus* (1768-1772); Franz V. Reinhard, *Essay upon the Plan which the Founder of the Christian Religion Adopted for the Benefit of Mankind* (1781); Ernst A. Opitz, *History of Jesus* (1812); and Johann G. von Herder, *Redeemer of Men* (1797).

[15] *Optics,* p. 378.

[16] Burtt, *op. cit.,* p. 293ff.

[17] The English work of Tindal, *Christianity as Old as the Creation,* is important in speaking of German rationalism, for once translated into German by Schmidt, it exercised considerable influence. In 1752 J. W. Hecker pub-

lished, in Berlin, *Die Religion des Vernunft*, which was made up of ideas then popular in England. Reimarus and Semler both wrote on religion, insisting that the Bible was only a repetition of the laws of nature. Wolff's rational religion, however, was more positive. He assumed, first, that the essence of religion consists in the affirmation of those more or less independent realities— "God, freedom and immortality," and secondly, that the first of these, or the existence of God, is supported by three distinct lines of argument—"the ontological, cosmological and teleological proof." It is worth remembering, at this point, that Kant refuted the arguments for the existence of God as crystallized by Wolff, but he in no way touched the Scholastic arguments, for he apparently did not know them. There would have been much less authority attributed to the Kantian critique if this had been kept in mind.

[18] Christopher Dawson, *Progress and Religion*, p. 190.
[19] *Observations on Man*, chap. i.
[20] *The Making of the Modern Mind*, p. 309.
[21] *Treatise on Civil Government*, chap. ii, sec. 2.
[22] *Ibid.*, chap. x, sec. 22.
[23] At a later date and at the turning point of rationalism and romanticism, there appeared another social philosophy which, while romantic in its general inspiration, nevertheless contained at least some trace of rationalism, and that was the philosophy of Jean Jacques Rousseau, who in 1762 published his *Social Contract*. Politics for him was a kind of quasi-mathematical science. Its fundamental principle, which held sway throughout the whole realm of government, was that of liberty, from which, by vigorous logic, all other axioms were deduced.
[24] *De l'Esprit*, III, chap. xxii.
[25] *Writings* (1869 ed.) VII, 407.
[26] *The Rise of American Civilization*, I, 449.
[27] *A History of Political Theories from Rousseau to Spencer*, p. 126.
[28] Cf. John Howe, "The Redeemer's Tears," *The Great Sermons of the World*, ed. McCartney, p. 131.
[29] *A History of English Literature*, tr. W. D. MacIunes and Author, Vol. II.
[30] *The History of Music*, II, 201.

CHAPTER II

[1] "The work of the earlier philosophic movement had already destroyed the spiritual foundation of the post-Reformation society and had prepared men's minds for the coming of a new order; its actual realization was due to the influence of Rousseau which supplied the necessary dynamic of religious conviction and enthusiasm. This is the real source of the revolutionary movement on the continent. Social and political revolution has become so common a feature of modern European life that we are apt to forget how rare such movements are in history. They occur only when a culture is undergoing a process of internal transformation. Social revolution is an index of spiritual change. Thus the French Revolution was not so much a revolt against misgovernment and oppression as an attempt to restore the unity of European society on the foundation of new ideas." Christopher Dawson, *Religion and Progress*, p. 194.
[2] *Confessions*, VIII, Second letter to M. de Malesherbes.
[3] Masson, II, 84.

[4] "General ideas and abstract ideas are the source of the greatest errors of men: never once has the jargon of metaphysics discovered a single truth." *Emile*, Vol. IV.

"Reasoning far from illumining us, blinds us." Masson, II, 55, Second letter to Sophie.

"Provided that you feel that I am right, I have no further need of proving anything for us." *Ibid.*

[5] John Baillie, *The Interpretation of Religion*, p. 202.

[6] *Three Reformers*, p. 128.

[7] Maritain, *op. cit.*, p. 144.

[8] *Discours sur l'inégalité*, sec. 2.

[9] *Social Contract*, chap. xvi.

[10] *Critique of Pure Reason*, chap. xix.

[11] *Ueber die Fortschritte der Metaphysik seit Leibnitz und Wolff, Werke*, III, 130. Kant, as a matter of fact, accepted Hume's criticism of the knowability of the nature of things, even before he undertook his own critical inquiry into human knowledge. More than this, Kant showed himself to have some attachment to rationalist religion in his definition of religion as the recognition of all duties as divine commands. This definition avoids entirely the existence of God, and avoids all suggestion that special duties (*Hofdienste*) or "court services" were due to God over and above our duties to our fellowmen.

[12] Peroration of *Träume eines Geistersehers*.

[13] *Immanuel Kant*, pp. 18-21.

[14] *History of Modern Philosophy*, II, 34.

[15] *Werke*, VIII, 624.

[16] The same sentimental approach is to be found in the writings of John August Neander. Never a man of very strong prejudices, he is violent at only one time in his writings, and that is when he touches upon the destructive nature of rationalism. He declared, "I shall never cease to protest against the one-sided intellectualism, that fanaticism of the understanding which is spreading more and more and which threatens to change man into an intelligent over-wise beast." His whole theological system and life career are to be found in his motto, "*Pectus est quod theologum facit.*" The Germans called his creed "Pectoralism," in view of the inner basis of his faith.

[17] *Gesammelte Werke*, V, 5.

[18] *Esquisse d'une philosophie de religion* (9th ed.), p. 382.

[19] Alfred Loisy, *L'Evangile et L'Eglise*, p. 66.

[20] *Varieties of Religious Experience*, p. 431.

[21] Samuel Alexander, *Space, Time, and Deity*, II, 352, 374, 382, 385.

[22] Gurnhill, *Christian Philosophy*, p. 31.

Henri Bergson, *L'Evolution Créatrice*, pp. 170, 197.

E. L. Roy, *Dogme et Critique*.

[23] Sir Henry Jones, *A Faith That Enquires*, p. 49.

[24] Hans Vaihinger, *The Philosophy of As-If*, tr. E. K. Ogden.

[25] Creed and Boysmith, *Religious Thought in the Eighteenth Century*.

[26] Albrecht Ritschl, *Justification and Reconciliation*, English translation, II, 199.

[27] *Three Philosophical Poets*, p. 188.

[28] *Dramatic Art and Literature*, Lecture 22.

[29] Irving Babbitt, *Rousseau and Romanticism*.

[30] Emile Legouis and Louis Cazamian, *A History of English Literature*, p. 209.

81 Carlton Hayes, *A Political and Cultural History of Modern Europe*, II, chap. xxvii.

32 W. J. Sparrow-Simpson, *Religious Thought in France in the 19th Century*.

33 V. L. Parrington, *Romantic Revolution in America*, II, 322.

34 A. G. Newcomer, *American Literature*, p. 175.

35 "The years from about 1780 to 1830 in Germany and Austria mark the struggle of the rising romantic spirit with the still powerful classical spirit, a struggle finally decided after the death of Beethoven and Goethe in favor of romanticism." Hugo Leichtentritt, *Music, History and Ideas*, p. 198.

CHAPTER III

1 Carlton Hayes, *A Generation of Materialism*, chap. iv.

2 William Cecil Dampier-Whetham, *A History of Science*, pp. 310-311.

3 J. B. S. Haldane, *Science and Philosophy*, pp. 36, 37.

4 Robert C. Binkley, *Realism and Naturalism*, pp. 1-57.

5 The word "positivism" was widely known in England when the term "agnosticism" was in its infancy. Spencer objected to the name, though J. S. Mill did not. The latter had considerable philosophical kinship with Comte. He denied the existence of causality and universal and necessary concepts, inventing a positivistic logic in which he dismisses the syllogism as a *"petitio principi,"* and in its place offers induction through simple enumeration. Mill had completed about two-thirds of his *System of Logic* when he fell upon the first two volumes of *Cours de Philosophie Positive*, wherein he found assistance for elaborating his theory of "the Inverse Deductive Method as the one chiefly applicable to the complicated subjects of History and Statistics." *Autobiography of Mill*, pp. 209-210.

6 Antonio Aliotta, "Science and Religion in the Nineteenth Century," *Science, Religion and Reality*, p. 160.

7 Antonio Aliotta, *The Idealistic Reaction Against Science*, p. 3.

8 *Controverted Questions*, p. 450.

9 Ralph Barton Perry, *Philosophy of the Recent Past*, p. 41. Among other forms of materialism may be mentioned: in Germany, Jacob Moleschott's *Kreislauf des Lebens* (1852), the first systematic exposition of what is called scientific materialism; Karl Vogt's *Lectures on Man* (1863); Ludwig Büchner, *Matter and Force* (1855), *Nature and Science* (1862), and *Man's Place in Nature* (1869); Edward Lowenthal, *System and History of Naturalism* (1861), the purpose of which was to establish an international freethinkers' association or a *Cogitatenthum*. In France, scarcely any work of merit appeared on materialism. A Communist author, A. Blanqui, wrote *L'Eternité par les Astres* (1872), in which he held that matter is both infinite in extension and duration; and finally, M. Lefèvre's *La Philosophie* (1879), which was a history of philosophy from the materialistic point of view.

10 "The 18th century philosophers even when they were materialists, placed man in a category above and apart from the rest of nature, and hypostatized human reason into a principle of world development. But the new evolutionary theory put man back into nature, and ascribed his development to the mechanical operation of the same blind forces which ruled the material world. Thus Reason becomes merely an organ that has been developed by man's effort to adapt himself to his environment, and is as essentially related to his

struggle for existence as is the speed of a deer or the scent of the beast of prey." Christopher Dawson, *Religion and Progress*, p. 19.

[11] As quoted in William Cecil Dampier-Whetham, *A History of Science*, p. 299.

[12] Arthur Cushman McGiffert, *The Rise of Modern Religious Ideas*, pp. 177-178.

[13] Alfred North Whitehead, *Science and the Modern World*, pp. 147-148. Cf. George H. Mead, *Movements of Thought in the Nineteenth Century*, p. 243. Edward C. Moore, *An Outline of Christian Thought since Kant*, p. 162.

CHAPTER IV

[1] De Bonald, *Sur un dernier ouvrage de M. l'Abbé de Lamennais*, I, 645; *Recherches philosophiques*, pp. 63, 68, 69. Lamennais, *Essai sur l'indifférence*, pp. 203-4.

[2] Bautain, *Philosophie du Christianisme*.

[3] Ubaghs, *Essai d'idéologie ontologique, Logicae seu philosophiae rationalis elementa*.

[4] Bonnetty, *Annales de philosophie chrétienne* (1830-55).

[5] Denziger, 1650ff.

[6] Gioberti, *Introduzione allo studio della filosofia* (1840). Cf. Denziger, nn. 1890-1930. Brownson's Works, I, 267.

[7] *Über die physikalische und die philosophiche Atomenlehre*.

[8] *Microcosmos*, Bk. 12, n. 2.

[9] *Prolegomena to Ethics; Works*, 3 vols. For a full treatment of this period, cf. Ralph Barton Perry, *The Philosophy of the Recent Past*, Pt. 3.

[10] *Appearance and Reality; Truth and Reality*.

[11] *The World and the Individual*.

[12] *L'Essai sur les données immediates de la conscience*, p. 3.

[13] *L'Evolution Créatrice*.

[14] *Darwinism Today*, pp. 18-21.

[15] *Essays upon Heredity*, English translation (1889); *The Evolution Theory*, 2 vols., English translation (1904).

[16] *William Bateson, Naturalist*, Memoir by Beatrice Bateson, p. 32.

[17] Driesch, *History of the Theory of Vitalism; Philosophy of the Organism*. Cf. Julian Drachman, *Studies in Literature and Natural Science*, p. 63. William McDougall, *Modern Materialism and Emergent Evolution*, p. 109.

[18] *The Sciences and Philosophy*, pp. 54, 90.

[19] *Ibid.*, p. 66.

[20] *Contingence des Lois de la Nature*, p. 154.

[21] *The Reaction Against Idealism*, p. 56.

[22] *Science and Religion*.

[23] *La Valeur de la Science* (28th ed.); *La Science et l'Hypothese* (36th ed.).

[24] *Physik und Hypothese; Grundlagen der Physik*, p. 172.

[25] *Anatomy of Science*, p. 6.

[26] James Jeans, *The Mysterious Universe*, p. 23.

[27] Arthur Lynch, *Leading and Mis-leading*, p. 82ff. M. Luckiesh, *Foundations of the Universe*, p. 166ff. *Science and Religion, a Symposium*, p. 117. A. S. Eddington, *The Philosophy of Physical Science*, chaps. 5, 6. Eddington, *Science and the Unseen World*, p. 48ff. Richard Doyle, *The Faith and Modern Science*, p. 63ff.

[28] "There has been a substitution of relativity for absoluteness in all departments of thought.... There is no final and infallible authority in religion, in ethics, any more than in science." *Op. cit.*, p. 185.

[29] *The General Principle of Relativity*, pp. 21-23.

[30] Herbert Samuel, "The New Doctrine of Eddington and Jeans," *The Contemporary Review* (Jan., 1931), p. 8.

[31] *The Mysterious Universe*, p. 36.

[32] *The Expanding Universe*, p. 295.

[33] *Where Is Science Going?*, p. 12.

[34] *Op. cit.* Thomas Kelly, *Explanation and Reality in the Philosophy of Emile Meyerson.* Herbert Dingle, *Through Science to Philosophy*, p. 288. C. E. M. Joad, *Philosophical Aspects of Modern Science*, p. 226. D. J. B. Hawkins, *Causality and Implication*, p. 89.

[35] *Op. cit.*, p. 32.

[36] *Zeitschrift, f. Phy.*, p. 43.

[37] Reichenbach, *Kausalkultur der Welt.*

[38] A. E. Baker, *Christianity and Science in the Twentieth Century*, p. 74. Leslie J. Walker, S.J., *Science and Revelation*, p. 42. J. W. N. Sullivan, *The Bases of Modern Science*, p. 245. Max Planck, *The Philosophy of Physics*, p. 43. John MacMurray, *The Boundaries of Modern Science*, p. 72.

[39] *Space, Time, and Deity*, I, pp. 36, 44, 213.

[40] *Op. cit.*, Bk. 3, chap. ii.

[41] *Science and the Modern World*, p. 23.

[42] Whitehead, *op. cit.*, p. 94ff.

[43] A. N. Whitehead, *Religion in the Making*, p. 100.

[44] Langdon-Davies, *op. cit.*, pp. 50, 51.

[45] *Ibid.*, p. 106

[46] *Ibid.*, p. 109.

[47] *Ibid.*, pp. 129-137.

[48] *Ibid.*, pp. 170, 177, 181.

[49] *Ibid.*, p. 261.

[50] For further evidence of temporalism in literature, cf. Wyndham Lewis, *Time and the Western Man.*

CHAPTER V

[1] Comte, *Cours de Philosophie Positive* (1877 ed.), IV, 267.

[2] Engels, *Correspondence*, p. 475.

[3] Lenin, *Collected Works*, II, 47.

[4] Sorel, *Reflections on Violence*, p. 350.

[5] *Ibid.*, p. 295.

[6] Hermann Rauschning, *The Revolution of Nihilism.*

[7] Pius XI, *Caritate Compulsi.*

[8] Roscoe Pound, *Interpretations of Legal History*, pp. 95, 152-157.

[9] Adams, *Centralization and Law*, p. 35. Frank, *Law and the Modern Mind*, p. 103. Cf. Lon L. Fuller, *The Law in Quest of Itself*, chap. i.

[10] *Lectures on Jurisprudence* (4th ed., 1879), p. 226.

[11] *Pathway of the Law* (1897); for a refutation of Holmes' theory of law, see *The Fundamentals of Holmes' Juristic Philosophy* (1941), by John C. Ford, S.J.

[12] *Education Between Two Worlds*, pp. 200-207.

13 Meiklejohn, *op. cit.*

14 Bertrand Russell, *The Scientific Outlook*, pp. 94-5.

15 Russell, *op. cit.*, p. 71.

16 *Religion in the Making*, p. 71.

17 A. S. Eddington, *The Nature of the Physical World*, pp. 296-97.

18 *The Enduring Quest*, pp. 147-48.

19 "Believe what is in the line of your needs, for only by such beliefs is the need fulfilled." James, *The Will to Believe*, p. 49, and *A Pluralistic Universe*, p. 328; Schiller, *Axioms as Postulates*, p. 88; Jacks, *Religious Perplexities*, p. 95; Sir Henry Jones, *A Faith that Enquires*, p. 104. "The world would be consistent with God; it would also be consistent without God; whichever hypothesis a man adopts will fit experience equally well; neither one, so far as accounting for facts is concerned, works better than the other." Hocking, *The Meaning of God in Human Experience*, p. 143; Lewis, *God and Ourselves*, p. 31; Beibitz, *Belief, Faith and Proof*, p. 16; McGiffert, *The Rise of Modern Religious Ideas*, p. 136; Kilpatrick, *Education for a Coming Civilization*, p. 14; Burtt, *Religion in an Age of Science*, p. 125; Brightman, *The Problem of God*, p. 25.

20 "Whether God stands above the things or lives in the things themselves, whether there is one God or many, remains a consideration of secondary importance." Munsterberg, *Eternal Values*, p. 362.

21 *Op. cit.*, p. 789.

22 Drawbridge, *The Religion of Scientists*, p. 11.

23 Eddington, *The Nature of the Physical World*, p. 11.

24 Jeans, *The Mysterious Universe*.

25 A. S. Eddington, *The Universe Around Us*, p. 7. Reiser, *Philosophy and the Concepts of Modern Science*, pp. 55-57, 89, 110-113, 120.

26 Eddington, *op. cit.*, pp. 253, 254, 262, 263; Jeans, *op. cit.*, pp. 135-138.

27 Jeans, *The New Background of Science*, pp. 8, 9.

28 "And if today you ask a physicist what he has finally made out aether or the electron to be . . . he will point instead to a number of symbols. What do the symbols stand for? The physicist has no means of probing beneath the symbolism." Jeans, *Science and the Universe*, p. 20.

29 Whitehead, *Religion in the Making*, p. 90.

30 *Science and the Modern World*, pp. 249-57. A further idea of Whitehead's conception of the universe and reality may be gained from the following—and again it may not—"There are many ways of analyzing the universe, conceived as that which is comprehensive of all that there is. In a description it is thus necessary to correlate these different routes of analysis. First, consider the analysis into the actual world, passing in time; those elements which go into its formation. Such formative elements are not themselves actual and passing; they are the factors which are either non-actual or non-temporal, disclosed in the analysis of what is both actual and temporal. They constitute the formative character of the actual temporal world. We know nothing beyond this temporal world and the formative elements which jointly constitute its character. The temporal world and its formative elements constitute for us the all-inclusive universe. These formative elements are: (1) The creativity whereby the actual world has its character of temporal passage to novelty. (2) The realm of ideal entities, or forms, which are in themselves not actual, but are such that they are exemplified in everything that is actual, according to some proportion of relevance. (3) The actual but non-temporal entity whereby the indetermination of mere creativity is transmuted into a

determinate freedom. This non-temporal actual entity is what men call God—the super God of rationalized religion." *Religion in the Making*, pp. 89, 90. "Apart from the actual world with its creativity, there would be no rational explanation of the idea vision which constitutes God." *Ibid.*, p. 157. "It is not true that God is in all respects infinite." *Ibid.*, p. 153. For an excellent refutation of Whitehead's philosophy, cf. Leo A. Foley, *A Critique of the Philosophy of Being of Alfred N. Whitehead in the Light of Thomistic Philosophy* (Catholic University of America Press).

[31] Whitehead, *Process and Reality*, p. 529.

[32] *The Wrestle of Religion with Truth*, p. 182.

[33] *Is There a God?* 1st conversation.

[34] Wieman, *The Wrestle of Religion with Truth*, p. 48.

[35] *Ibid.*, p. 49.

[36] *Ibid.*

[37] Jeans, *The Mysterious Universe*, pp. 140, 143, 144.

[38] *Ibid.*, pp. 120-21.

[39] Jeans, *op. cit.*, p. 138.

[40] Jeans, *op. cit.*, p. 131.

[41] *Ibid.*, p. 132. "The anthropomorphic fallacy is very obvious in the conclusion that the Great Architect is a super-mathematician, in short, a Being well fitted to become President of the Royal Society—a colleague of Jeans himself." Stebbing, *Philosophy and the Physicists*, p. 15. This study by Dr. Stebbing is a sustained and trenchant criticism of the unfortunate excursion of Jeans and Eddington into the field of philosophy. Jeans fails to establish the point that because the universe can be explained in mathematical terms, it *is* itself mathematical. This same fallacy of exclusive prediction is also present in his discussion of God's nature. The Divine Mind may, among other aspects, think mathematically, but it does not follow that it is resolvable into a mathematical formula. "That the Creator thinks in terms of mathematics, if He does, is not, therefore, a reason for supposing that He Himself is mathematical, as Sir James Jeans seems to suggest. Nor, to return to the former point, is the presence of mathematical law in the world a reason for supposing that he even thinks in term of mathematics, unless the presence of beauty and goodness is also a reason for supposing that he thinks in terms of esthetics and ethics." Joad, *Philosophical Aspects of Modern Science*, p. 74.

[42] Jeans, *op. cit.*, p. 136.

[43] Bertrand Russell, *The Scientific Outlook*, p. 111.

[44] Jeans, *op. cit.*, p. 137.

[45] Eddington, *The Nature of the Physical World*, p. 321-22.

[46] *Ibid.*, p. 327.

[47] *Ibid.*, p. 337.

[48] *Ibid.*

[49] *Science and the Unseen World*, p. 42.

[50] *Ibid.*, p. 50.

[51] Eddington, *Science and Religion—A Symposium*, p. 129.

[52] *Ibid.*, p. 127.

[53] *Space, Time, and Deity*, Vol. II.

[54] *Ibid.*, II, 318.

[55] *Ibid.*, II, 362.

[56] Alexander, *op. cit.*, II, 345, 361-62.

[57] *Ibid.*, pp. 418-19. Cf. General Smuts' *Holism and Evolution*. General Smuts defines a doctrine of progress in the universe as a movement from

simpler to more complex wholes. The stuff of the universe is not matter, but events and Space-Time. The event takes up the matter, giving a richer content. Thus Space-Time finds its completion in organic evolution, and organic evolution finds its completion in mind or personality. The personality, however, which dominates the universe is not transcendent to it: "from the facts of evolution no inference to a transcendent mind is possible." *Op. cit.*, p. 350.

58 *Two Sources of Morality and Religion*, p. 270.

59 *Ibid.*, p. 206.

60 *Ibid.*, p. 216.

61 *Ibid.*, p. 206.

62 Bergson, *op. cit.*, p. 216.

63 *Ibid.*, p. 216.

64 *Sum. theol.*, i, q. 9, a. 1, ad. 1.

65 Bergson, *op. cit.*, p. 188.

66 *Ibid.*, p. 245.

67 Carr, *The Philosophy of Change*, p. 187; Sheldon, *Pantheistic Dilemmas*, p. 107.

68 William James, *A Pluralistic Universe*, p. 318.

69 *God, the Invisible King*, p. 67.

70 *Faith that Enquires*, p. 360. Cf. Reeman, *Do We Need a New Idea of God?*, pp. 24-28; Overstreet, "God in the Common Will," *Hibbert Journal* (Oct., 1914), p. 155.

71 Van Dusen, "Contemporary Threads in Theism," *Religion in Life* (Spring Number, 1932), p. 187.

72 Brightman, *The Problem of God*, p. 29.

73 Brightman, *op. cit.*, p. 30.

74 *Ibid.*, p. 134.

75 *Ibid.*, pp. 126-37.

76 Montague, *op. cit.*, p. 84.

77 H. A. Overstreet, *The Enduring Quest*, pp. 264-65.

78 Cf. *Theism and the Modern Mood*, pp. 104, 117, 128.

79 *Op. cit.*, p. 125.

80 *Religion*, p. 173.

81 *Religion*, p. 178.

82 *Ibid.*, p. 187.

83 In Germany and France there has also been a belief in the finite God, e.g., Marneck, *Glaubenslose Religion;* Hamburger, *Die Religion in Ihrer Domatischen und Ihrer Reinen Form;* Benda, *La Fin de l'éternel;* Monod, *Dieu dans l'univers.*

84 Cf. Maritain, *Three Reformers*, p. 83.

85 Descartes expressed this mathematical ideal forcibly and confidently in a letter to Père Vatier, dated February 22, 1638: "Believing that I can deduce my thoughts by way of the first principles of my metaphysics, I have deliberately neglected all other kinds of proof." *Oeuvres*, ed. Adam-Tannery, I, 564. To the revolution in our order of thinking which this conception of a *mathesis universalis* effected can be traced the exclusive emphasis which modern philosophy has placed upon the viewpoint of the subject, and its subjection of metaphysics to the standards of nonmetaphysical procedure and evidence. When the criterion of knowledge is no longer to be found in the object itself but only in the quality of our concepts, it is impossible to maintain the proper hierarchy of the sciences. For the order of sciences is based upon the nature of the objects studied, and apart from the objective approach the primacy of meta-

physics cannot be rationally justified. Cf. Gilson, *Etudes sur le rôle de la pensée medievale dans la formation du système Cartesien*, p. 200. "Every idealism of the Cartesian type, from the fact that it identified *a priori* the philosophical method with that of a particular science, ends necessarily by emptying philosophy of all proper content and condemns it to scientism." Gilson, *Le réalisme methodique*, p. 12.

[86] "The very object of the critique of pure speculative reason consists in this attempt at changing the old procedure of metaphysics, and imparting to it the secure method of a science, after having completely revolutionized it, following the example of geometry and physical science . . . it is therefore the first and most important task of philosophy to deprive metaphysics, once for all, of its pernicious influence, by closing up the sources of its error." Kant, Introduction to the second edition of *Critique of Pure Reason*, tr. Max Miller (New York, 1896), pp. 696-70. The error which Kant conceived metaphysics to be laboring under was the ineradicable conviction that it could attain to realities which surpassed the deliverances of the senses. The only cure for this stubborn realism was to follow the lead of the empirical sciences in limiting knowledge to sensible appearances and the quantitative aspect of experience. Once metaphysics gave up its pretensions to knowing things in themselves, it might be reconstituted on a new and more modest basis.

[87] Gilson, *The Unity of Philosophical Experience*, p. 277. This excellent work, better than any other, traces the successive repudiation of reason by philosophers from Abelard to the present day.

[88] Hocking, *What Man Can Make of Man*, p. 32. Cf. Gasset, *Toward a Philosophy of History*, p. 199.

[89] *Op. cit.*, (Int. Pub. ed.), XIII, 100.

[90] Lenin, *op. cit.*, p. 296.

[91] *Ibid.*

CHAPTER VI

[1] *Op. cit.*, p. 329.

[2] *Science and Personality*, p. 81.

[3] *A Struggling God*, as quoted in Joseph Newton's *My Idea of God*, p. 122.

[4] Ames, *My Conception of God*, as quoted in Newton, *ibid.*, p. 243.

[5] *A Materialistic Theory of Emergent Evolution*, as quoted in *Essays in Honor of John Dewey*, pp. 272-73. Cf. Alexander, *Space, Time, and Deity*, II, passim.

[6] Cf. Whitehead, *Religion in the Making*, p. 157.

[7] "Nihil movetur nisi secundum quod est in potentia ad illud quod movetur, movet autem aliquid, secundum quod est in actu." *Sum. theol.*, i, q. 2, a. 3. *Physics*, lib. i, cap. 8; *Meta.*, lib. ix.

[8] "Aristotelis enim proprie accepit motum, secundum quod est actus existentis in potentia secundum quod hujusmodi." *Contra Gentiles*, lib. i, cap. 13.

[9] *Sum. theol.*, i, q. 79, a. 4.

[10] *Sum. theol.*, i, q. 45, a. 5, ad. 3.

[11] *The Universe Around Us*, p. 317.

[12] Cf. *Contra Gentiles*, lib. ii, cap. 35; *Sum. theol.*, i, q. 46, a. 1; *De Potentia*, q. 3, a. 17.

[13] *Evolution and Creation*, p. 15.

[14] "Movetur ab eo qui movet naturam." *Sum. theol.*, i-ii, q. 9, a. 4, ad. 1.

[15] *Sum. theol.*, dist. i, q. 37, a. 1.

[16] E. l. Watkin, *Theism, Agnosticism and Atheism*, pp. 86, 87.

[17] *Sum theol.*, i, q. 46, a. 2, ad. 7.

[18] *Ibid.*, i, q. 2, a. 3.

[19] Jeans, *The Mysterious Universe*, p. 141.

[20] *Contra Gentiles*, lib, ii, cap. 38; *De Potentia*, q. 6, a. 6.

[21] "The Vindication of Religion," in *Essays Catholic and Critical*, p. 50.

[22] "Id quod movet instrumentaliter non potest movere, nisi sit aliquid, quod principaliter moveat. Sed si in infinitum procedatur in moventibus et motis, omnia erunt quasi *instrumentaliter moventia*, quia ponenetur sicut moventia mota; nihil autem erit principale movens; ergo, nihil movebitur." *Contra Gentiles*, lib. i, cap. 13.

[23] "Esse autem in quantum est esse, non potest esse diversum, potest enim diversificare per aliquid quod est praeter esse, sicut esse lapidis est aliud ab esse hominis." *Contra Gentiles*, lib. ii, cap. 52.

[24] "Omne autem quod est per participationem causatur ab eo qui est per essentiam." *Sum. theol.*, i, q. 44, a. 1; *Ibid.*, q. 1, a. 61; *Contra Gentiles*, lib. ii, cap. 15. The argument is not that the greater or less participation prove of themselves the absolute, but rather that the diversity of degree of participation proves that a thing does not possess it by itself and essentially.

[25] "Oportet quod omnis talis res, cujus esse est aliud a natura sua, quod habeat esse ab alio." *De Ente et Essentia*, cap. 5, q. 10.

[26] Morgan, *Emergent Evolution*, p. 33.

[27] *Ibid.*, p. 36.

[28] *Space, Time, and Deity*, II, 353, 366.

[29] *Is There a God?*, p. 13.

[30] *Process and Reality*, p. 521.

[31] Eddington, *Nature of the Physical World*, p. 77.

[32] *In Meta.*, lib. vi, lect. 3.

[33] "Id quod casus est entis, eo quod cadit a principiis entitatis dicitur per accidens esse secundum suum nomen." Albert the Great, *Meta.*, lib. vi-xi.

[34] *Sum. theol.*, i, q. 115, a. 6.

[35] *Ibid.*, i, q. 116, a. 1.

[36] *Ibid.*, Cf. *Contra Gentiles*, lib. ii, cap. 39. Cf. Garrigou-Lagrange, *Le Réalisme du Principe de Finalité*.

[37] Sertillanges, *Dieu ou Rien*, p. 46.

[38] Barclay M. Newman, *Science Rediscovers God*, p. 132.

[39] *The Purpose of God*, pp. 73-75.

[40] *De Veritate*, q. 5, a. 2, ad. 5.

[41] Haldane, *The Philosophical Basis of Biology*, p. 11.

[42] *Anti-Dühring*, p. 79.

[43] *Sum. theol.*, i-ii, q. 109, a. 1.

[44] "The science of mathematics treats its object as though it were abstracted mentally, whereas it is not abstract in reality. Although the object of mathematics has an efficient cause, still, its relation to that cause is not the reason why it is brought under the consideration of the mathematician, who therefore does not demonstrate that object from its efficient cause." *Ibid.*, i, q. 44, a. 1, ad. 1. Cf. *Meta.*, lib. iii, lect. 4, and *De Potentia*, q. 5, a. 1.

[45] Garrigou-Lagrange, *op. cit.*, p. 118ff; Maritain, *Sept Leçons*, lect. 4 and 5; Garrigou-Lagrange, *God*, English translation, p. 356ff.

[46] *Sum. theol.*, i, q. 44, a. 4.

[47] *Sum. theol.*, i, q. 18, a. 3.

[48] *Ibid.*, i-ii, q. 6, a. 2.

⁴⁹ *Ibid.*, i, q. 18, a. 3.

⁵⁰ Macfie, *Science Discovers God*, p. 262.

⁵¹ *Sum. theol.*, i, q. 44, a. 4.

⁵² *Ibid.*, i-ii, q. 109, a. 6.

⁵³ Macfie, *op. cit.* This is truly a remarkable book on the theodicy of science in which dozens of arguments can be found for finality. Cf. also Best, *From the Seen to the Unseen*. Both of these works are more up to date than Janet's *Final Causes*, which, however, still remains a classic. Cf. *The Great Design*, ed. Frances Mason, which has interesting and uncorrelated facts. Cf. also Shearman, *The Natural Theology of Evolution*. *Simple Science* by Huxley and Androde is replete with teleological facts in the universe, but divorced from their obvious conclusions.

⁵⁴ *Contra Gentiles*, lib. ii, cap. 24.

⁵⁵ Jeans, *Through Space-Time*, p. 13.

⁵⁶ Jeans, *The Mysterious Universe*. Cf. Bragg, *The Universe of Light*, and H. S. Allen, *Electrons and Waves*.

⁵⁷ *Final Causes*, p. 55.

⁵⁸ *Sum. theol.*, i-ii, q. 1, a. 2.

⁵⁹ Quod. q. 7, a. 2.

⁶⁰ *Contra Gentiles*, lib. iii, cap. 112.

⁶¹ Professor A. N. Whitehead admits that God must decide which new patterns will enter into the process, but this God he puts inside the universe itself, which of course gives rise to the question of who orders God in the process and determines that he shall have such and such material neighbors and be a member of its process.

⁶² "Quod non est suum esse, non est per se necesse est. Deus autem est per se necesse esse. Ergo Deus est suum esse." *Contra Gentiles*, lib. i, cap. 22.

⁶³ *Sum. theol.*, i, q. 18, a. 3.

⁶⁴ *Ibid.*, q. 14, a. 2.

CHAPTER VII

¹ "Unumquodque nobilius invenitur in causa quam in effectu." *Contra Gentiles*, lib. i, cap. 23. Cf. Sylvester Ferrariensis, n. 7. *De Malo*, q. 4, a. 1, ad. 15. "Similia quidem, secundum quod imitantur ipsum, prout contigit eum imitari qui non perfecte imitabilis est; dissimilia vero, secundum quod deficiunt a sua causa, non solum secundum intentionem et remissionem sicut minus album deficit a magis albo, sed quia non est convenentia rei secundum speciem nec secundum genius." *Sum. theol.*, i, q. 4, a. 3, ad. 1.

² Cf. *De Potentia*, q. 3, a. 5, ad. 1; *De Veritate*, q. 21, a. 5.

³ *Sum. theol.*, i, q. 19, a. 4, ad. 4.

⁴ The text most often quoted in connection with the Immanence of God is *Sum. theol.*, i, q. 8, a. 3, in which St. Thomas says God is present: (1) "per potentiam in quantum omnia eius potestati subduntur; (2) per praesentiam in quantum omnia nuda sunt et aperta oculis eius; (3) per essentiam in quantum adest omnibus ut causa essendi." Cajetan comments on this passage as follows: "(1) Per potentiam, scilicet immediatione virtutis; (2) per praesentiam scilicet suo intuitu; (3) per essentiam, scilicet immediatione suppositi." In an earlier work, i, disc. 37, q. 1, a. 2, St Thomas defines Presence as Divine Operation, Power as Divine Action, and Essence as both Action and Power, for they are one in essence. We have chosen the text in i, q. 9, a. 4, in preference to i, q. 8, a. 3, principally because the former seems more metaphysical and

fundamental, inasmuch as it reduces the immanence of God to the three causes. There is, however, no contradiction between the texts. i, q. 8, a. 3 emphasizes the immanence by creation. Both are aspects of the same reality.

5 "Deus dicitur esse in re aliqua dupliciter. Uno modo, per modum causae agentis, et sic est in omnibus rebus creatis ab ipso. Alio modo, sicut objectum operationis est in operante." *Sum. theol.*, i, q. 8, a. 3c.

6 "Creatura autem accipit a Deo unde ei sit similis." *Contra Gentiles*, lib. i, cap. 29. "Divinitas est esse omnium, ostendit quod a Deo in omnibus quaedam divini esse similitudo reperitur." *Contra Gentiles*, lib. i, cap. 26. "Sed artifex per ordinem suae sapientiae, et intellectus artificiata in esse producit; ergo et Deus omnes creaturas per ordinem sui intellectus facit." *Contra Gentiles*, lib. i, cap. 24.

7 *Sum. theol.*, i, q. 15, a. 2c.

8 "Scientia Dei est causa rerum. Sic enim scientia Dei se habet ad omnes creaturas, sicut scientia artificis se habet ad artificiata." *Ibid.*, i, q. 14, a. 8c. *Ibid.*, q. 44, a. 4c. "Essentia divina in quantum est absolute perfecta, potest accipi ut propria *ratio singulorum*." *Contra Gentiles*, lib. i, cap. 54.

9 "Necesse est quod in mente divina sit forma ad similitudinem cujus mundus est factus. Et in hoc consistit ratio ideae." *Sum. theol.*, i, q. 15, a. 1c. "In divina sapientia sunt rationes omnium rerum, quas sunt ideae ad est, formas exemplares in mente divina existentes." *Ibid.*, i, q. 44, a. 4c.

10 It must not be thought that God makes merely the form of things without the matter; Plato fell into such an error, believing that matter was not created. Matter was created by God, but never without a form. Matter too has its Archetypal Idea in the mind of God, but not apart from the idea of the composite thing, i.e., matter and form. "Materia, secundum se, neque esse habet, neque cognoscibilis est." *Sum. theol.*, i, q. 15, a. 3, ad. 3. "Materia non sit causata sine forma." *Ibid.*, i, q. 44, a. 3, ad 3. "Hoc igitur quod Deus est causa rerum, inquantum sunt entia, oportet esse causam rerum, non solum secundum quod sunt *talia*; per formas accidentales; nec secundum quod sunt haec per formas substantiales; nec secundum omne illud quod pertinet ad esse illorum quocumque modo. Et sic oportet ponere etiam materiam primam causatam ab universali causa entium." *Ibid.*, i, q. 44, a. 3.

11 *Contra Gentiles*, lib. iii, cap. 20.

12 "Dicendum quod res naturales sunt mediae inter scientiam Dei et scientiam nostram. Nos enim scientiam accipimus a rebus naturalibus, quarum Deus per suam scientiam causa est. Unde, sicut scibilia naturalia sunt priora quam scientia nostra, et mensura ejus; ita scientia Dei est prior quam res naturales, et mensura ipsorum; sicut etiam aliquo domus est medio inter scientiam artificis qui eam fecit, et scientiam illius qui ejus cognitionem ex ipsa jam facta capit." *Sum. theol.*, q. 14, a. 8, ad. 3.

13 *Ibid.*, i, q. 16, a. 1c.

14 *Ibid.*, i, q. 16, a. 5.

15 "Sicut enim omnes rationes rerum intelligibiles primo existunt in Deo, et ab eo derivantur in alios intellectus ut actu intelligant; sic etiam derivantur in creaturas ut subsistent. *Sum. theol.*, i, q. 104, a. 3. "Id quod per animam cognitum est, verum est, in quantum illius divinae veritatis quam Deus cognoscit, similitudo quaedam existit in ipso." *Contra Gentiles*, lib. iii, cap. 47. In this sense, St. Augustine says that all things have a triple existence—"scilicet in exemplari aeterno, et in intellectu creato, et in ipso mundo." *Sent.*, i, dist. 36, a. 2, q. 2, conc.

[16] "Dicendum quod agere propter indigentiam non est nisi agentis imperfecti, quod natum est agere et pati. Sed Deo non competit. Et ideo ipse solus est maxime liberalis: quia non agit propter suam utilitatem, sed solum propter suam bonitatem." *Sum. theol.*, i, q. 44, a. 4, ad. 1.

[17] Hence everything has an intrinsic end, which is its perfection, and an extrinsic end, which is God. "Diversimodo se habet ad bonitatem Deus et creaturae, secundum duplicem modum bonitatis quae in creaturis potest considerari.... Secundum duplicem perfectionem et finem creaturae attenditur duplex ejus bonitas. Attenditur enim quaedam creaturae perfection ipsius attenditur quam consequitur per suum motum vel operationem." *Comp. Theol.*, cap. 109. "Unaquaeque creatura intendit consequi suam perfectionem, quae est similitudo perfectionis et bonitatis divinae. Sic ergo divina bonitas est finis rerum omnium." *Sum. theol.*, i, q. 44, a. 1, ad. 1.

[18] "Deus est in omnibus, sed in quibusdam per participationem suae bonitatis ut in lapide et aliis hujusmodi, et talia non sunt Deus, sed habent in se aliquid Dei, non ejus substantiam, sed similitudinem ejus bonitatis." In *Epis. ad Col.*, lect. 2, cap. 2, *Contra Gentiles*, lib. iii, cap. 20.

[19] "Aliquid dicitur operari vel moveri propter finem; sicut sagitta movetur directa ad signum a sagittante, qui cognoscit finem, non autem sagitta." *Sum. Theol.*, i, q. 103, a. 1, ad. 1. *Contra Gentiles*, lib. iii, cap. 24.

[20] "Non potest Deus sic esse finis rerum quasi aliquid constitutum, sed solum quasi aliquid praexistens obtinendum.... Deus sit finis rerum non quod aliquid ei a rebus acquiratur, sed hoc solo modo quia ipse rebus acquiratur." *Contra Gentiles*, lib. iii, cap. 18.

[21] "Et sic, eorum quae Deum appetunt; quaedam cognoscunt ipsum secundum se ipsum, quod est proprium creaturae rationalis; quaedam vero cognoscunt aliquos participationes suae bonitatis, quod etiam extenditur ad cognitionem sensibilem; quaedam vero appetitum naturalem habent absque cognitione, utpote inclinata ad suos fines ab alis superiori cognoscente." *Sum. theol.*, i, q. 6, a. 1, ad. 2. *Ibid.*, i, q. 60, a. 1c.

[22] "Amor naturalis nihil aliud sit quam inclinatio naturae indita ab auctore naturae." *Sum. theol.*, i, q. 60, a. 1, ad. 3.

[23] "Deus est prima causa in ordine causarum finalium, quum sit summum in ordine bonorum. Est igitur magis finis uniuscujusque rei quam aliquis finis proximus." *Contra Gentiles*, lib. ii, cap. 37.

[24] "Deligere autem Deum super omnia est quidam connaturale homini, et etiam cuilibet creaturae, non solum rationali sed irrationali, et etiam inanimatae, secundum modum amoris qui unicuique competere potest." *Sum. theol.*, i-ii, q. 109, a. 3. "Deus est primum desideratum." *Contra Gentiles*, lib. i, cap. 37. "Deus est primum desideratum." *Contra Gentiles*, lib. i, cap. 37.

[25] "Dicendum quod necesse est dicere omne quod quocumque modo est, a Deo esse. Si enim aliquid invenitur in aliquo per participationem, necesse est quod causatum in ipso ab eo cui essentialiter convenit: sicut ferrum fit ignitum ab igne." *Sum. theol.*, i, q. 44, a. 1c. "Non ergo propter hoc solum requitur causa agens, quia effectus potest non esse; sed quia effectus non esset, si causa non esset, si causa non esset." *Ibid.*, ad. 2. "Ex hoc quod aliquid per participationem est ens, sequitur quod sit causatum ab alio." *Ibid.*, ad. 1.

[26] *Sum theol.*, i, q. 8, a. 1c.

[27] "Immensitate suae virtutis attingit omnia quae sunt in loco, quum sit universalis causa essendi." *Contra Gentiles*, lib. iii, cap. 68.

[28] "Hunc autem effectum causat Deus in rebus, non solum quando primo esse incipiunt, sed quamdiu in esse conservantur; sicut lumen causatur in aere

a sole, quamdiu aer illuminatus manet. Quamdiu igitur res habet esse, tamdiu oportet quod Deus adest ei secundum modum quo esse habet." *Sum. theol.*, i, q. 8, a. 1c. "Nec esse rei potest remanere, cessante actione agentis quod est causa effectus non solum secundum fieri, sed etiam secundum esse." *Ibid.*, i, q. 104, a. 1c, 2c. *De Potentia*, q. 5, a. 2, ad. 6.

29 "Omnes creaturae indigent divina conservatione. Dependet enim esse cujuslibet creaturae a Deo, ita quod nec ad momentum subsistere divinae virtutis conservarentur in esse." *Sum. theol.*, i, q. 104, a. 1c. *De Potentia*, q. 3, a. 8, ad. 15.

30 "Dicendum quod nullius agentis, quantumcumque virtuosi, actio procedit ad aliquid distans, nisi in quantum in illud per media agit. Hoc autem ad maximam virtutem Dei pertinent, quod inmediate in omnibus agit. Unde nihil est distans ab eo, quasi in se illud Deum non habeat." *Sum. theol.*, i, q. 8, a. 1, ad. 3.

31 *Ibid.*, i, q. 8, a. 1c.

32 "Causa prima magis influit in effectum quam secunda." *De Potentia*, q. 3, a. 8, ad. 15.

33 "In ipsa rerum creatione ordinem in rebus instituit, ut quaedam ab aliis dependerent, per quas secundario conservarentur in esse; praesupposita tamen principali conservatione quae est ab ipso." *Sum. theol.*, i, q. 104, a. 2, ad. 1.

34 *De Potentia*, q. 3, a. 7. It must not be thought that because God is the Principle of Activity, He is also the Author of Evil. Evil is not a positive entity, but a privation of some good. It has only a *causa per accidens*. *Ibid.*, i, q. 49, a. 1c. A lame man may walk; the act of walking is caused by the motion formally immanent in the soul which gives life to his body. But the lameness is caused by some defect in his bones. In like manner, whatever is active or existential in an evil action belongs to God as a cause; but what is evil in the action is caused not by God but by a defective secondary cause, e.g., an evil will. *Ibid.*, i, q. 49, a. 2c. "Dicendum est quod in causis mali non est procedere in infinitum; sed est reducere omnia mala in aliquam causam bonam, ex qua sequitur malum per accidens. *Ibid.*, i, q. 49, a. 3, ad. 6.

35 *Sum. theol.*, i, q. 8, a. 2.

36 "In substantiis autem incorporeis non est totalitas, nec per se, nec per accidens, nisi secundum perfectam rationem essentiae. Et ideo sicut anima est tota in qualibet parte corporis, ita Deus totus est in omnibus et singulis." *Ibid.*, i, q. 8, a. 2, ad. 3.

37 "Deus est supra omnia per excellentiam suae naturae. Et tamen est in omnibus rebus ut causam omnium esse." *Ibid.*, i, q. 8, a. 1, ad. 1. "Dicendum quod aliquid potest dici praesens alicui, inquantum subjacet ejus conspectui, quod tamen distat ab eo secundum suam substantiam. Et ideo oportuit duos modos poni, scilicet per essentiam, et praesentiam." *Ibid.*, i, q. 8, a. 3, ad. 2.

38 "Secundum scientiam et voluntatem, magis res sunt in Deo, quam Deus in rebus. Sed de ratione potentiae est quod sit principium agendi in aliud. Unde, secundum potentiam, agens comparatur rei exteriori. Et sic per potentiam potest dici agens esse in alio." *Ibid.*, i, q. 8, a. 4c.

39 With the aid of revelation, the Scholastics were wont to look for vestiges of the Trinity in Creation. *Sum. theol.*, i, q. 45, a. 7.

CHAPTER VIII

[1] For a fuller description of these changes cf. Fulton J. Sheen, *Philosophy of Science*, chap. ii; M. Luckiesh, *The Foundation of the Universe*, p. 81; David Dietz, *The Story of Science*, chap. xxii (Quantum Theory); William Bragg, *The Universe of Light;* Emile Berlot, *Enseignements de la Cosmogonie Moderne;* Ernest Zimmer, *The Revolution in Physics*, tr. H. S. Hatfield, p. 177; J. Arthur Thomson, *Science Today*, p. 213; W. F. Swann, *The Architecture of the Universe*, chaps. viii, ix. J. W. N. Sullivan, *The Bases of Modern Science*, p. 29; Harold Richards, *The Universe Surveyed*, chap. x; Max Planck, *The Universe in the Light of Physics;* F. Sherwood Taylor, *A World of Science;* Louis Trenchard More, *Isaac Newton;* Albert Eagle, *The Philosophy of Religion Versus the Philosophy of Science*, p. 225.

[2] *The Universe Around Us*, p. 83.

[3] The science of physics of the Middle Ages is not exactly like the science of the present day, but more of a natural philosophy.

[4] "Quaedam igitur sunt speculabilia quae dependent a materia secundum esse, quia non nisi in materia esse possunt et haec distinguuntur quia dependent quaedam a materia secundum esse et intellectum, sicut, illa in quorum definitione ponitur materia sensibilis: unde sine materia sensibili intelligi non possunt ut in definitione hominis oportet accipere carnem et ossa, et de his est physica sive scientia naturalis. Quaedam vero quamvis dependeant a materia secundum esse, non tamen secundum intellectum quia in eorum definitionibus non ponitur materia sensibilis, ut linea et numerus, et de his est mathematica. Quaedam vero sunt speculabilia quae non dependent a materia secundum esse, quia sine materia esse possunt, sive numquam sint in materia, sicut Deus et angelus, sive in quibusdam sint in materia, et in quibusdam non, ut substantia, qualitas et actus unum et multa, et hujusmodi, de quibus est theologia, id est divina scientia, qui praecipuum cognitorum in ea est Deus. Alio nomine dicitur metaphysica, id est transphysica, quia post physiciam discenda occurrit nobis, quibus es sensibilibus competit in insensibilia devenire. Dicitur etiam philosophia prima in quantum scientiae aliae ab ea principia sua accipientes eam sequuntur." *De Trinitate Boetii*, q. 5, a. 1.

[5] Mathematical physics, it was stated above, is a *scientia media* between physics and mathematics. In the very nature of things, physics is posterior to metaphysics, because it adds something to being considered in the abstract state, namely, quantity and mobility. As St. Thomas says: "Sed scientiae particulares sunt posteriores secundum naturam universalibus scientiis, quia subjecta eorum addunt ad subjecta scientiarum universalium; sicut patet, quod ens mobile de quo est naturalis philosophia addit supra ens simpliciter, de quo est metaphysica, et supra maxime universalibus est certissima." *In Meta.*, lib. i, lect. 2. The unity of mathematical physics is not real but mental.

[6] *In De Trinitate Boetii*, q. 5, aa. 3, 5.

[7] *In De Trinitate Boetii*, q. 6, a. 2.

[8] "The Vindication of Religion," in *Essays Catholic and Critical.*

[9] "In divinis neque ad sensum, neque ad imaginationem debemus deduci; in mathematicis autem et imaginationem et non ad sensum; in naturalibus autem etiam adsensum. Et propter hoc peccant, qui uniformiter in tribus speculativae partibus procedere nituntur." *De Trinitate Boetii*, q. 6, a. 2.

[10] *In De Trinitate Boetii*, q. 5. a. 1. Kurt Riezler, *Physics and Reality.*

[11] *Broadcast Minds*, pp. 211-212.

[12] J. W. N. Sullivan, *The Bases of Modern Science*, p. 233.

[13] Max Planck, *Where Is Science Going?*, p. 116.

[14] Max Planck, "Causality in the World of Nature," in *Science Today*, p. 345.

[15] *The Nature of the Physical World*, p. 297.

[16] Eddington, *op. cit.*, p. 303.

[17] *Ibid.*, p. 299.

[18] *The Freedom of Man*, p. 39.

[19] "Non acquiruntur per ratiocinationes sed solum per hoc quod eorum termini innotescunt, quod quidem fit per hoc quod a sensibilibus accipitur memoria, a memoria experimentum et ab experimento illorum terminorum cognitio. *In Meta.*, lect. 6. "Sensibilia sunt prima principia cognitionis humanae." *Sum. theol.*, ii, q. 173, a. 3. "Intellectus humanus est in potentia respectu intelligibilium." *Ibid.*, i, q. 79, a. 2. "Quaedam statim a principio naturaliter homini innotescunt absque studio et investigatione: et hujusmodi sunt prima principia." *Quaes. Disput., De Virtutibus*, q. 1, a. 8.

[20] *In de Caelo et Mundo*, lib. i, lect. 17.

[21] *Sum. theol.*, i-ii, q. 35, a. 6.

[22] *Ibid.*, i, q. 60, a. 5; ii-ii, q. 26, a. 3.

[23] *Ibid.*, i, q. 62, a. 6.

[24] In *Hebrews*, cap. 10, lect. 2.

[25] Herbert Samuel, *Contemporary Review* (Jan., 1931), p. 8.

[26] Jeans, *The Mysterious Universe.*

[27] Eddington, *The Nature of the Physical World*, p. 310. Arthur A. Compton, *The Freedom of Man.*

[28] Max Planck, *Where Is Science Going?*, pp. 210-211. H. Levy, *The Universe of Science*, pp. 165-170. Cf. Bertrand Russell, *The Scientific Outlook*, pp. 103-104.

[29] McWilliams, in *The Modern Schoolman* (Jan., 1935), p. 40.

[30] "Soli vero substantiae intellectivae attribuitur voluntas; et quanto est immaterialior, tanto ei magis competit ratio voluntas." *Sum. theol.*, i, q. 19, a. 1—*De Veritate*, q. 23, a. 1.

[31] *Sum. theol.*, i, q. 79, a. 3.

[32] Maher's *Psychology*, pp. 414-415. "As regards finite goods it is obvious that, either in the difficulty of their acquisition, or in the uncertainty of their possession, or in their possible incompatibility with our highest good, there is always something on account of which they are undesirable, and for which man may turn away from them to seek the *infinite* good—God himself. At the same time it is equally clear that man is not at present drawn inevitably in this latter direction. The inadequate and obscure notion of God possessed in this life, the difficulty of duty, the conflict of man's pride and sensuality with virtue, all make the pursuit of our true good disagreeable in many respects to human nature, so that we can only too easily and freely abandon it. The clear apprehension of an Infinite Good, such as is given in the Beatific Vision of the blessed in Heaven, would, theologians teach, remove this freedom. The blessed cannot help loving God above all things; we, however, though necessitated to seek after good in some shape or other, are at liberty to reject any particular form of it presented to us. Our Freedom, accordingly, lies in our power of choosing between the manifold kinds of good, which are ever conceivable by the Intellect; it is, in fact, a free acceptance of intellectual judgments concerning the desirability of thoughts and external action."

[33] *The Nature of the Physical World*, p. 254.

[34] *Ibid.*, p. 317.
[35] *Ibid.*, p. 327.
[36] *The Mysterious Universe*, p. 254.
[37] Eddington, *The Nature of the Physical World*, p. 321.
[38] *Ibid.*, p. 330.
[39] *Ibid.*, pp. 321, 330, 337, 338.
[40] Bergson, *The Two Sources of Morality and Religion*, p. 246.
[41] *Ibid.*, p. 233.
[42] Bergson, *op. cit.*, pp. 226, 234.
[23] Bergson, *op. cit.*, p. 216.
[44] Bergson, *op. cit.*, pp. 236, 237.

CHAPTER IX

[1] H. Pinard de la Boullate, S.J., *L'Etude Comparée des Religions*, II, 14.
[2] *Etudes d'histoire religieuse*, Pt. II, chap. i, p. 77ff.
[3] *The Study of Religion*, p. 28.
[4] H. L. Mencken, *Treatise on the Gods*, p. 176.
[5] *Op. cit.*, chap. vi.
[6] M. G. Foucart, *Histoire des Religions*, p. 376ff.
[7] *Op. cit.*, p. 150.
[8] B. Bosanquet, *Individuality and Value*, pp. 24, 59, 299.
[9] *The Scientific Outlook*, p. 253.
[10] *Treatise on the Gods*, pp. 12-13.
[11] Constitution of Clement XI (1713), entitled "Unigenitus." Bull of Pius V (1507), "Ex omnibus afflictionibus."
[12] De Broglie, *Problèmes et Conclusions*, chap. viii, pt. 5.
[13] *De Lege*, I, cap. 24.
[14] Cf. Brunsmann-Preuss, *Fundamental Theology*, I, 132ff. W. St. Clair Tisdall, *Christianity and Other Faiths*, chap. ii. S. P. T. Prideaux, *Man and His Religion*, chap. viii.
[15] Cf. Herman Dieckmann, *De Revelatione Christiana*.
[16] "Cum homo a Deo tamquam creatore et Domino suo totus dependeat, et ratio creata increatae Veritati penitus subiecta sit, plenum revelanti Deo intellectus et voluntatis obsequium praestare tenetur." Council of Vatican. Denziger (1789).
[17] *Sum. theol.*, ii-ii, q. 2, a. 3.
[18] *Ibid.*, iii, q. 11, a. 1; q. 1, a. 3, ad. 3.
[19] A. N. Whitehead, *Religion in the Making*, p. 22.
[20] J. B. Pratt, *The Pilgrimage of Buddhism*, p. 325ff. Relation of de Rubruquis, Ambassador of St. Louis, to the Khan of Tartar, quoted in De Broglie's *Histoire des Religions*, p. 254.
[21] *The Everlasting Man*, pp. 85-89. Cf. *Orthodoxy*, pp. 240-242.
[22] Pinard de la Boullate, *op. cit.*, Vol. II.
[23] P. Radin, *Primitive Man as a Philosopher*, p. 345. Cf. Robert H. Lowie, *An Introduction to Cultural Anthropology*.
[24] E. B. Taylor shares with Spencer in the dubious honor of being the father of evolutionary anthropology, although Taylor was much more scientific and far better grounded in anthropological data.
[25] A. A. Goldenweiser, "Cultural Anthropology," in *The History of the Social Sciences*, ed. H. E. Barnes, p. 222.

[26] Radin, *op. cit.*, p. 373.

[27] *Primitive Marriage.*

[28] *Ancient Society.*

[29] *The History of Human Marriage.*

[30] A. A. Goldenweiser, *op. cit.*, p. 225.

[31] A. A. Goldenweiser, *op. cit.*, p. 226. "It is very important to remember that the three primary cultures did not arise generally one after another, so that every people, or even the majority of people, must needs have passed through them all. On the contrary, a part of the tribes having primitive culture developed with the higher totemistic hunting stage, another part became cattle breeders, the third horticulturists. It was not till later, by means of crossings, which of course took place in different degrees of strength of the various components, that elements of one or both the other cultures could be taken up by a third; the internal development of each culture always went on independently." W. Schmidt, *The Origin and Growth of Religion*, tr. H. J. Rose.

[32] *In Ethics*, lib. i, lect. 2.

[33] L. P. Jacks, *My Neighbour the Universe*, p. 77ff.

[34] William James, *Varieties of Religious Experience*, pp. 201, 223.

[35] *Ibid.*, pp. 390, 407.

[36] A. R. Uren, *Recent Religious Psychology*, pp. 72, 73.

[37] J. H. Leuba, *A Psychological Study of Religion*, p. 272.

[38] R. H. Thouless, *Introduction to the Psychology of Religion*, pp. 261, 262.

[39] J. B. Pratt, *The Religious Consciousness*, p. 457ff.

[40] *Ibid.* "The psychology of religion must take a much humbler position than that which some of its devotees desire for it. It must content itself with a description of human experiences, while recognizing that there may well be spheres of reality to which these experiences refer and with which they are possibly connected, which yet cannot be investigated by science." J. B. Pratt, quoted in John Baillie, *The Interpretation of Religion*, p. 139. Another writer says: "One fault in some psychological literature ... is the introduction of judgments of worth into what are apparently intended to be descriptive accounts of facts." W. K. Wright, *The Relation of the Psychology of Religion to the Philosophy of Religion*, as quoted in John Baillie, *op. cit.*, p. 139. And still another holds: "In view of the confident ontological pronouncements of certain of the American investigators, it becomes necessary to state with firmness that psychology is not entitled to be heard on questions of metaphysics. Psychology is a natural science proceeding by the empirical method, which has taken as its special department of study the phenomena of the mental life. The psychology dealing with the religious phenomena of the human consciousness ought, then, to be simply empirical and descriptive. This religious psychology may gather factual data, and may proceed from this data to classifications, generalizations, and laws; this far and no further my it go. It must stop short at the problem of the objective validity of the facts of religious experience." A. R. Uren, *Recent Religious Psychology*, p. 274.

[41] *The Psychological Foundation of Belief in Spirits.*

[42] *Christian Religious Experience*, pp. 222-23.

[43] *Varieties of Religious Experience*, p. 431.

[44] *Psychology of the Unconscious*, chap. iii.

[45] *An Introduction to the Psychology of Religion*, chap. i.

[46] *De Veritate*, q. 10, a. 11, ad. 6.

[47] *The New Psychology and Religious Experience*, p. 148.

[48] John of St. Thomas, t. II, pt. i, q. 1, a. 3.

[49] *Ibid.*, i-ii, q. 109, a. 3.

[50] "Cognitio existendi Deum dicitur omnibus naturaliter inserta." *De Veritate*, q. 10, a. 12, ad. 1.

[51] *Contra Gentiles*, lib. iii, cap. 50.

[52] Wisdom 13:9.

[53] "Habere propriam cognitionem de rebus, est cognoscere res non solum in communi, sed secundum quod sunt ab invicem distinctas." *Sum. theol.*, i, q. 14, a. 6.

[54] *Contra Gentiles*, lib. ii, cap. 38.

[55] *Ibid.*

[56] Auguste de Broglie, *Religion et Critique*, p. 109ff.

[57] *A Preface to Morals*, p. 216ff.

[58] Plotinus, II, 208.

[59] S. L. Frank, *God With Us*, p. 185.

[60] Acts 4:12.

[61] I Cor. 10:12.

[62] I Timothy 2:5.

[63] "Socrates quidem cum rogaretur civitatem se esse diceret, mundanum inquit." Cicero *Tusc. Disp.* V, 37, 108.

CHAPTER X

[1] *The Meaning of History.*

[2] Arnold J. Toynbee, *A Study of History*, IV, 259.

[3] *The Crisis of Our Age.*

[4] *Meteora*, I, xiv. Cf. P. Duhem, *Le Système du Monde.*

[5] *Meteora*, I, iii.

[6] Nicholas Berdyaev, *The Meaning of History*, p. 34.

[7] A. E. Haydon, "What is Humanism?" *The University Review*, III, 238.

[8] William James, *Will to Believe*, p. 61.

[9] John B. Bury, *The Idea of Progress*, p. 5.

[10] W. Godwin, *Inquiry Concerning Political Justice*, II, 528.

[11] *The Meaning of Faith.*

[12] *Darwinism and What It Implies*, p. 39.

[13] *The Work, Wealth, and Happiness of Mankind.*

[14] Nicholas Berdyaev, *The Meaning of History*, pp. 188, 190.

[15] F. Engels, *Ludwig Feuerbach* (Martin Lawrence ed.), p. 28.

[16] "Theses on Feuerbach," Engels, *Ludwig Feuerbach*, p. 73.

[17] *Matériaux d'une Théorie du Proletariat* (3rd ed., Paris, 1929), p. 314.

[18] *Die Heilige Familie*, p. 238.

[19] *Communist Manifesto.*

[20] *The Poverty of Philosophy.*

[21] *Capital*, Vol. I.

[22] Marx, *Contribution to Critique of Political Economy*, p. 11. "The course of history is governed by inner general laws." Engels, *Ludwig Feuerbach*, p. 58. Cf. pp. 59, 60, for a fuller treatment of the Marxist thesis.

[23] *Communist Manifesto.*

[24] *Ibid.*

[25] *Marx–Engels* (critical edition published by the Karl Marx Institute, Moscow), I, i (2), p. 615.

26 *Marx—Engels* (historical critical ed.), I, i, p. 590.

27 *German Ideology.*

28 *Ibid.*

29 *Ibid.*

30 Charles J. McFadden, *The Philosophy of Communism;* E. I. Watkin, *Mean and Tendencies,* pp. 246-290; Edwin R. A. Seligman, *The Economic Interpretation of History.*

31 Tr. Charles Francis Atkinson (Knopf ed., 1939, N. Y.).

32 Preface to the first edition.

33 Preface to the revised edition.

34 *Ibid.*

35 *Ibid.*

36 *Travel Diary of a Philosopher.*

37 *Ibid.*

38 *Decline of the West,* I, 23.

39 *Ibid.,* p. 25.

40 Preface to revised edition.

41 *Ibid.,* I, 24.

42 *Decline of the West,* I, 25.

43 *Ibid.,* p. 4.

44 *Ibid.,* pp. 5, 6.

45 *Ibid.,* p. 6.

46 *Ibid.,* p. 8.

47 *Ibid.,* p. 7.

48 *Decline of the West,* I, 183.

49 *Ibid.,* p. 291.

50 *Ibid.,* p. 45.

51 *Ibid.,* p. 374.

52 *Ibid.,* p. 40.

53 *Ibid.,* p. 44.

54 *Decline of the West,* II, 507.

55 *Experience and Nature,* chap. x. *Human Nature and Conduct,* Pt. iv, sec. 9.

56 W. E. Hocking, *What Man Can Make of Man,* p. 32.

57 "It must necessarily be allowed that the principle of intellectual operation which we call the soul, is a principle both incorporeal and subsistent. For it is clear that by means of the intellect man can have knowledge of all corporeal things. Now whatever knows certain things cannot have any of them in its own nature; because that which is in it naturally would impede the knowledge of anything else. Thus we observe that a sick man's tongue being vitiated by a feverish and bitter humor, is insensible to anything sweet, and everything seems bitter to it. Therefore, if the intellectual principle contained the nature of a body, it would be unable to know all bodies. Now every body has its own determinate nature. Therefore it is impossible for the intellectual principle to be a body. It is likewise impossible for it to understand by means of bodily organ; since the determinate nature of that organ would impede knowledge of all bodies; as when a certain determinate colour is not only in the pupil of the eye, but also in a glass vase, the liquid in the vase seems to be of that same colour. Therefore the intellectual principle which we call the mind or the intellect has an operation *per se.* For nothing can operate but what is actual: wherefore a thing operates according as it is; for which reason we do not say that heat imparts heat, but that what is hot gives heat. We must conclude,

therefore, that the human soul, which is called the intellect or mind, is something incorporeal and subsistent." *Sum. theol.*, i, q. 75, a. 2.

58 G. K. Chesterton, *The Everlasting Man*, pp. 16, 17, 18, 20, 21, 22.

59 Pitirim Sorokin, *Social and Cultural Dynamics*, IV, 666.

60 *The Basic Works of Aristotle*, ed. Richard McKeon, *Physics*, Bk. ii, chap. 3, 194-B, 195-A.

61 *Sum. theol.*, i-ii, q. 1, a. 1c.

62 From letter of Engels to J. Bloch, quoted by Hook, *Toward an Understanding of Karl Marx*, p. 179.

63 *Capital*, p. 8.

64 *Sum. theol.*, i, q. 14, a. 2c. *Ibid.*, i-ii, q. 3, a. 2, ad. 3.

65 *Contra Gentiles*, Bk. iv, cap. 11.

66 Arnold J. Toynbee, *A Study of History*, II, 223.

67 *Sum. theol.*, i-ii, q. 21, a. 4c.

68 *Sum. theol.*, i, q. 15, a. 1. Creatures proceed from God in virtue of this double similitude. "Aut quantum ad id quod habet in natura sua, sicut homo generat hominem; aut quantum ad id quod habet in intellectu suo, sicut artificiatum. Utroque modo procedit creatura a Deo in similitudinem ejus. Primo modo, quia ab ente sunt entia, et vivo viventia; secundo modo quia procedunt a rationibus aeternis." *Ibid.*, ii, dist. 16, q. 1, a. 2, ad. 2.

69 "Deus secundum essentiam suam est similitudo omnium rerum. Unde idea in Deo nihil est aliud quam Dei essentia." *Ibid.*, i-ii, q. 15, a. 1, ad. 3.

70 "Ipse enim essentiam suam perfecte cognoscit, unde cognoscit eam secundum omnem modum quo cognoscibilis est. Potest autem cognosci non solum secundum quod in se est, sed secundum quod est participabilis secundum aliquem modum similitudinis a creaturis." *Ibid.*, i, q. 15, a. 2c.

71 "Quae quidem, licet multiplicentur secundum respectum ad res, tamen non sunt realiter aliud a divina essentia, prout ejus similitudo a diversis participari potest diversimode. Sic igitur Deus ipse est Primum Exemplar Omnium." *Ibid.*, i, q. 44, a. 3.

72 "Idea enim graece, latine forma dicitur. Unde per ideas intelliguntur formae aliarum rerum, praeter ipsas res existentes. Forma autem alicujus rei praeter ipsam existens, ad duo esse potest; vel ut sit exemplar ejus cujus dicitur forma, vel ut sit secundum principium cognitionis ipsius, secundum quod formae cognoscibilium dicuntur esse in cognoscente." *Ibid.*, i, q. 15, 1c. "Et secundum quod est principium factionis rerum exemplar dici potest, et ad practicam cognitionem pertinet. Secundum autem quod principium cognoscitium est proprie dicitur ratio, et potest etiam ad scientiam speculativam pertinere." *Ibid.*, i, q. 15, 3c. *Meta.*, lib. v, lect. 2.

73 *Sum. theol.*, ii, dist. 16, q. 1, a. 2, ad. 2.

74 Cajetan in i, q. 14, a. 1.

75 A. D. Sertillanges, *Mélanges Thomistes*, p. 182.

76 *Sum. theol.*, i, q. 14, a. 8, ad. 3.

77 "Species intelligibiles, quae participat noster intellectus, reducuntur, sicut in primam causam, in aliquod principium per suam essentiam intelligibiles, scilicet, in Deum. Sed ab illo principio procedunt mediantibus formis rerum sensibilium et materialium, a quibus scientiam colligimus, ut Dionysius dicit." *Div. Norm.*, cap. 7. *Sum. theol.*, i, q. 84, a. 4, ad. 1. *Ibid.*, i, q. 15, a. 3; Quod. viii, q. 1, a. 3; *De Spirit. Creat.*, a. 10.

78 A. D. Sertillanges, *St. Thomas*, II, 165.

79 *Sum. theol.*, i, q. 44, a. 3c.

80 *Sum. theol.*, i-ii, q. 2, a. 8c.

81 *De Legibus*, lib. ii, chaps. 4, 5.

82 *Lysis*, chap. x, p. 107.

83 Douglas Jerrold, *The Future of Freedom*, p. 39.

84 W. E. Hocking, *What Man Can Make of Man*, pp. 24-27.

85 Apocalypse 21:3-4.

86 Arnold J. Toynbee, *A Study of History*, IV, 162.

87 *Sum. theol.*, i-ii, q. 91.

88 "Law being a rule and a measure, can be in a person in two ways; in one way, as in him that rules and measures; and in another way, as in that which is ruled and measured, since a thing is ruled and measured, insofar as it partakes of the rule or measure. Wherefore, since all things subject to Divine Providence are ruled and measured by the Eternal Law, it is evident that all things partake somewhat of the Eternal Law, insofar as, namely, it being imprinted on them, they derive their respective inclinations to their proper acts and ends. Now among all others, the rational creature is subject to Divine Providence in the most excellent way, insofar as it partakes of a share of providence, by being provident both for itself and others. Wherefore, it has a share of the Eternal Reason, whereby it has a natural inclination to its proper act and end, and this participation of the Eternal Law in the rational creature is called the rational law. . . . The light of natural reason whereby we discern what is good and what is evil, which is the function of the natural law, is nothing else than an imprint on us of the Divine Light. It is therefore evident that the natural law is nothing else than the rational creature's participation of the eternal law." *Ibid.*, i-ii, q. 91, a. 2.

89 *Sum. theol.* i, q. 29, a. 3.

90 *Ibid.*, i, q. 91, a. 1.

91 As Berdyaev explains: "Personality is the creator and the bearer of superpersonal values and this is the only source of its wholeness, unity and eternal significance. But this must not be taken to mean that personality has no intrinsic value. It is itself an absolute and exalted value, but it can only exist in virtue of superpersonal values. In other words, the existence of personality presupposes the existence of God; its value presupposes the supreme value— God. If there is no God as the source of superpersonal values, personality as a value does not exist either; there is merely the individual entity subordinate to the natural life of the genus. Personality is the moral principle, and our relation to all other values is determined by reference to it. Hence the idea of personality lies at the basis of ethics. An impersonal system of ethics is a *contradictio in adjecto*. Ethics is to a great extent the theory of personality. Moral life is centered in the person and not in generalities. Personality is a higher value than the state, the nation, mankind or nature, and indeed it does not form part of that series." *The Destiny of Man*, p. 72.

92 *Sum. theol.*, i, q. 95, a. 1, ad. 2.

93 Acts 17:22-28.

94 Isa. 44:28-45; 1:2-6.

95 *Les Deux Sources de la Morale et de la Religion*, p. 333.

96 *Laws*, 951 B-C.

97 Matt. 10:34-36.

98 Mark 6:34.

99 Herbert Agar, *A Time for Greatness*, p. 47.

100 Lewis Mumford, *Faith for Living*, pp. 38, 39.

101 *Ibid.*, pp. 300-301.

102 Henri Bergson, *Morality and Religion*, pp. 86, 223.

[103] Plato's *Letters*, No. 7, 341 B-E.

[104] *Sum. theol.*, iii, q. 42, a. 4c.

[105] *De Fide*, Bk. i, chap. 5.

[106] *Sermo.*, 197.

[107] Eugen Rosenstock—Huessy, *The Christian Future*, p. 83.

[108] Reinhold Niebuhr, *Reflections on the End of an Era*, p. 163. D. R. Davies, *On to Orthodoxy*, chap. iii. Nicholas Berdyaev, *The Meaning of History*, p. 169. Charles Clayton Morrison, *The Christian and the War*.

[109] Jeremias 2:13.

[110] Amos 6:15.

[111] Isa. 10:5.

[112] Isa. 10:15.

[113] Isa. 13:17, 19.

[114] Jeremias 18:4.

[115] I Cor. 11:31.

[116] *Sum. theol.* ii-ii, q. 48, a. 1. For Aristotle's view of Providence, cf. *Meteora*, I, chap. iii. For Plato's view, cf. *Republic*, VI.

[117] *De Civitate Dei*, Bk. i, chap. 36.

[118] *De Civitate Dei*, Bk. xiii, chaps. 1, 2, 5. Cf. Christopher Dawson, *Enquiries*, p. 198.

[119] Here he differed from St. Thomas, who was in favor of many taking part in government. "Ut omnes aliquam partem habeant in principatu: per hoc enim conservatur pax populi." *Sum. theol.*, i-ii, q. 105, a. 1.

[120] *The Dialogues of Plato*, tr. B. Jowett, II, 383.

[121] *Ibid.*, *Phaedrus*, I, 223ff. Cf. *Ibid.*, Vol. II; *Laws*, Bk. iv, p. 477ff.

[122] "Some say that all the virtues are forms of practical wisdom, and that is why Socrates in one respect was on the right track, while in another he went astray; in thinking that all the virtues were forms of practical wisdom he was wrong, but in saying they implied practical wisdom he was right. This is confirmed by the fact that even now all men, when they define virtue, after naming the state of character and its objects, add, 'that (state) which is in accordance with the right rule': now the right rule is that which is in accordance with practical wisdom." *Ethics*, Bk. v, chap. 12.

[123] *Ibid.*

[124] *Eiss.* II, 16, 46.

[125] *Ep.*, pp. 21, 87.

[126] For further development of pagan ideas, cf. William Chase Greene, *Moira*, pp. 296, 362ff; Werner Jaeger, *Paideia*, 3 vols.

[127] *Republic*, p. 363.

[128] *Republic*, p. 606.

[129] Christopher Hollis, *Noble Castle*, p. 42.

[130] Aristotle, *Ethics*, pp. 1, 2.

[131] Aeschylus, *The Suppliants*, p. 26, lines 513-537 (Random House ed. of *The Complete Greek Drama*, Vol. II, ed. by Oates and O'Neill).

[132] *Ibid.*, p. 28, lines 578-604.

[133] Aeschylus, *The Persians*, p. 75, lines 800-837, *The Complete Greek Drama*, Vol. I.

[134] Aeschylus, *The Seven Against Thebes*, p. 121, lines 1068-1184, *The Complete Greek Drama*, Vol. I.

[135] Aeschylus, *Prometheus Bound*, p. 143, lines 562-594, *The Complete Greek Drama*, Vol. I.

[136] Aeschylus, *Agamemnon*, p. 192, lines 759-795, *The Complete Greek Drama*, Vol. I.

[137] *Ibid.*, p. 179, lines 349-372.

[138] *Ibid.*, p. 218, lines 1478-1506.

[139] Aeschylus, *Ibid.*, p. 220, lines 535-1566, *The Complete Greek Drama*, Vol. I.

[140] Aeschylus, *The Eumenides*, p. 279, lines 226-248, *The Complete Greek Drama*, Vol. I.

[141] *Ibid.*, p. 287, lines 443-476.

[142] Aeschylus, *Prometheus Bound*, p. 156, lines 1001-1048, *The Complete Greek Drama*, Vol. I.

[143] Sophocles, *Oedipus the King*, p. 415, lines 1465-1515, *The Complete Greek Drama*, Vol. I.

[144] Sophocles, *Oedipus the King*, pp. 416-417, lines 1516-1527, 1528-1530, *The Complete Greek Drama*, Vol. I.

[145] Charles Norris Cochrane, *Christianity and Classical Culture*, chap. x. T. R. Glover, *The Ancient World*, p. 333.

CHAPTER XI

[1] Personality: "Personality is more primary than being." Nicholas Berdyaev, *Slavery and Freedom*, p. 75. There has been an attempt to revive metaphysics in *The Nature of Metaphysical Thinking* by Dorothy M. Emmet, but only as a philosophy of relationships.

[2] *Collected Papers*, Vol. V, chap. iv, "An Introductory Lecture in Psychoanalysis."

[3] *Either/Or*, II, 177-178. *Concept of Dread*, p. 111.

[4] Karl Barth, *The Theology of Crisis*, p. 90.

[5] *The Meaning of History*, p. 189.

[6] *Ibid.*, p. 60.

[7] C. E. M. Joad, *God and Evil*, p. 14.

[8] *Ibid.*, p. 19.

[9] *Beyond Tragedy. Christianity and Power Politics. Children of Darkness and the Children of Light. Nature and Destiny of Man*, 2 vols.

[10] *Moral Man and Immoral Society*, p. 11.

[11] *Nature and Destiny of Man*, I, 3-4.

[12] *Christianity and Power*, p. 37.

[13] G. U. Plekhanov, *The Role of the Individual in History*.

[14] *Sum. theol.*, i, q. 91, a. 1; i, q. 96, a. 2; i-ii, q. 17, a. 8, ad. 2.

[15] *Ibid.*, ii, dist. 1, q. 2, a. 3; ii, dist. 47, q. 2, a. 1, q. 1; *Contra Gentiles*, lib. iii, q. 112.

[16] *Sum. theol.*, i, q. 3, a. 1, ad. 2.

[17] *Sum. theol.*, i, dist. 1, q. 2, a. 3, ad. 3.

[18] *Ibid.*, ii-ii, q. 122, a. 2.

[19] *Ibid.*, iv, dist. 15, q. 4, a. 1, q. 1c.

[20] *Ibid.*, i, q. 96, a. 3. *Ibid.*, ii-ii, q. 64, a. 1.

[21] *Ibid.*, i, q. 29, a. 3.

[22] *Ibid.*, i-ii, q. 1, a. 8.

[23] *De Potentia*, q. 3, a. 18, ad. 5; *De Malo*, q. 16, a. 4, ad. 16; *Sum. theol.*, i-ii, q. 3, a. 4.

[24] *Sum. theol.*, i-ii, q. 1, aa. 5, 3.

[25] *Ibid.*, i-ii, q. 2, a. 3, ad. 3.

[26] *Ibid.*, i-ii, q. 2, a. 4.

[27] "Esse enim hominis consistit in anima et corpore et quamis esse corporis dependet ab anima, esse tamen humanae animae non dependet a corpore." *Sum. theol.*, i-ii, q. 2, a. 5.

[28] *Ibid.*, i-ii, q. 5, a. 8.

[29] Cf. A. E. Taylor, *The Faith of a Moralist*, 2 vols., for description of the temporal and eternal tension.

[30] *Sum. theol.*, i-ii, q. 22.

[31] *Ibid.*, i-ii, q. 23, a. 1.

[32] Modern psychologists could find much sound direction in St. Thomas' treatise on the cause of love—goodness, knowledge, and similarity. *Sum. theol.*, i-ii, q. 28. These articles, and the treatise of Bossuet on *Concupiscence* are the most profound treatments of the subject of passion in philosophical and psychological literature.

[33] *Sum. theol.*, i-ii, q. 40-48.

[34] *Science and the Idea of God*, p. 49.

[35] *Sum. theol.*, i-ii, q. 75, a. 1.

[36] *Ibid.*, i-ii, q. 76.

[37] *Ibid.*, i-ii, q. 80.

[38] *Ibid.*, i-ii, q. 81.

[39] Freud, *Introductory Lectures*, p. 43.

[40] *Psychological Types.*

[41] *Sum. theol.*, i, q. 100, a. 1; i-ii, q. 81, a. 1.

[42] *Ibid.*, q. 82, a. 3. *De Malo*, q. 4, a. 2, ad. 4.

[43] *Contra Gentiles*, lib. iv, cap. 52.

[44] *Ibid.*, lib. iv, cap. 54.

[45] *Ibid.*, lib. iv, cap. 54.

[46] *Contra Gentiles*, lib. iv, cap. 55.

[47] *Contra Gentiles*, lib. iii, cap. 71.

Index

397

(6)